These are the contents for *Fairy Tail* volume 1!
EATH PENDANT
:KATOU:
400,000J
3,000
FISH
17,000
60,000J

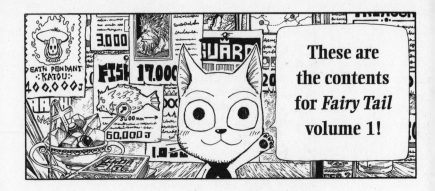

Hello!
To first-time readers...
To longtime readers...
To those who just realized
they bought the wrong book...
To those who are saying,
"Who're you?"...
I hope you have fun reading this.
This is a classic story of the
friendship between humans
and cats.
Yes.
I got in a lie right from the start!

—Hiro Mashima

FAIRY TAIL

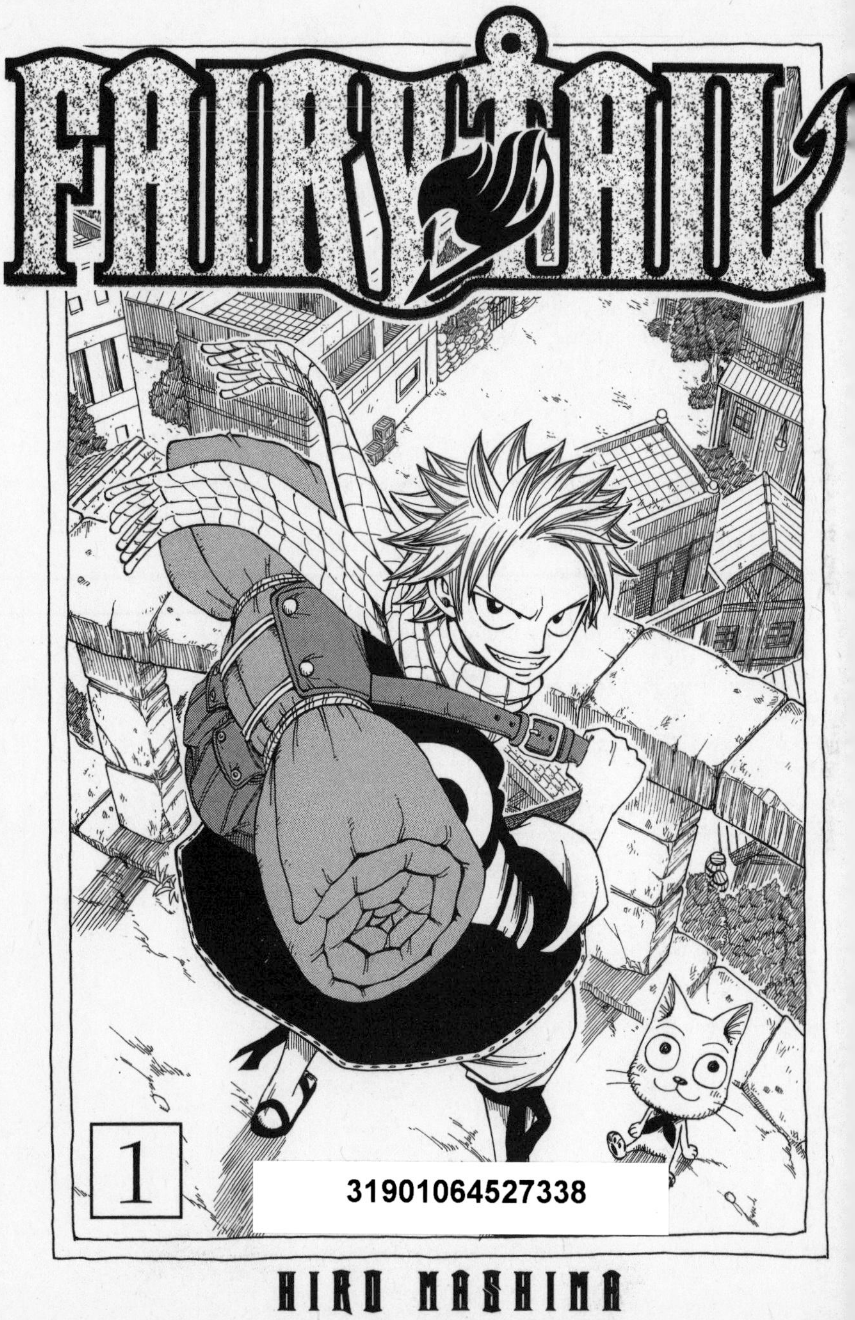

1

HIRO MASHIMA

Fairy Tail volume 1 is a work of fiction. Names, characters, places, and incidents are the products of the author's imagination or are used fictitiously. Any resemblance to actual events, locales, or persons, living or dead, is entirely coincidental.

A Kodansha Comics trade Paperback Original

Published in the United States by Kodansha Comics, an imprint of Kodansha USA Publishing, LLC., New York.

Publication rights for this English edition arranged through Kodansha Ltd., Tokyo.

First published in Japan in 2006 by Kodansha Ltd., Tokyo

ISBN 978-1-612-62276-7

Printed in the United States of America

www.kodanshacomics.com

19 18 17 16 15 14 13 12 11 10

Translator/Adapter—William Flanagan
Lettering—North Market Street Graphics

Honorifics Explained

Throughout the Kodansha Comics books, you will find Japanese honorifics left intact in the translations. For those not familiar with how the Japanese use honorifics and, more important, how they differ from honorifics in American English, we present this brief overview.

Politeness has always been a critical facet of Japanese culture. Ever since the feudal era, when Japan was a highly stratified society, use of honorifics—which can be defined as polite speech that indicates relationship or status—has played an essential role in the Japanese language. When addressing someone in Japanese, an honorific usually takes the form of a suffix attached to one's name (example: "Asuna-san"), is used as a title at the end of one's name, or appears in place of the name itself (example: "Negi-sensei," or simply "Sensei!").

Honorifics can be expressions of respect or endearment. In the context of manga and anime, honorifics give insight into the nature of the relationship between characters. Many English translations leave out these important honorifics and therefore distort the feel of the original Japanese. Because Japanese honorifics contain nuances that English honorifics lack, it is our policy at Kodansha not to translate them. Here, instead, is a guide to some of the honorifics you may encounter in Kodansha Comics.

-san: This is the most common honorific and is equivalent to Mr., Miss, Ms., or Mrs. It is the all-purpose honorific and can be used in any situation where politeness is required.

-sama: This is one level higher than "-san" and is used to confer great respect.

-dono: This comes from the word "tono," which means "lord." It is an even higher level than "-sama" and confers utmost respect.

-kun: This suffix is used at the end of boys' names to express familiarity or endearment. It is also sometimes used by men among friends, or when addressing someone younger or of a lower station.

-chan: This is used to express endearment, mostly toward girls. It is also used for little boys, pets, and even among lovers. It gives a sense of childish cuteness.

Bozu: This is an informal way to refer to a boy, similar to the English terms "kid" and "squirt."

Sempai/ Senpai: This title suggests that the addressee is one's senior in a group or organization. It is most often used in a school setting, where underclassmen refer to their upperclassmen as "sempai." It can also be used in the workplace, such as when a newer employee addresses an employee who has seniority in the company.

Kohai: This is the opposite of "sempai" and is used toward underclassmen in school or newcomers in the workplace. It connotes that the addressee is of a lower station.

Sensei: Literally meaning "one who has come before," this title is used for teachers, doctors, or masters of any profession or art.

-[blank]: This is usually forgotten in these lists, but it is perhaps the most significant difference between Japanese and English. The lack of honorific means that the speaker has permission to address the person in a very intimate way. Usually, only family, spouses, or very close friends have this kind of permission. Known as *yobisute*, it can be gratifying when someone who has earned the intimacy starts to call one by one's name without an honorific. But when that intimacy hasn't been earned, it can be very insulting.

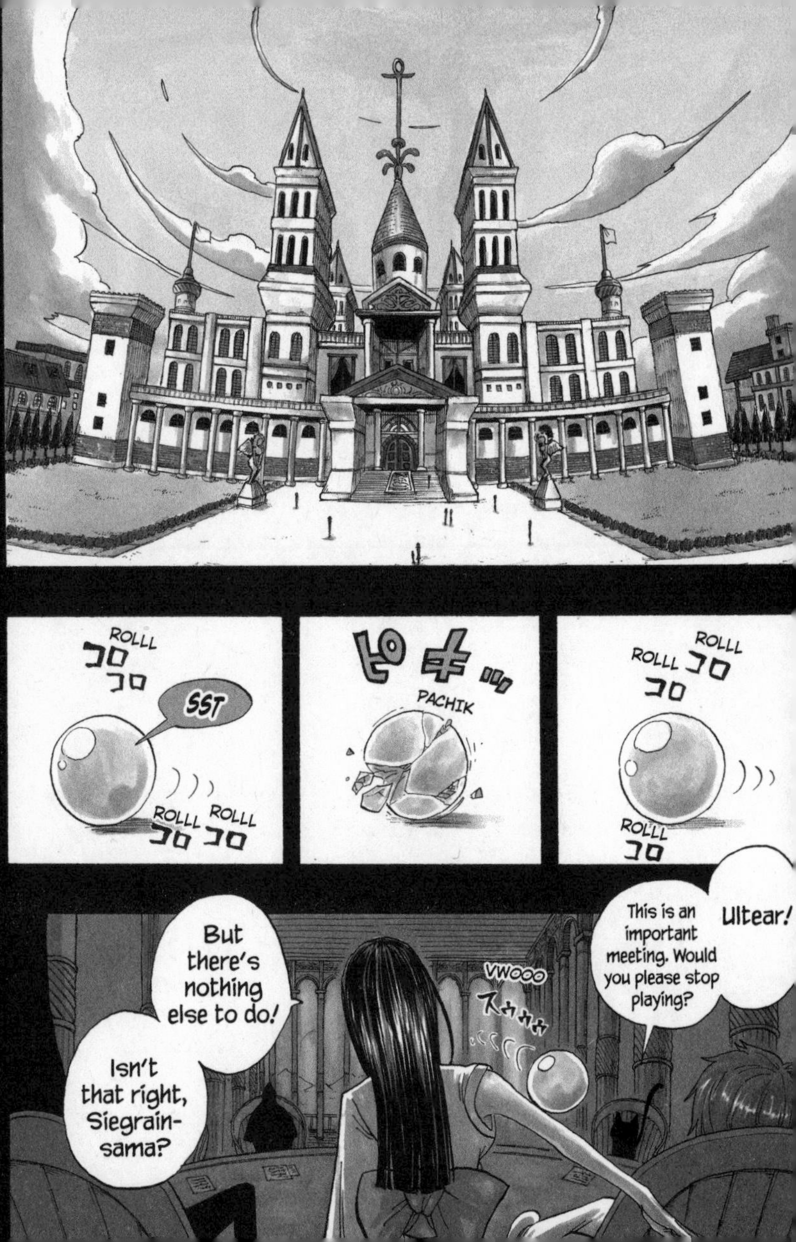

ROLLL
コロ
ROLLL
コロ
PACHIK
ROLLL
コロ
コロ
SST
ROLLL
コロ
ROLLL
コロ
Ultear!
This is an important meeting. Would you please stop playing?
VWOOO
But there's nothing else to do!
Isn't that right, Siegrain-sama?

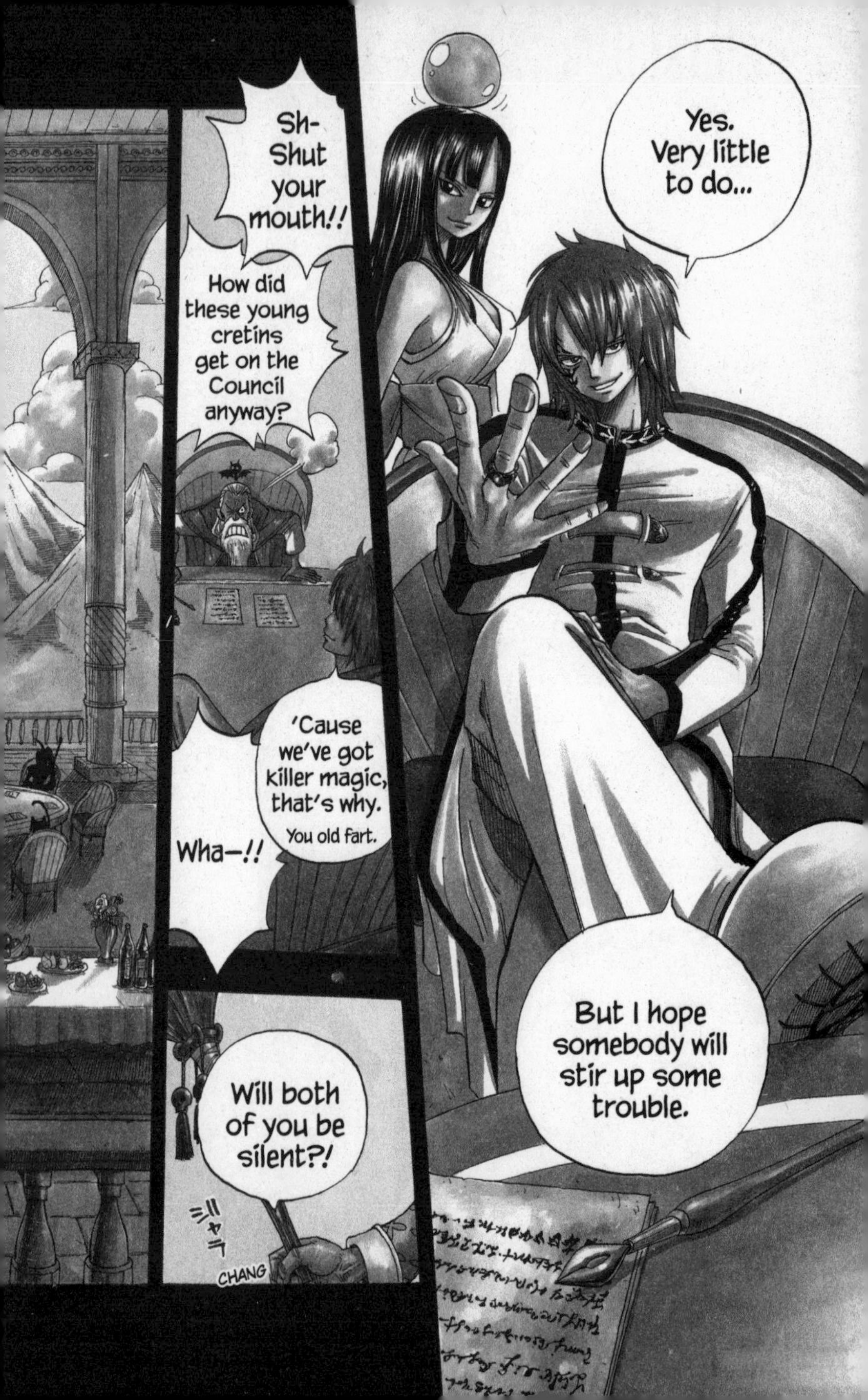
Yes. Very little to do...
But I hope somebody will stir up some trouble.
Sh-Shut your mouth!!
How did these young cretins get on the Council anyway?
'Cause we've got killer magic, that's why.
You old fart.
Wha-!!
Will both of you be silent?!
CHANG

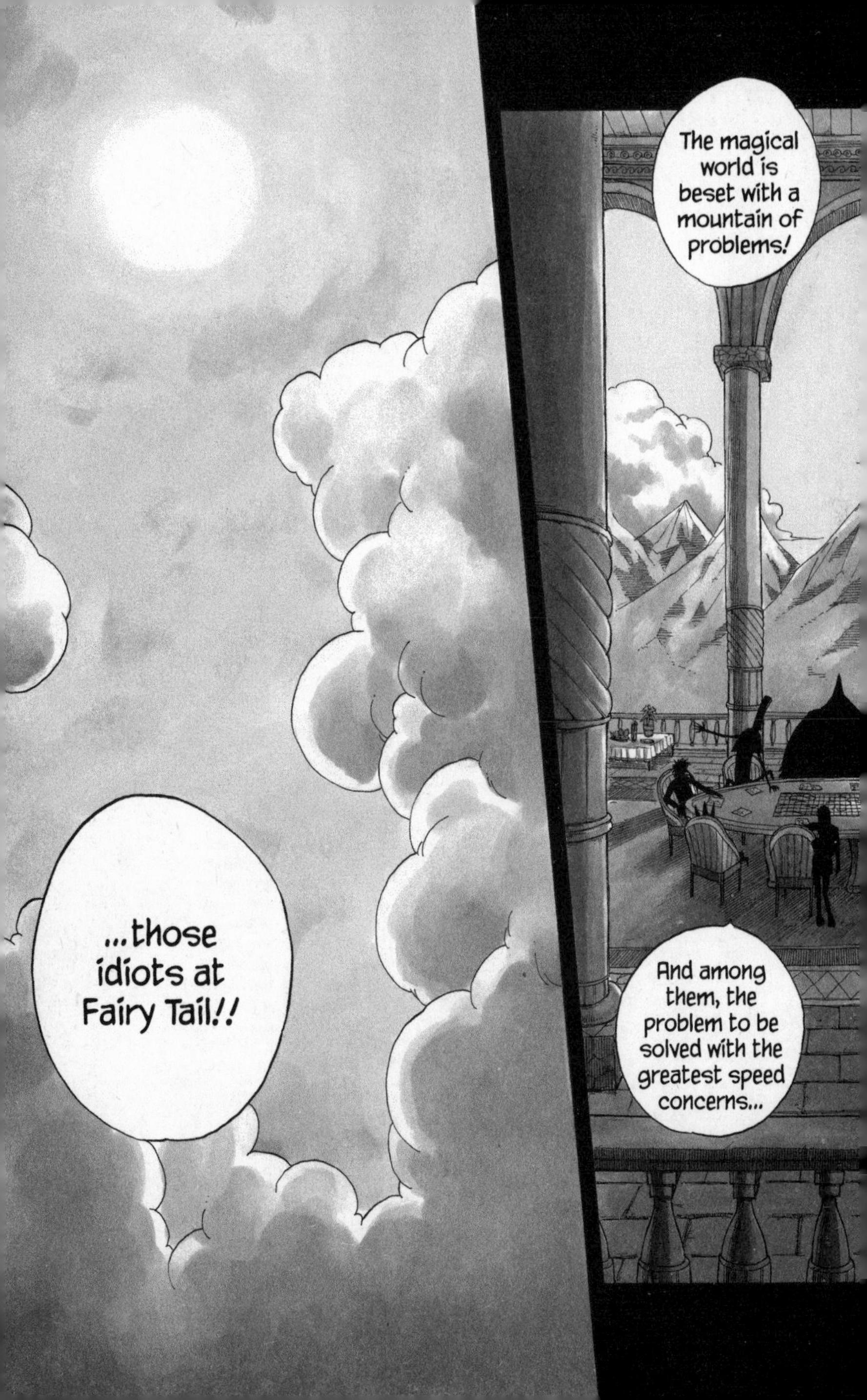
The magical world is beset with a mountain of problems!
And among them, the problem to be solved with the greatest speed concerns...
...those idiots at Fairy Tail!!

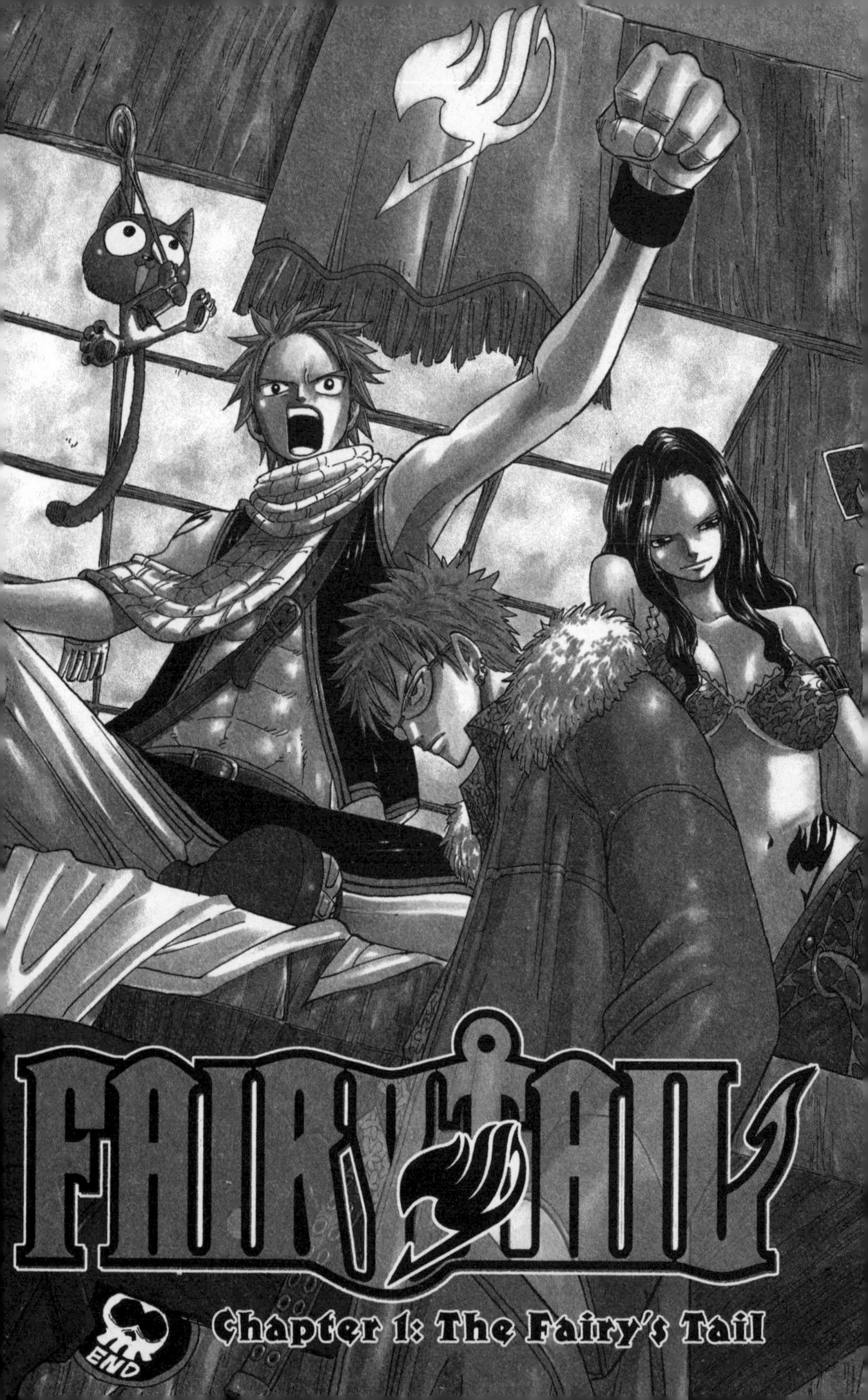

FAIRY TAIL
Chapter 1: The Fairy's Tail
END

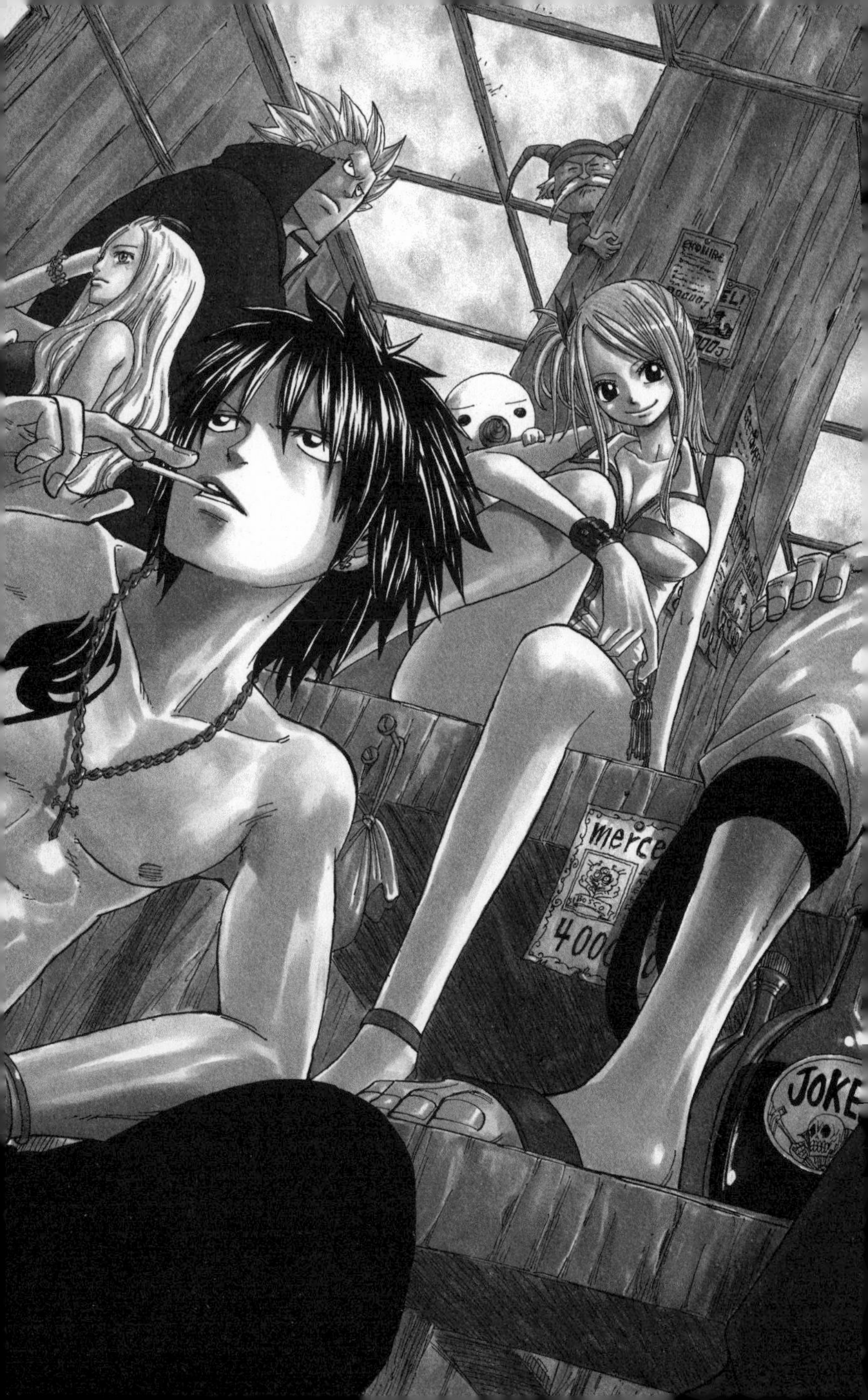
merce
JOKE

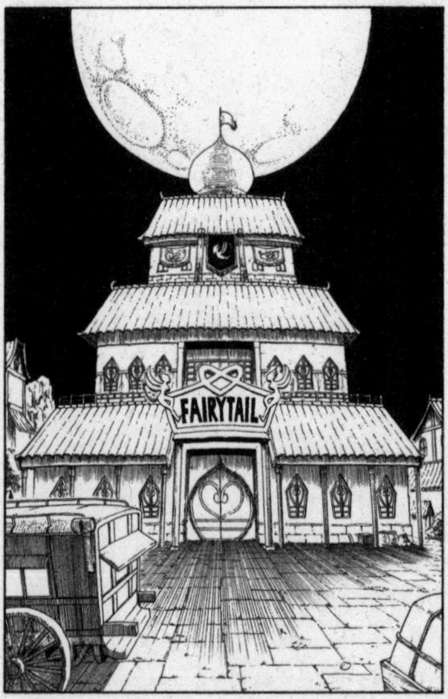
FAIRYTAIL

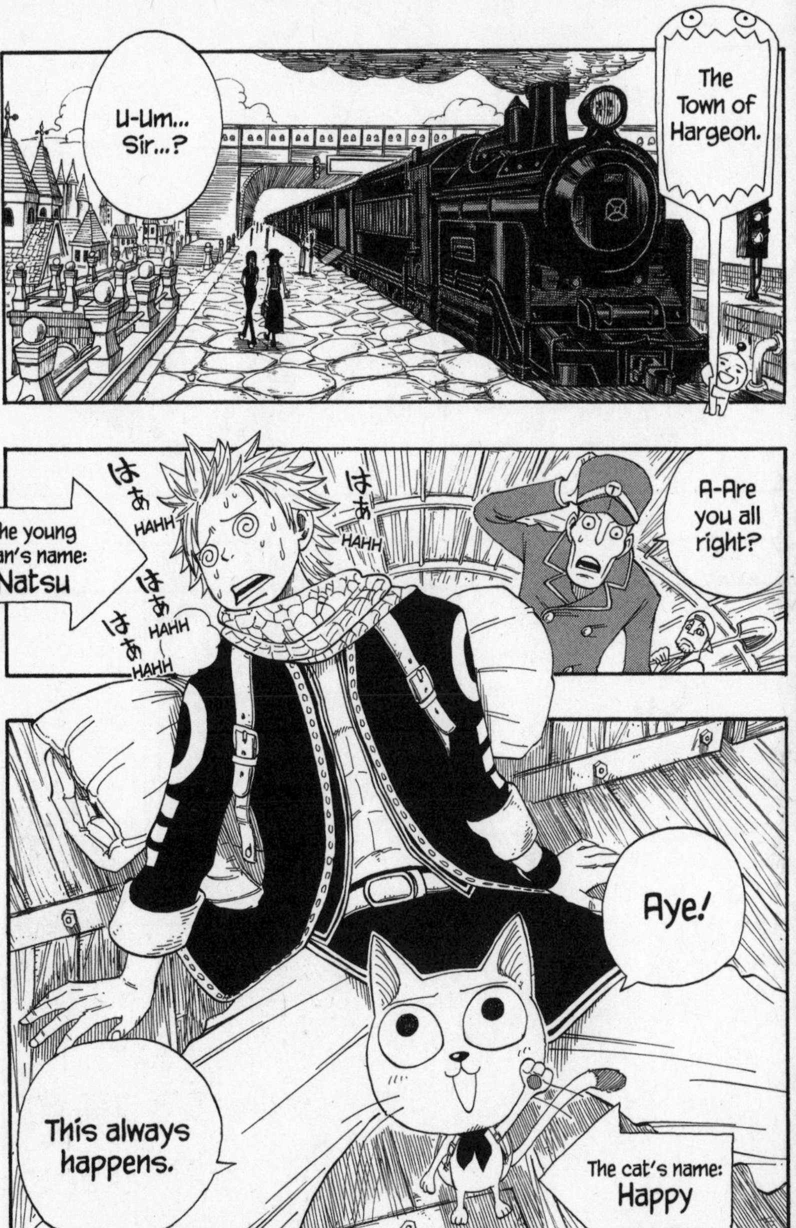
The Town of Hargeon.
U-Um... Sir...?
A-Are you all right?
はぁ HAHH
はぁ HAHH
はぁ HAHH
はぁ HAHH
The young man's name: Natsu
Aye!
The cat's name: Happy
This always happens.

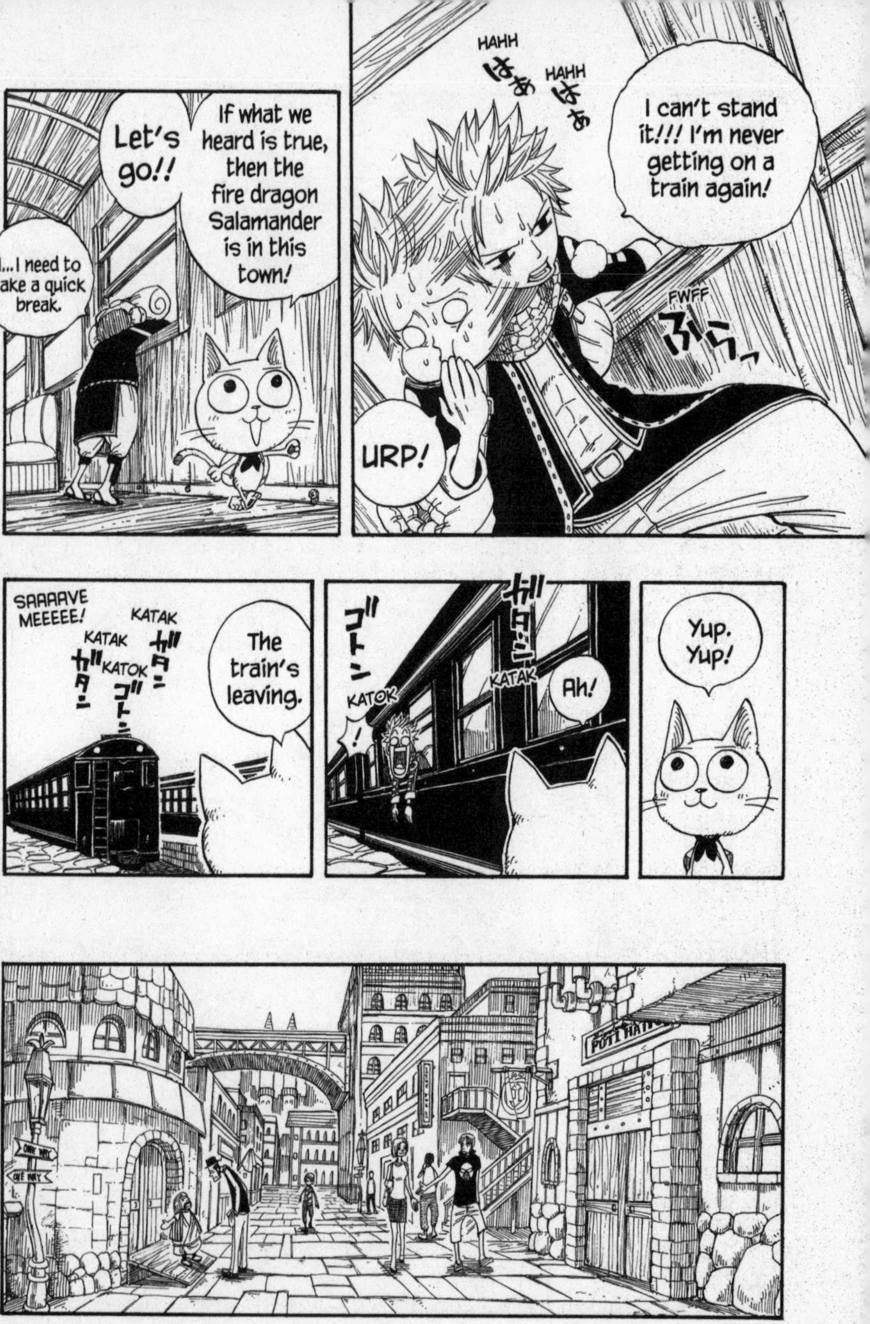
HAHH
はあ
HAHH
はあ
I can't stand it!!! I'm never getting on a train again!
FWFF
ふら
URP!
If what we heard is true, then the fire dragon Salamander is in this town!
Let's go!!
I...I need to take a quick break.
Yup. Yup!
ガタン
KATAK
Ah!
ゴトン
KATOK
!
The train's leaving.
KATAK
ガタン
KATAK
ガタン
KATOK
ゴトン
SAAAAVE MEEEEE!

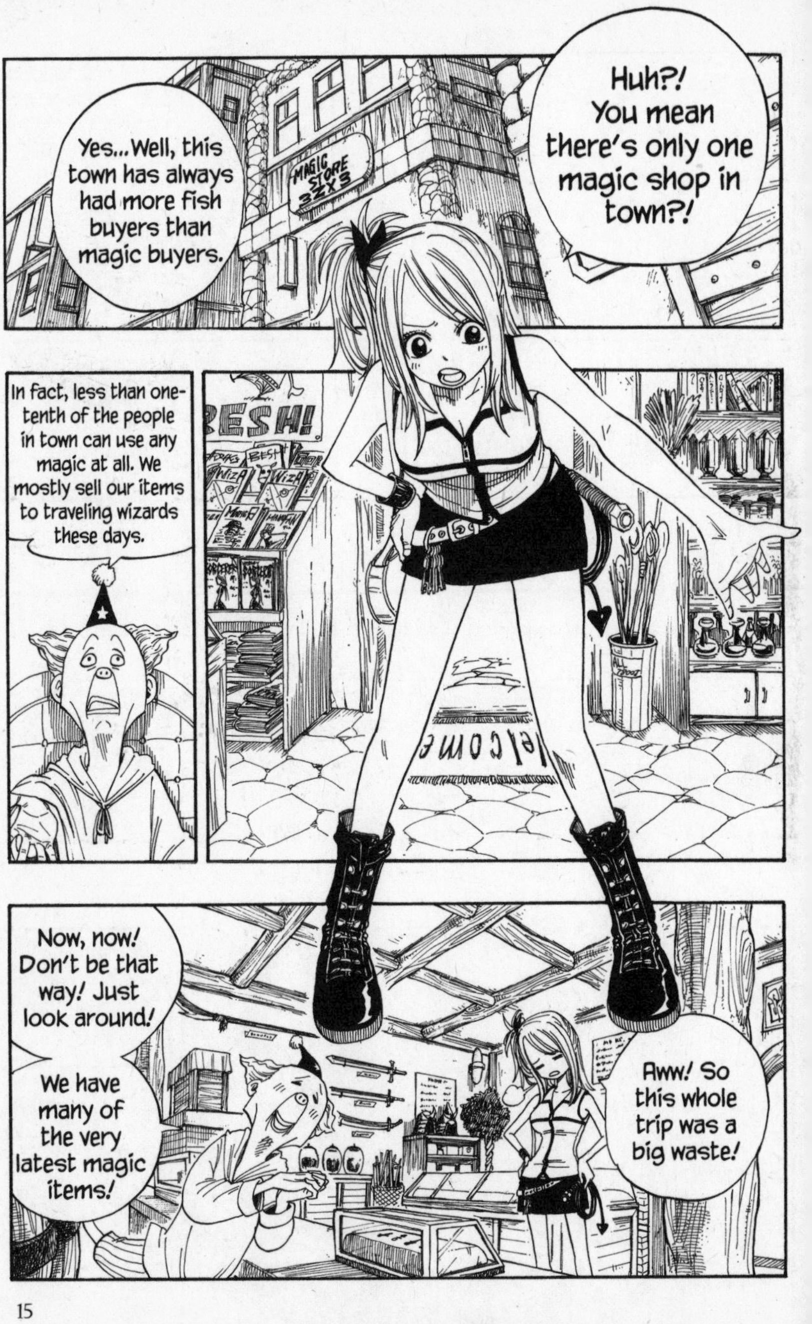
Huh?! You mean there's only one magic shop in town?!
MAGIC STORE
Yes...Well, this town has always had more fish buyers than magic buyers.
In fact, less than one-tenth of the people in town can use any magic at all. We mostly sell our items to traveling wizards these days.
Aww! So this whole trip was a big waste!
Now, now! Don't be that way! Just look around!
We have many of the very latest magic items!

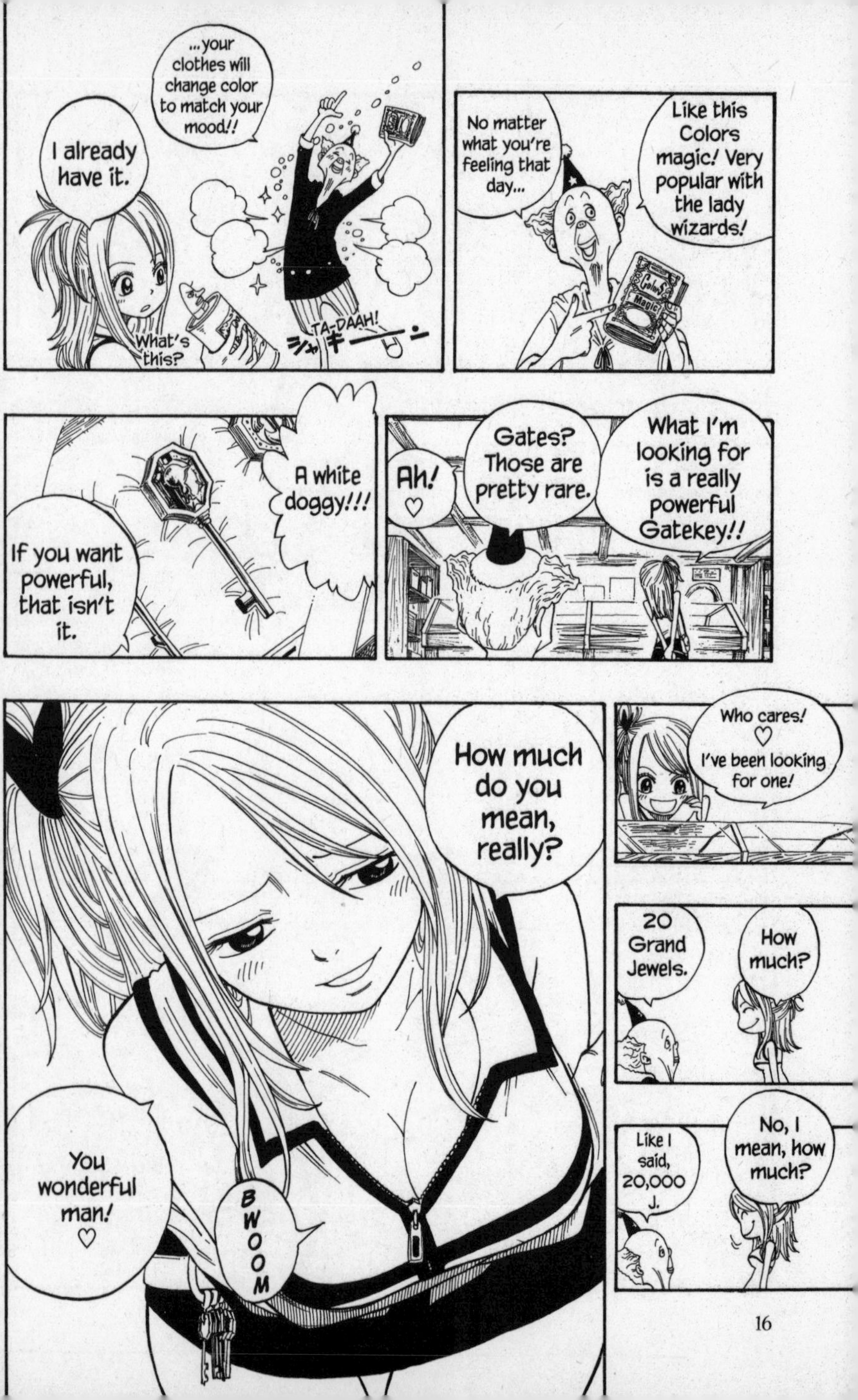
Like this Colors magic! Very popular with the lady wizards!
No matter what you're feeling that day...
...your clothes will change color to match your mood!!
TA-DAAH!
I already have it.
What's this?
What I'm looking for is a really powerful Gatekey!!
Gates? Those are pretty rare.
Ah! ♡
A white doggy!!!
If you want powerful, that isn't it.
Who cares! ♡ I've been looking for one!
How much?
20 Grand Jewels.
No, I mean, how much?
Like I said, 20,000 J.
How much do you mean, really?
BWOOM
You wonderful man! ♡

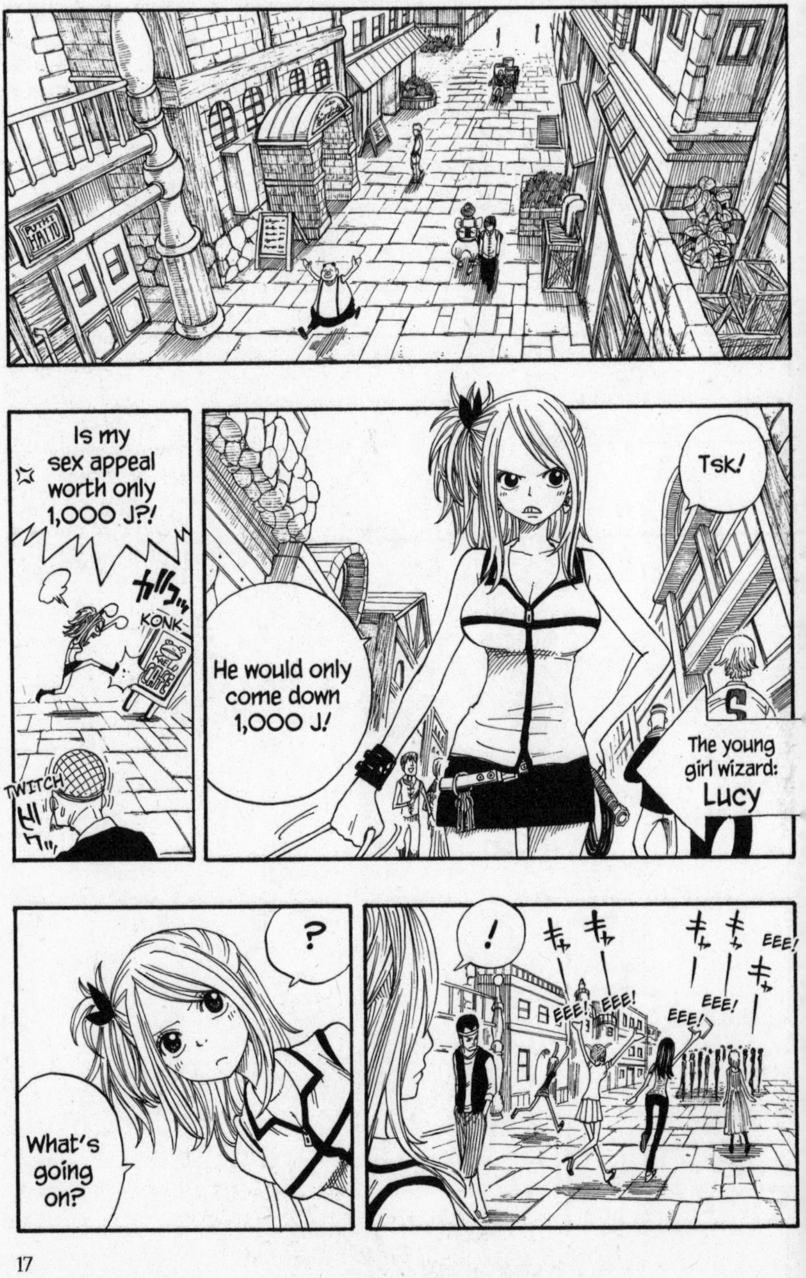
Tsk!
He would only come down 1,000 J!
The young girl wizard: Lucy
Is my sex appeal worth only 1,000 J?!
KONK
TWITCH
!
EEE!
EEE!
EEE!
EEE!
EEE!
EEE!
?
What's going on?

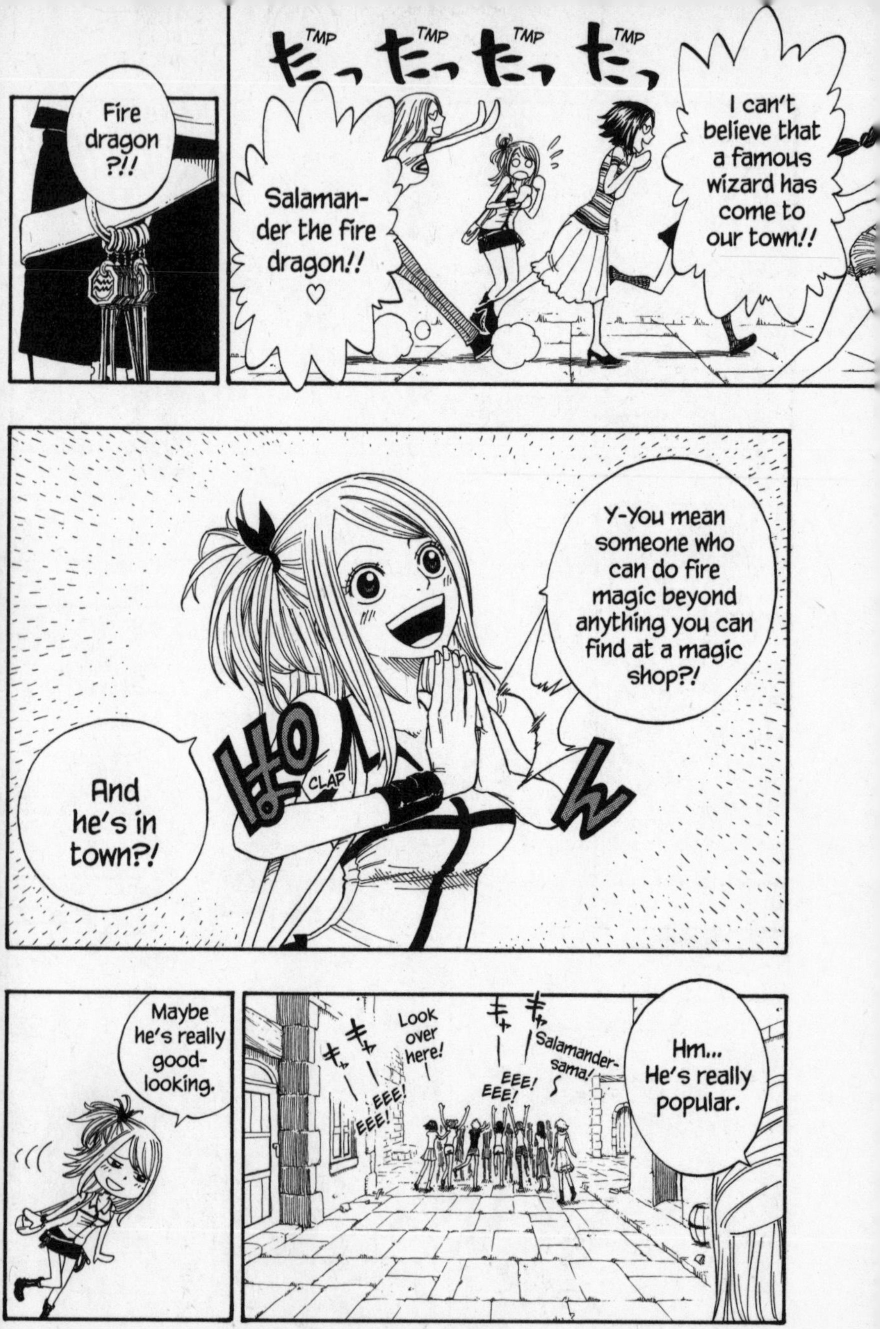
TMP TMP TMP TMP
I can't believe that a famous wizard has come to our town!!
Salamander the fire dragon!! ♡
Fire dragon ?!!
Y-You mean someone who can do fire magic beyond anything you can find at a magic shop?!
CLAP
And he's in town?!
Hm... He's really popular.
Salamander-sama!
EEE! EEE!
Look over here!
EEE! EEE!
Maybe he's really good-looking.

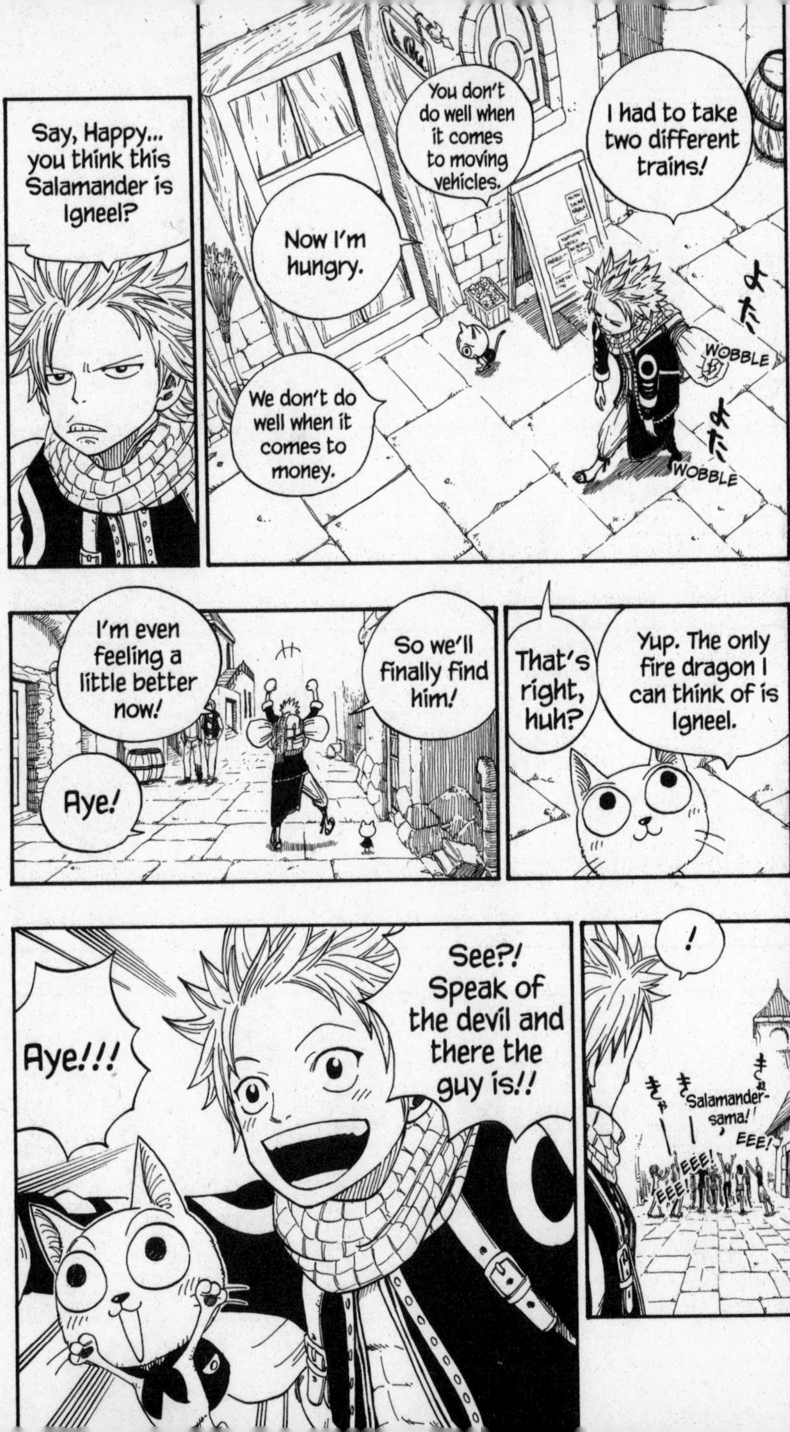
I had to take two different trains!
よた
WOBBLE
よた
WOBBLE
You don't do well when it comes to moving vehicles.
Now I'm hungry.
We don't do well when it comes to money.
Say, Happy... you think this Salamander is Igneel?
Yup. The only fire dragon I can think of is Igneel.
That's right, huh?
So we'll finally find him!
I'm even feeling a little better now!
Aye!
!
きゃー
Salamander-sama!
EEE!
EEE!
EEE!
See?! Speak of the devil and there the guy is!!
Aye!!!

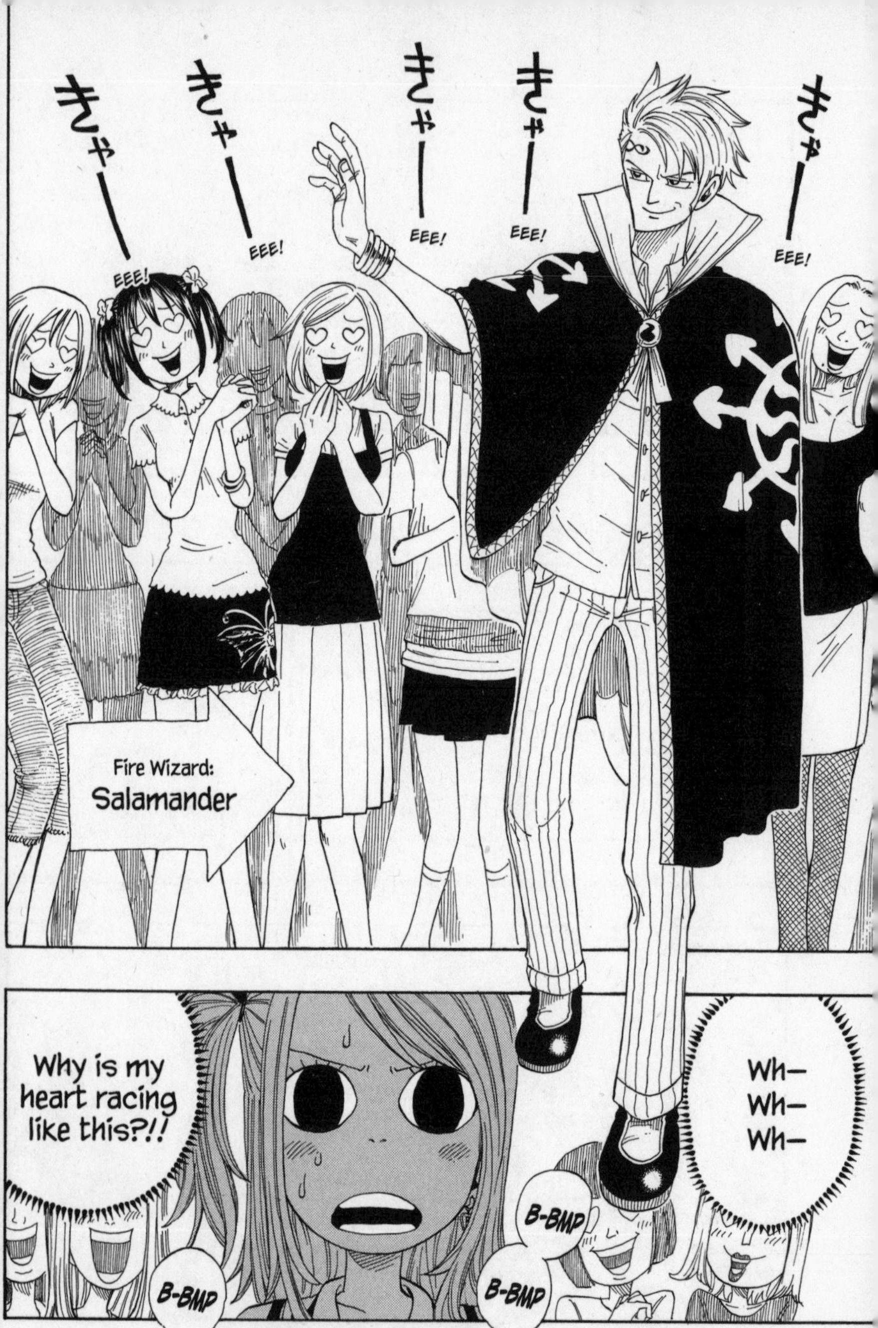
きゃー
EEE!
きゃー
EEE!
きゃー
EEE!
きゃー
EEE!
きゃー
EEE!
Fire Wizard:
Salamander
Wh-
Wh-
Wh-
B-BMP
B-BMP
B-BMP
Why is my heart racing like this?!!

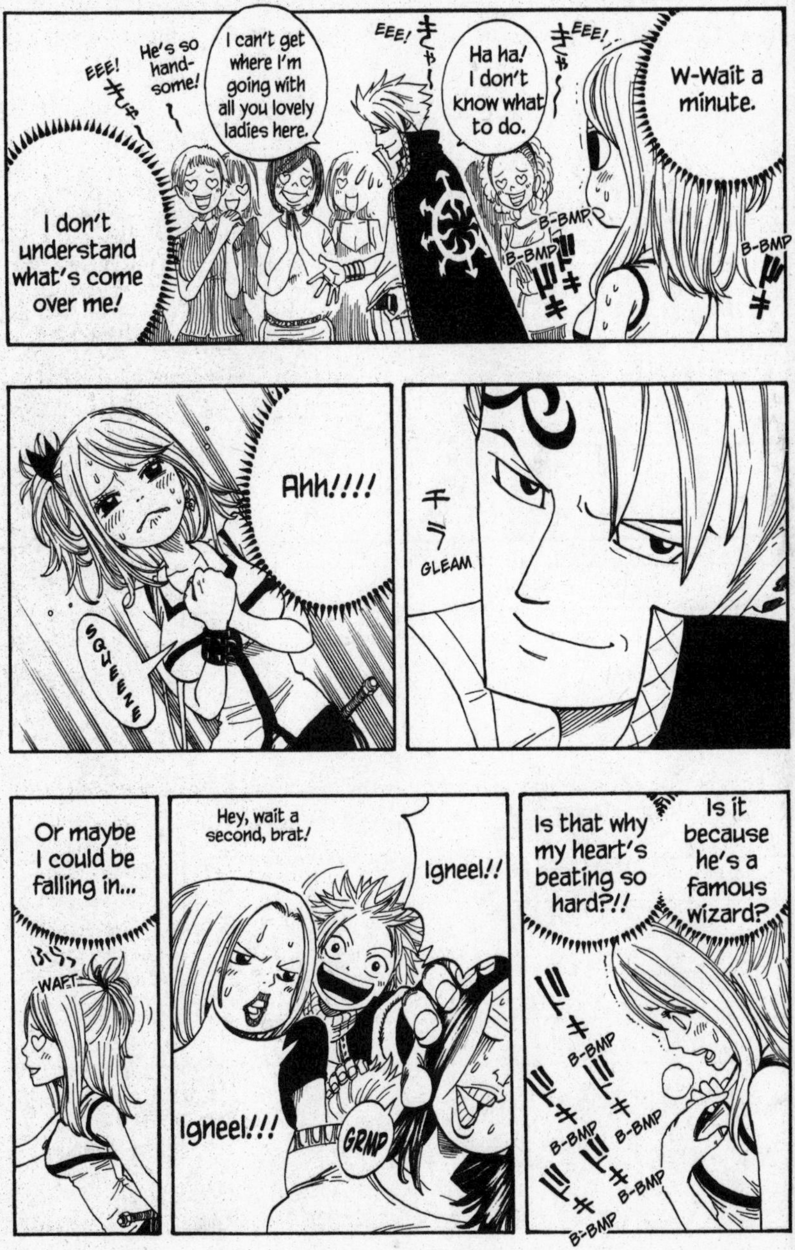
W-Wait a minute.
B-BMP
EEE! きゃ~
Ha ha! I don't know what to do.
B-BMP
B-BMP
EEE! きゃ~
I can't get where I'm going with all you lovely ladies here.
He's so hand-some!
EEE! きゃ~
I don't understand what's come over me!
チラ GLEAM
Ahh!!!!
SQUEEZE
Is it because he's a famous wizard?
Is that why my heart's beating so hard?!!
B-BMP
B-BMP
B-BMP
B-BMP
B-BMP
Igneel!!
Hey, wait a second, brat!
Igneel!!!
GRMP
Or maybe I could be falling in...
ふらっ WAFT

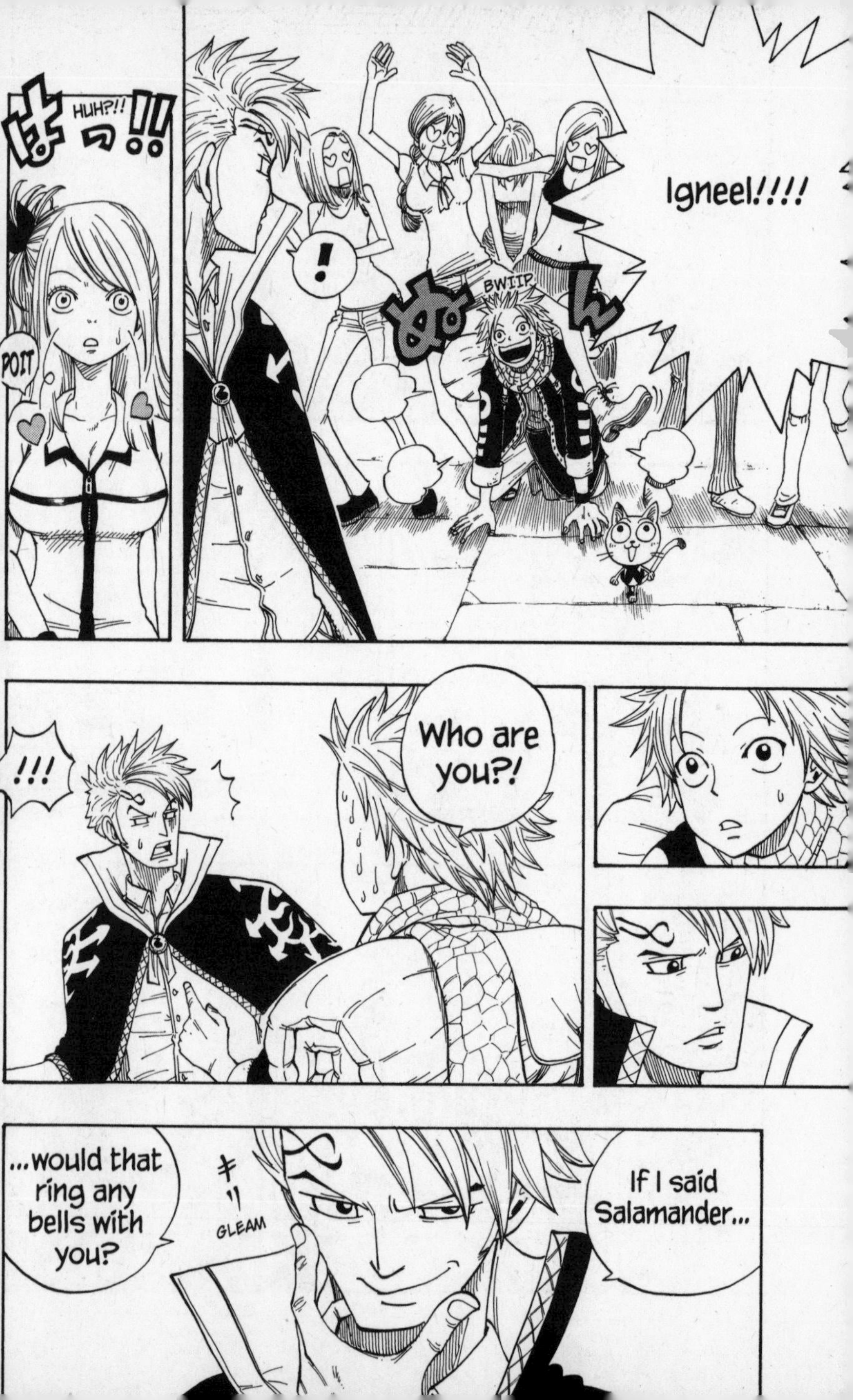
Igneel!!!!
BWIIP
!
HUH?!!
POIT
Who are you?!
!!!
If I said Salamander...
GLEAM
...would that ring any bells with you?

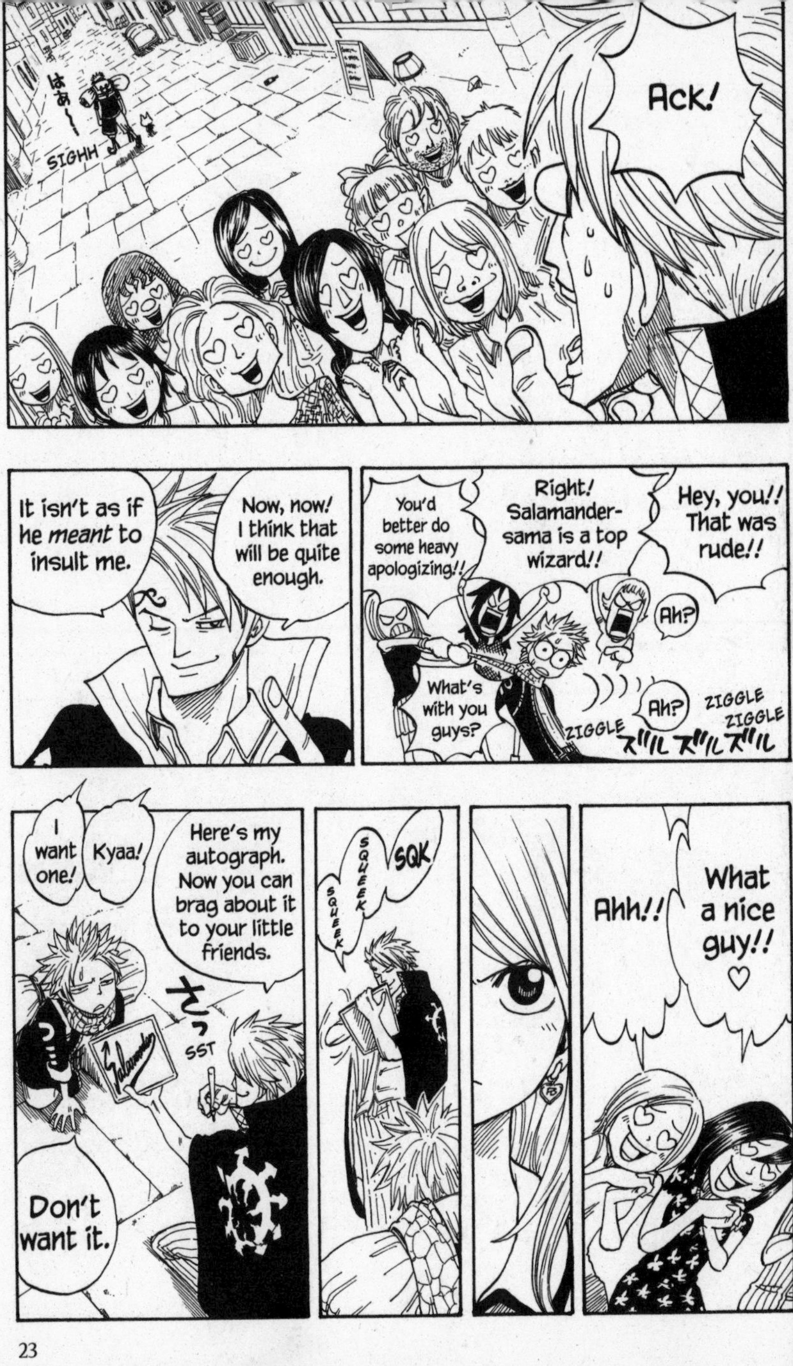
Ack!
はあ〜〜
SIGHH
Hey, you!! That was rude!!
Right! Salamander-sama is a top wizard!!
You'd better do some heavy apologizing!!
Ah?
Ah?
What's with you guys?
ZIGGLE ZIGGLE
ZIGGLE
ズルズルズル
Now, now! I think that will be quite enough.
It isn't as if he *meant* to insult me.
What a nice guy!! ♡
Ahh!!
SQK
SQUEEEK
SQUEEEK
Here's my autograph. Now you can brag about it to your little friends.
Kyaa!
I want one!
さっ
SST
Don't want it.

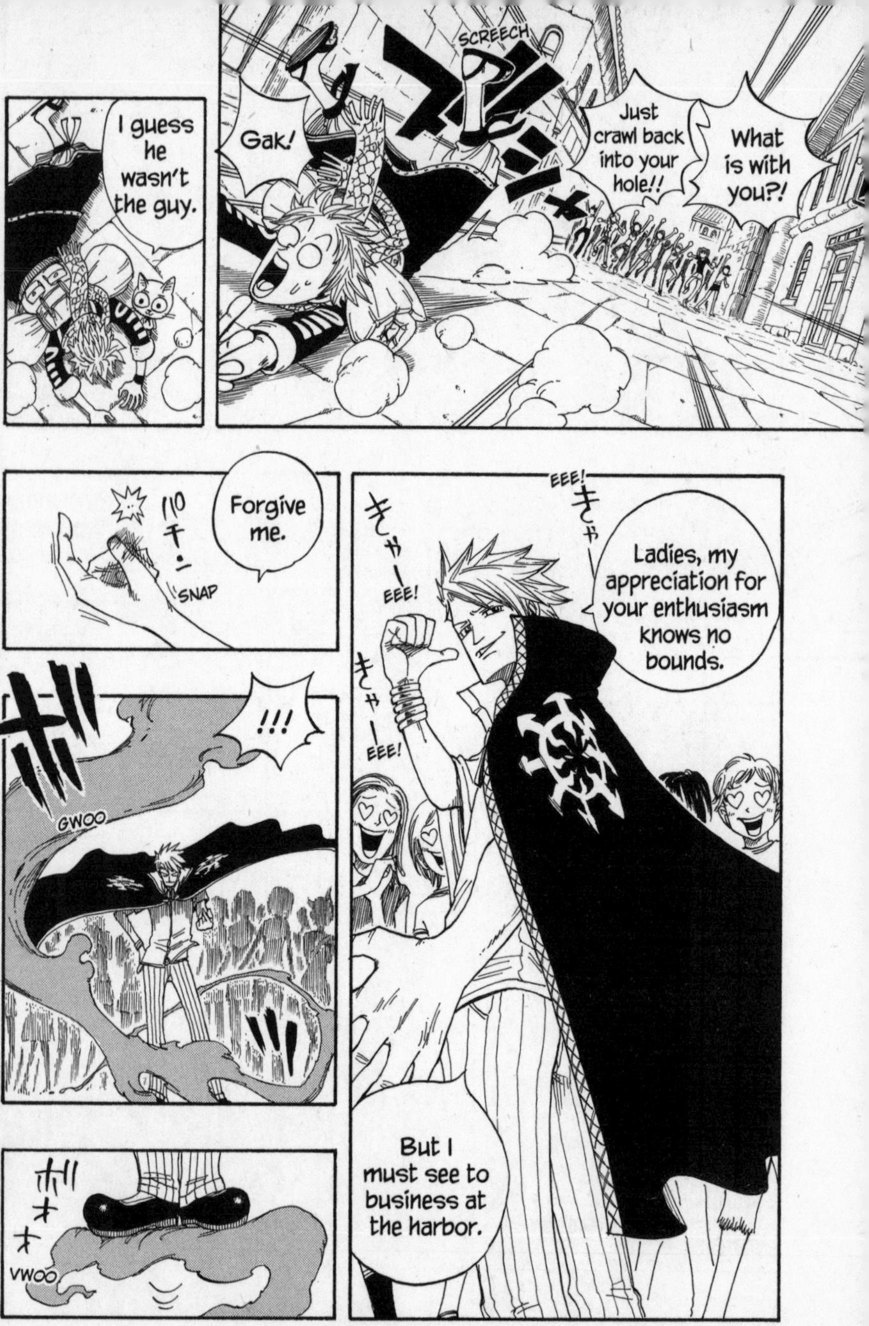
What is with you?!
Just crawl back into your hole!!
SCREECH
Gak!
I guess he wasn't the guy.
EEE!
Ladies, my appreciation for your enthusiasm knows no bounds.
EEE!
EEE!
But I must see to business at the harbor.
Forgive me.
SNAP
!!!
GWOO
VWOO

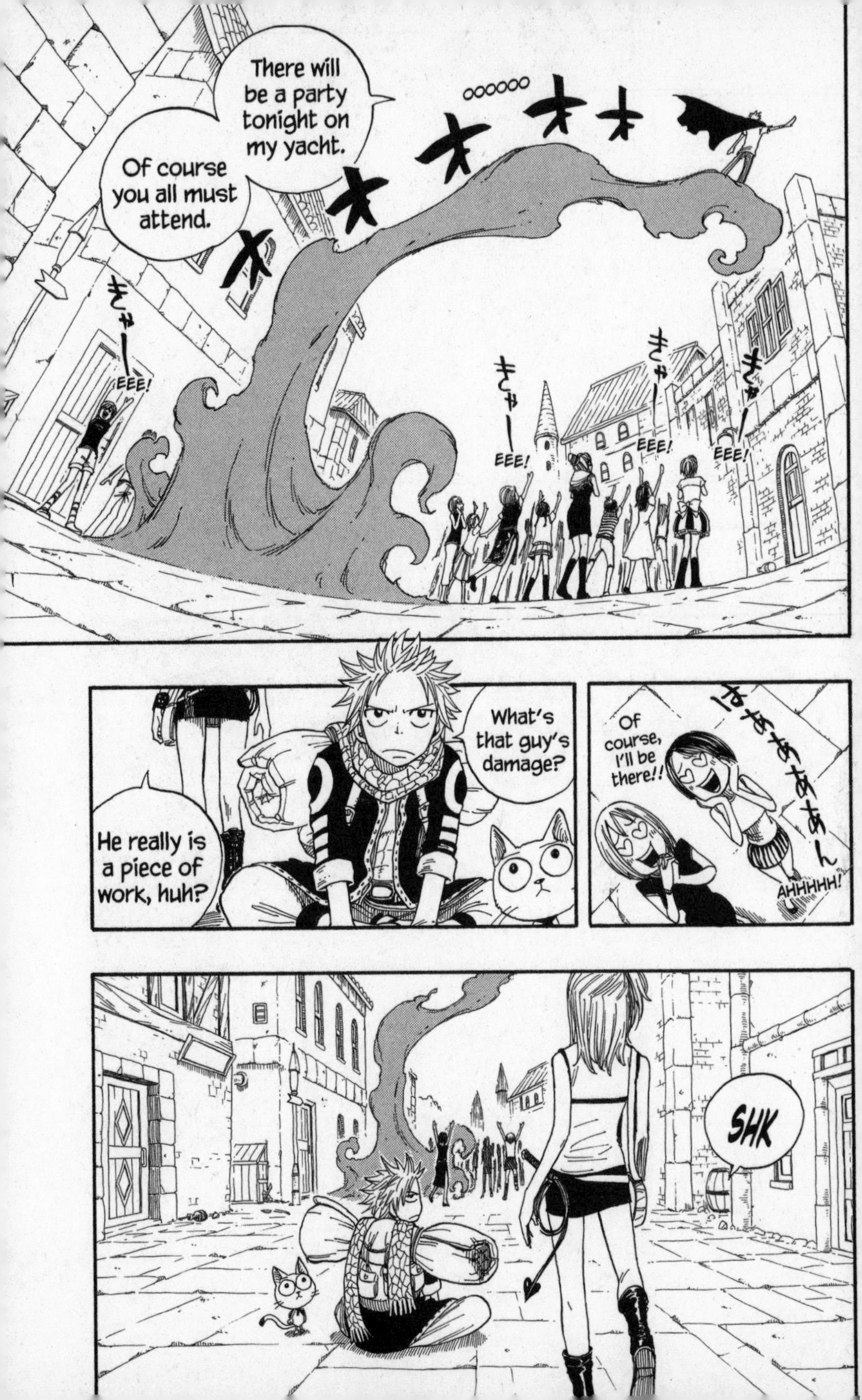
oooooo
There will be a party tonight on my yacht.
Of course you all must attend.
EEE!
EEE!
EEE!
EEE!
Of course, I'll be there!!
AHHHHHH!
What's that guy's damage?
He really is a piece of work, huh?
SHK

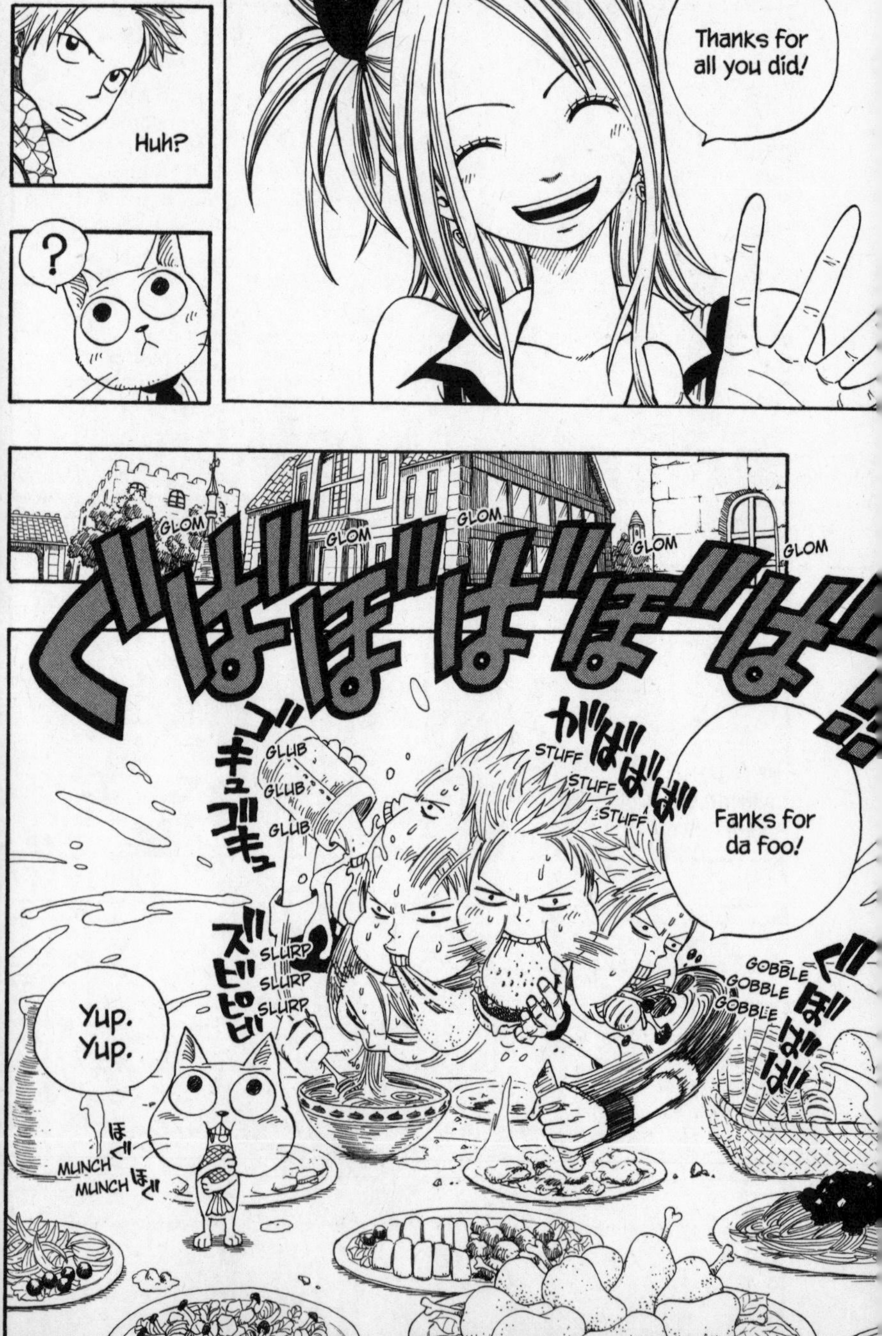
Thanks for all you did!
Huh?
?
GLOM GLOM GLOM GLOM GLOM
ぐばぼばぼば!!
Fanks for da foo!
がばばば
STUFF STUFF STUFF
ゴキュゴキュ
GLUB GLUB GLUB
ぐぼばば
GOBBLE GOBBLE GOBBLE
ズビビビ
SLURP SLURP SLURP
Yup. Yup.
ほぐほぐ
MUNCH MUNCH

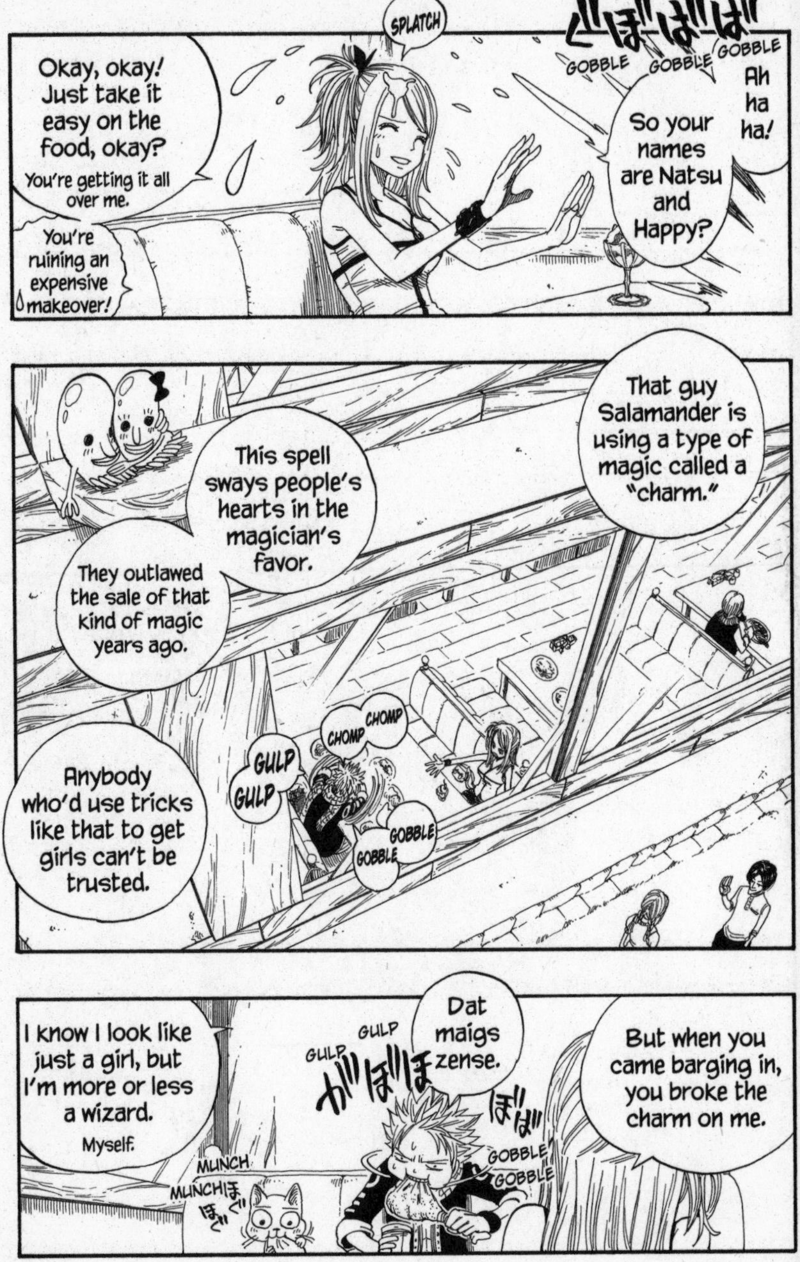
ぐぼばば
GOBBLE GOBBLE GOBBLE
Ah ha ha!
So your names are Natsu and Happy?
SPLATCH
Okay, okay! Just take it easy on the food, okay?
You're getting it all over me.
You're ruining an expensive makeover!
That guy Salamander is using a type of magic called a "charm."
This spell sways people's hearts in the magician's favor.
They outlawed the sale of that kind of magic years ago.
CHOMP CHOMP
GULP GULP
Anybody who'd use tricks like that to get girls can't be trusted.
GOBBLE GOBBLE
But when you came barging in, you broke the charm on me.
ぼば
GOBBLE GOBBLE
Dat maigs zense.
がぼほ
GULP GULP
I know I look like just a girl, but I'm more or less a wizard.
Myself.
MUNCH MUNCH ほぐほぐ

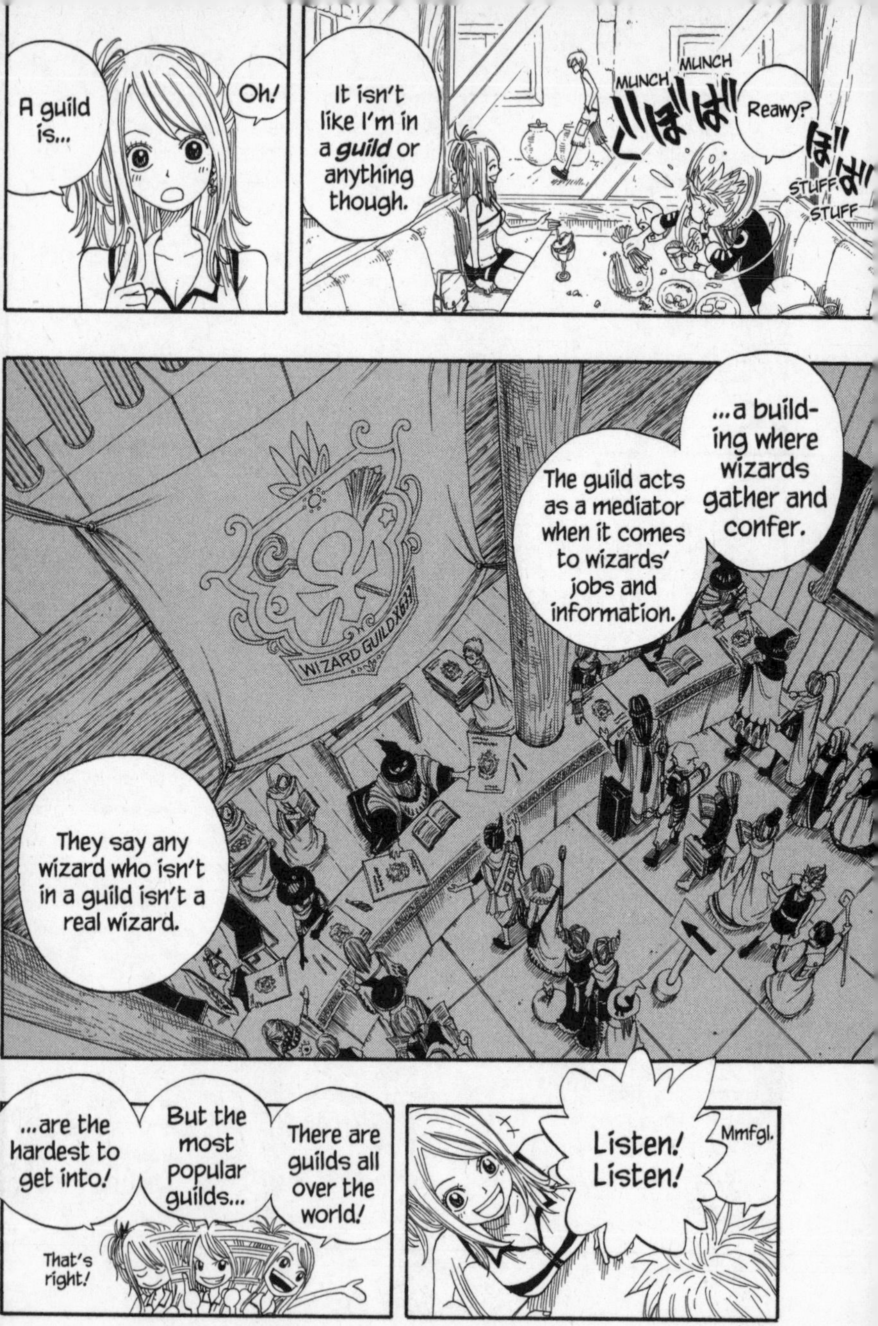
MUNCH
MUNCH
Reawy?
STUFF
STUFF
It isn't like I'm in a *guild* or anything though.
Oh!
A guild is...
...a building where wizards gather and confer.
The guild acts as a mediator when it comes to wizards' jobs and information.
They say any wizard who isn't in a guild isn't a real wizard.
Mmfgl.
Listen! Listen!
There are guilds all over the world!
But the most popular guilds...
...are the hardest to get into!
That's right!

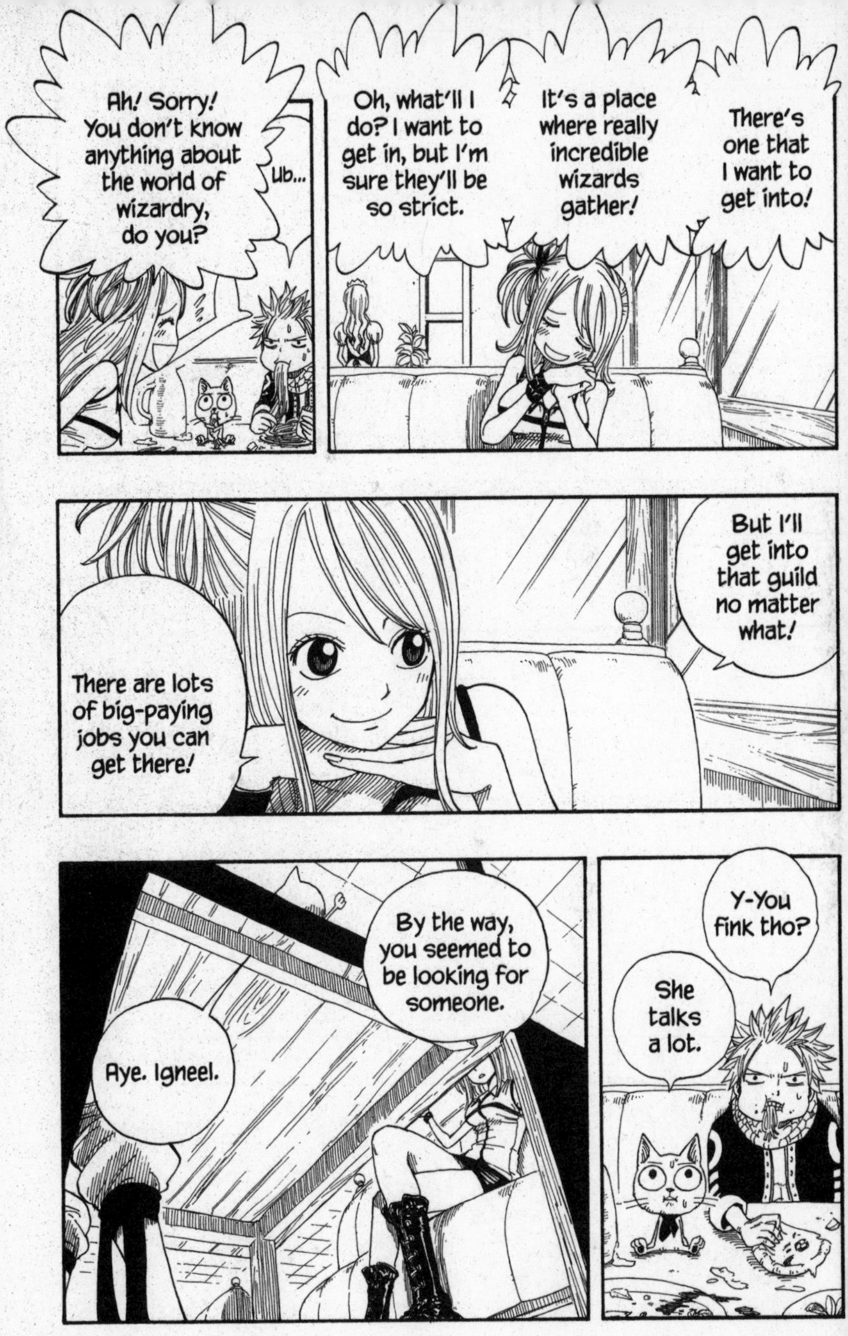
There's one that I want to get into!
It's a place where really incredible wizards gather!
Oh, what'll I do? I want to get in, but I'm sure they'll be so strict.
Ah! Sorry! You don't know anything about the world of wizardry, do you?
Uh...
But I'll get into that guild no matter what!
There are lots of big-paying jobs you can get there!
Y-You fink tho?
She talks a lot.
By the way, you seemed to be looking for someone.
Aye. Igneel.

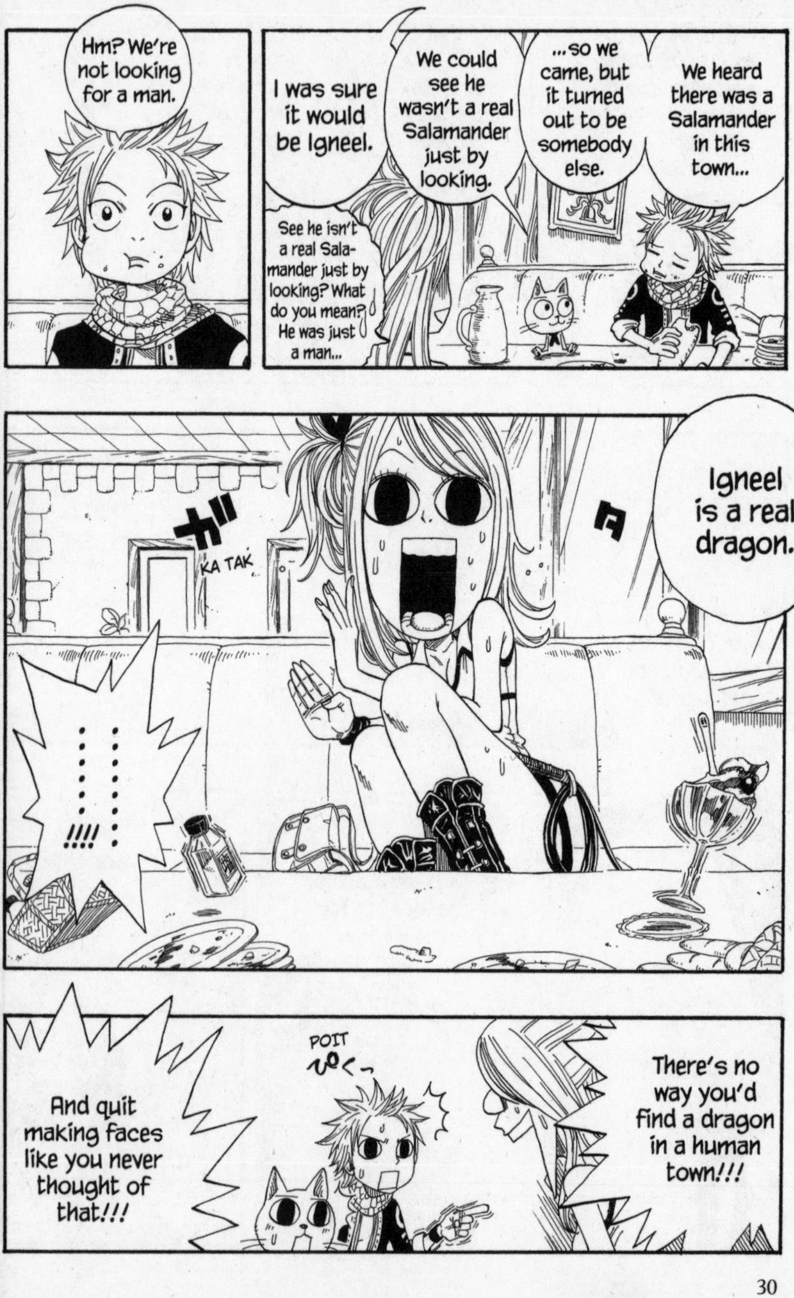
We heard there was a Salamander in this town...
...so we came, but it turned out to be somebody else.
We could see he wasn't a real Salamander just by looking.
I was sure it would be Igneel.
See he isn't a real Salamander just by looking? What do you mean? He was just a man...
Hm? We're not looking for a man.
Igneel is a real dragon.
ガ
KA TAK
!!!!
There's no way you'd find a dragon in a human town!!!
POIT
And quit making faces like you never thought of that!!!

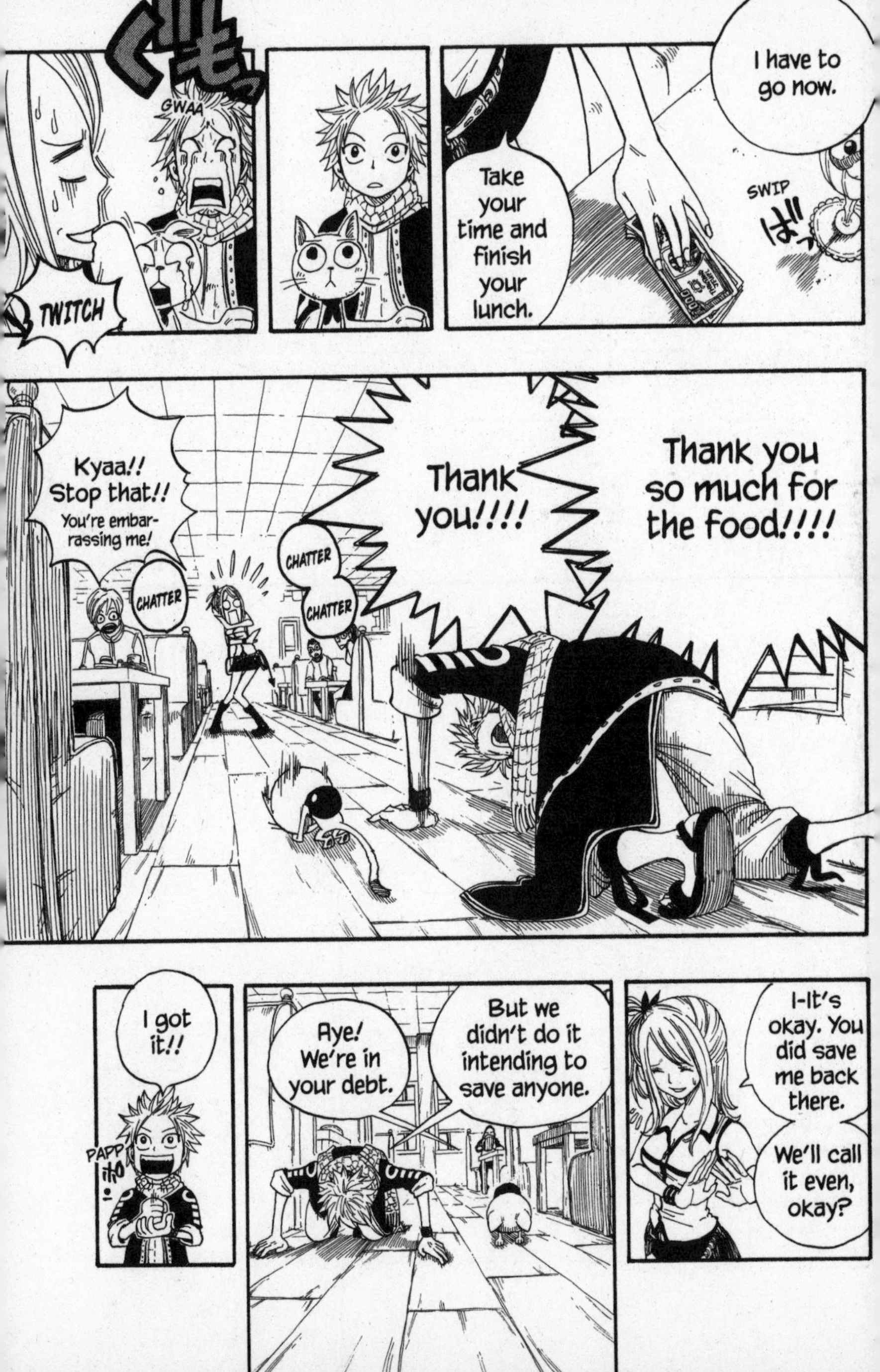
I have to go now.
SWIP
Take your time and finish your lunch.
GWAA
TWITCH
Thank you so much for the food!!!!
Thank you!!!!
CHATTER
CHATTER
Kyaa!! Stop that!! You're embarrassing me!
CHATTER
I-It's okay. You did save me back there.
We'll call it even, okay?
But we didn't do it intending to save anyone.
Aye! We're in your debt.
I got it!!
PAPP

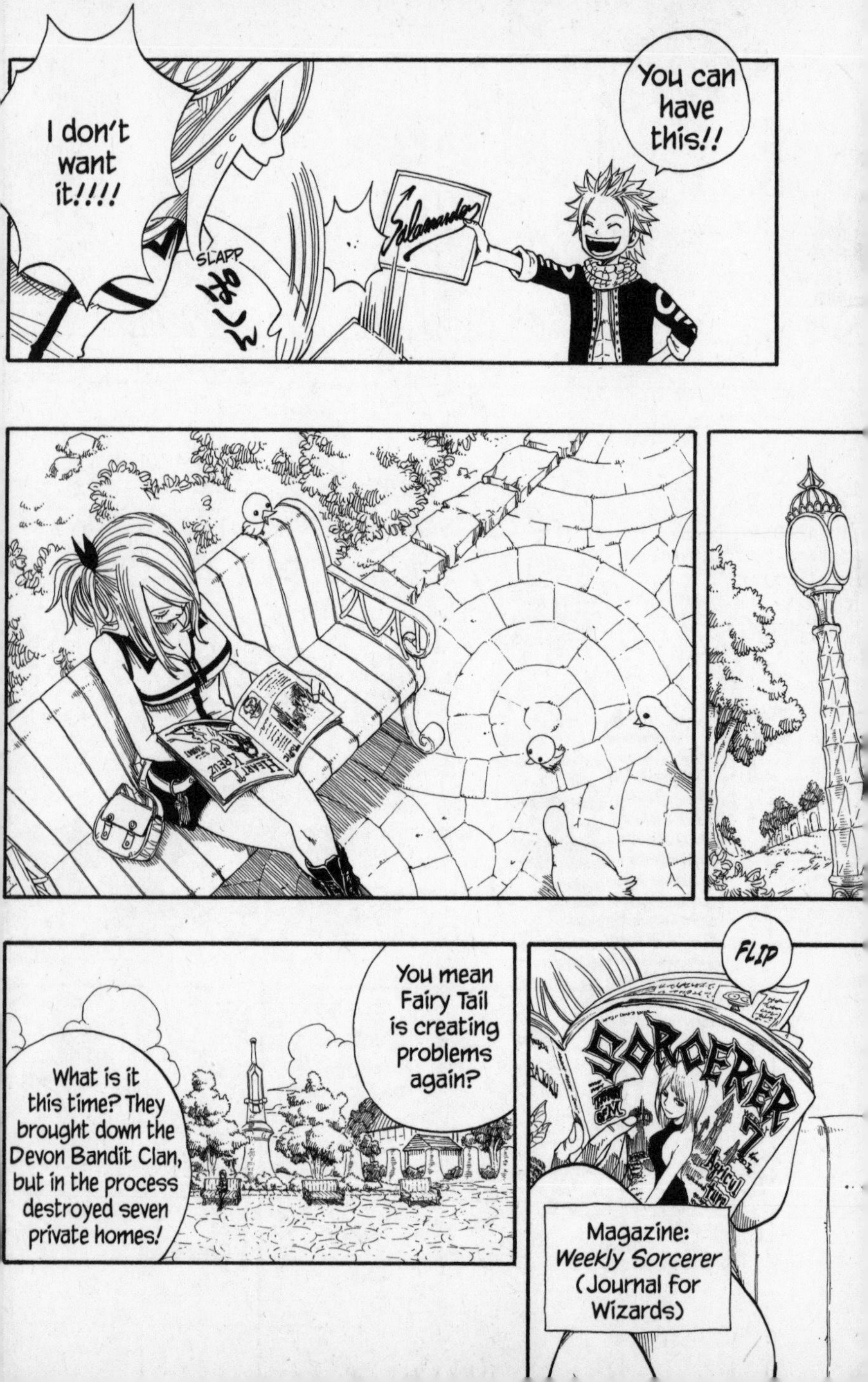
You can have this!!
I don't want it!!!!
SLAPP
FLIP
SORCERER
7
Magazine: Weekly Sorcerer (Journal for Wizards)
You mean Fairy Tail is creating problems again?
What is it this time? They brought down the Devon Bandit Clan, but in the process destroyed seven private homes!

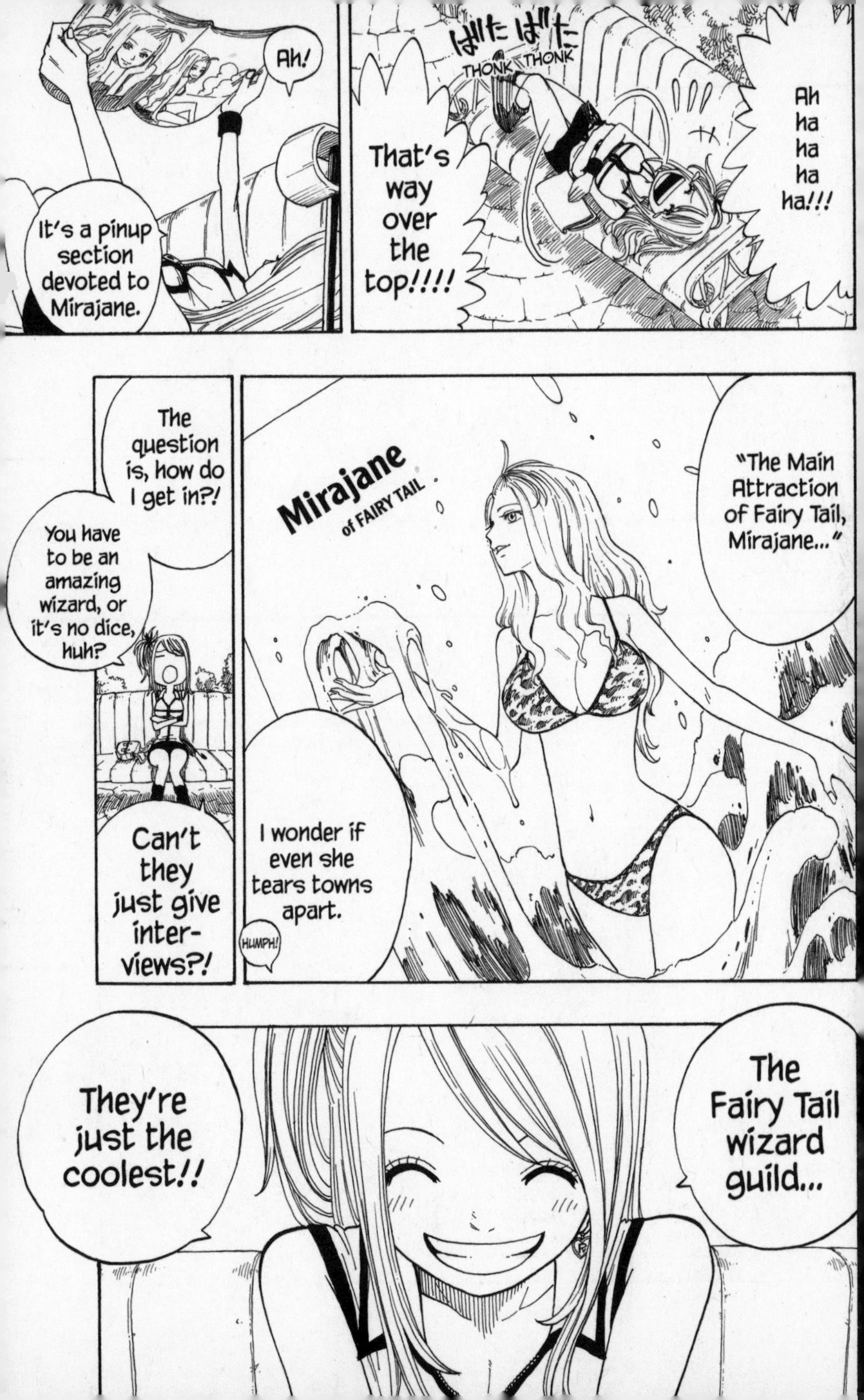
ばたばた
THONK THONK
Ah ha ha ha ha!!!
That's way over the top!!!!
Ah!
It's a pinup section devoted to Mirajane.
"The Main Attraction of Fairy Tail, Mirajane..."
Mirajane of FAIRY TAIL
I wonder if even she tears towns apart.
HUMPH!
The question is, how do I get in?!
You have to be an amazing wizard, or it's no dice, huh?
Can't they just give inter-views?!
The Fairy Tail wizard guild...
They're just the coolest!!

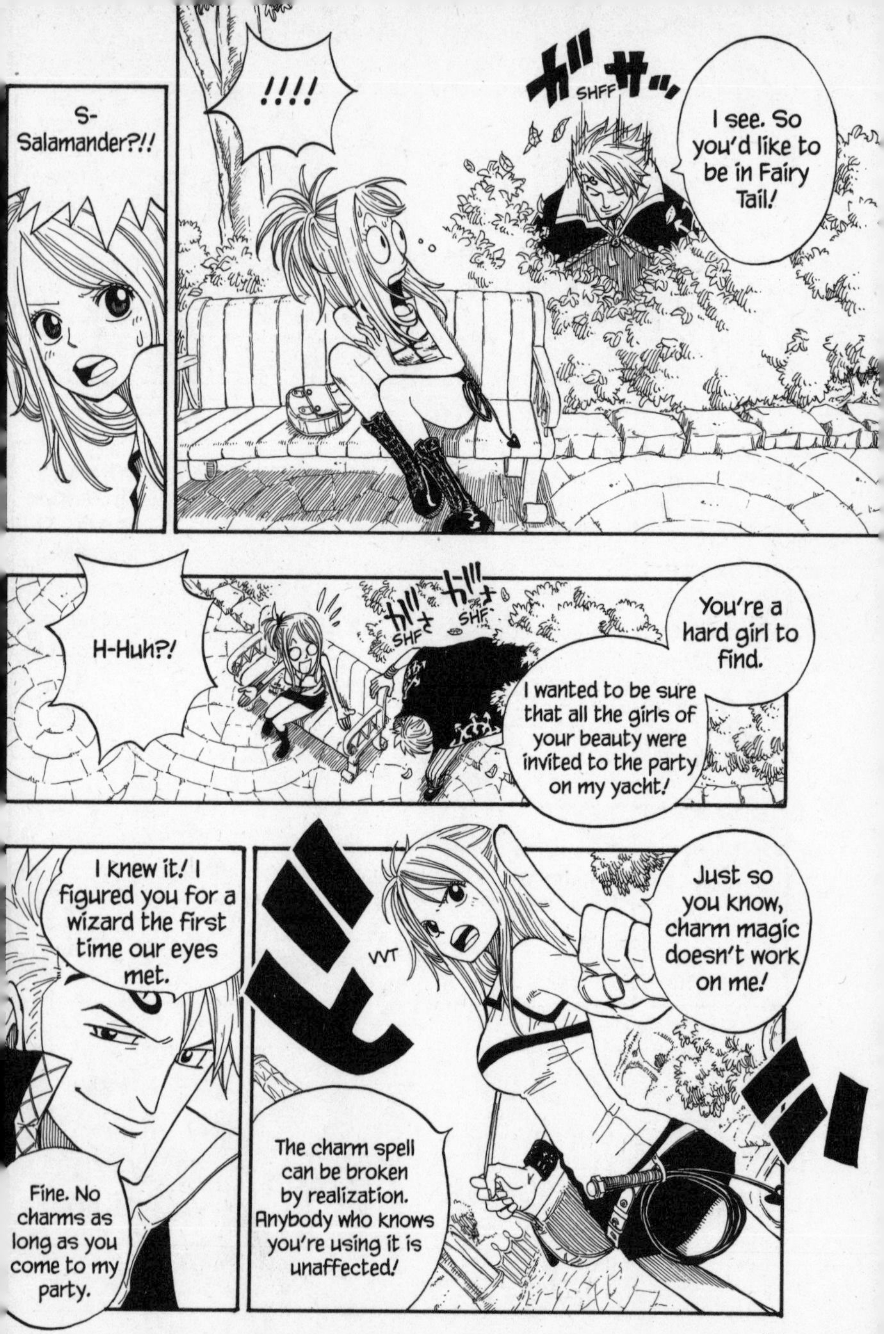
SHFF
I see. So you'd like to be in Fairy Tail!
!!!!
S-Salamander?!!
You're a hard girl to find.
I wanted to be sure that all the girls of your beauty were invited to the party on my yacht!
SHF
SHF
H-Huh?!
Just so you know, charm magic doesn't work on me!
VVT
The charm spell can be broken by realization. Anybody who knows you're using it is unaffected!
I knew it! I figured you for a wizard the first time our eyes met.
Fine. No charms as long as you come to my party.

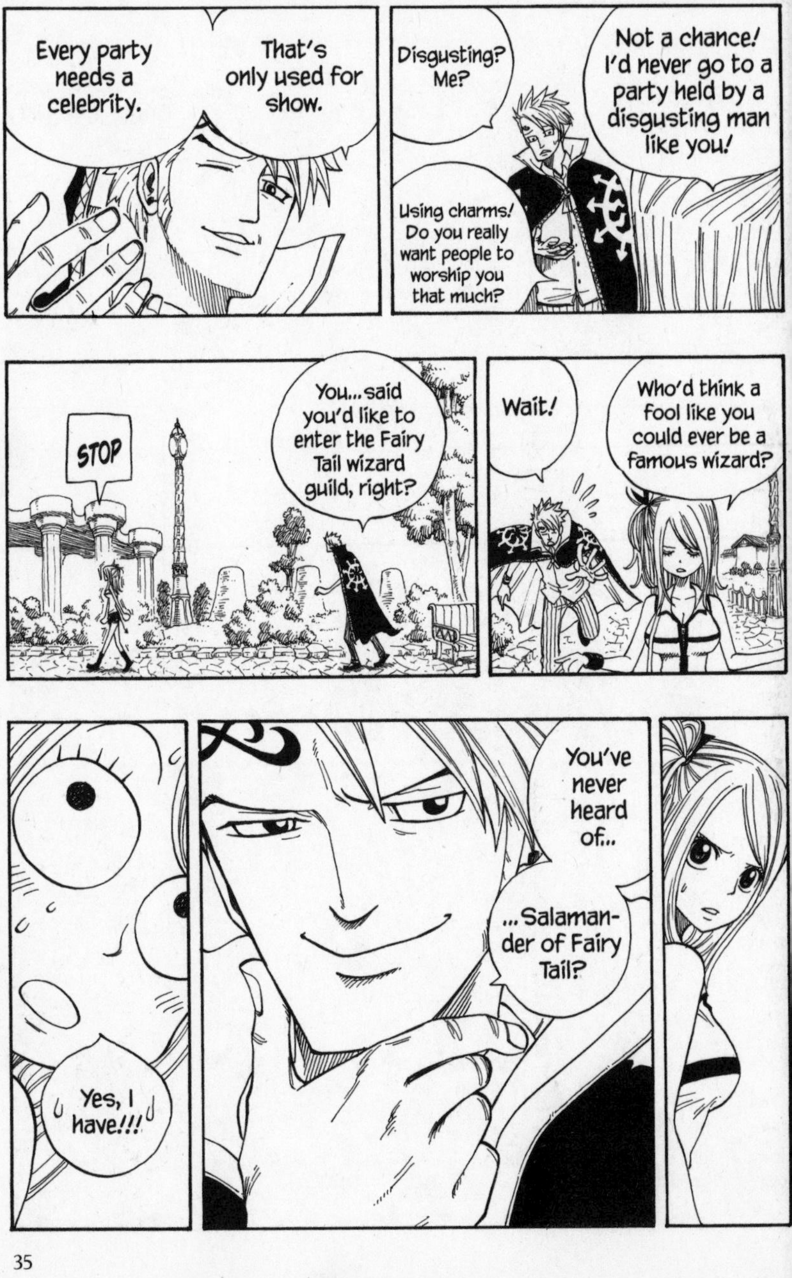
Not a chance! I'd never go to a party held by a disgusting man like you!
Disgusting? Me?
Using charms! Do you really want people to worship you that much?
That's only used for show.
Every party needs a celebrity.
Who'd think a fool like you could ever be a famous wizard?
Wait!
You... said you'd like to enter the Fairy Tail wizard guild, right?
STOP
You've never heard of...
... Salaman-der of Fairy Tail?
Yes, I have!!!

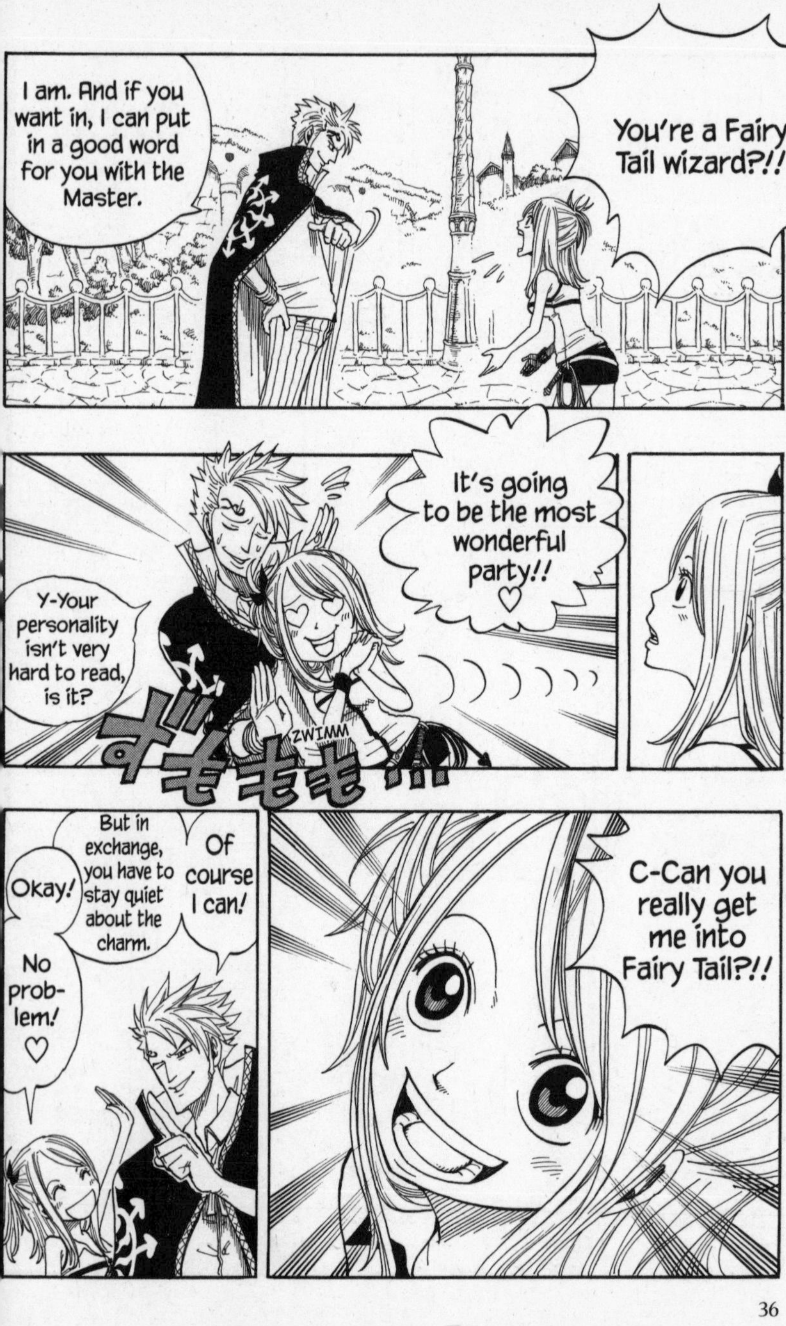
You're a Fairy Tail wizard?!!
I am. And if you want in, I can put in a good word for you with the Master.
It's going to be the most wonderful party!! ♡
Y-Your personality isn't very hard to read, is it?
ずももも…
ZWIMM
C-Can you really get me into Fairy Tail?!!
Of course I can!
But in exchange, you have to stay quiet about the charm.
Okay!
No problem! ♡

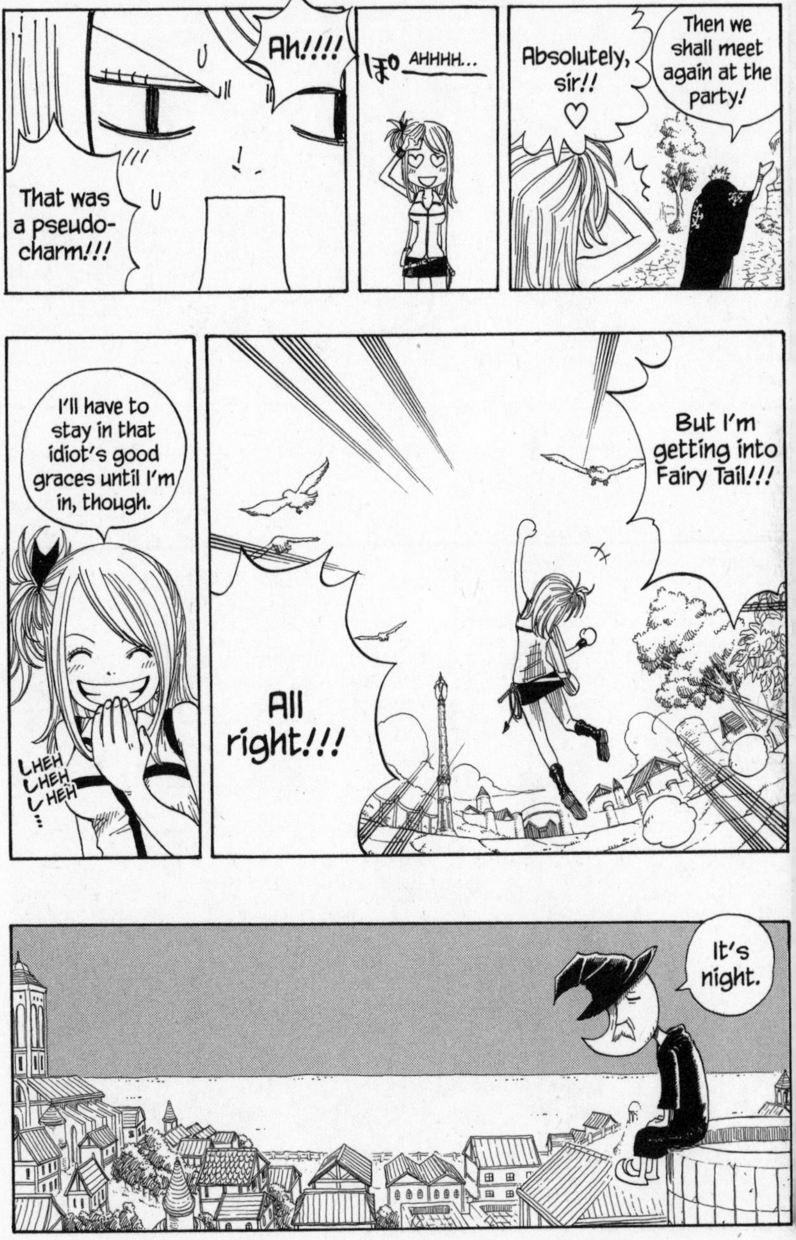
Then we shall meet again at the party!
Absolutely, sir!!
ぽ AHHHH...
Ah!!!!
That was a pseudo-charm!!!
But I'm getting into Fairy Tail!!!
All right!!!
I'll have to stay in that idiot's good graces until I'm in, though.
HEH HEH HEH...
It's night.

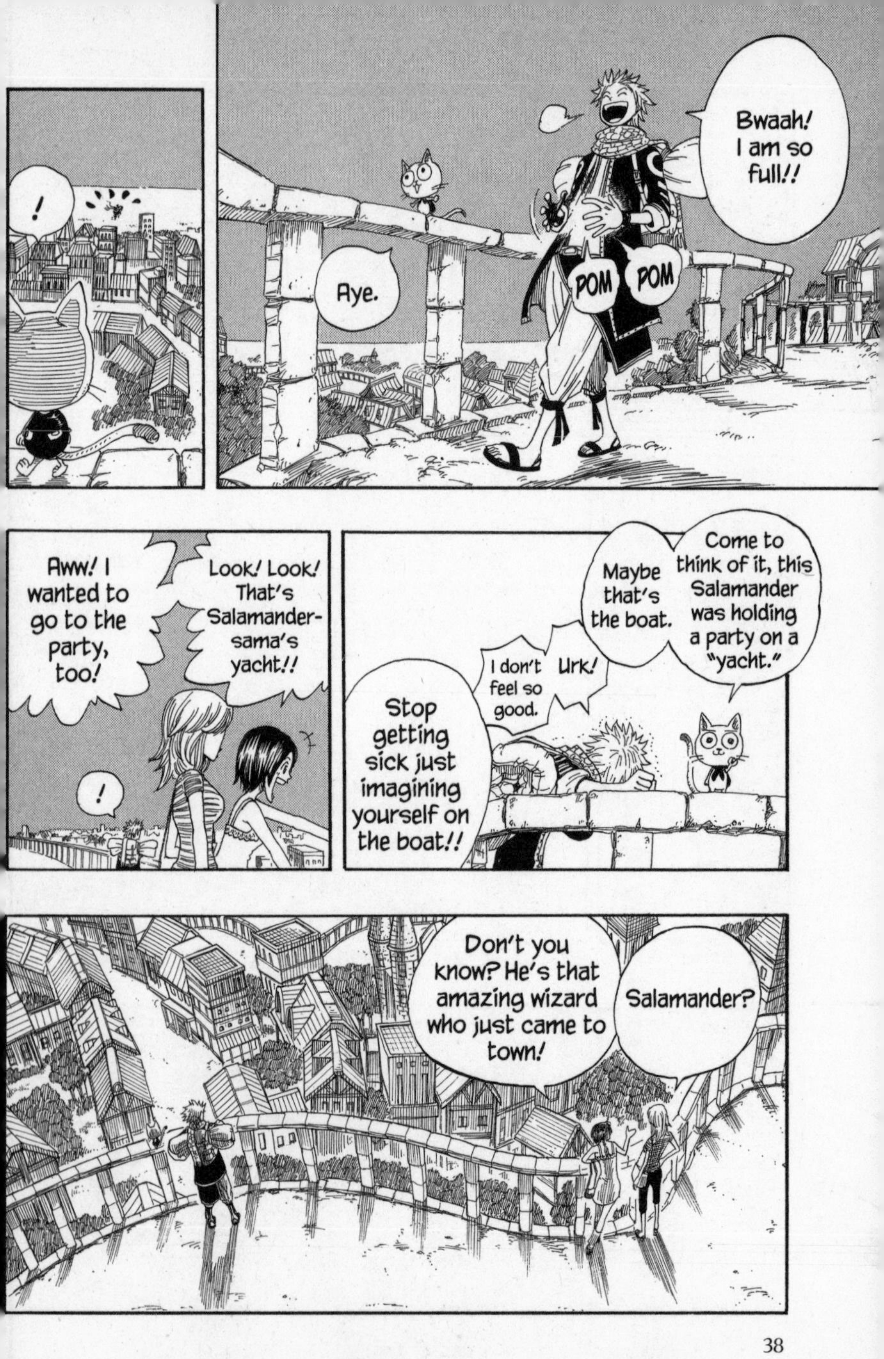
Bwaah! I am so full!!
POM
POM
Aye.
!
Come to think of it, this Salamander was holding a party on a "yacht."
Maybe that's the boat.
Urk!
I don't feel so good.
Stop getting sick just imagining yourself on the boat!!
Look! Look! That's Salamander-sama's yacht!!
Aww! I wanted to go to the party, too!
!
Salamander?
Don't you know? He's that amazing wizard who just came to town!

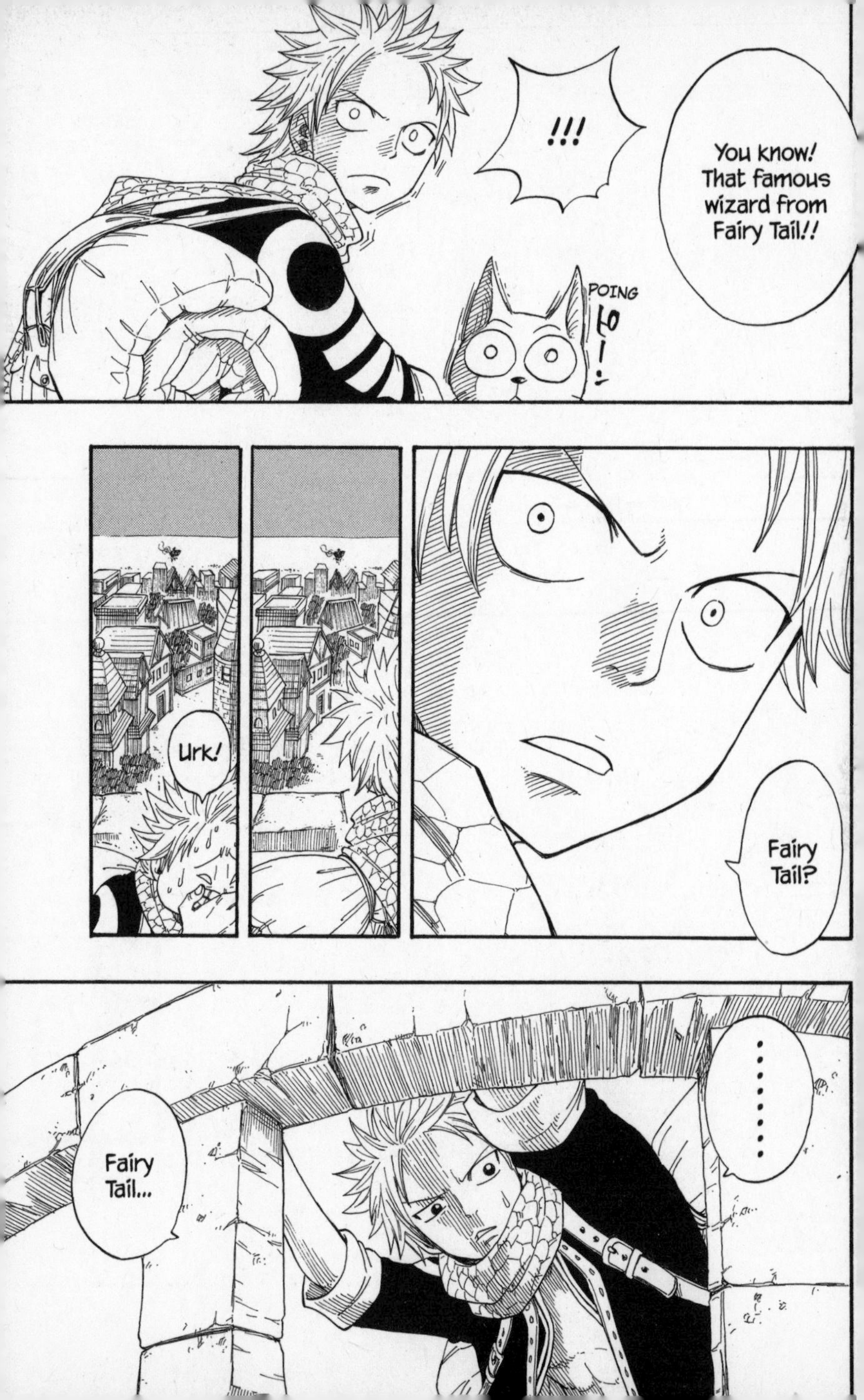
You know! That famous wizard from Fairy Tail!!
!!!
POING
Fairy Tail?
Urk!
Fairy Tail...
....

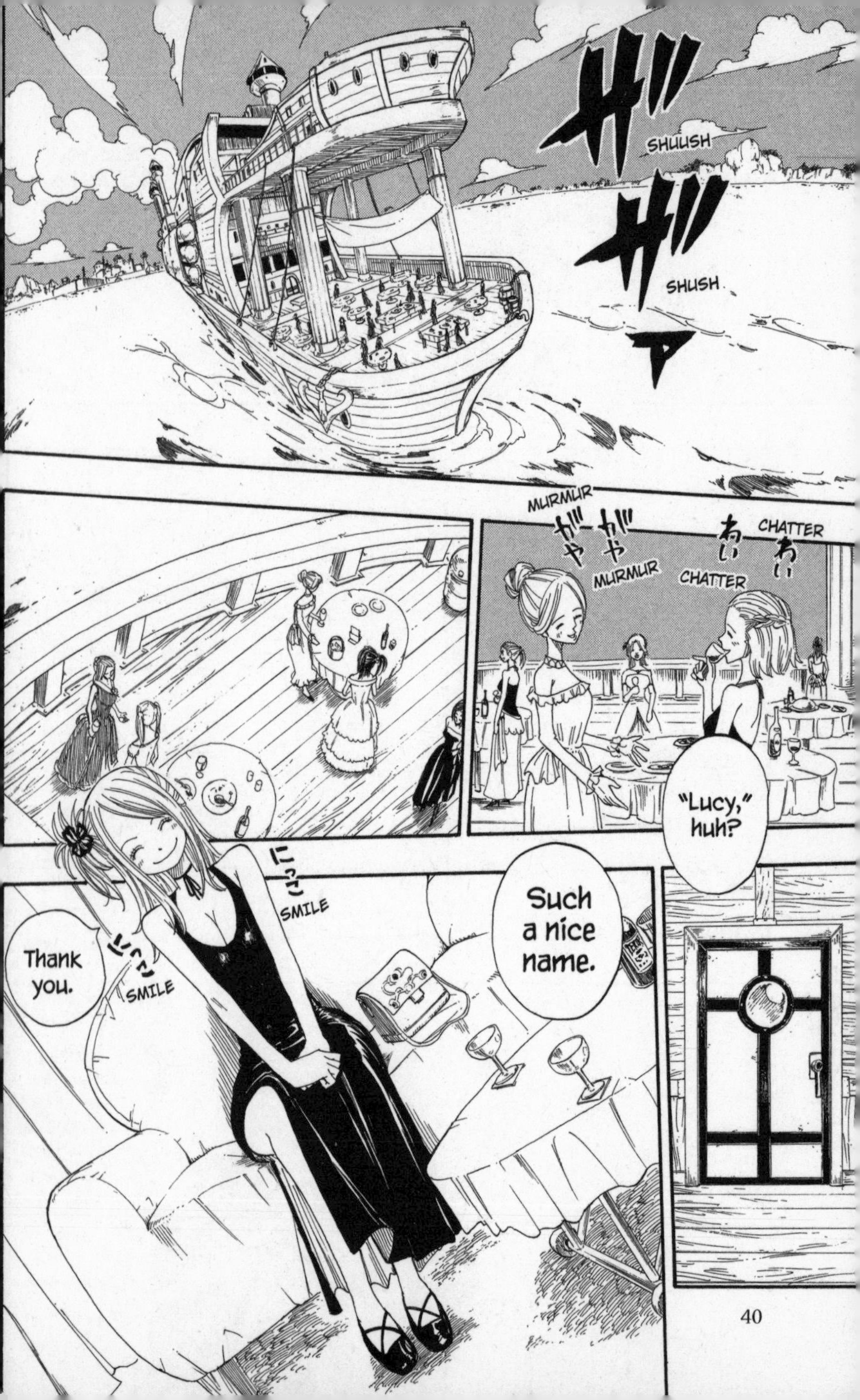
SHUUSH
SHUSH
MURMUR
MURMUR
CHATTER
CHATTER
"Lucy," huh?
Such a nice name.
SMILE
SMILE
Thank you.

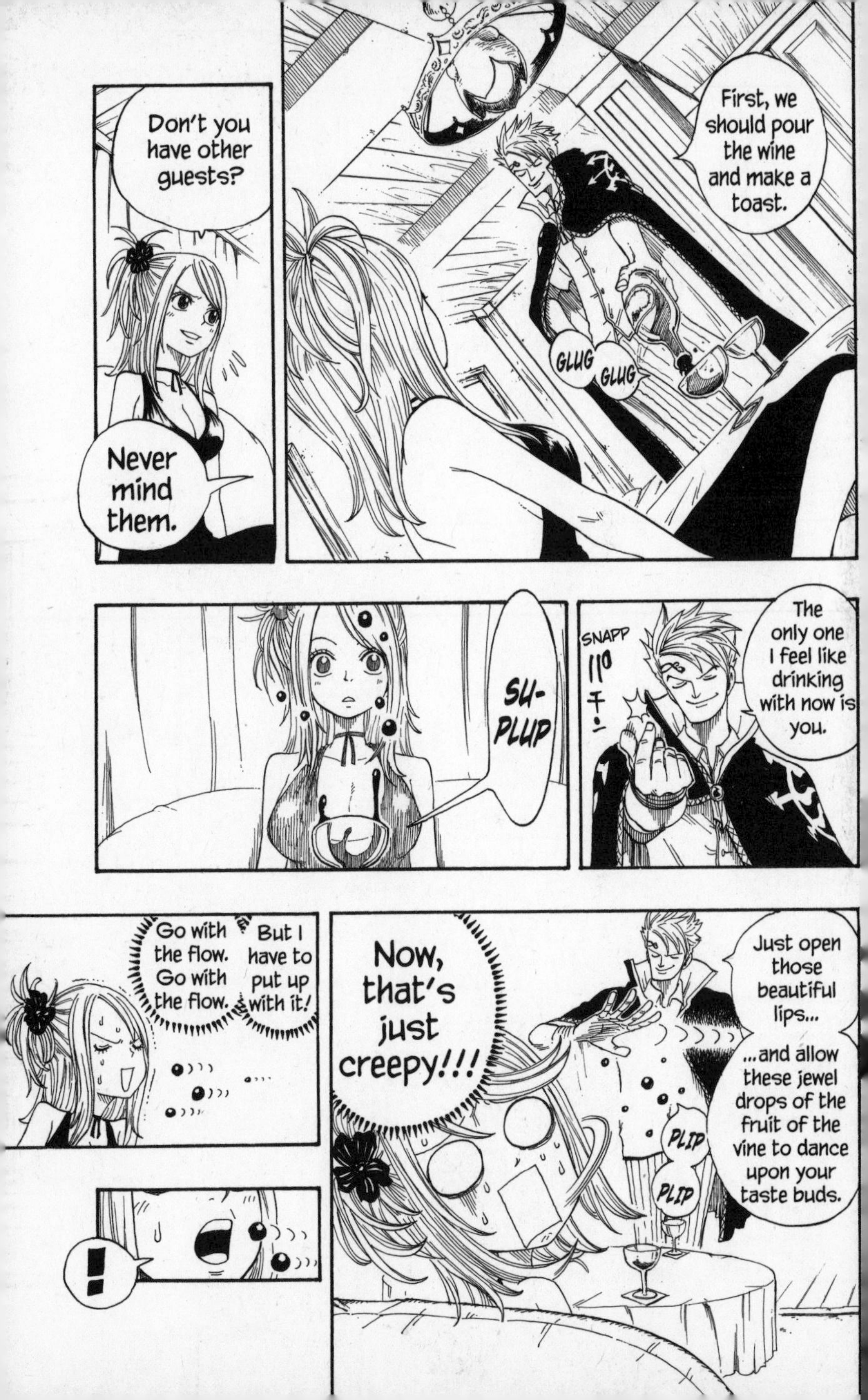
First, we should pour the wine and make a toast.
GLUG
GLUG
Don't you have other guests?
Never mind them.
The only one I feel like drinking with now is you.
SNAPP
SU-PLUP
Just open those beautiful lips...
...and allow these jewel drops of the fruit of the vine to dance upon your taste buds.
PLIP
PLIP
Now, that's just creepy!!!
But I have to put up with it!
Go with the flow. Go with the flow.
!

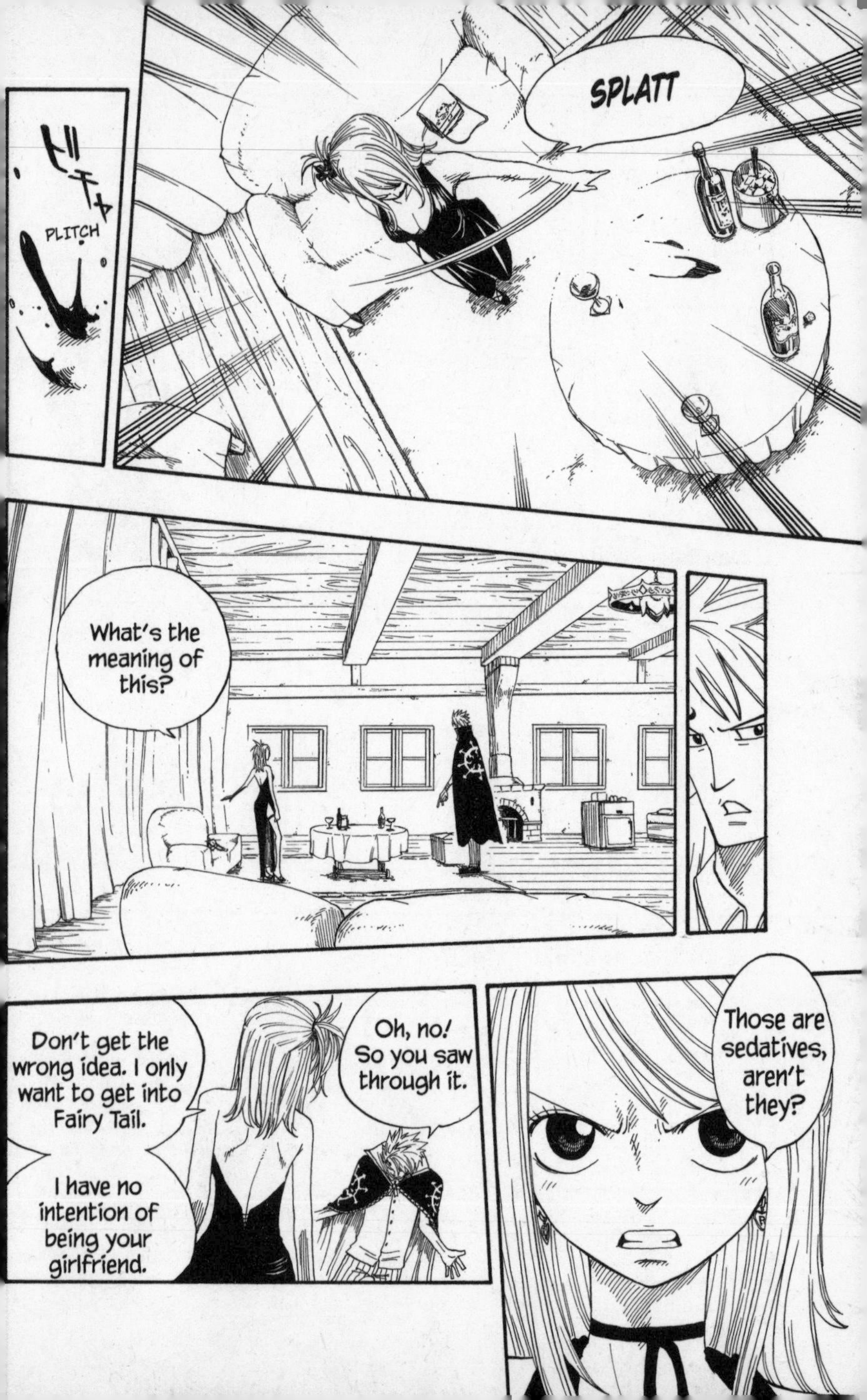
SPLATT
ビチャ
PLITCH
Those are sedatives, aren't they?
What's the meaning of this?
Oh, no! So you saw through it.
Don't get the wrong idea. I only want to get into Fairy Tail.
I have no intention of being your girlfriend.

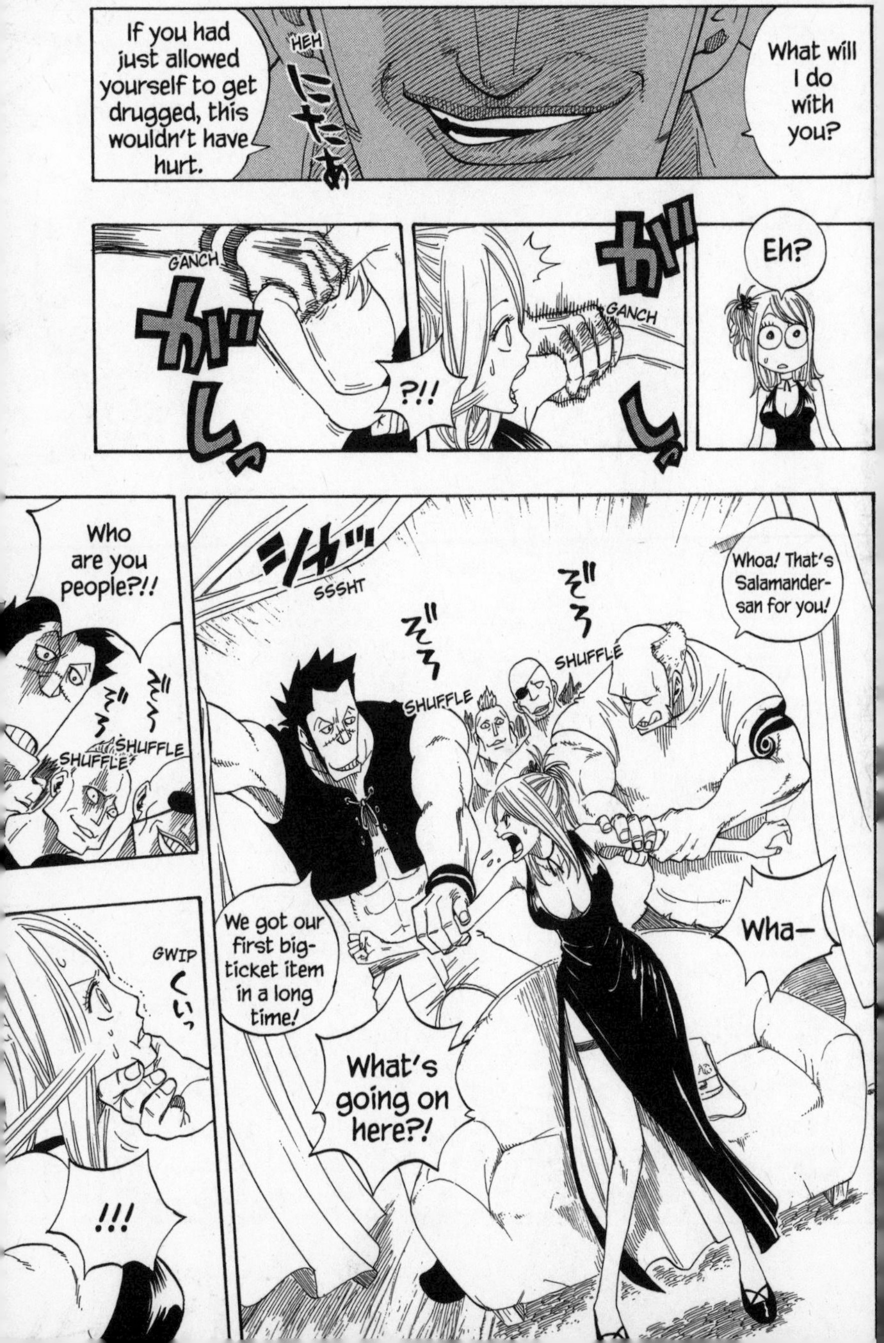
What will I do with you?
HEH
If you had just allowed yourself to get drugged, this wouldn't have hurt.
Eh?
GANCH
?!!
GANCH
Whoa! That's Salamander-san for you!
SHUFFLE
SSSHT
SHUFFLE
Wha-
We got our first big-ticket item in a long time!
What's going on here?!
Who are you people?!!
SHUFFLE
SHUFFLE
GWIP
!!!

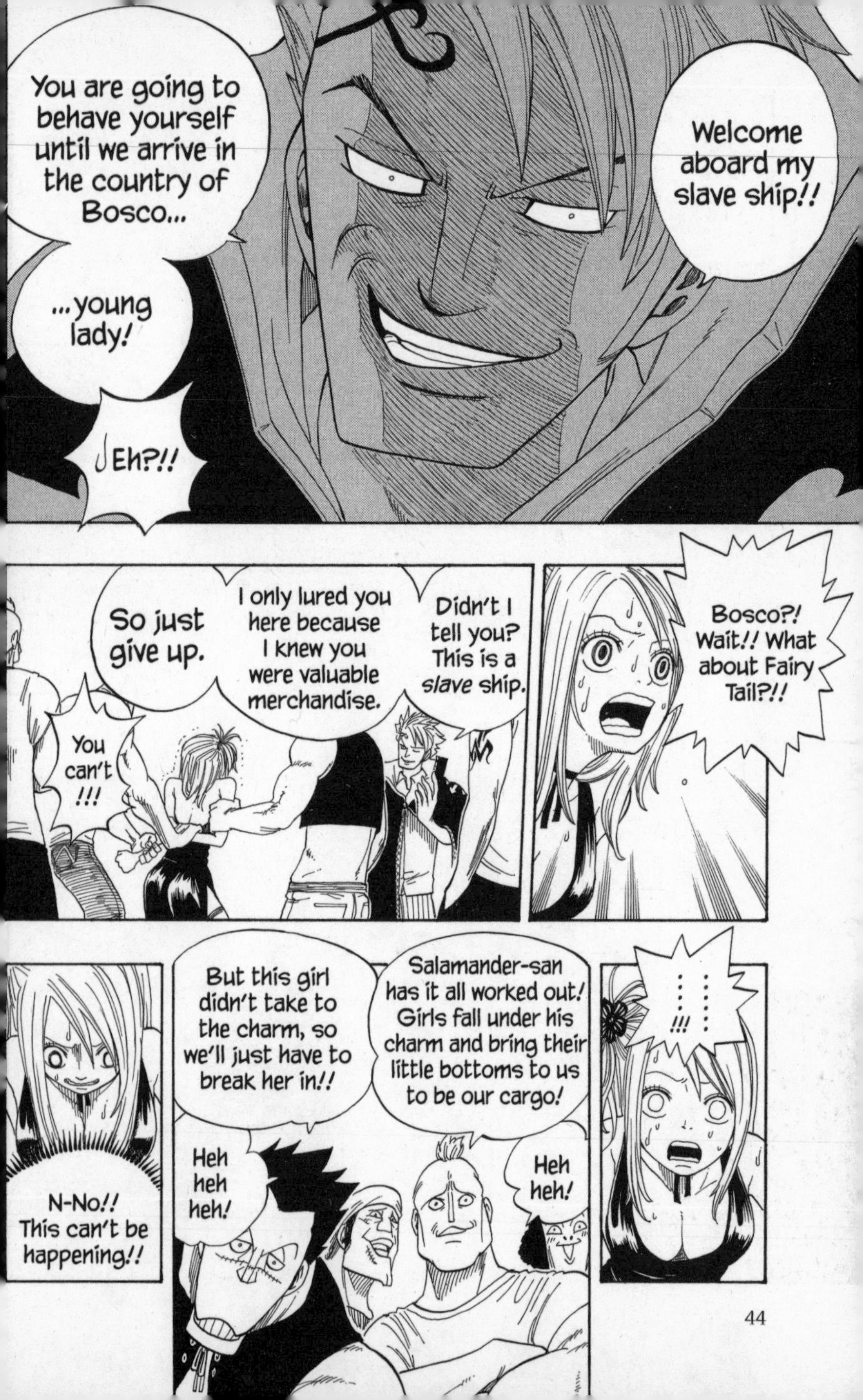
Welcome aboard my slave ship!!
You are going to behave yourself until we arrive in the country of Bosco...
...young lady!
Eh?!!
Bosco?! Wait!! What about Fairy Tail?!!
Didn't I tell you? This is a *slave* ship.
I only lured you here because I knew you were valuable merchandise.
So just give up.
You can't!!!
......!!!
Salamander-san has it all worked out! Girls fall under his charm and bring their little bottoms to us to be our cargo!
But this girl didn't take to the charm, so we'll just have to break her in!!
Heh heh!
Heh heh heh!
N-No!! This can't be happening!!

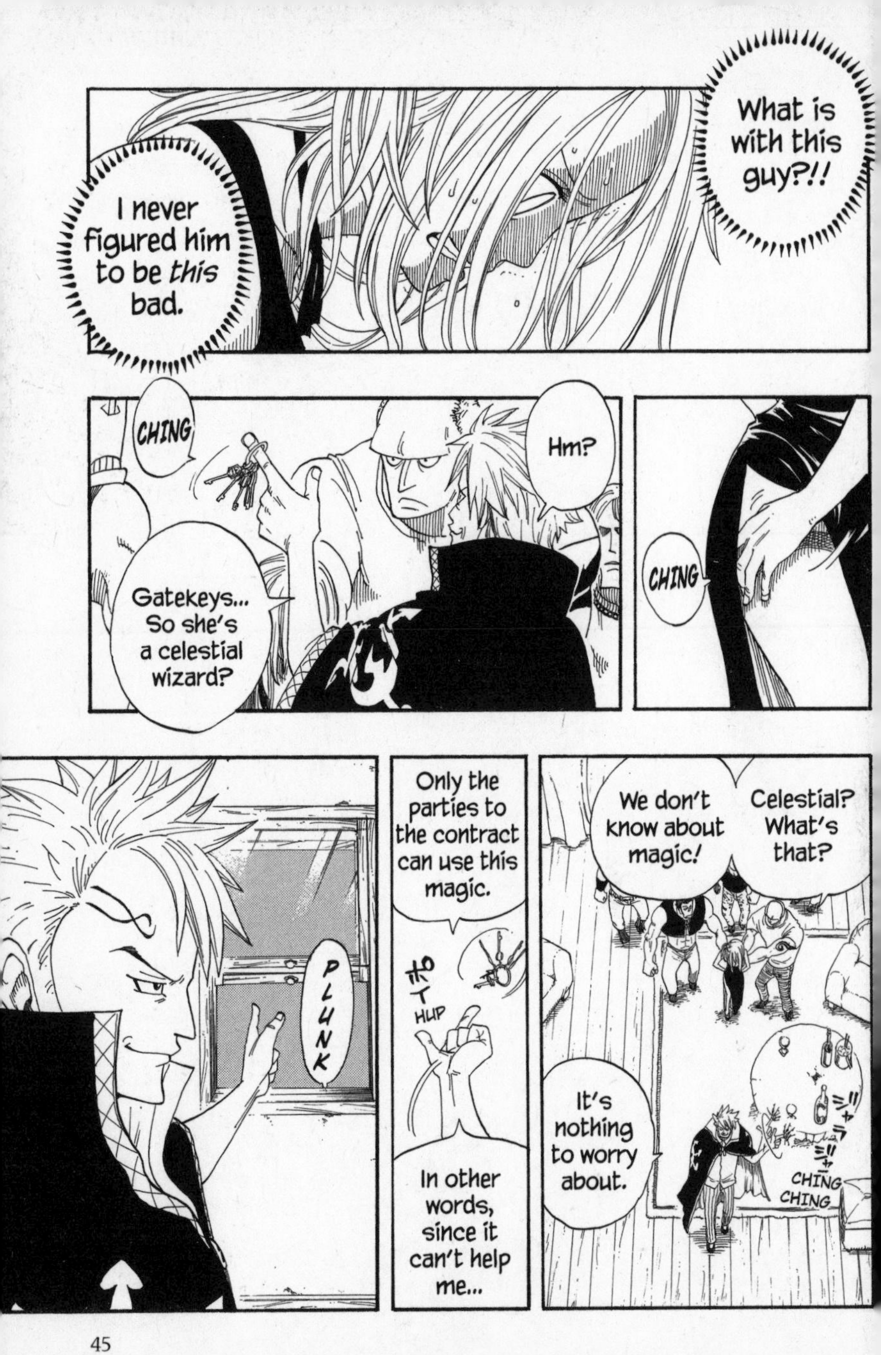
What is with this guy?!!
I never figured him to be *this* bad.
CHING
Hm?
CHING
Gatekeys... So she's a celestial wizard?
Celestial? What's that?
We don't know about magic!
It's nothing to worry about.
CHING CHING
Only the parties to the contract can use this magic.
HUP
In other words, since it can't help me...
PLUNK

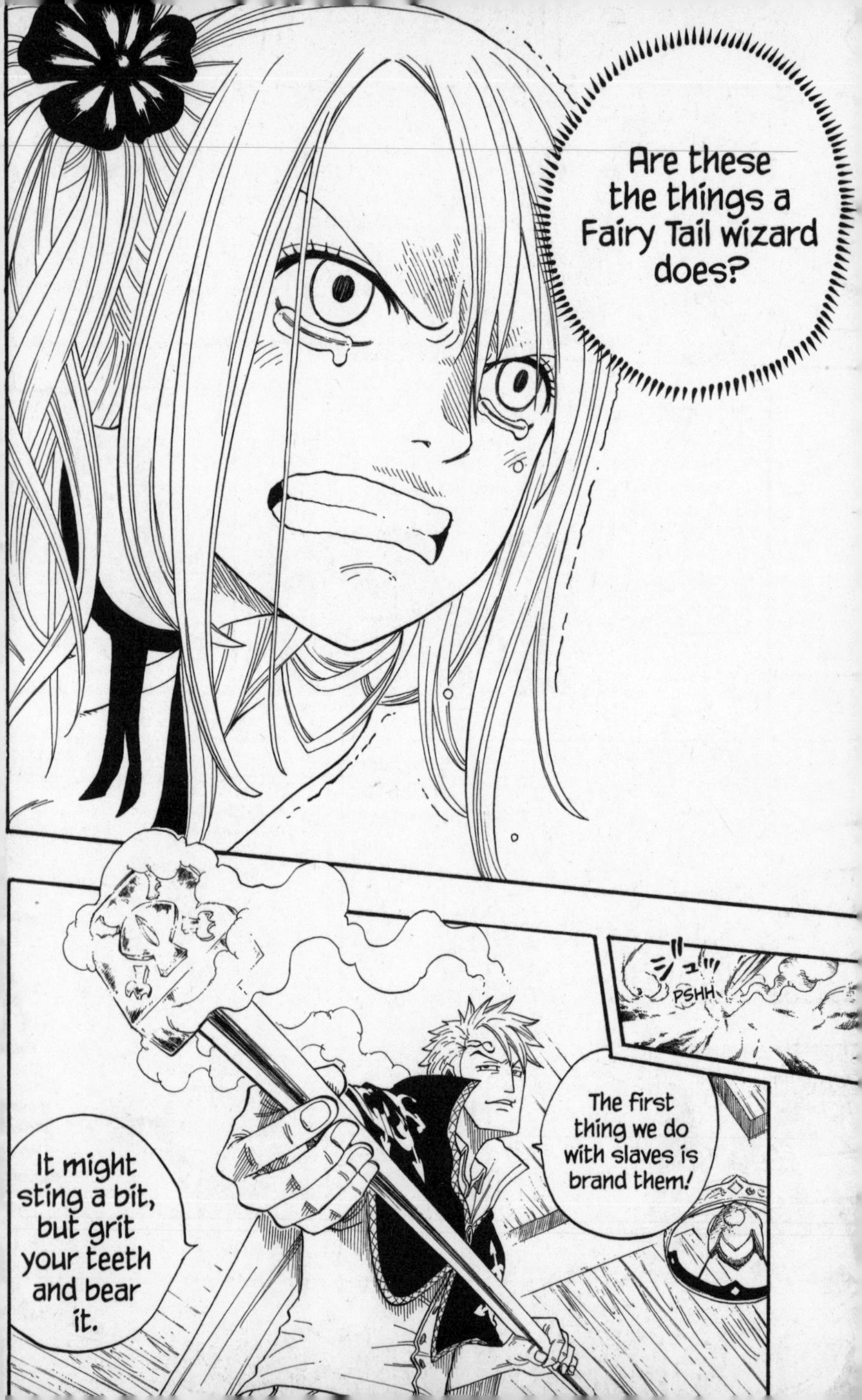

Are these the things a Fairy Tail wizard does?
PSHH
The first thing we do with slaves is brand them!
It might sting a bit, but grit your teeth and bear it.

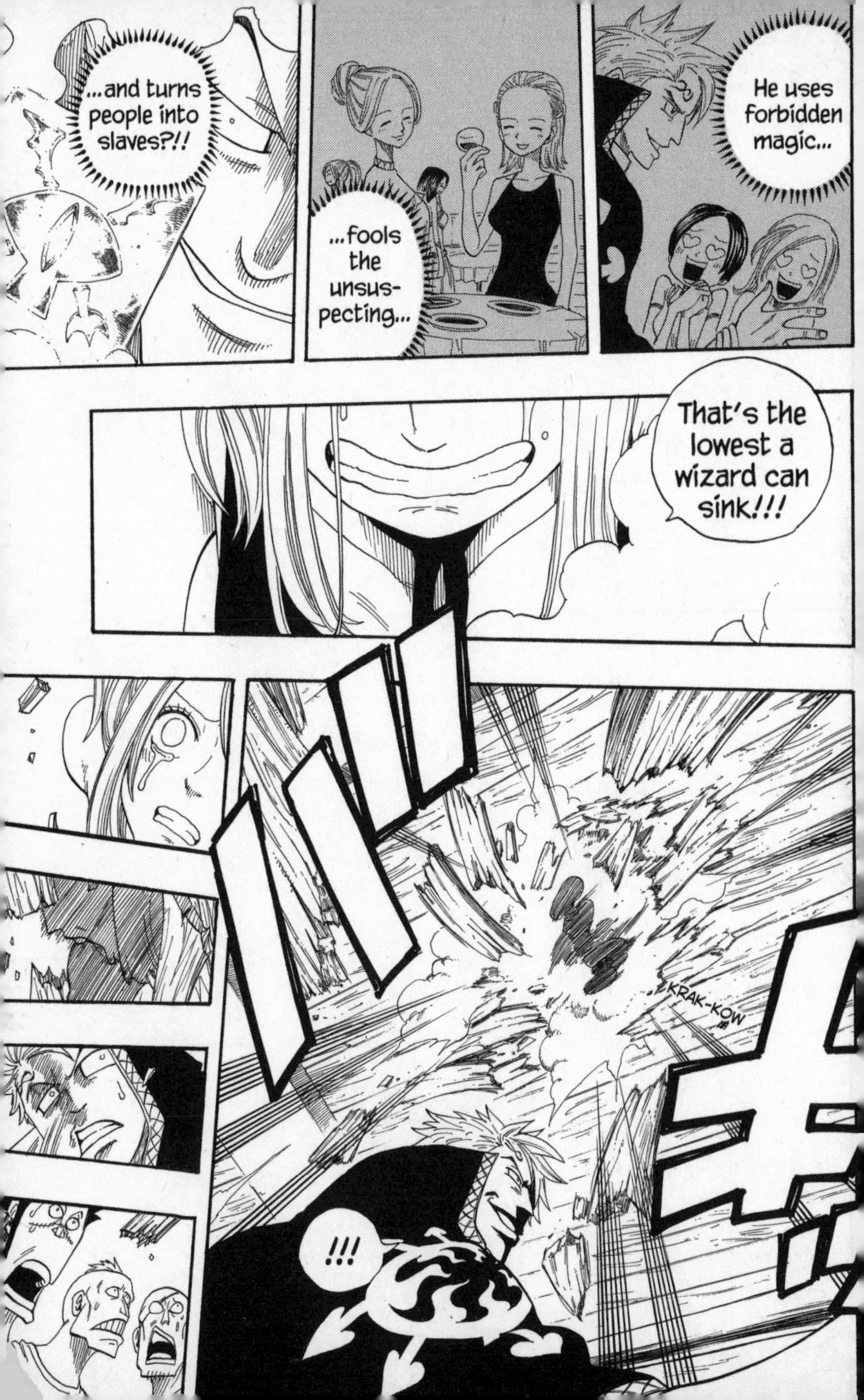
He uses forbidden magic...
...fools the unsus-pecting...
...and turns people into slaves?!!
That's the lowest a wizard can sink!!!
KRAK-KOW
!!!

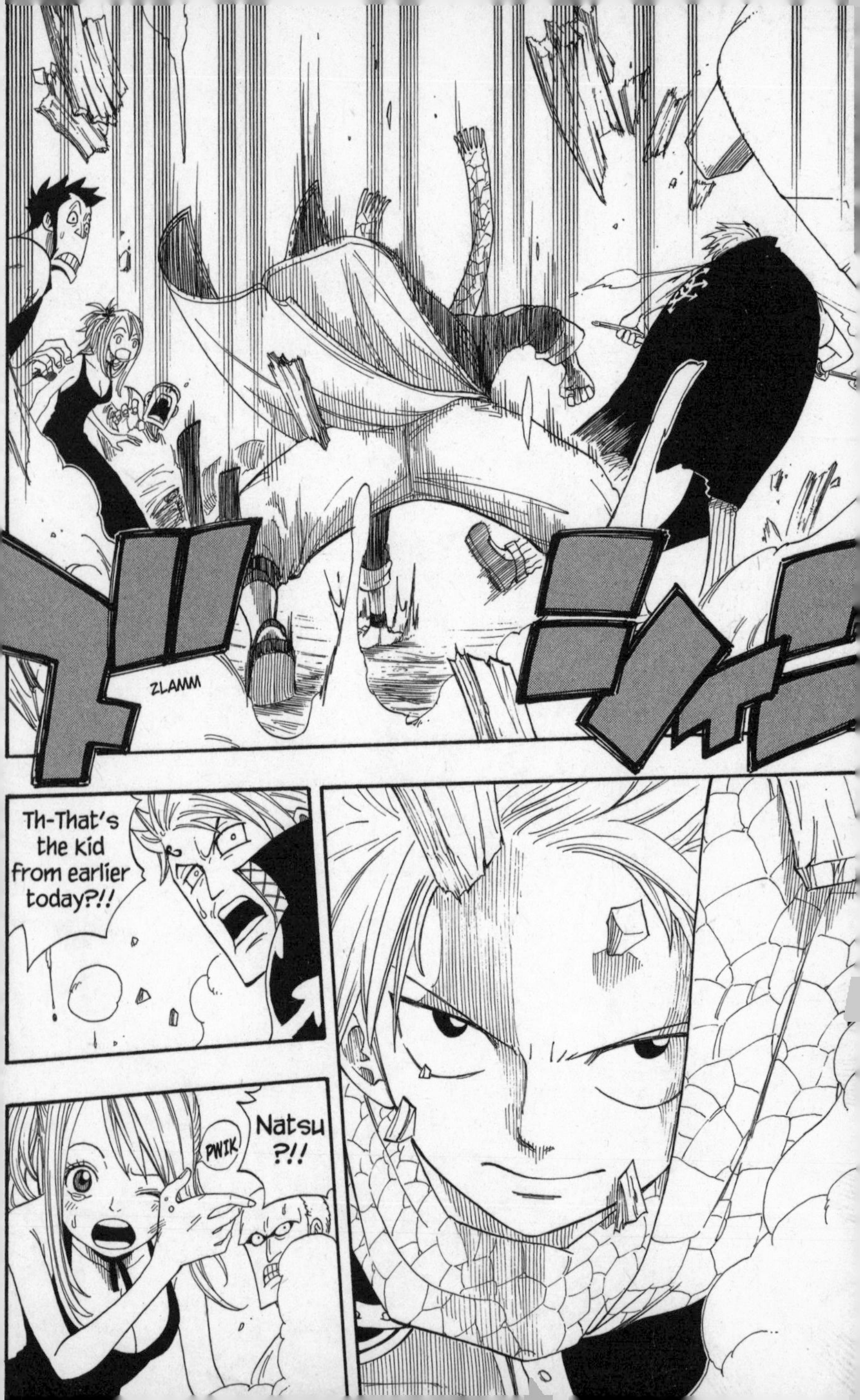
ZLAMM
Th-That's the kid from earlier today?!!
Natsu ?!!
PWIK

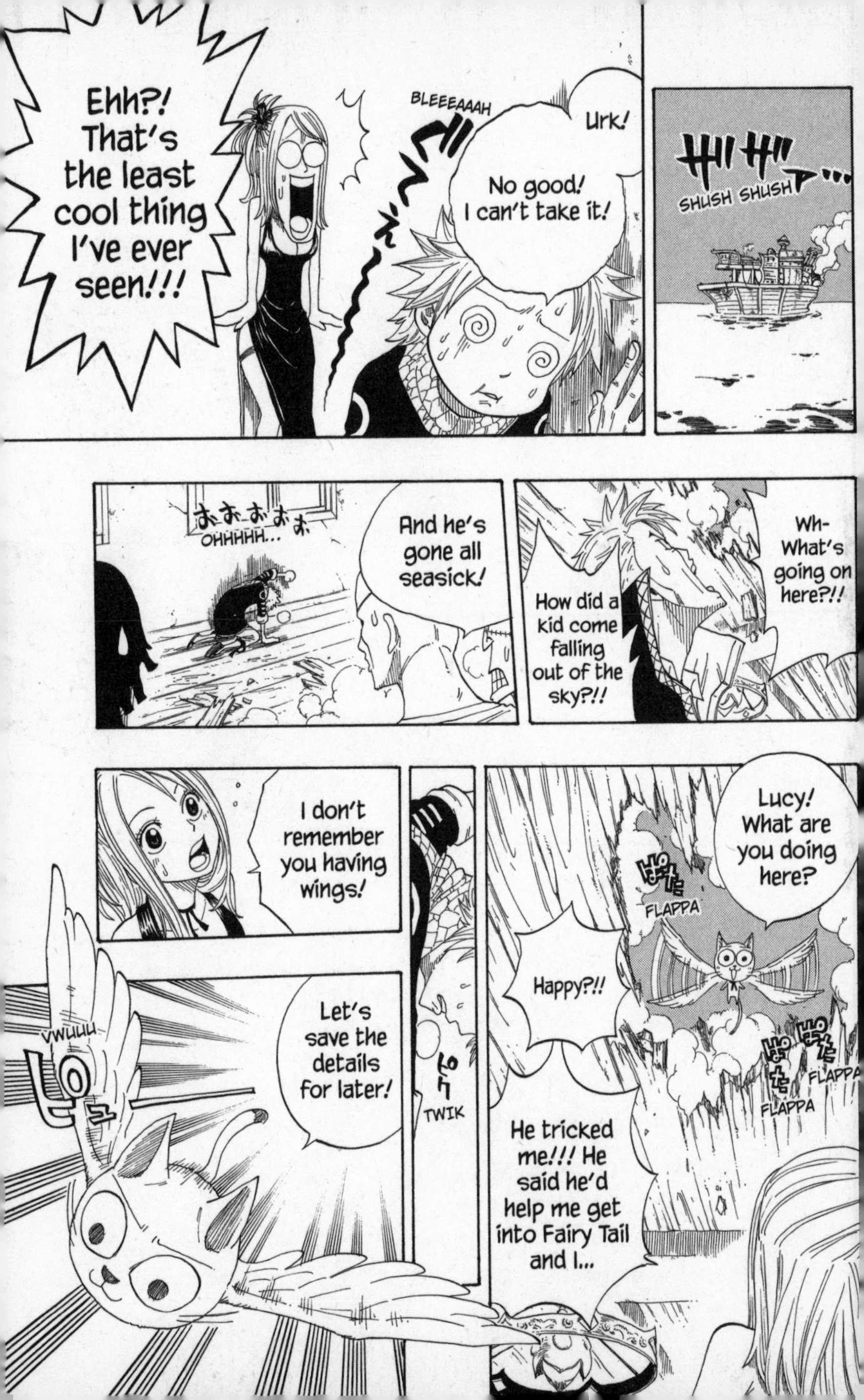
SHUSH SHUSH
BLEEEAAAH
Urk!
No good! I can't take it!
Ehh?! That's the least cool thing I've ever seen!!!
Wh- What's going on here?!!
How did a kid come falling out of the sky?!!
OHHHHH...
And he's gone all seasick!
Lucy! What are you doing here?
FLAPPA
Happy?!!
FLAPPA
FLAPPA
He tricked me!!! He said he'd help me get into Fairy Tail and I...
I don't remember you having wings!
TWIK
Let's save the details for later!
VWUUU

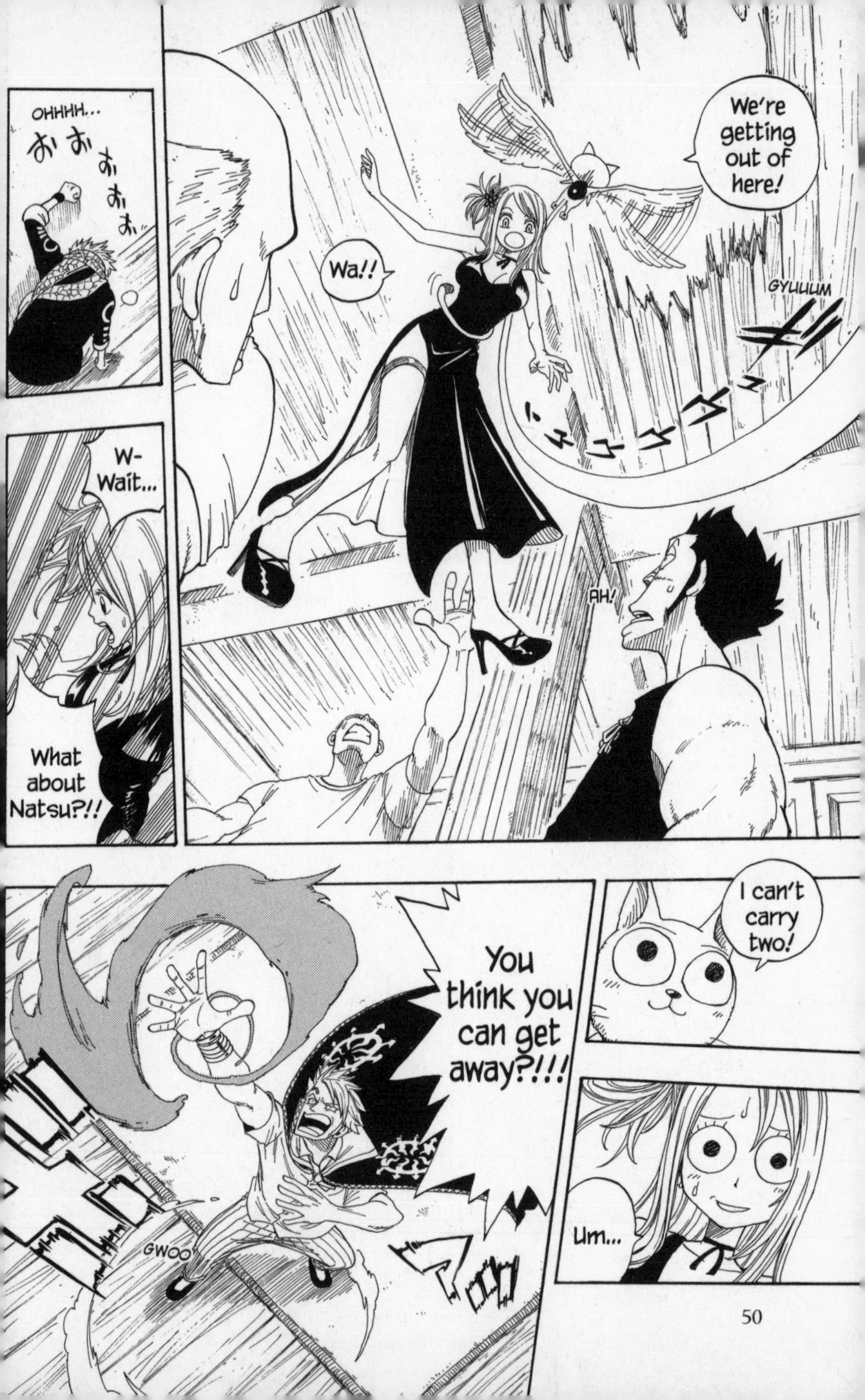
We're getting out of here!
Wa!!
GYUUUM
AH!
OHHHH...
おおおおお
W- Wait...
What about Natsu?!!
I can't carry two!
Um...
You think you can get away?!!!
GWOO

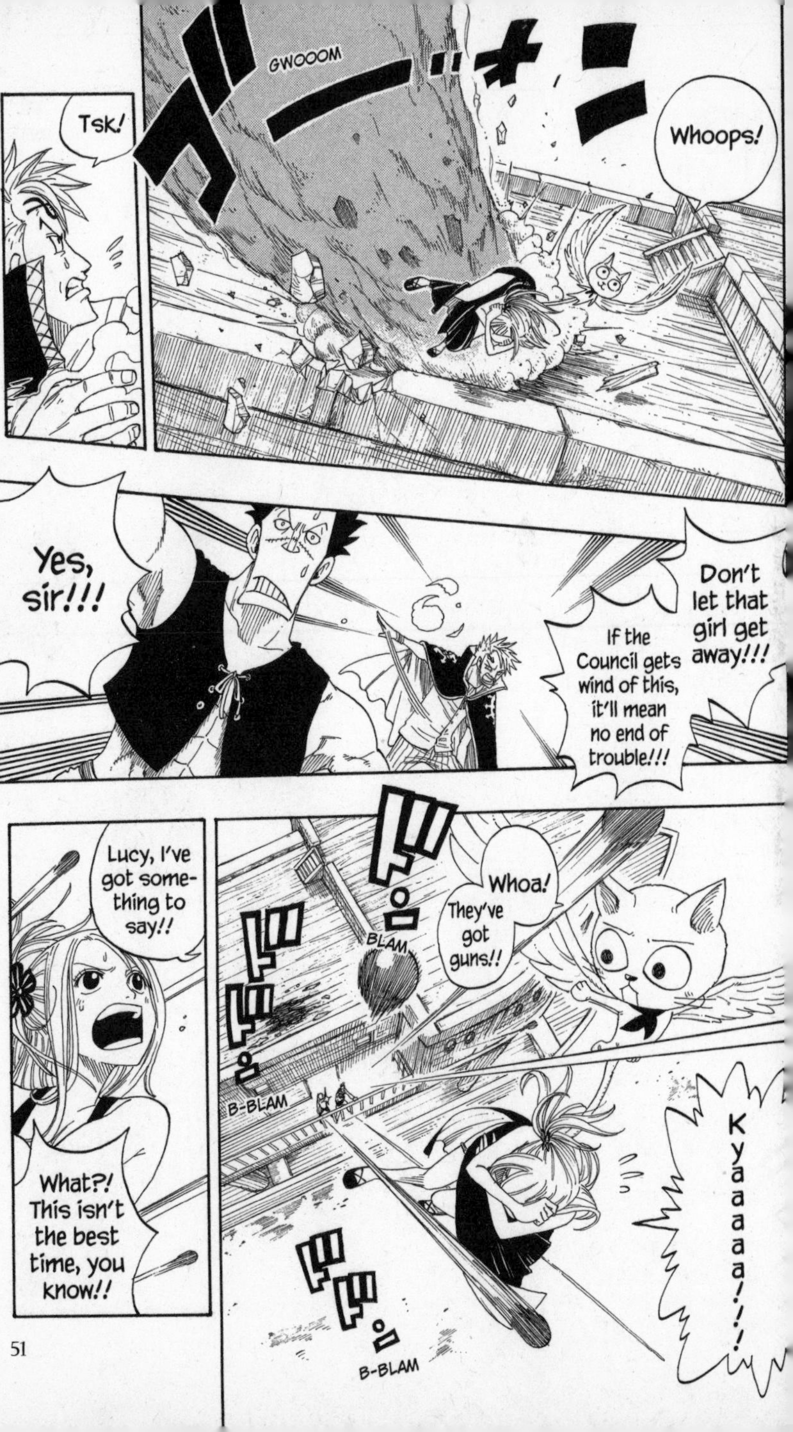
GWOOOM
Whoops!
Tsk!
Don't let that girl get away!!!
If the Council gets wind of this, it'll mean no end of trouble!!!
Yes, sir!!!
Kyaaaaa!!!
Whoa!
They've got guns!!
BLAM
B-BLAM
B-BLAM
Lucy, I've got some-thing to say!!
What?! This isn't the best time, you know!!

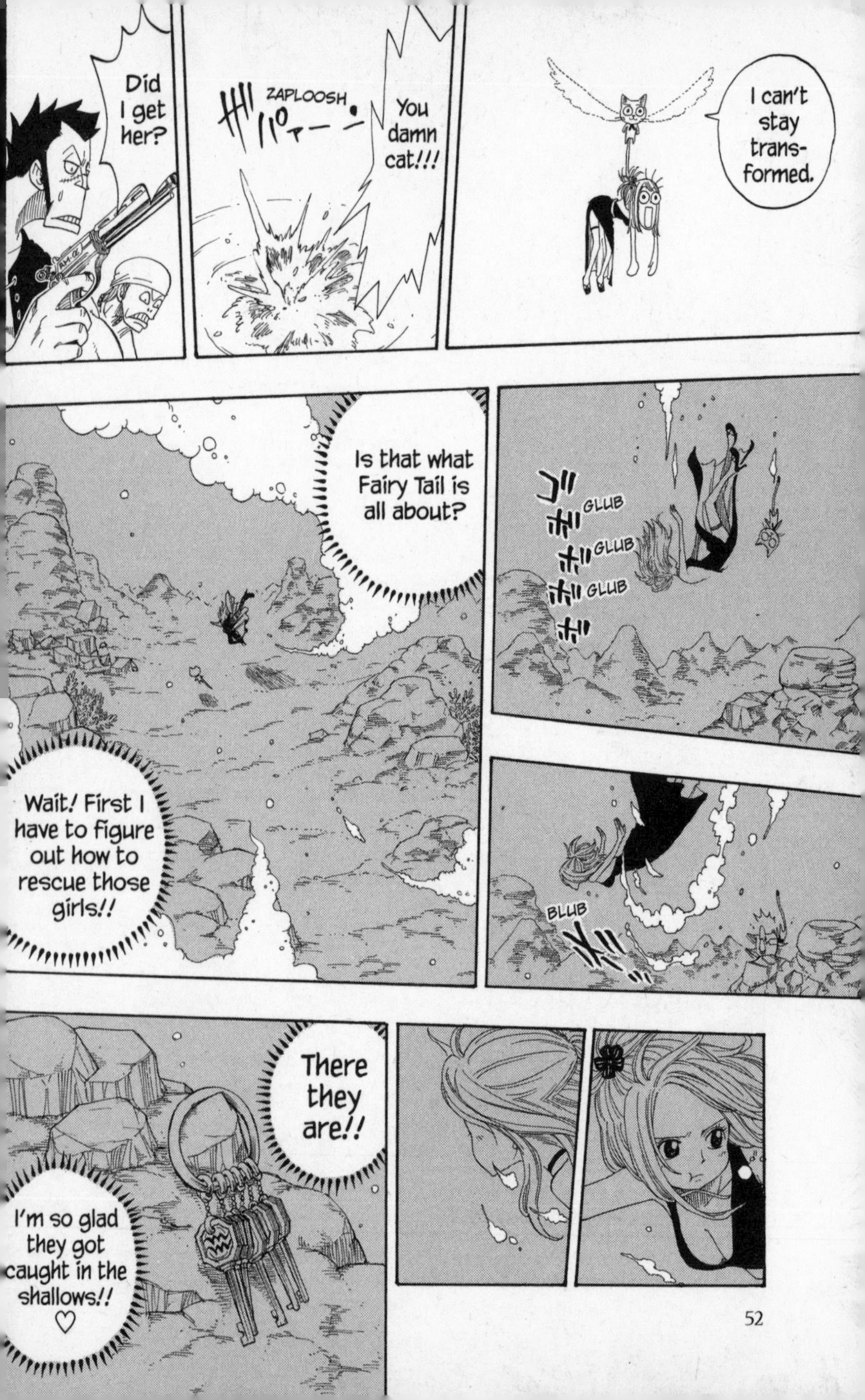
I can't stay trans-formed.
ZAPLOOSH
You damn cat!!!
Did I get her?
GLUB
GLUB
GLUB
BLUB
Is that what Fairy Tail is all about?
Wait! First I have to figure out how to rescue those girls!!
There they are!!
I'm so glad they got caught in the shallows!! ♡

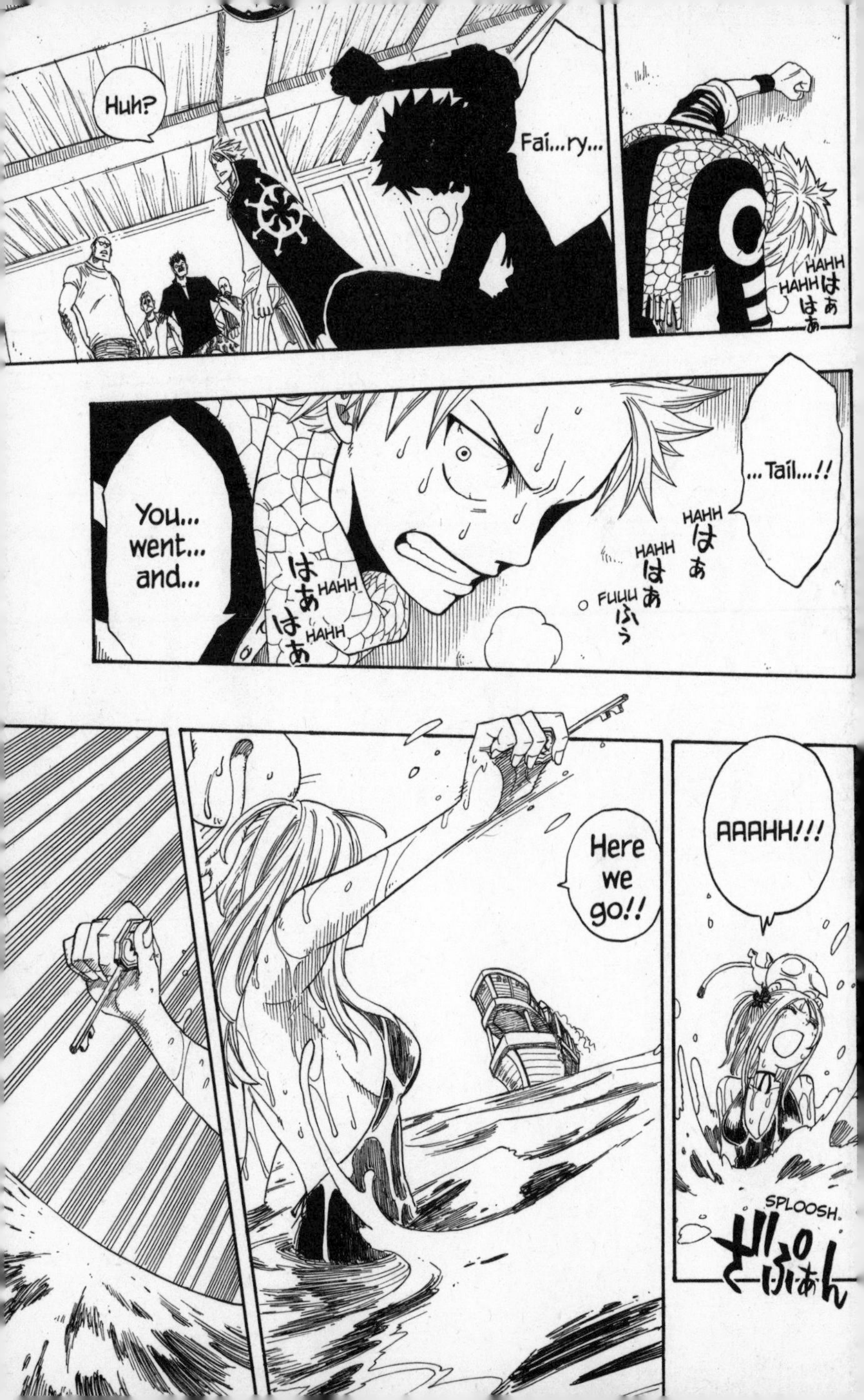
HAHH はぁ
HAHH はぁ
Fai...ry...
Huh?
...Tail...!!
HAHH はぁ
HAHH はぁ
FUUU ふぅ
HAHH はぁ
HAHH はぁ
You... went... and...
AAAHH!!!
SPLOOSH.
どぷぁん
Here we go!!

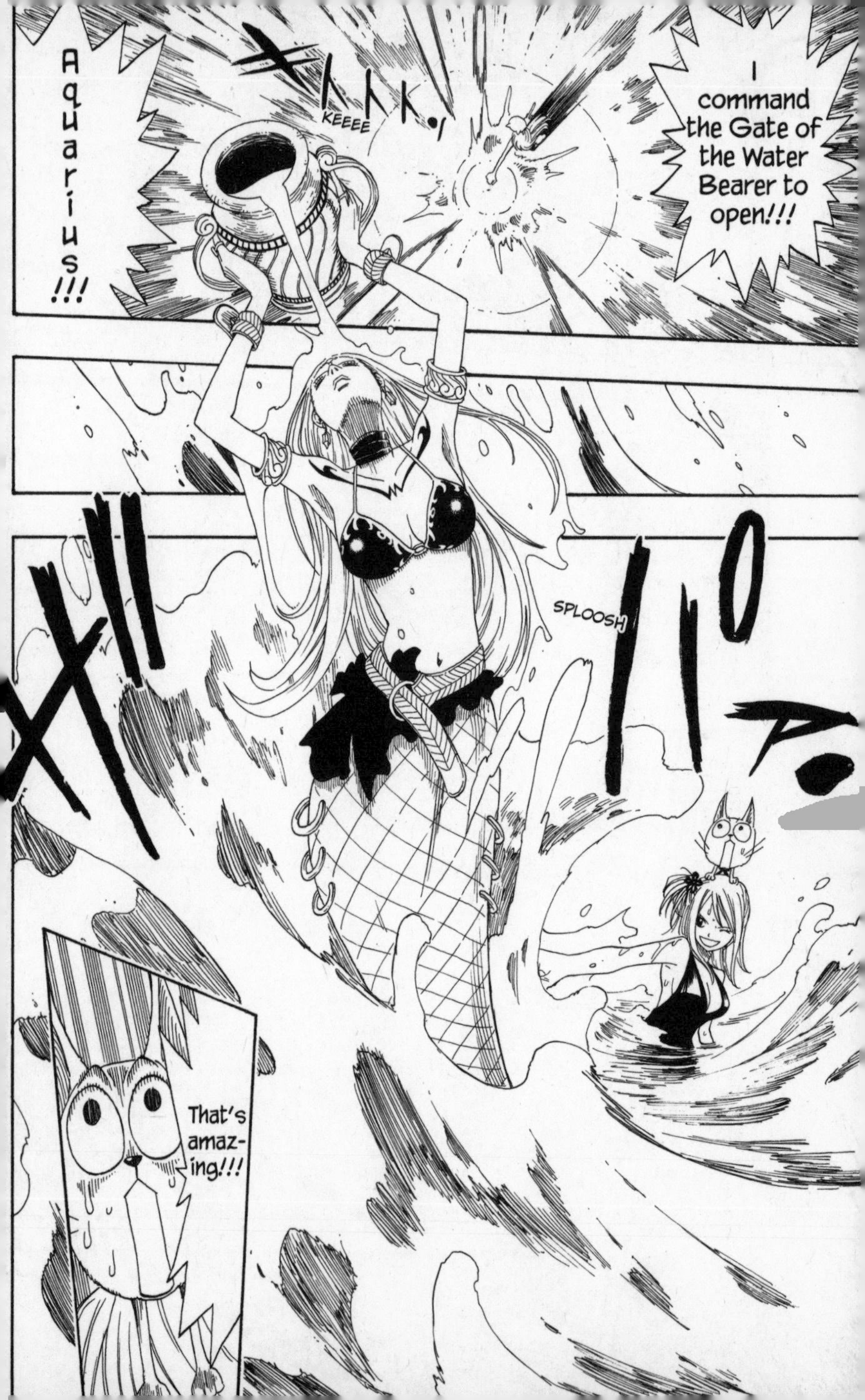

I command the Gate of the Water Bearer to open!!!
KEEEE
Aquarius!!!
SPLOOSH
That's amaz-ing!!!

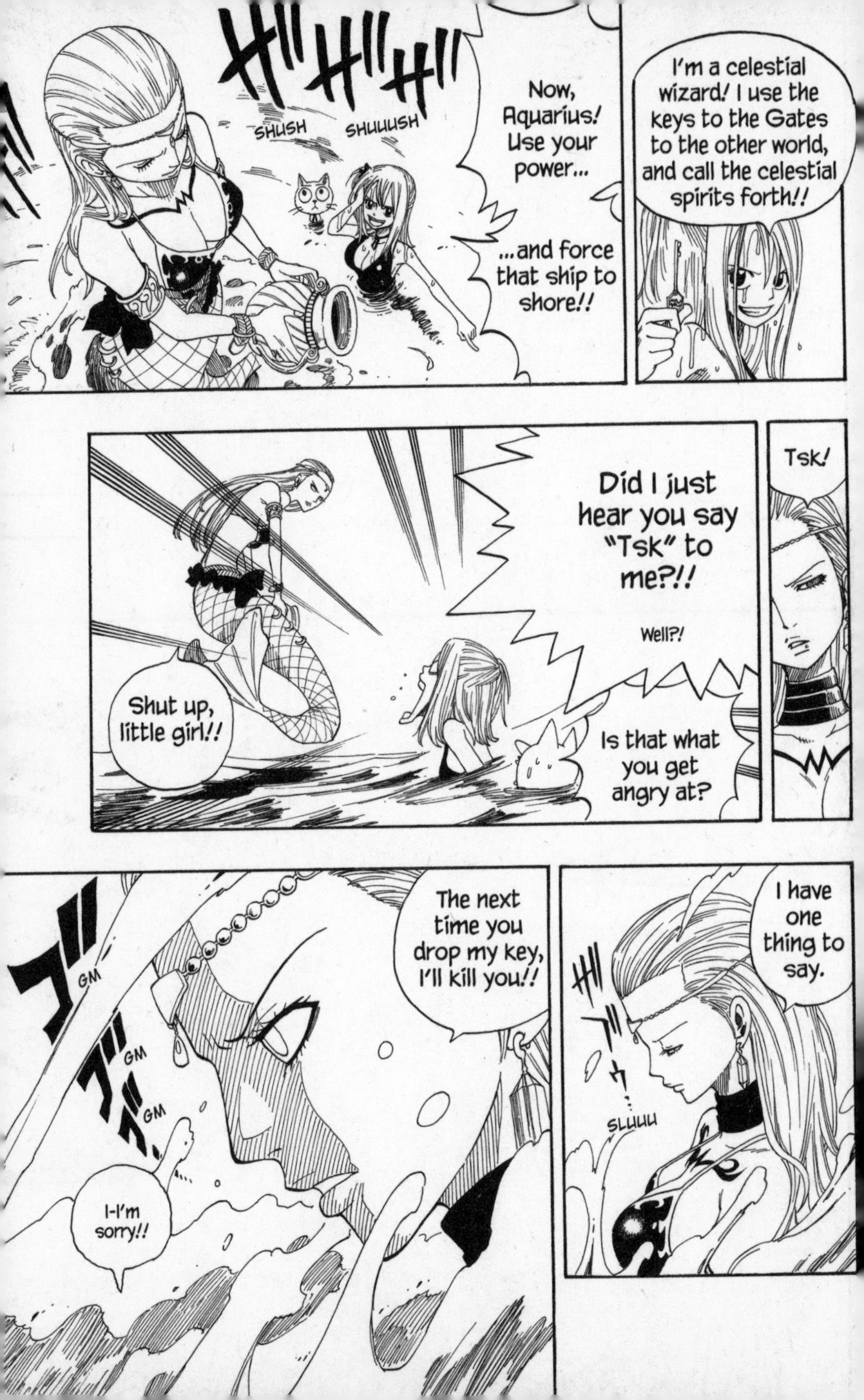
I'm a celestial wizard! I use the keys to the Gates to the other world, and call the celestial spirits forth!!
Now, Aquarius! Use your power...
...and force that ship to shore!!
SHUUUSH
SHUSH
Tsk!
Did I just hear you say "Tsk" to me?!!
Well?!
Is that what you get angry at?
Shut up, little girl!!
I have one thing to say.
SLUUU
The next time you drop my key, I'll kill you!!
GM
GM
GM
I-I'm sorry!!

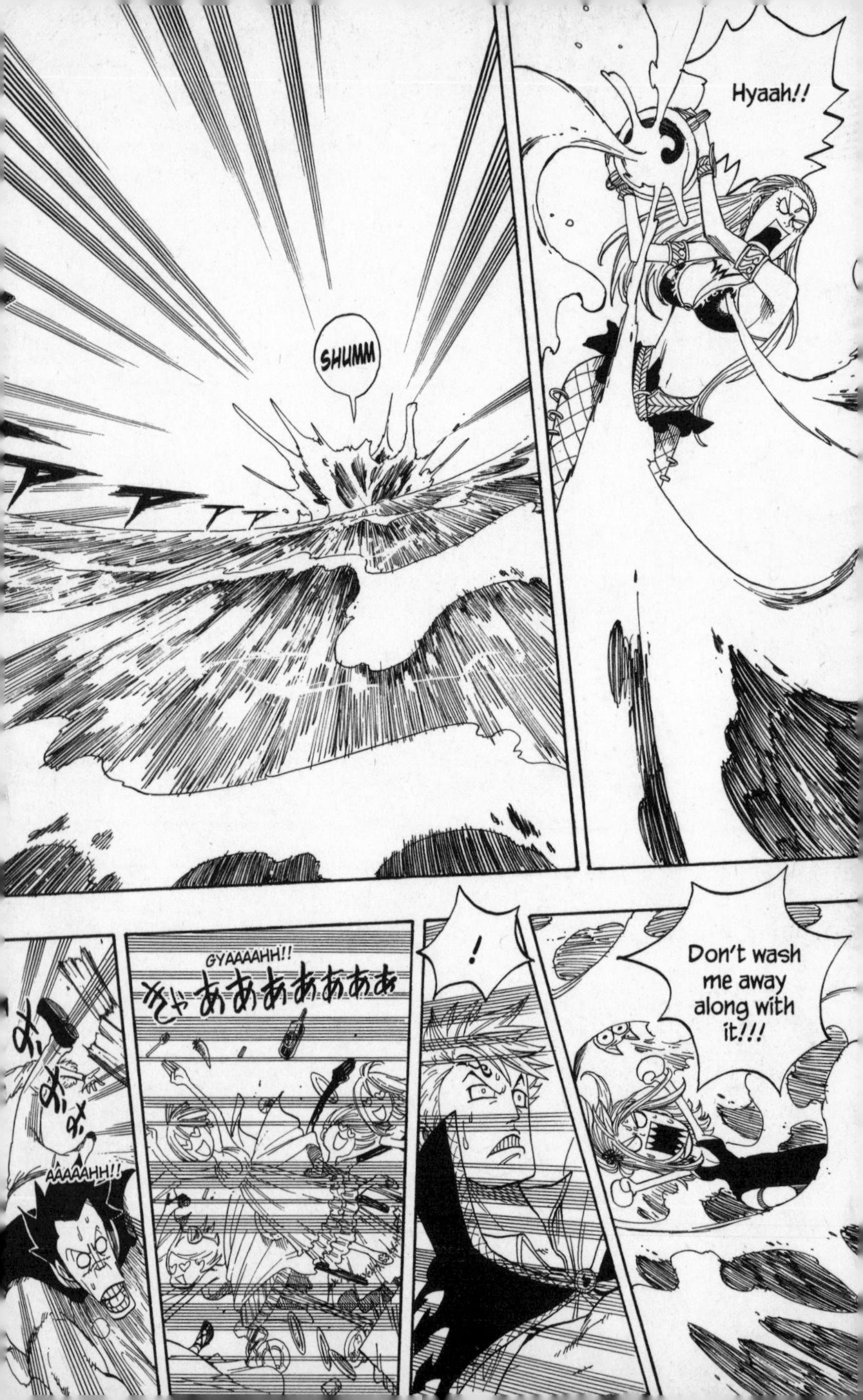
Hyaah!!
SHUMM
Don't wash me away along with it!!!
!
GYAAAAHH!!
AAAAAHH!!

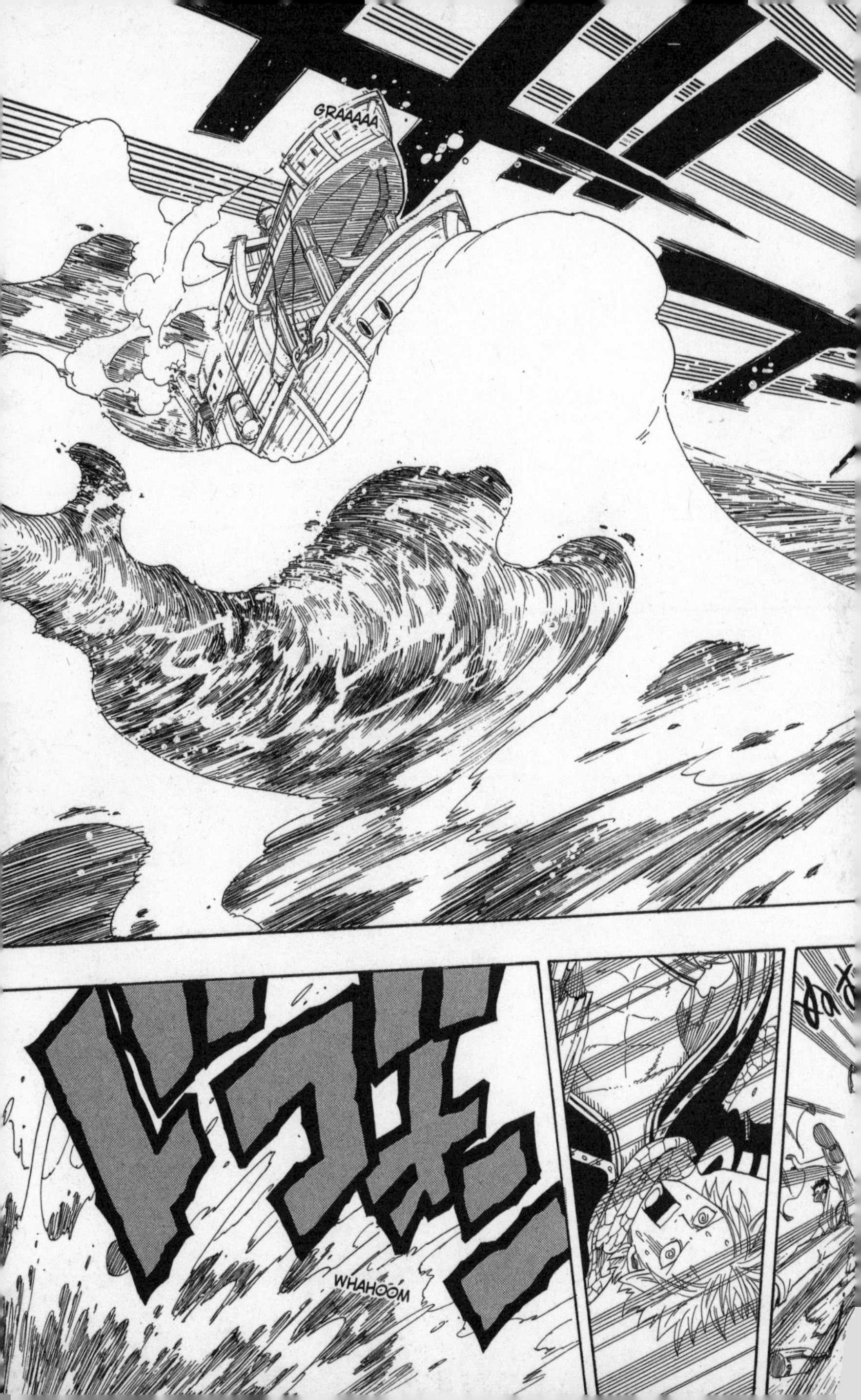
GRAAAAA
WHAHOOM

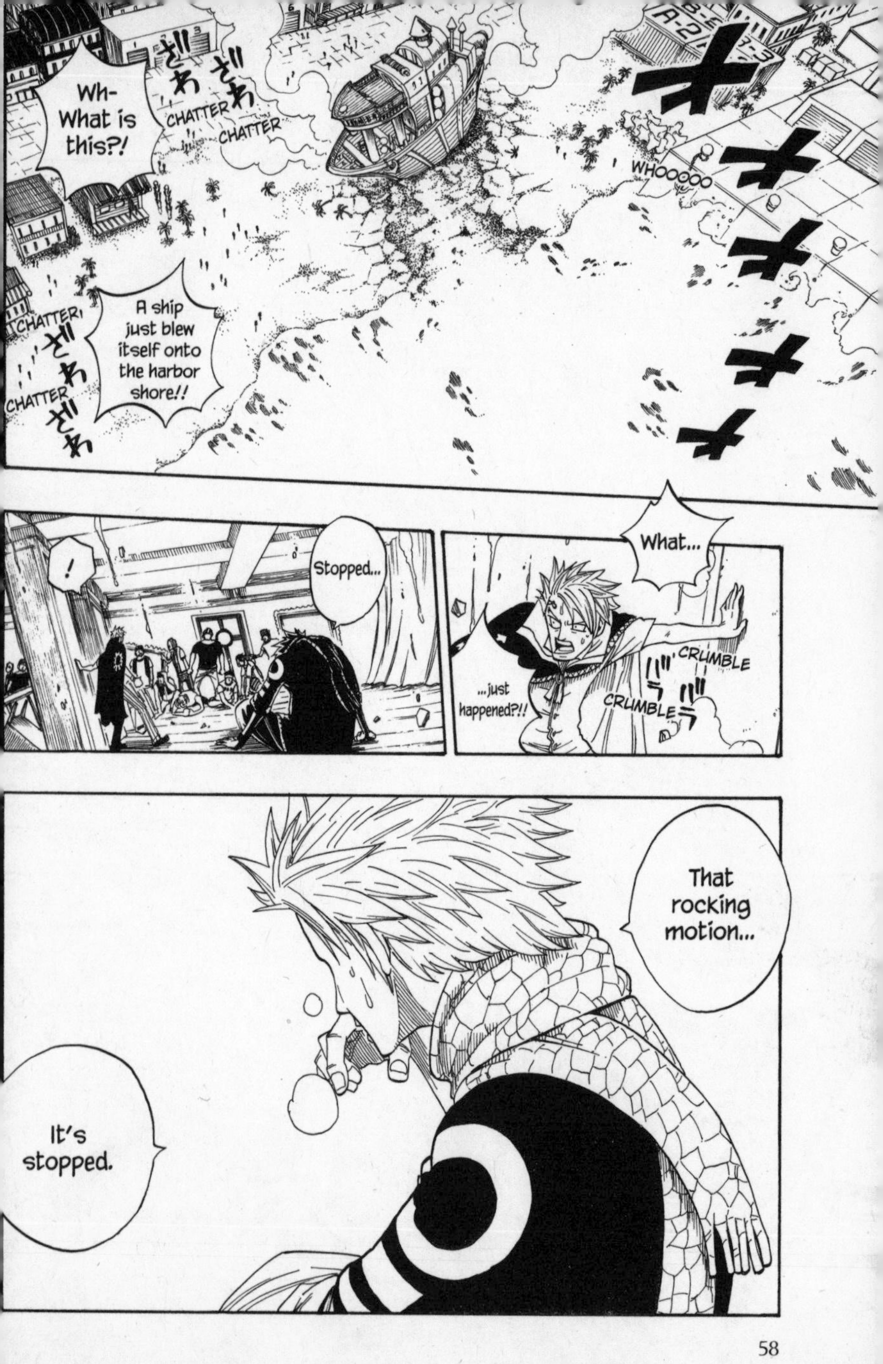
WHOOOOO
ざわざわ
CHATTER CHATTER
Wh- What is this?!
A ship just blew itself onto the harbor shore!!
ざわざわ
CHATTER, CHATTER
What...
CRUMBLE
CRUMBLE
...just happened?!!
Stopped...
!
That rocking motion...
It's stopped.

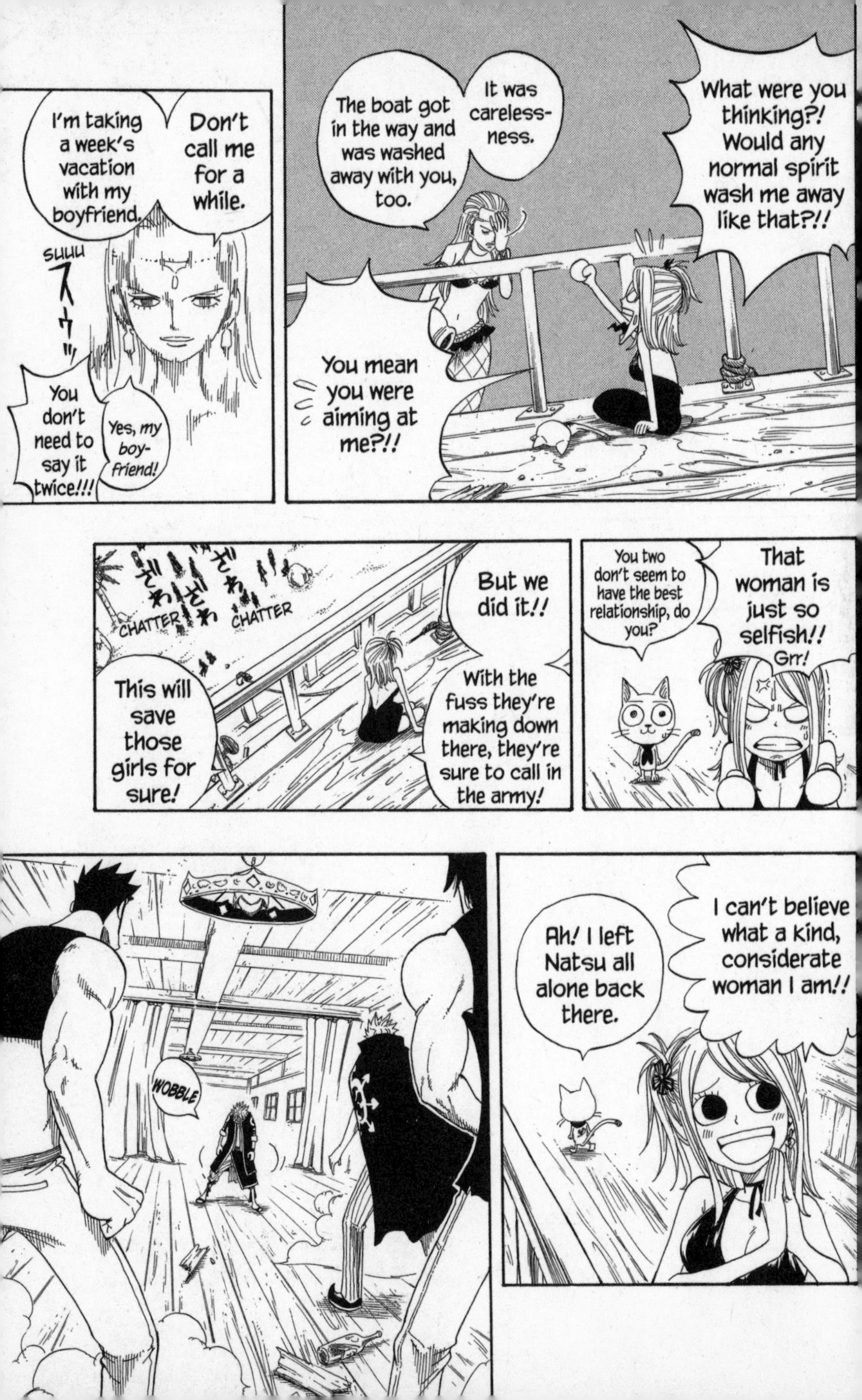
What were you thinking?! Would any normal spirit wash me away like that?!!
It was careless-ness.
The boat got in the way and was washed away with you, too.
You mean you were aiming at me?!!
Don't call me for a while.
I'm taking a week's vacation with my boyfriend.
SUUU
スゥッ
Yes, my boy-friend!
You don't need to say it twice!!!
That woman is just so selfish!!
Grr!
You two don't seem to have the best relationship, do you?
But we did it!!
With the fuss they're making down there, they're sure to call in the army!
ざわ ざわ ざわ ざわ
CHATTER CHATTER
This will save those girls for sure!
I can't believe what a kind, considerate woman I am!!
Ah! I left Natsu all alone back there.
WOBBLE

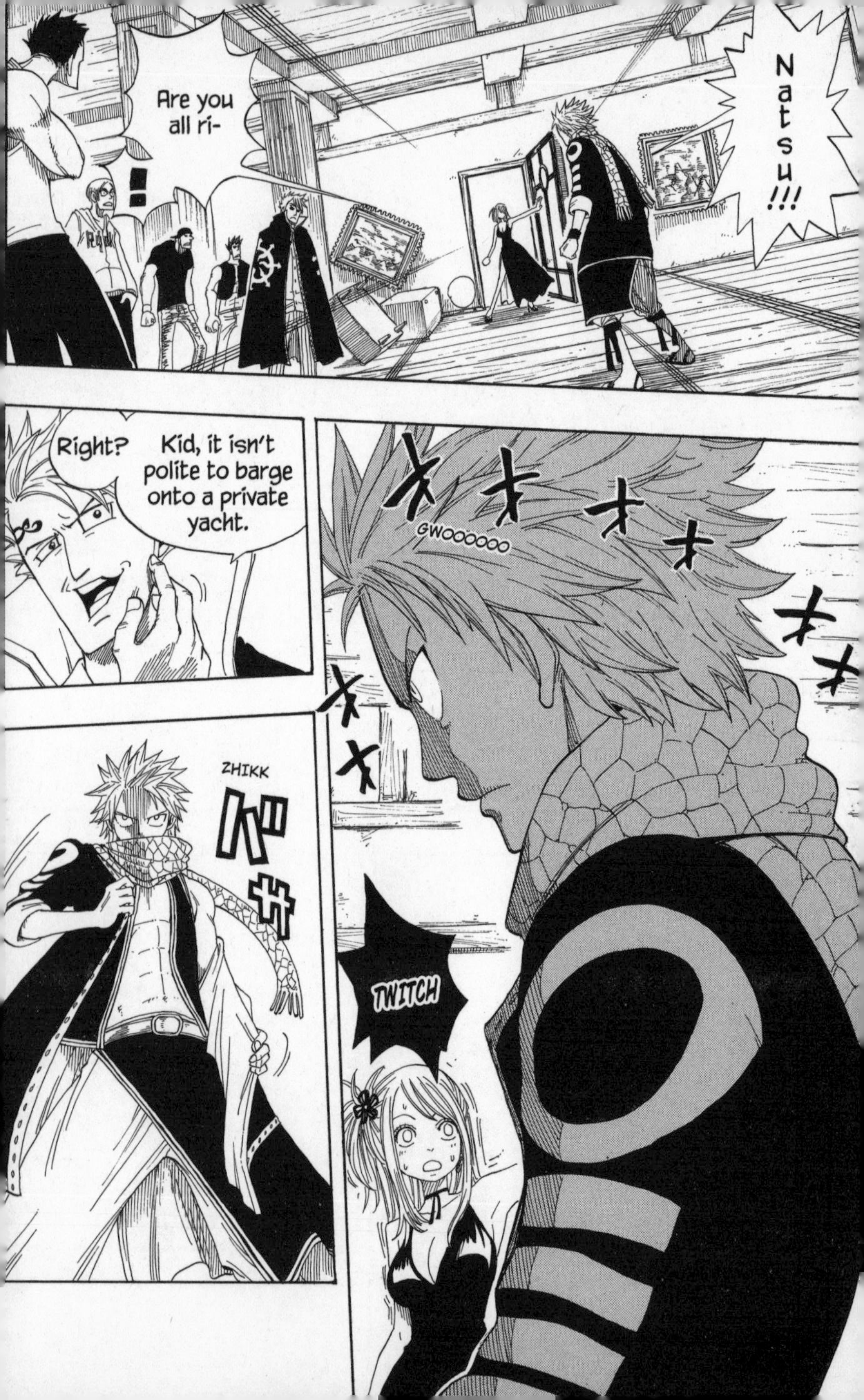
Natsu!!!
Are you all ri-
!
GWOOOOOO
TWITCH
Kid, it isn't polite to barge onto a private yacht.
Right?
ZHIKK

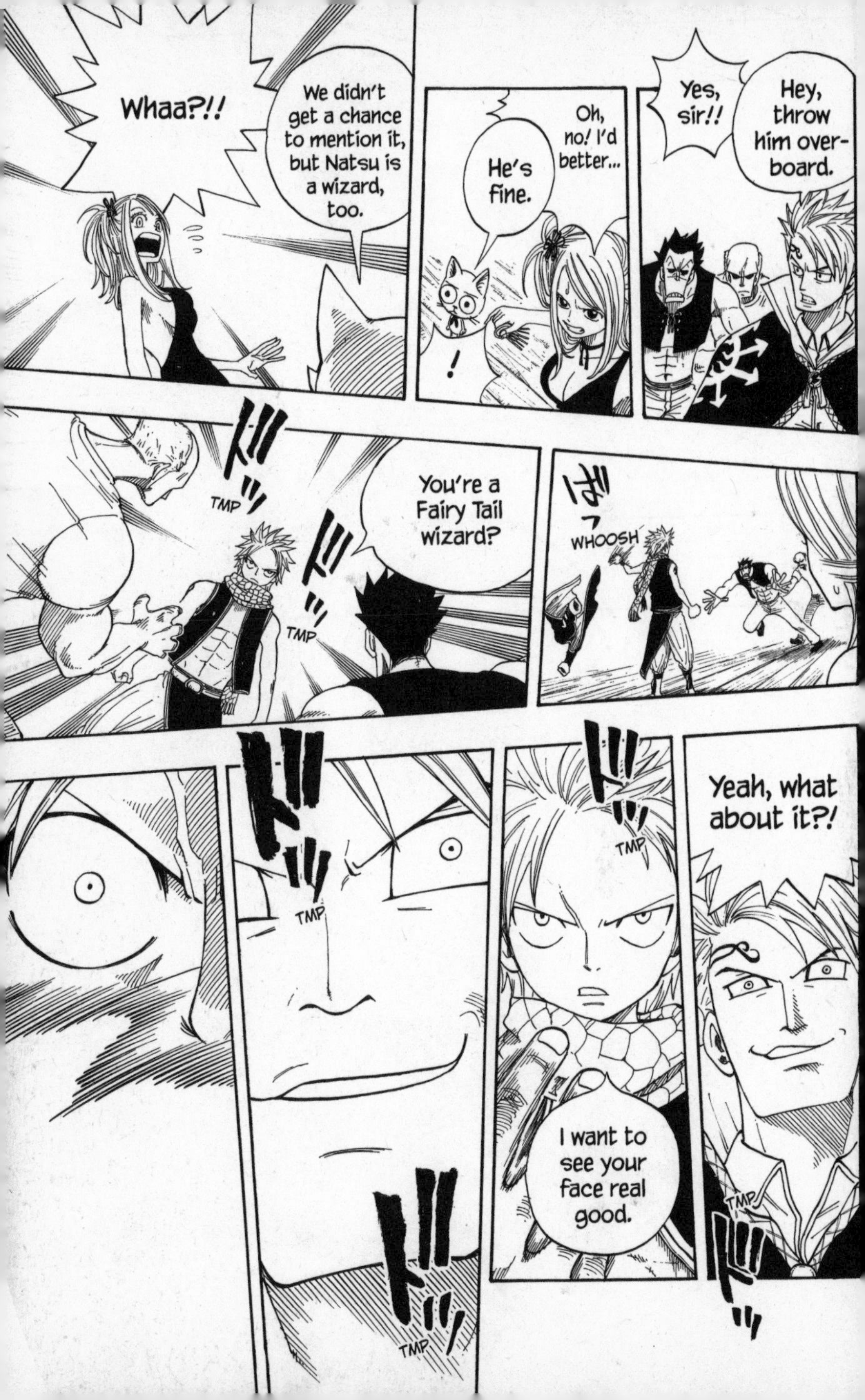

Hey, throw him overboard.
Yes, sir!!
Oh, no! I'd better...
He's fine.
!
We didn't get a chance to mention it, but Natsu is a wizard, too.
Whaa?!!
WHOOSH
You're a Fairy Tail wizard?
TMP
TMP
Yeah, what about it?!
TMP
TMP
I want to see your face real good.
TMP
TMP

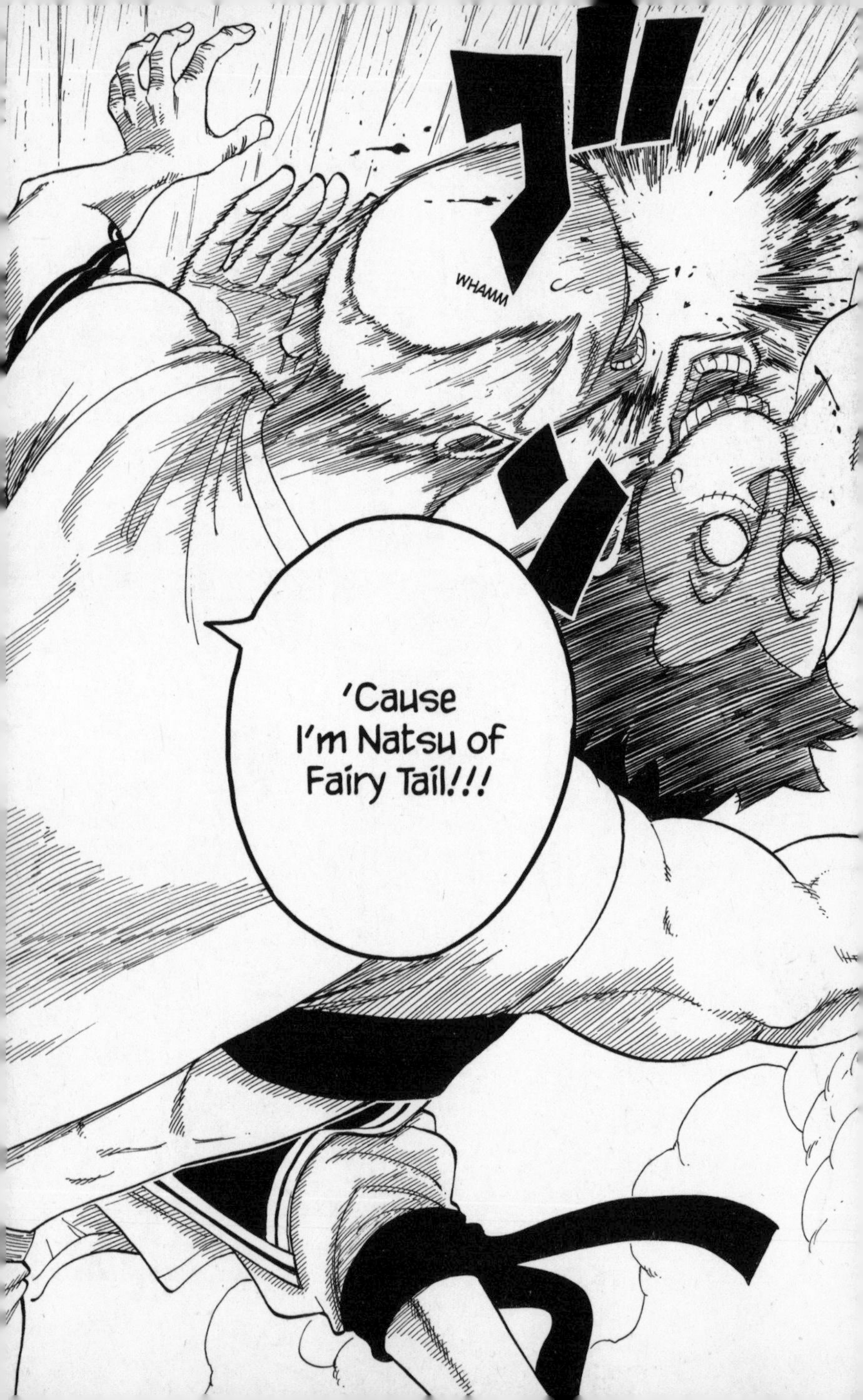
WHAMM
'Cause I'm Natsu of Fairy Tail!!!

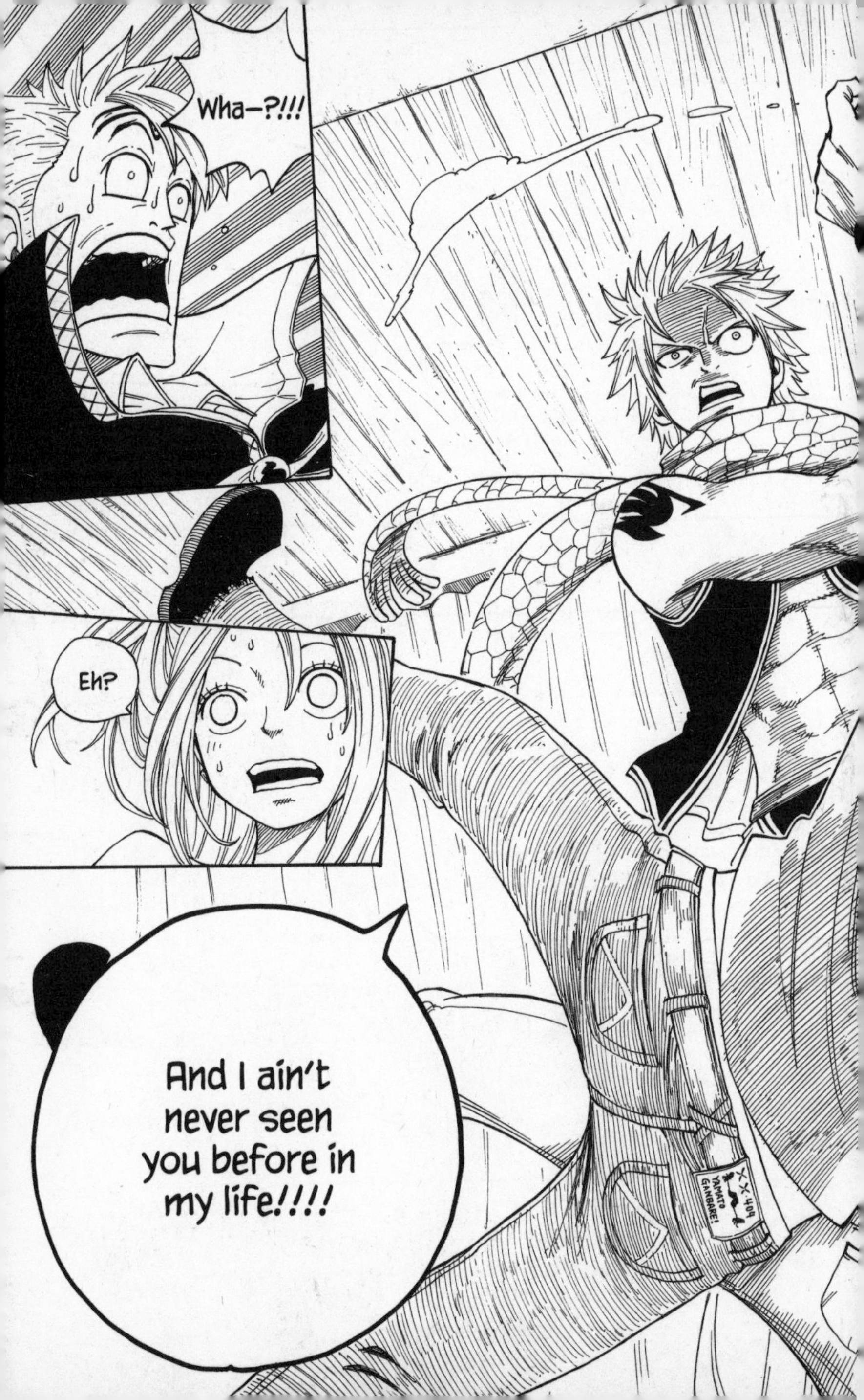
Wha-?!!!
Eh?
And I ain't never seen you before in my life!!!!

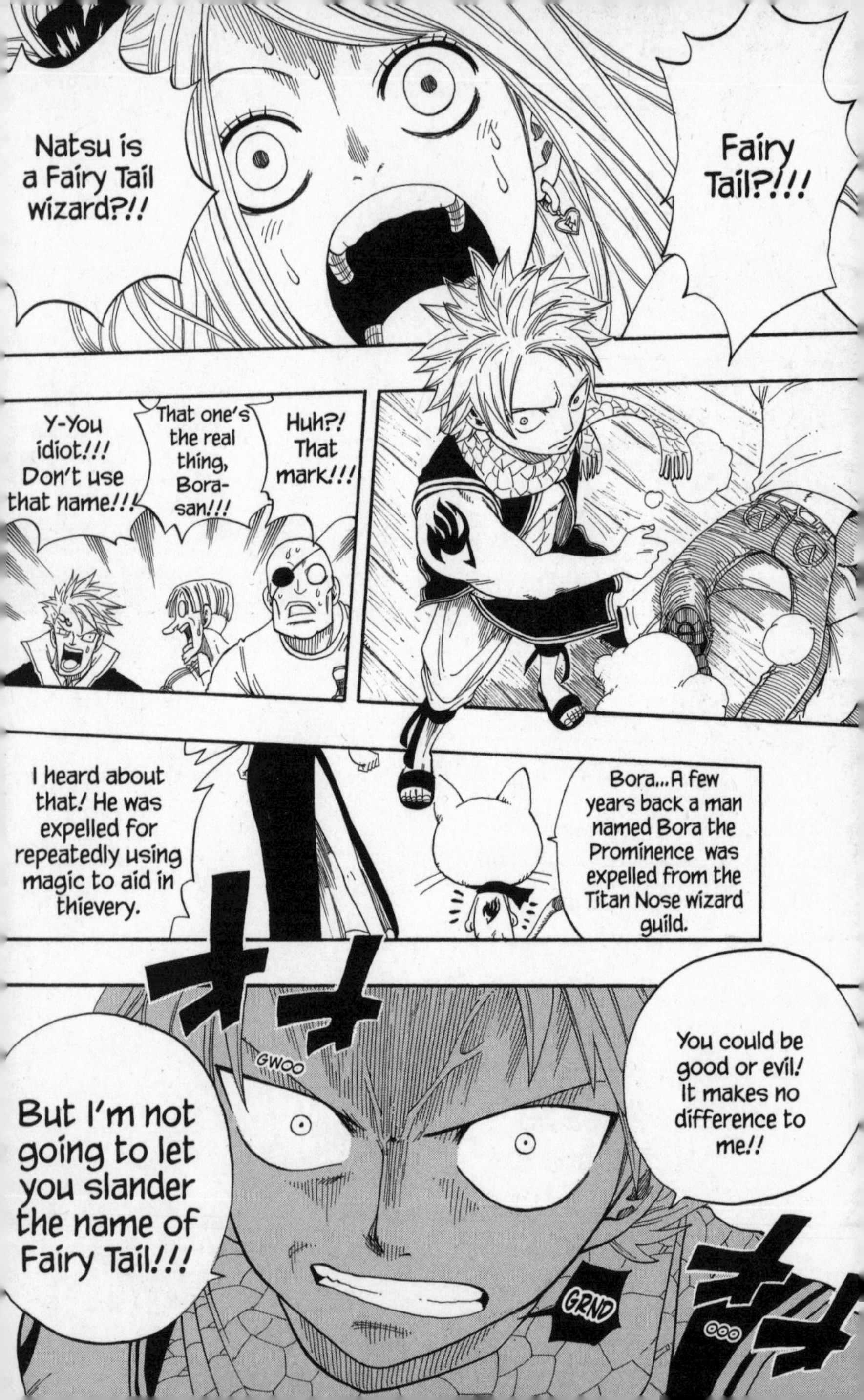
Fairy Tail?!!!
Natsu is a Fairy Tail wizard?!!
Huh?! That mark!!!
That one's the real thing, Bora-san!!!
Y-You idiot!!! Don't use that name!!!
Bora...A few years back a man named Bora the Prominence was expelled from the Titan Nose wizard guild.
I heard about that! He was expelled for repeatedly using magic to aid in thievery.
You could be good or evil! It makes no difference to me!!
GWOO
But I'm not going to let you slander the name of Fairy Tail!!!
GRND

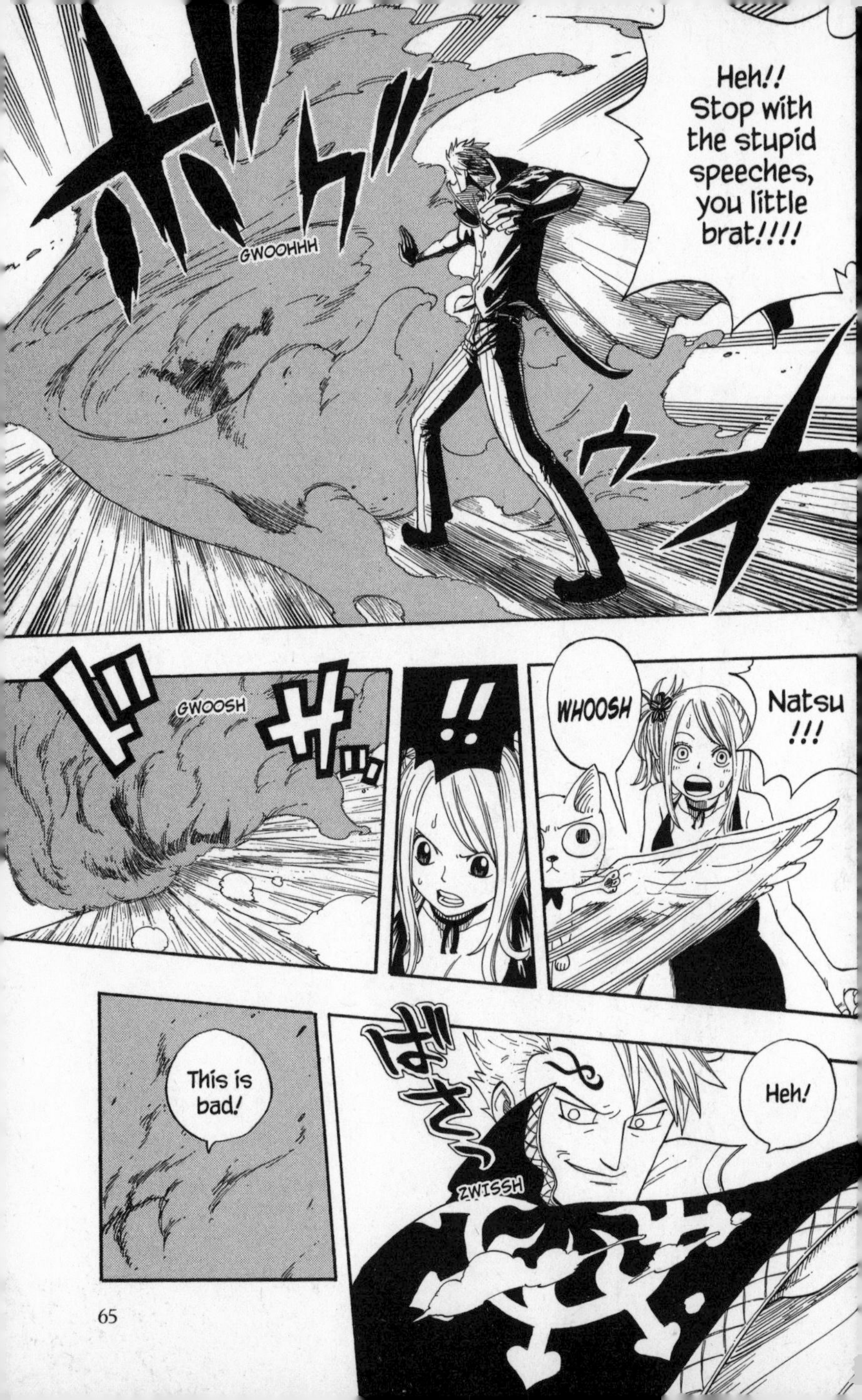
Heh!! Stop with the stupid speeches, you little brat!!!!
GWOOHHH
Natsu !!!
WHOOSH
!!
GWOOSH
Heh!
ZWISSH
This is bad!

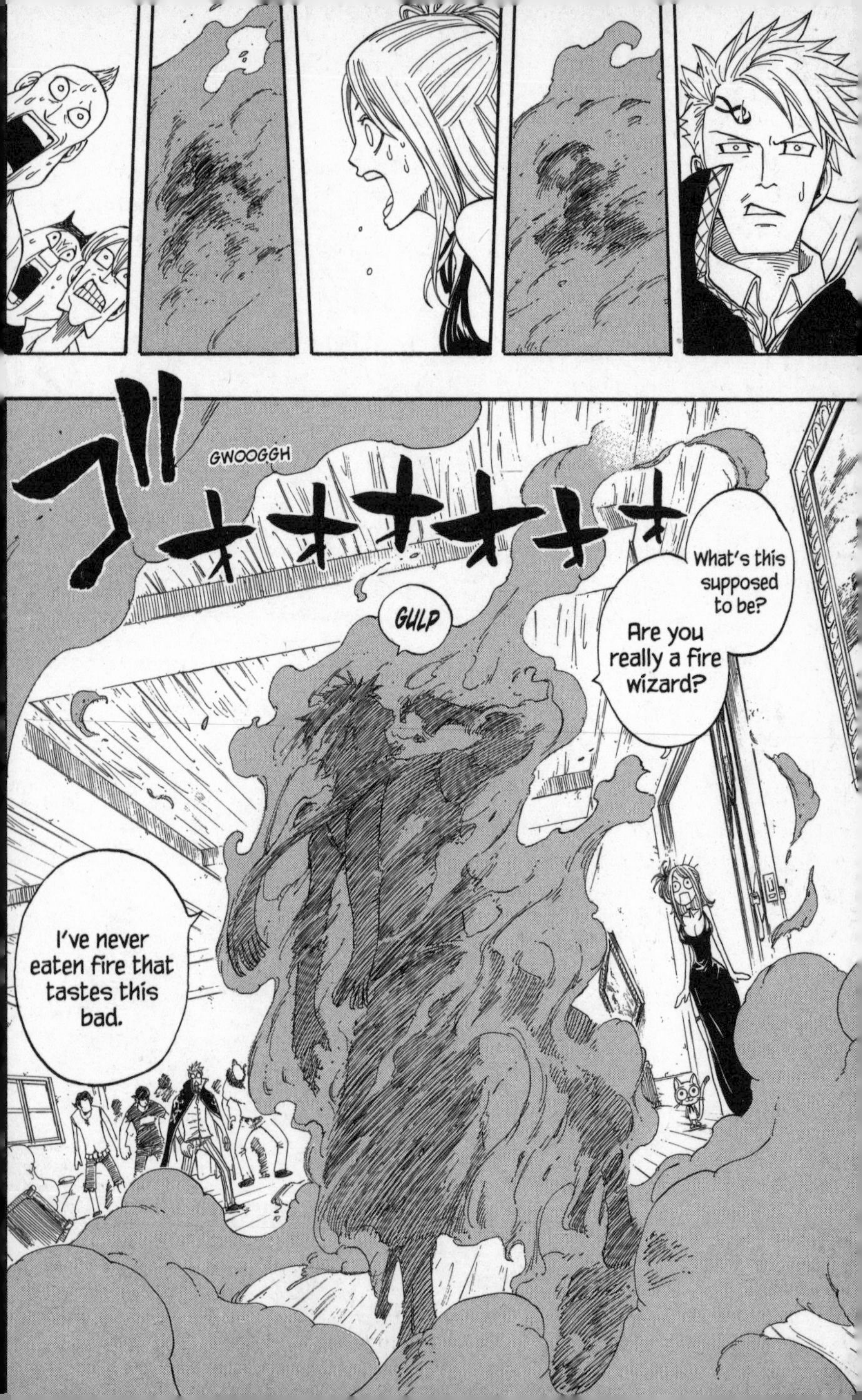
What's this supposed to be?
Are you really a fire wizard?
GWOOOGGH
GULP
I've never eaten fire that tastes this bad.

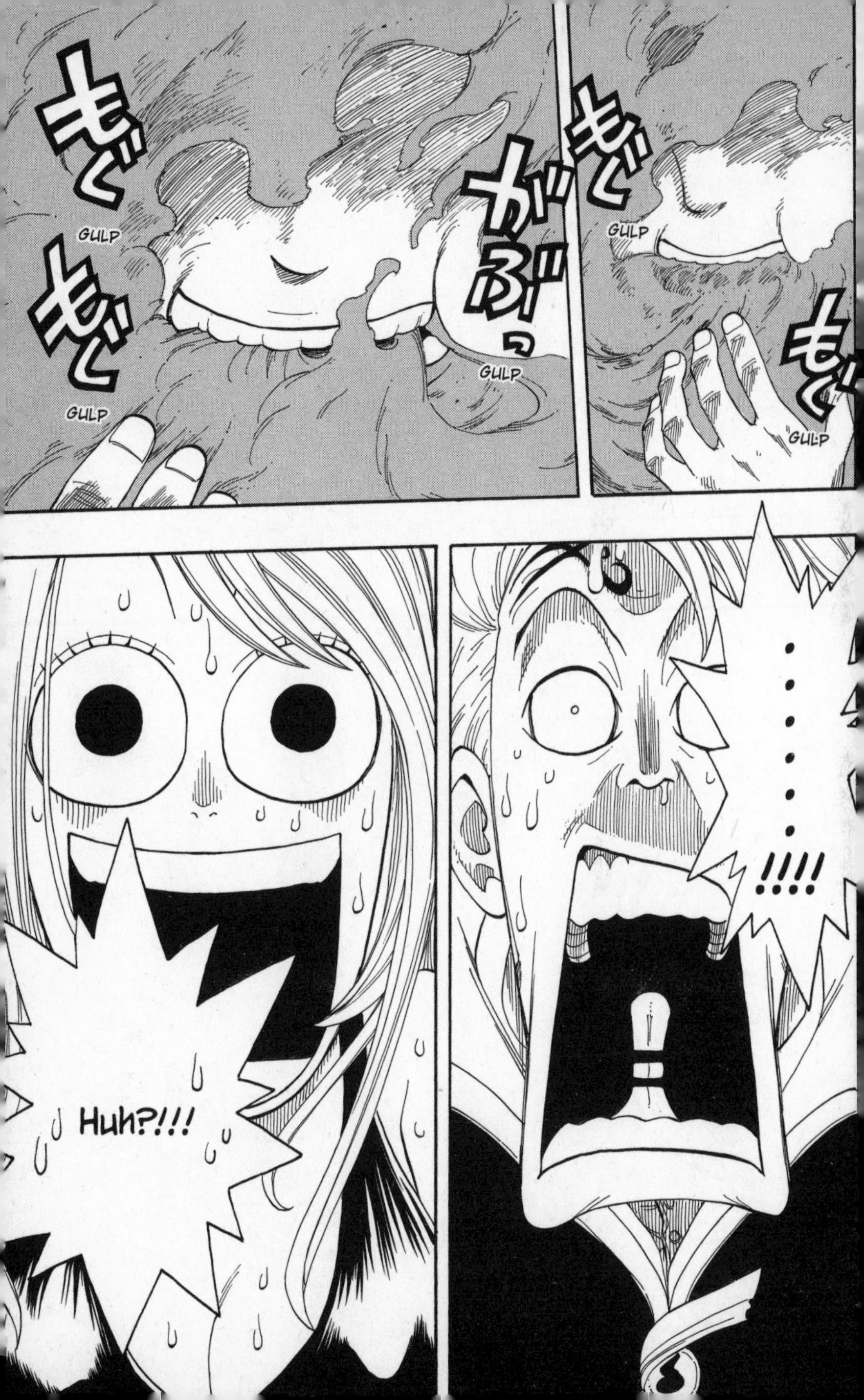
もぐ
GULP
もぐ
GULP
がぶっ
GULP
もぐ
GULP
もぐ
GULP
......!!!!
Huh?!!!

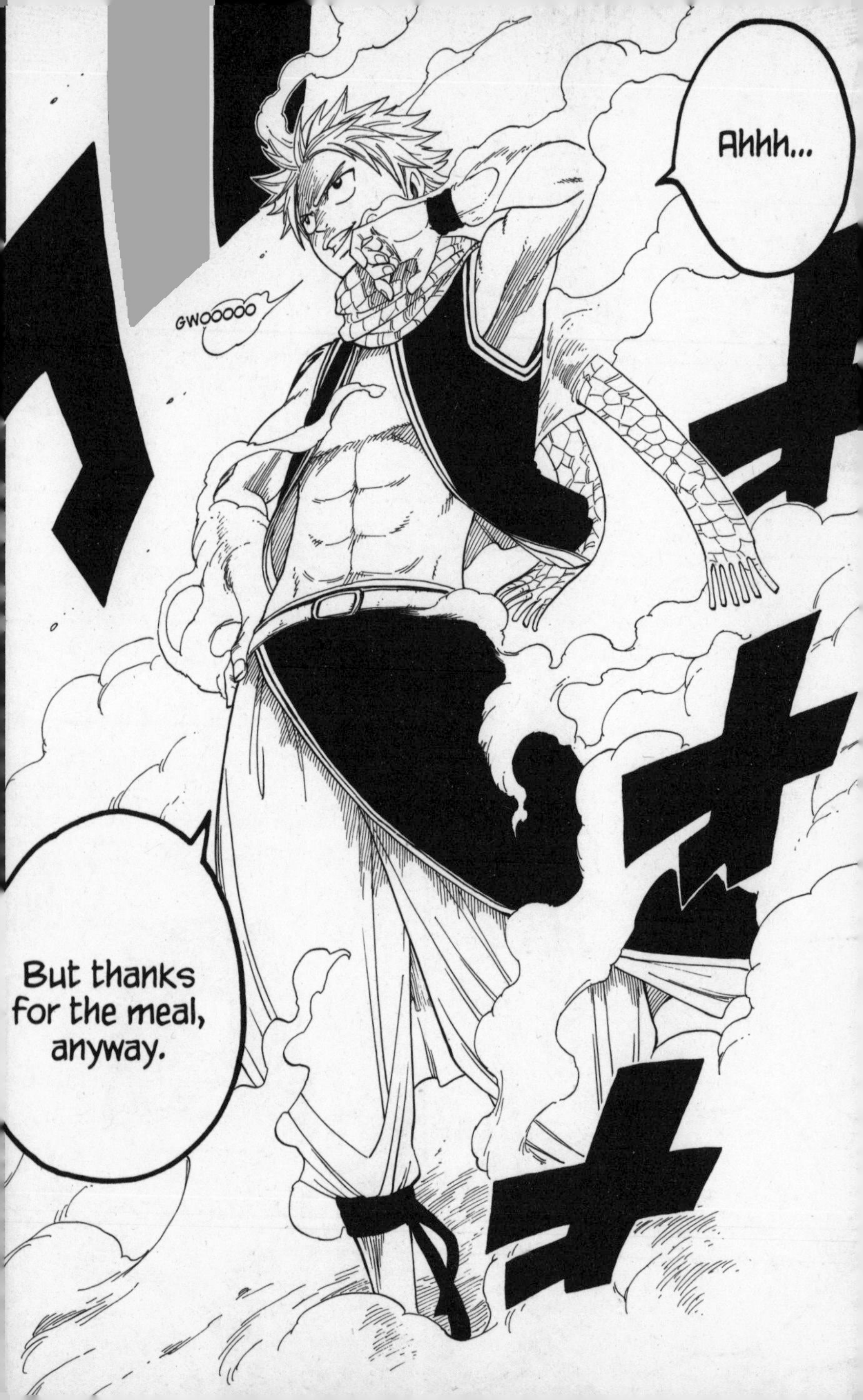
Ahhh...
GWOOOOO
But thanks for the meal, anyway.

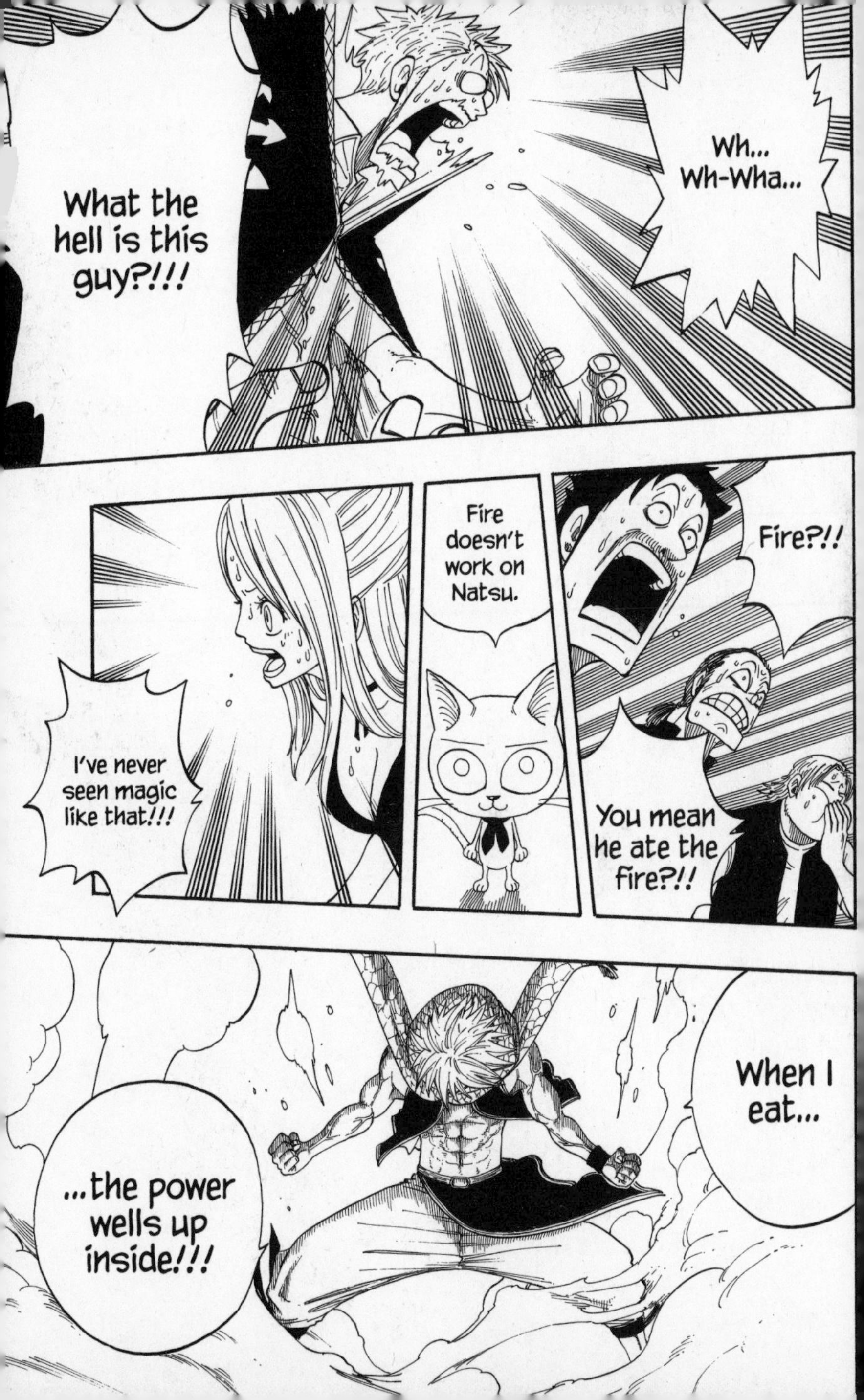
Wh... Wh-Wha...
What the hell is this guy?!!!
Fire?!!
You mean he ate the fire?!!
Fire doesn't work on Natsu.
I've never seen magic like that!!!
When I eat...
...the power wells up inside!!!

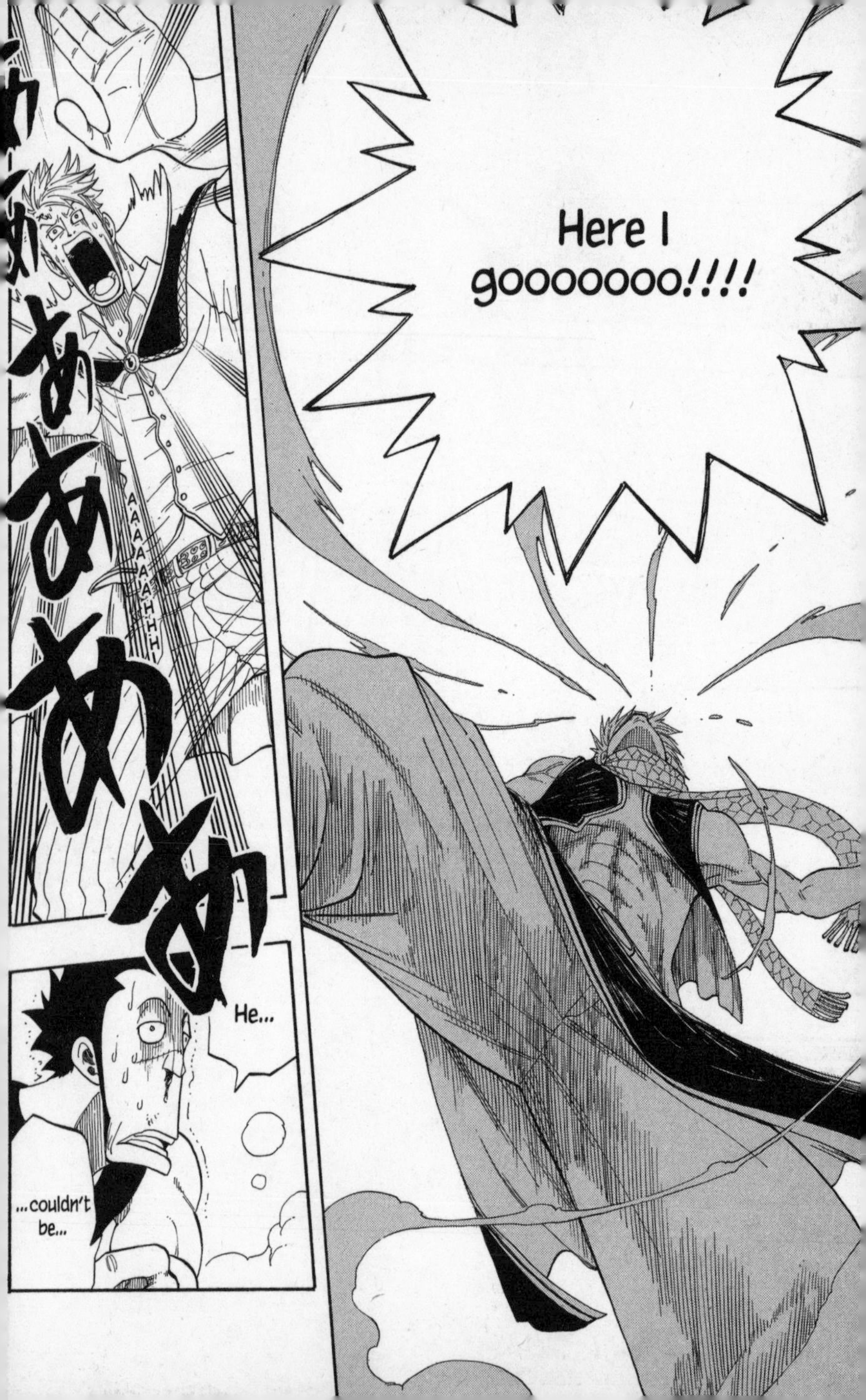
Here I goooooooo!!!!
AAAAAAAHHH
He...
...couldn't be...

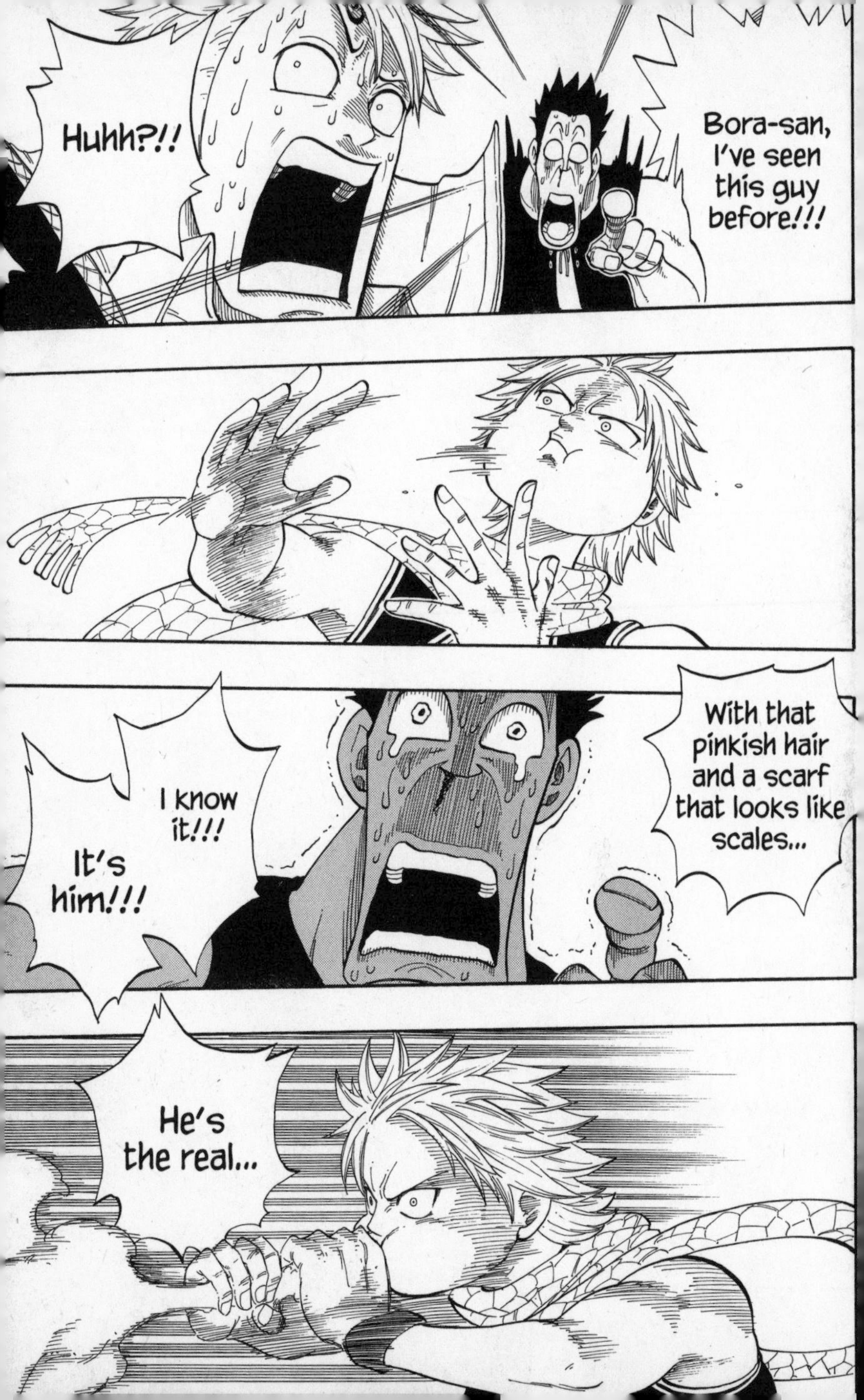
Bora-san, I've seen this guy before!!!
Huhh?!!
With that pinkish hair and a scarf that looks like scales...
I know it!!!
It's him!!!
He's the real...

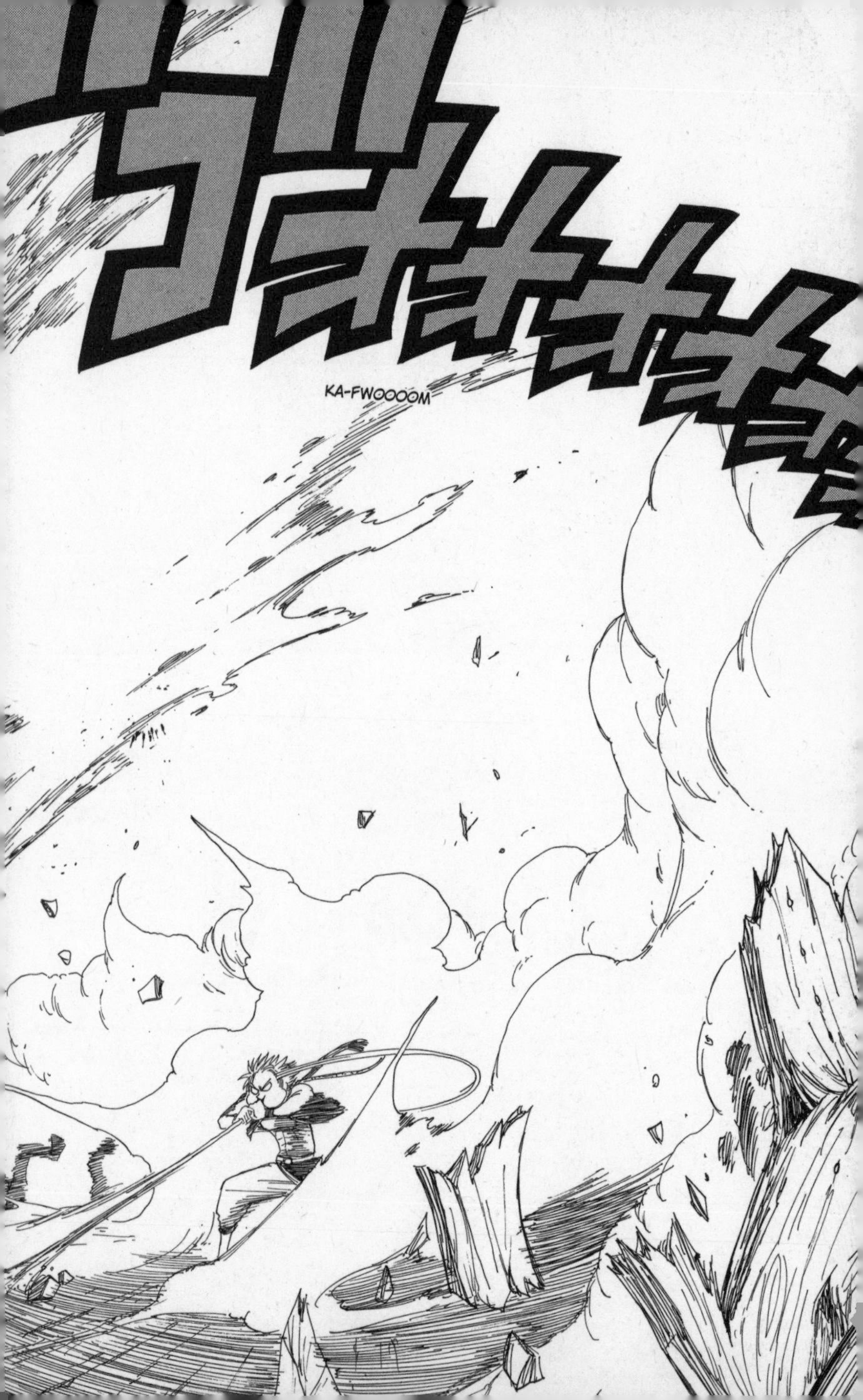
ゴォォォォォ
KA-FWOOOOM

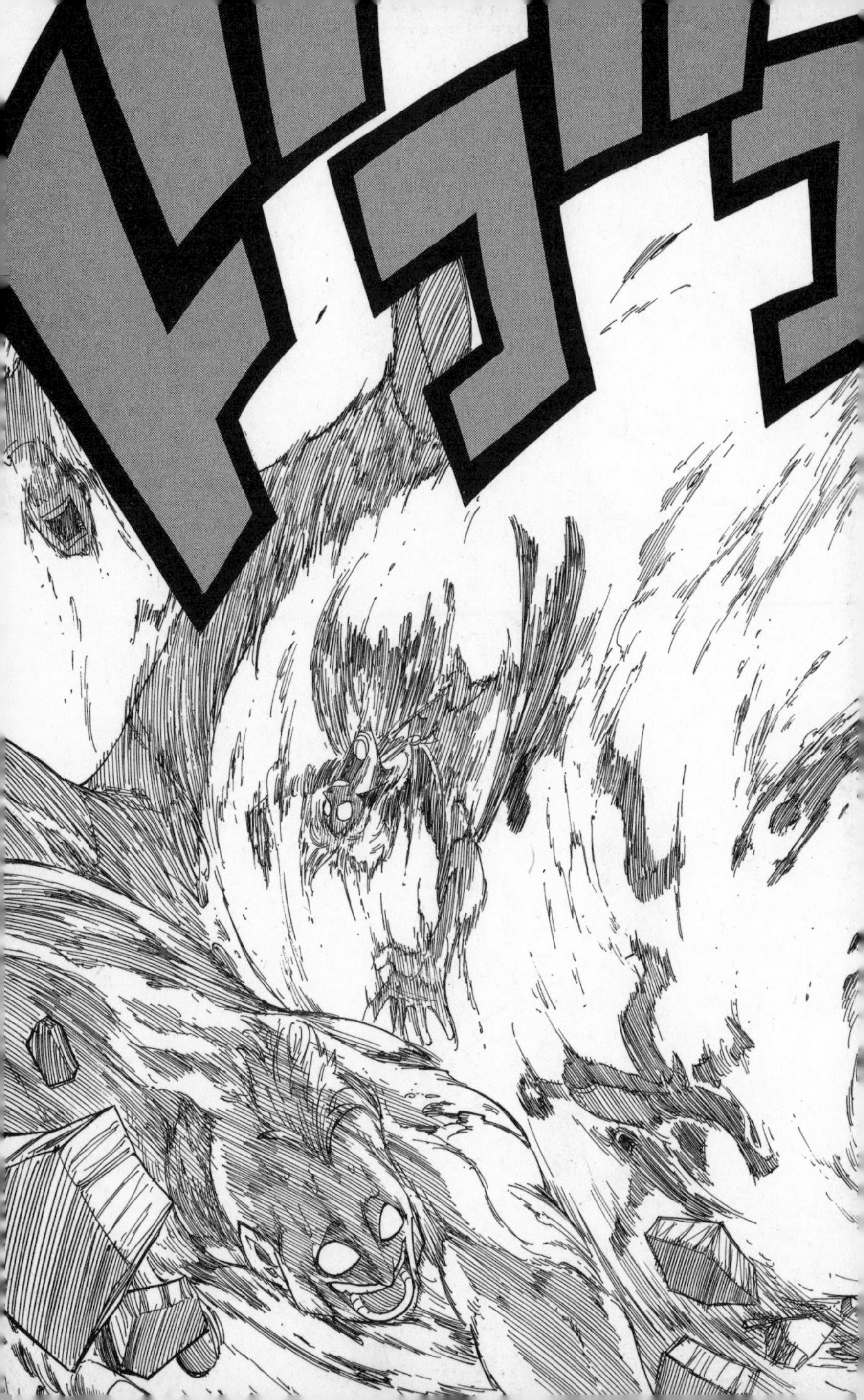

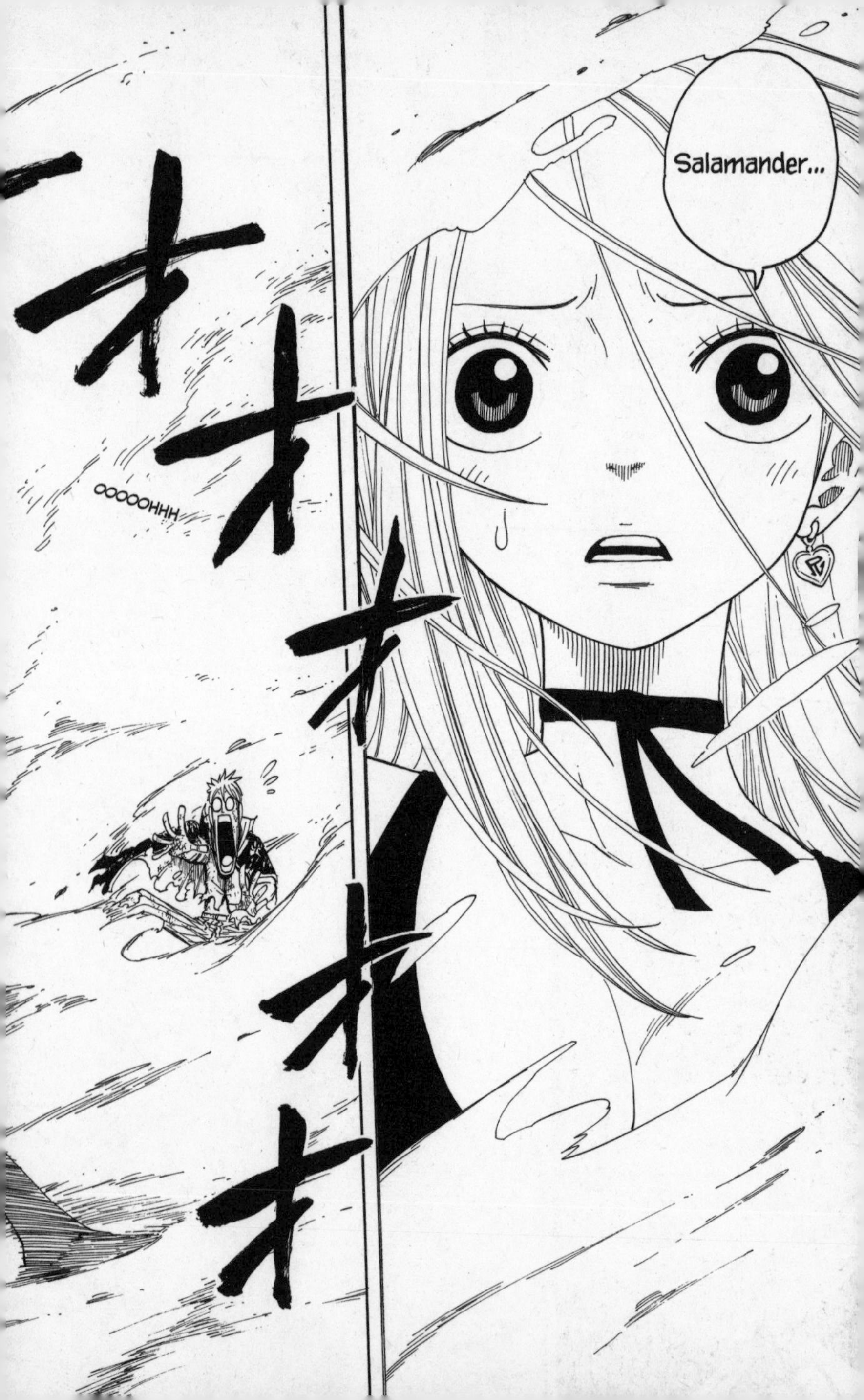
Salamander...
オオオオオ
OOOOOHHH

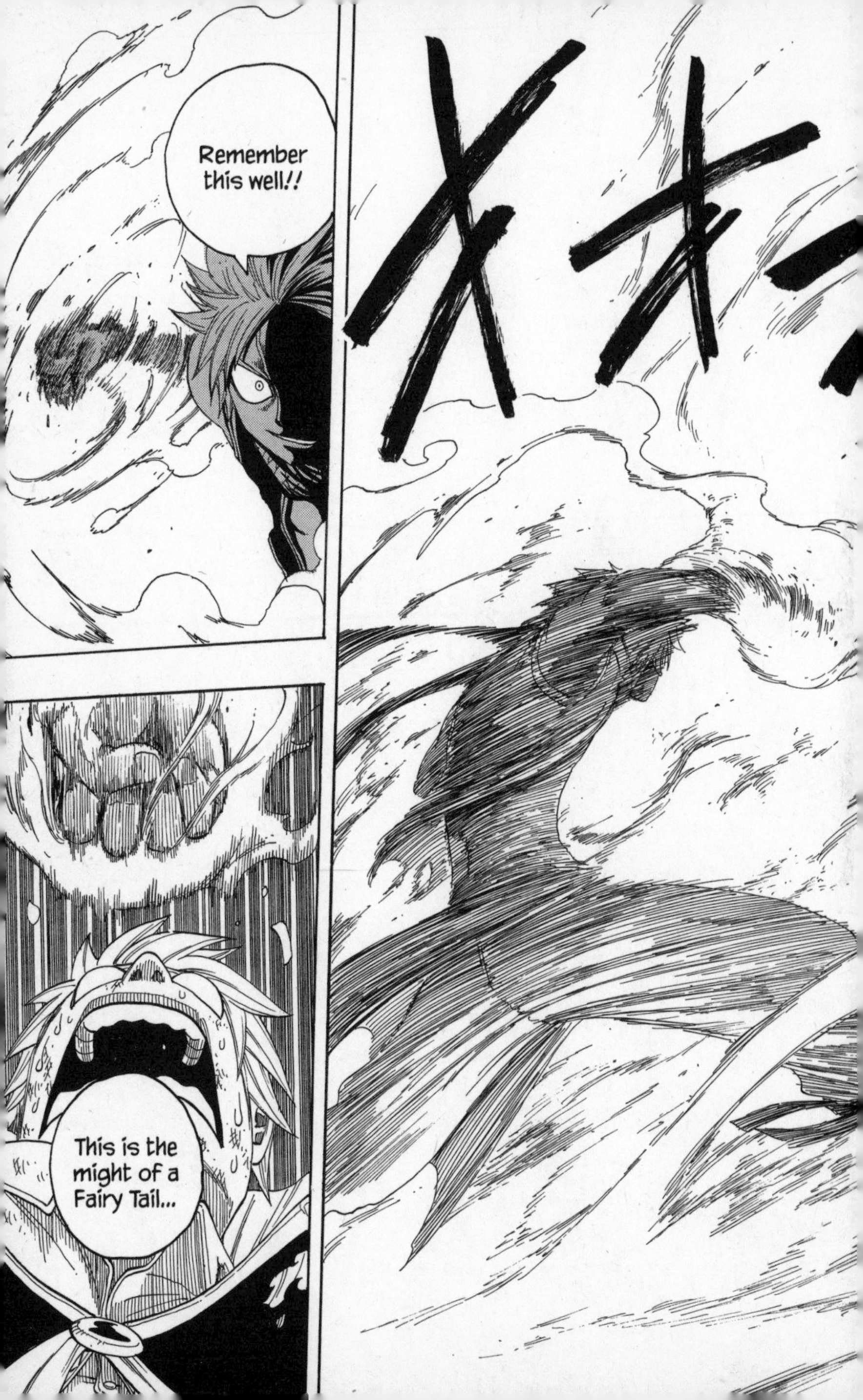

Remember this well!!
This is the might of a Fairy Tail...

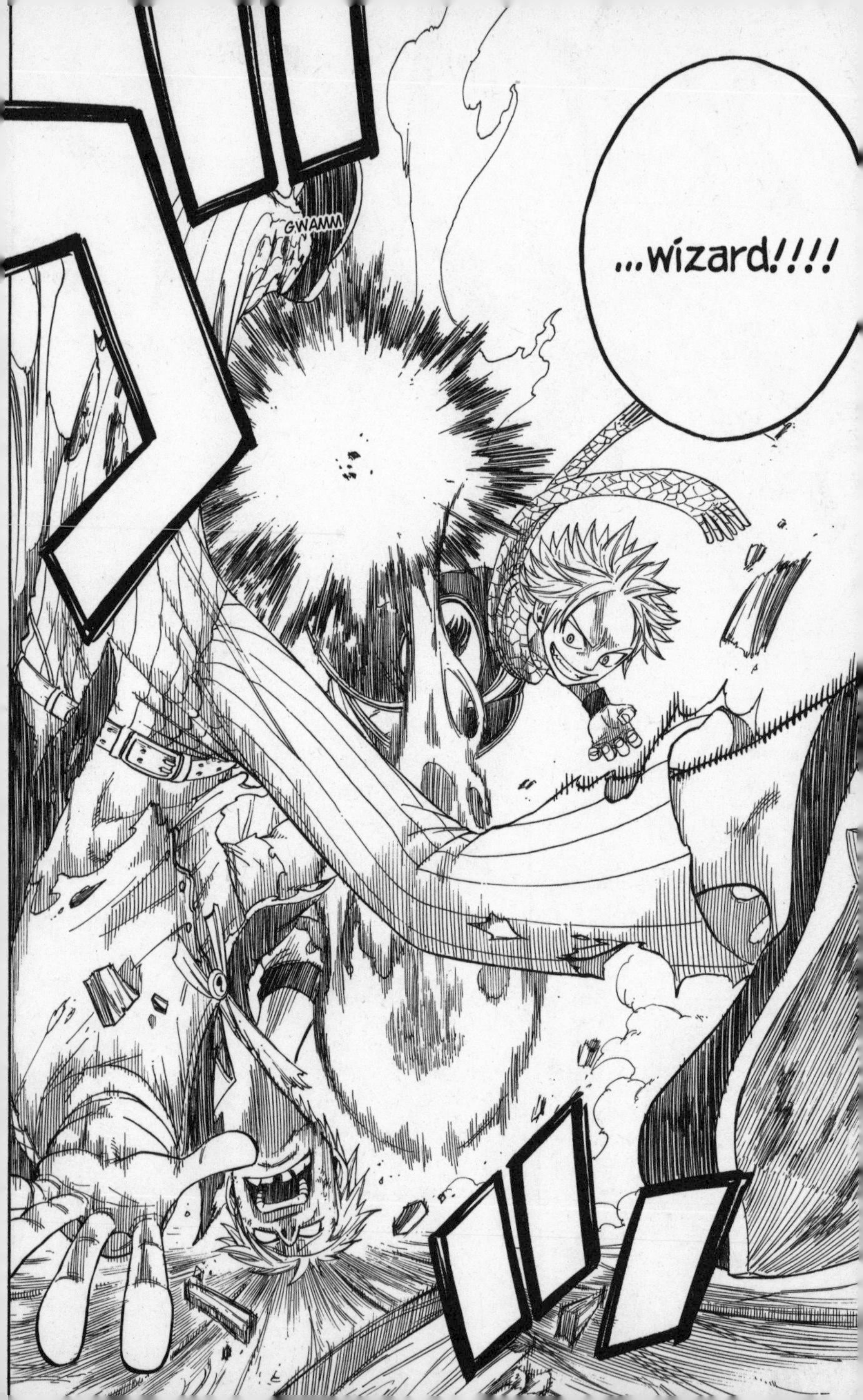
...wizard!!!!
GWAMM

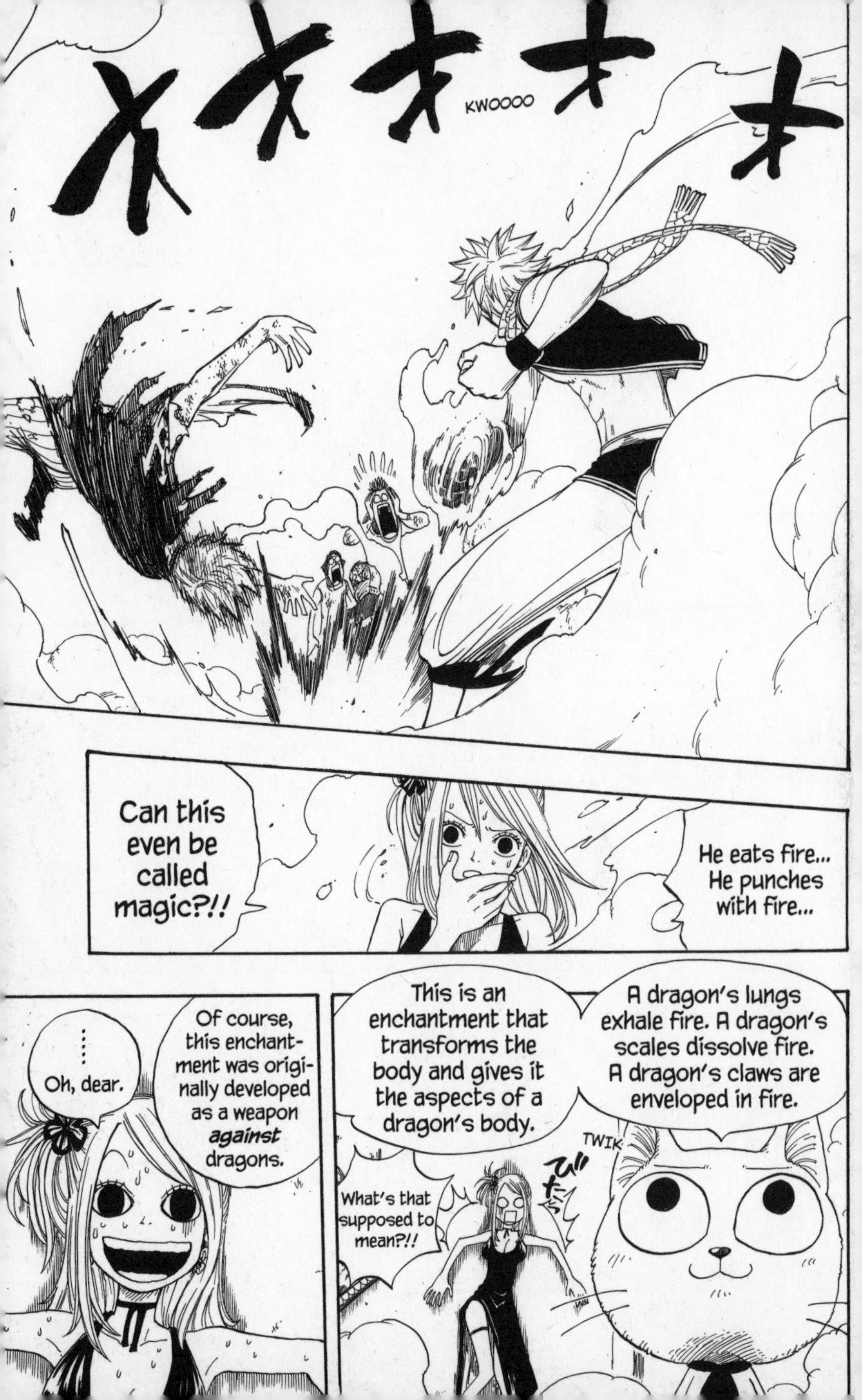

KWOOOO
He eats fire... He punches with fire...
Can this even be called magic?!!
A dragon's lungs exhale fire. A dragon's scales dissolve fire. A dragon's claws are enveloped in fire.
This is an enchantment that transforms the body and gives it the aspects of a dragon's body.
TWIK
What's that supposed to mean?!!
Of course, this enchantment was originally developed as a weapon *against* dragons.
...... Oh, dear.

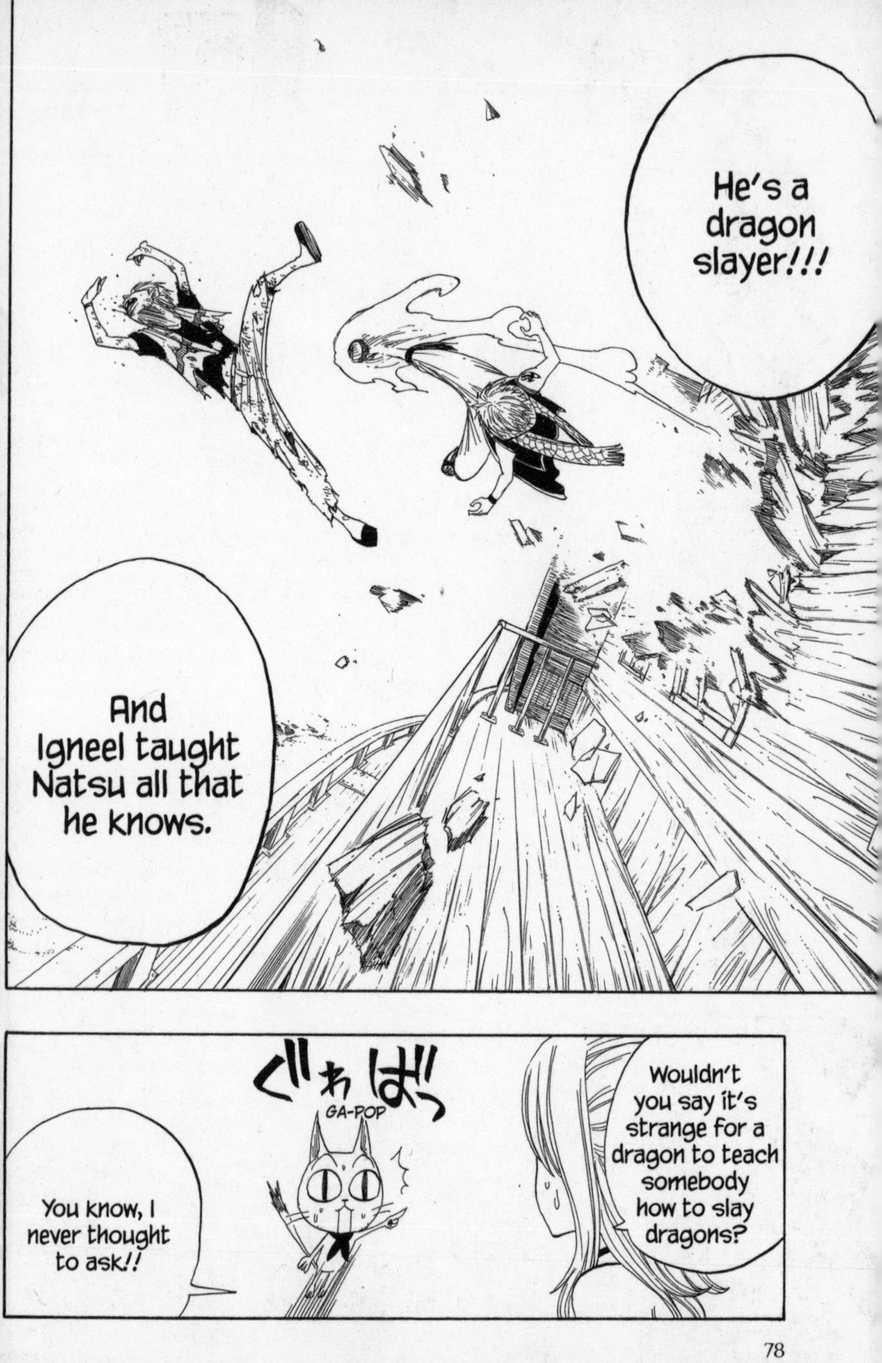
He's a dragon slayer!!!
And Igneel taught Natsu all that he knows.
Wouldn't you say it's strange for a dragon to teach somebody how to slay dragons?
ぐぁぱっ
GA-POP
You know, I never thought to ask!!

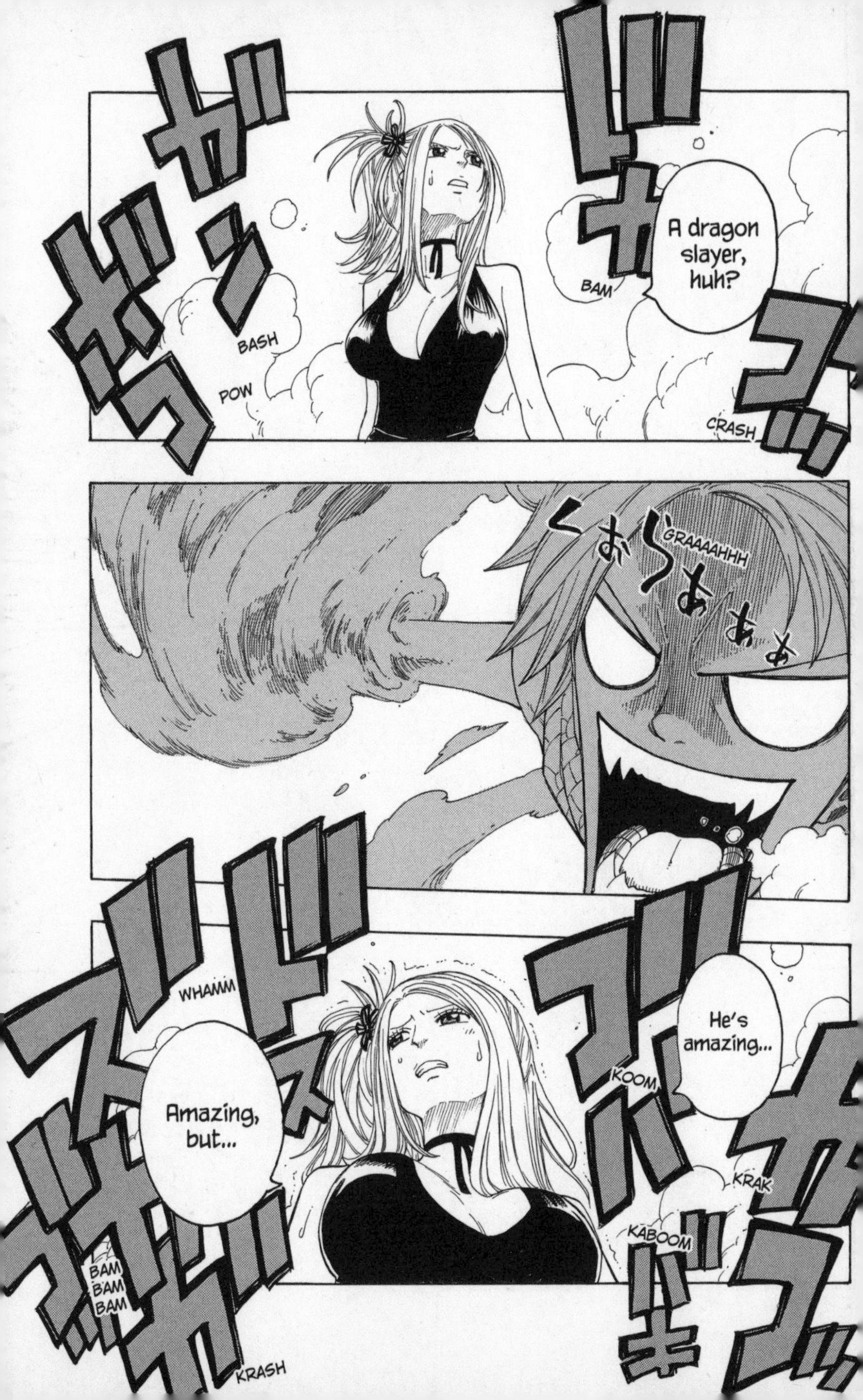
CRASH
A dragon slayer, huh?
BAM
BASH
POW
GRAAAAHHH
KRAK
KABOOM
He's amazing...
KOOM
WHAMM
Amazing, but...
BAM BAM BAM
KRASH

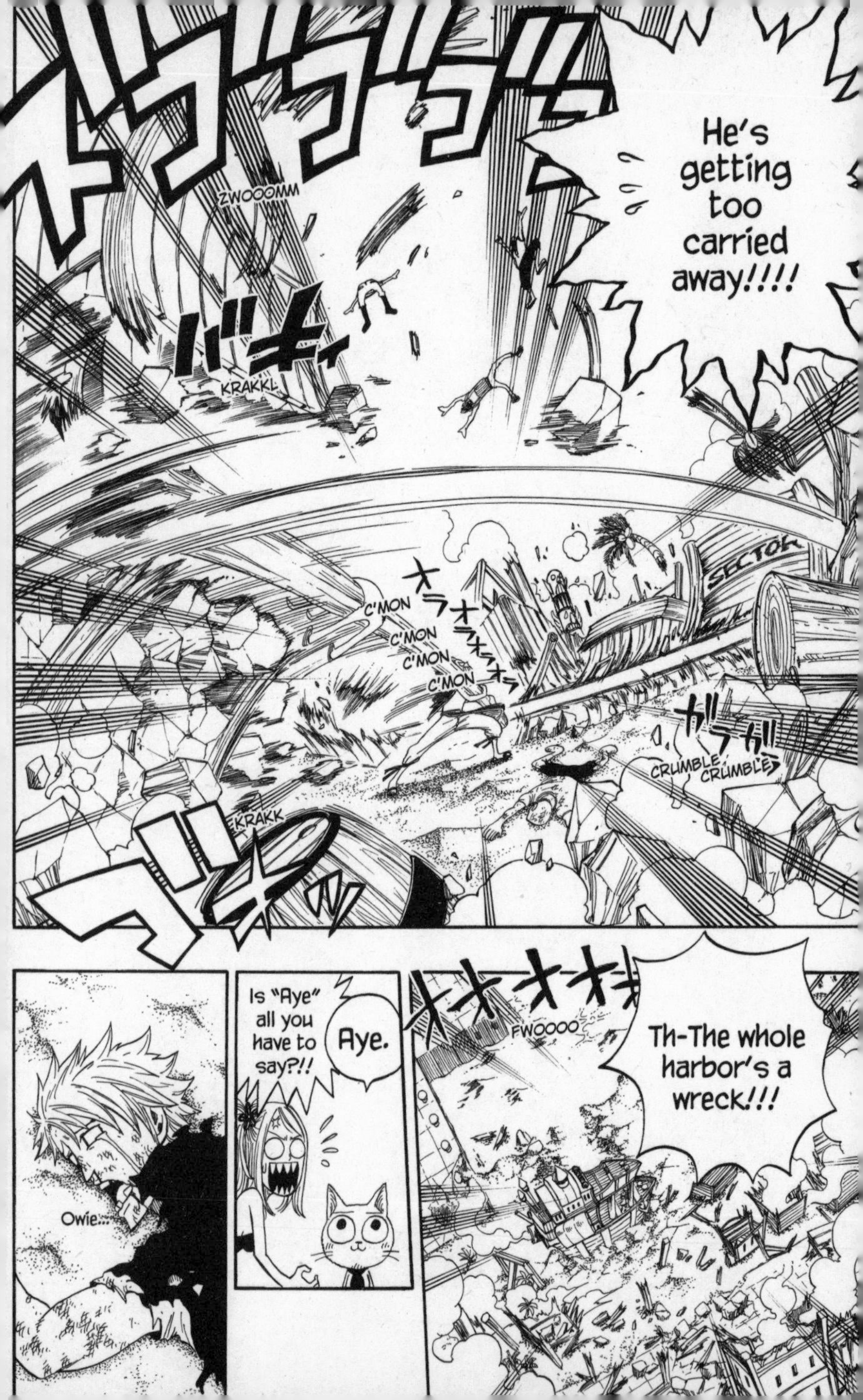
He's getting too carried away!!!!
ZWOOOMM
KRAKKL
C'MON
C'MON
C'MON
C'MON
CRUMBLE CRUMBLE
KRAKK
FWOOOO
Th-The whole harbor's a wreck!!!
Aye.
Is "Aye" all you have to say?!!
Owie...

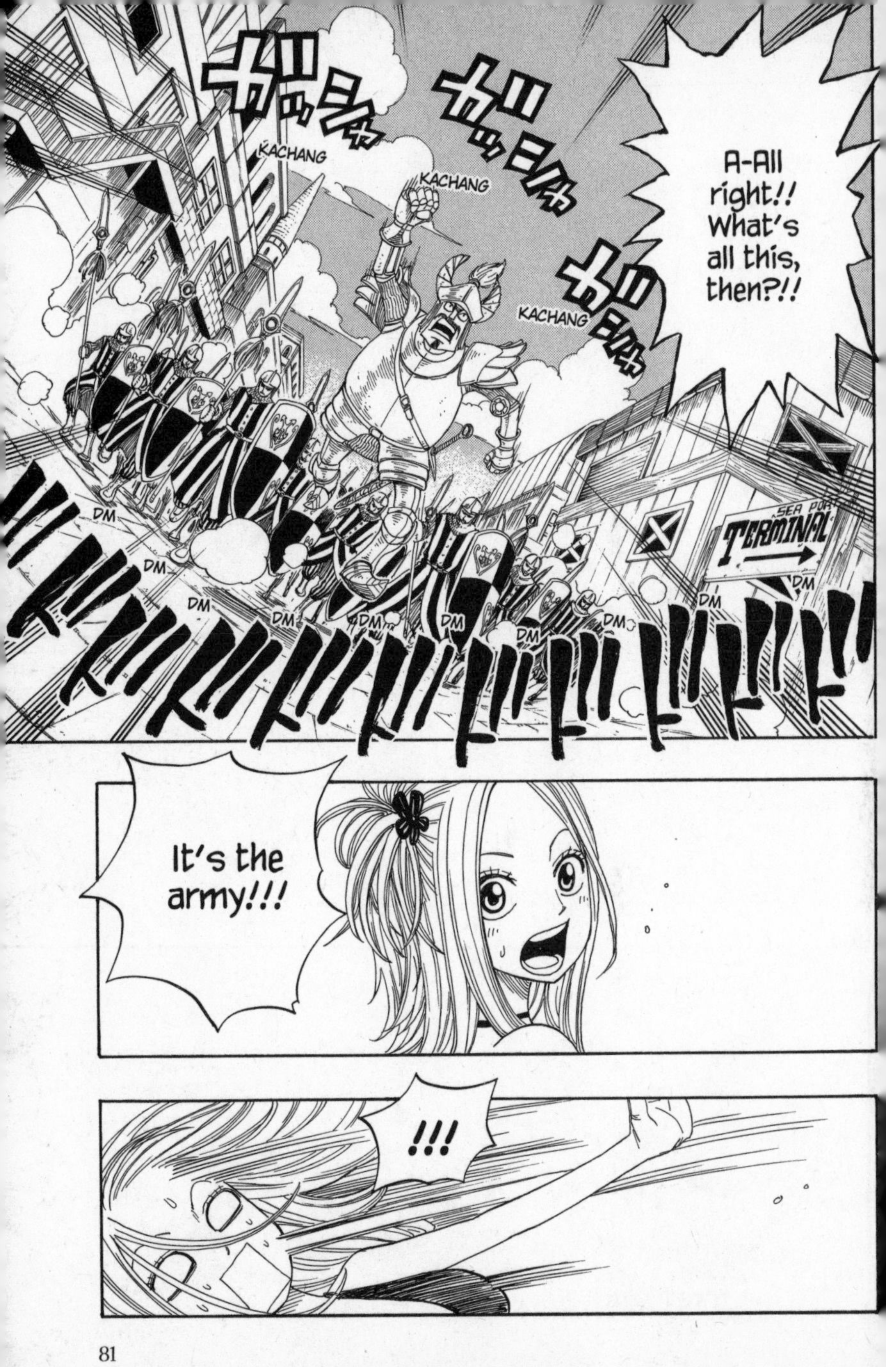
A-All right!! What's all this, then?!!
KACHANG
KACHANG
KACHANG
TERMINAL
DM
DM
DM
DM
DM
DM
DM
DM
DM
DM
It's the army!!!
!!!

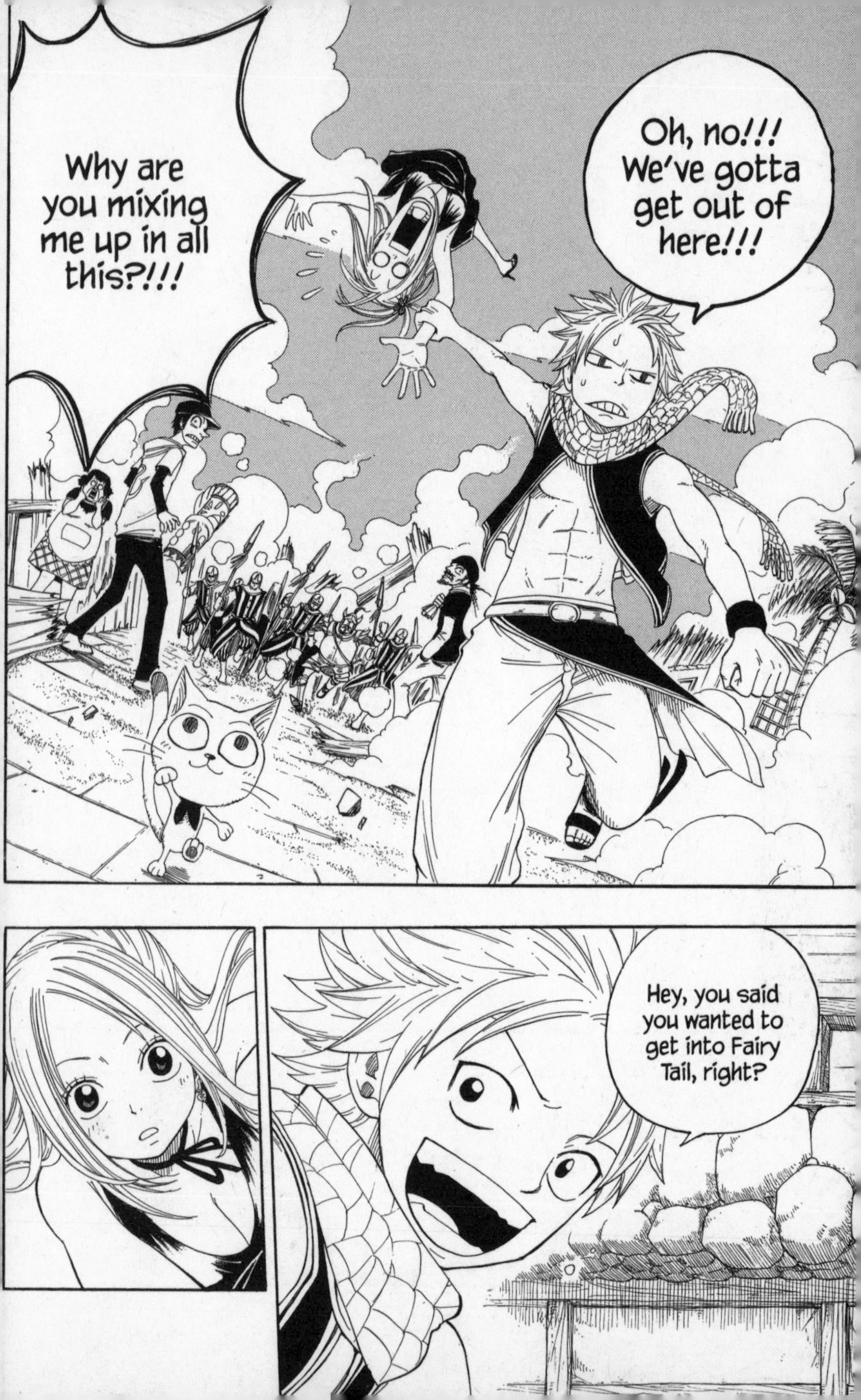
Oh, no!!! We've gotta get out of here!!!
Why are you mixing me up in all this?!!!
Hey, you said you wanted to get into Fairy Tail, right?

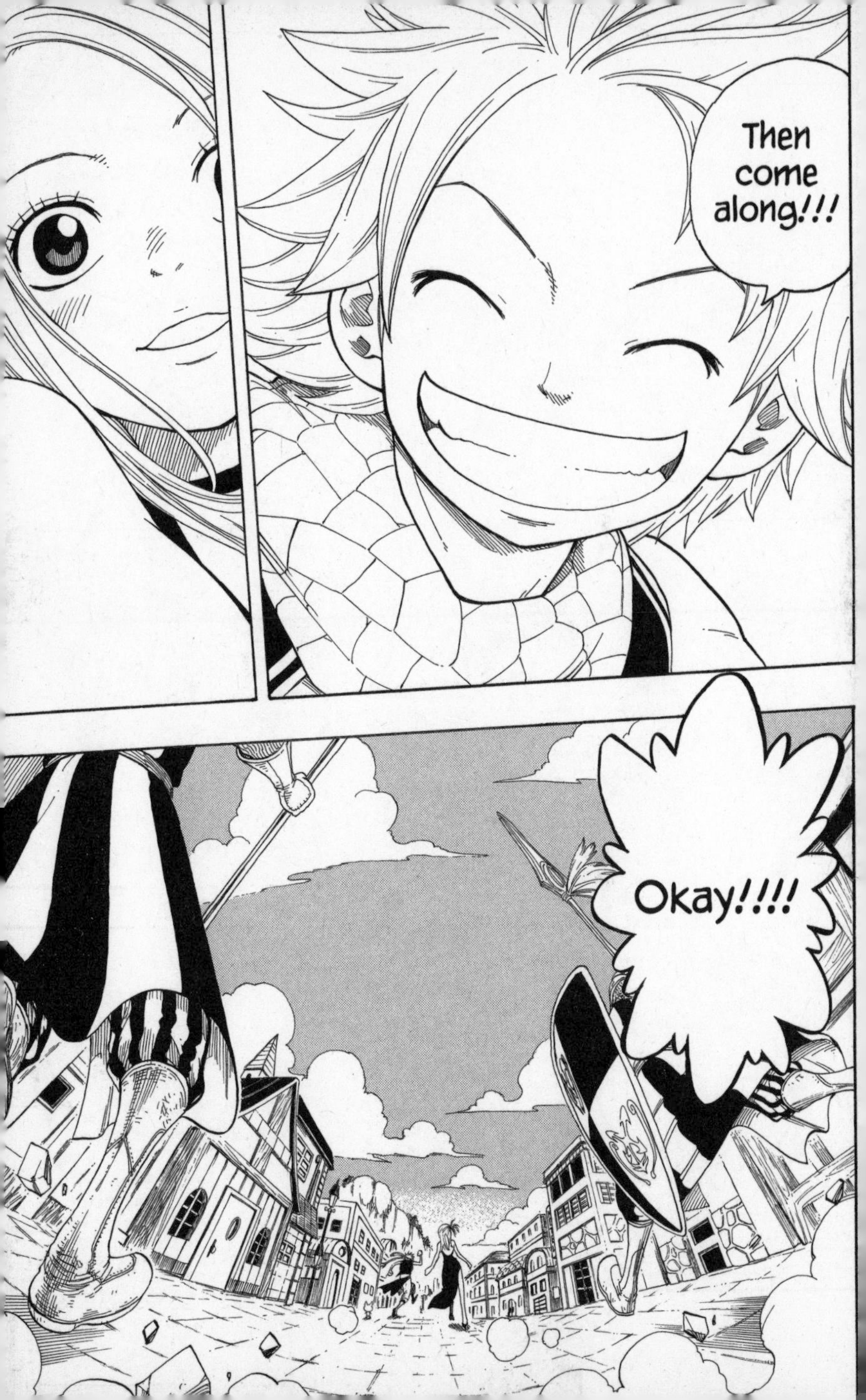
Then come along!!!
Okay!!!!

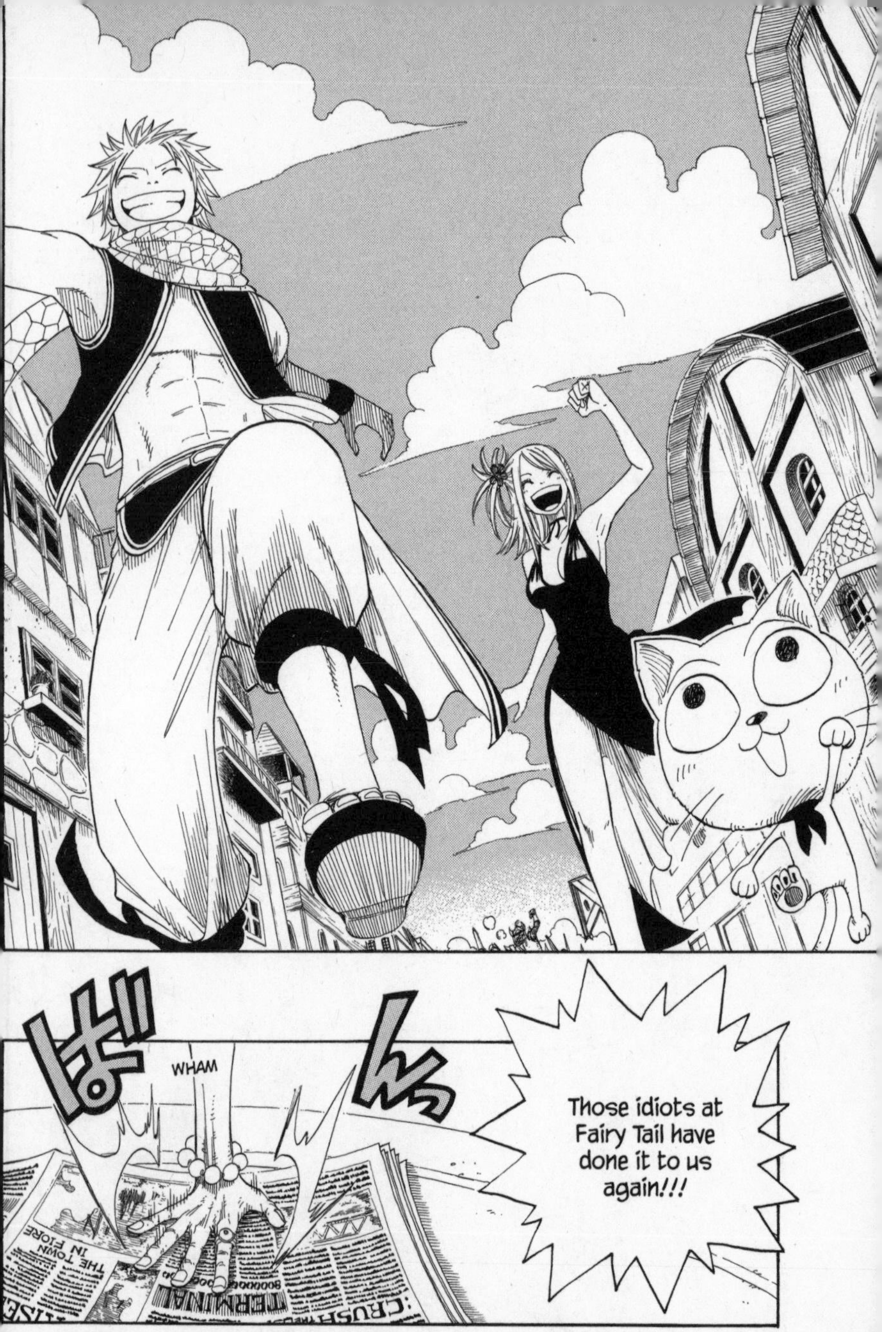
Those idiots at Fairy Tail have done it to us again!!!
WHAM

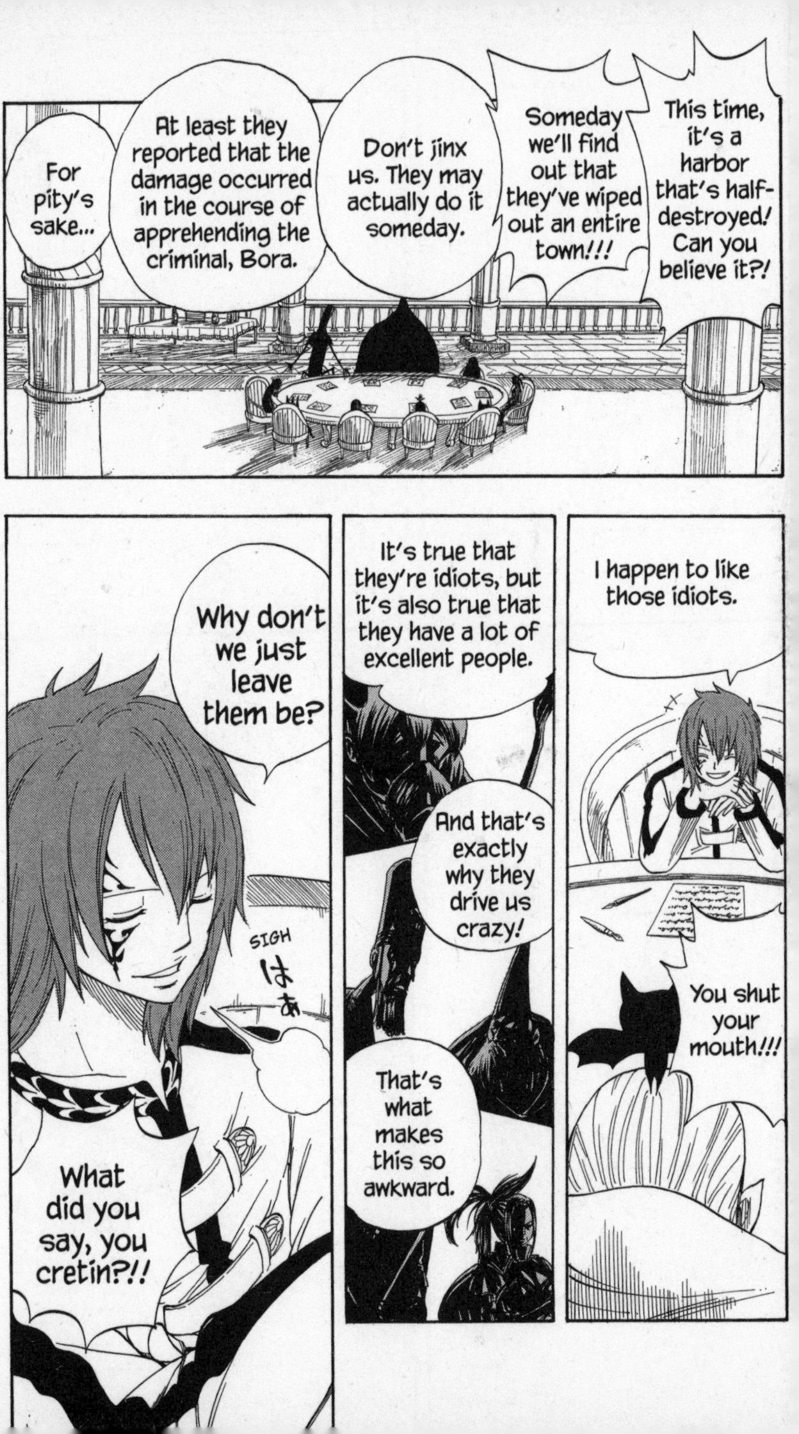
This time, it's a harbor that's half-destroyed! Can you believe it?!
Someday we'll find out that they've wiped out an entire town!!!
Don't jinx us. They may actually do it someday.
At least they reported that the damage occurred in the course of apprehending the criminal, Bora.
For pity's sake...
I happen to like those idiots.
You shut your mouth!!!
It's true that they're idiots, but it's also true that they have a lot of excellent people.
And that's exactly why they drive us crazy!
That's what makes this so awkward.
Why don't we just leave them be?
SIGH
はあ
What did you say, you cretin?!!

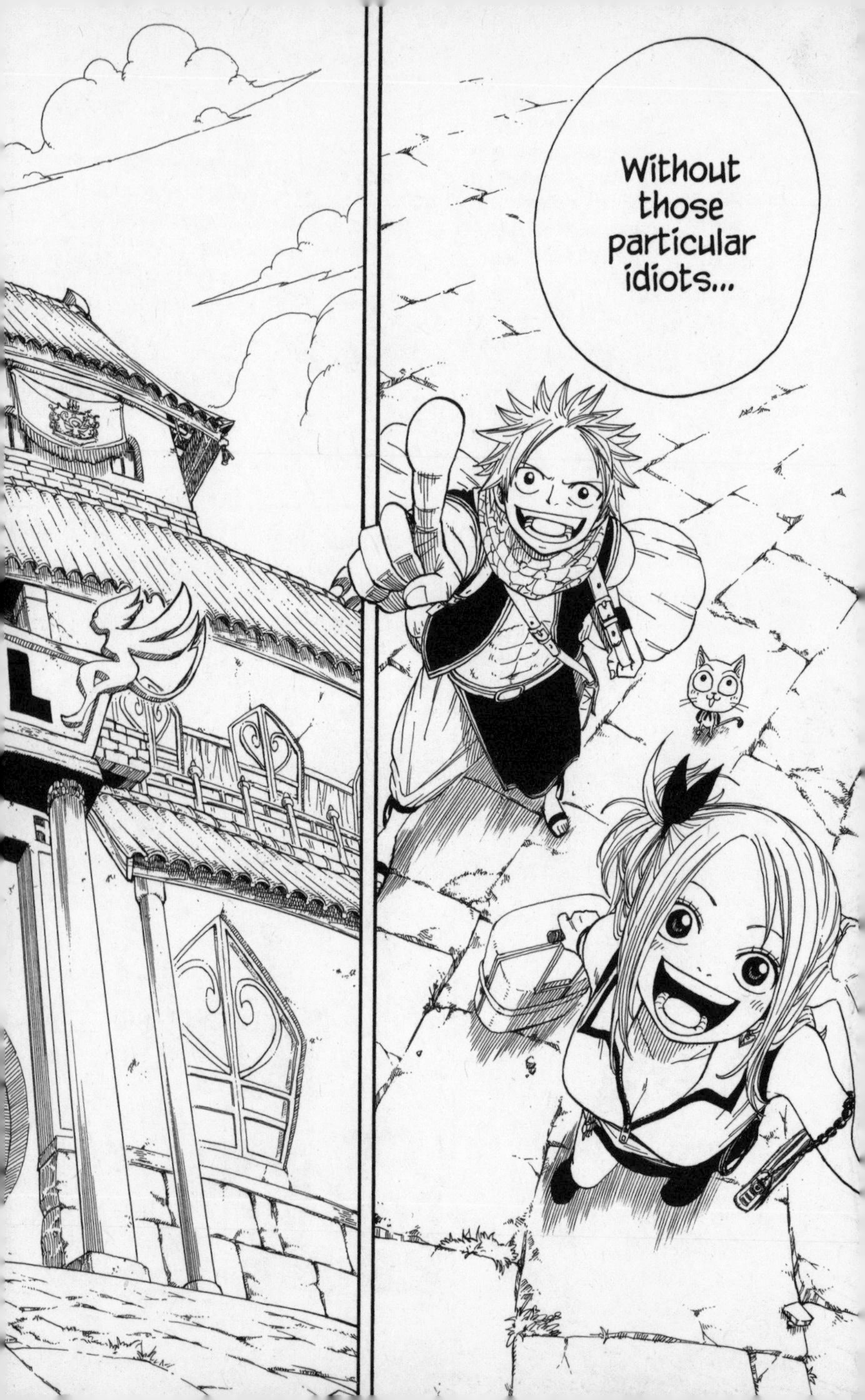
Without those particular idiots...

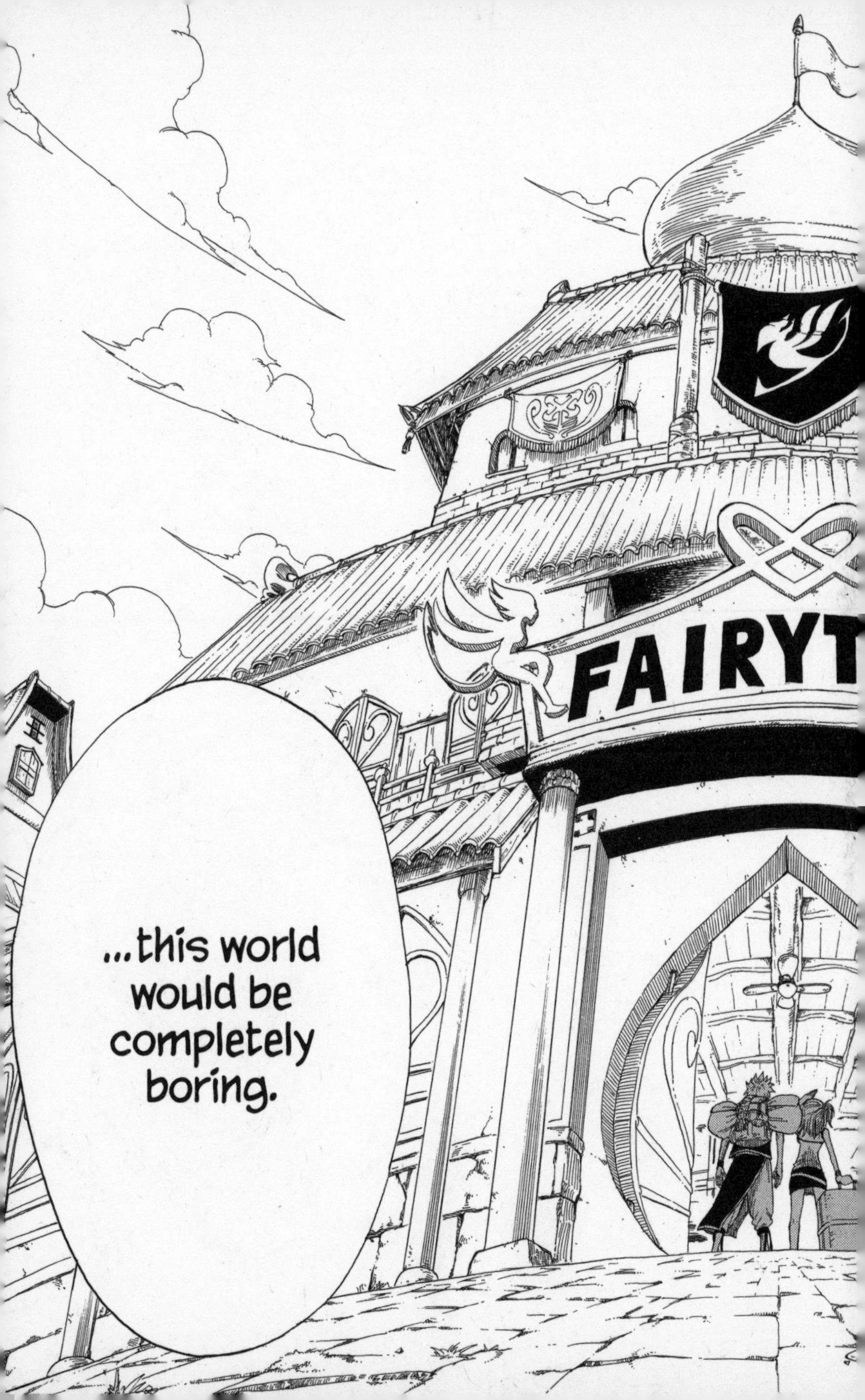

...this world would be completely boring.
FAIRYT

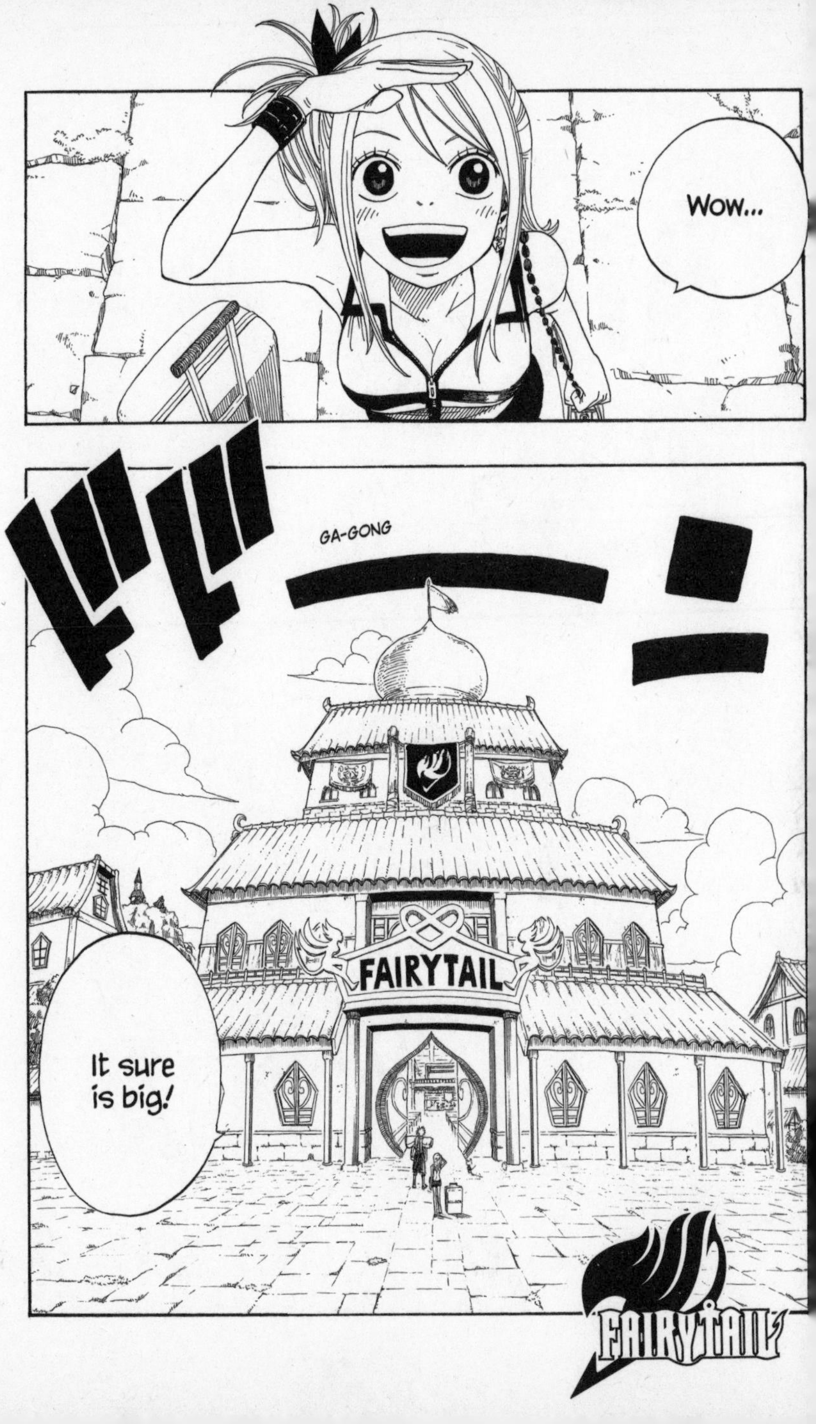
Wow...
GA-GONG
FAIRYTAIL
It sure is big!
FAIRYTAIL

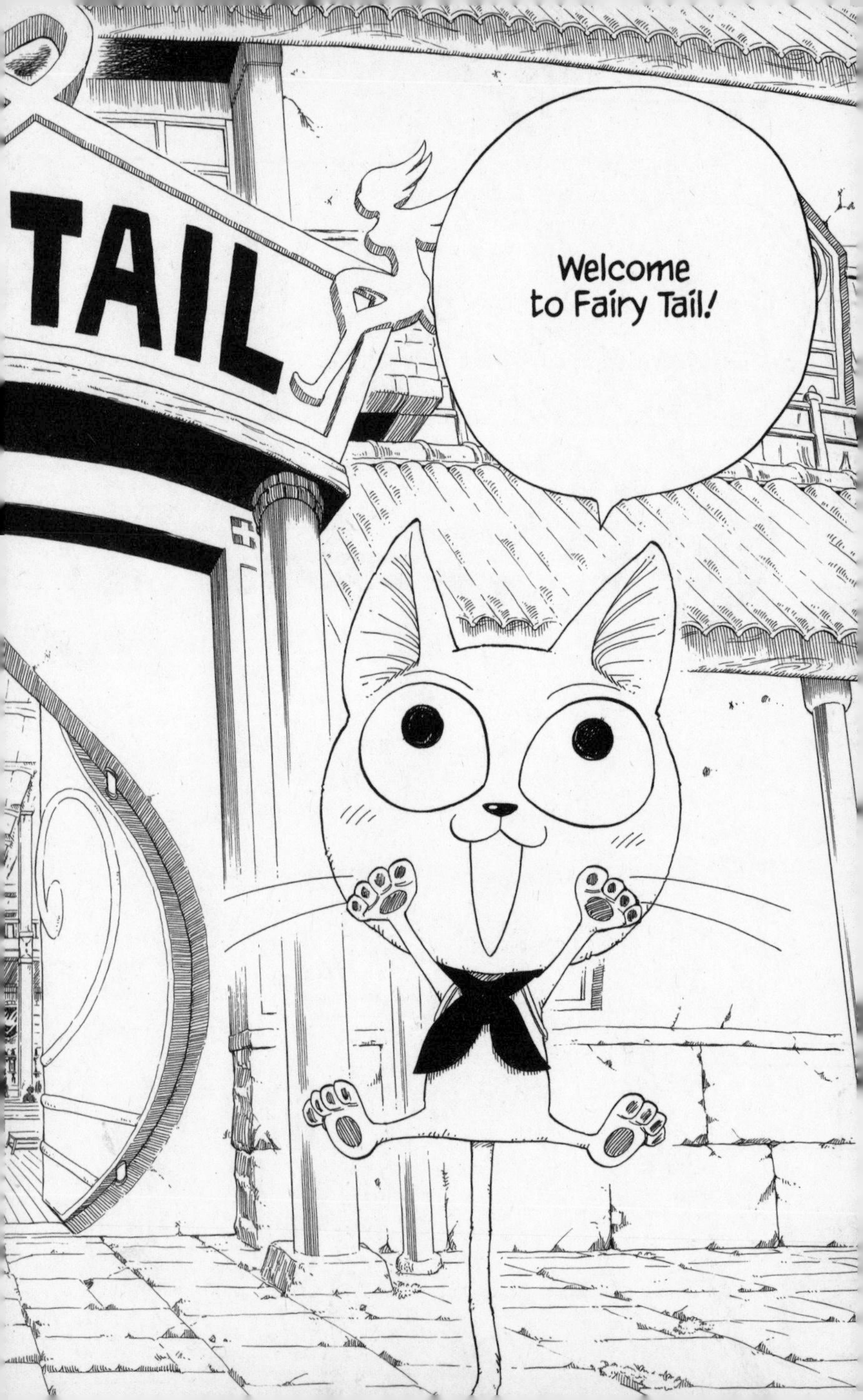
TAIL
Welcome to Fairy Tail!

Chapter 2: The Master Appears!

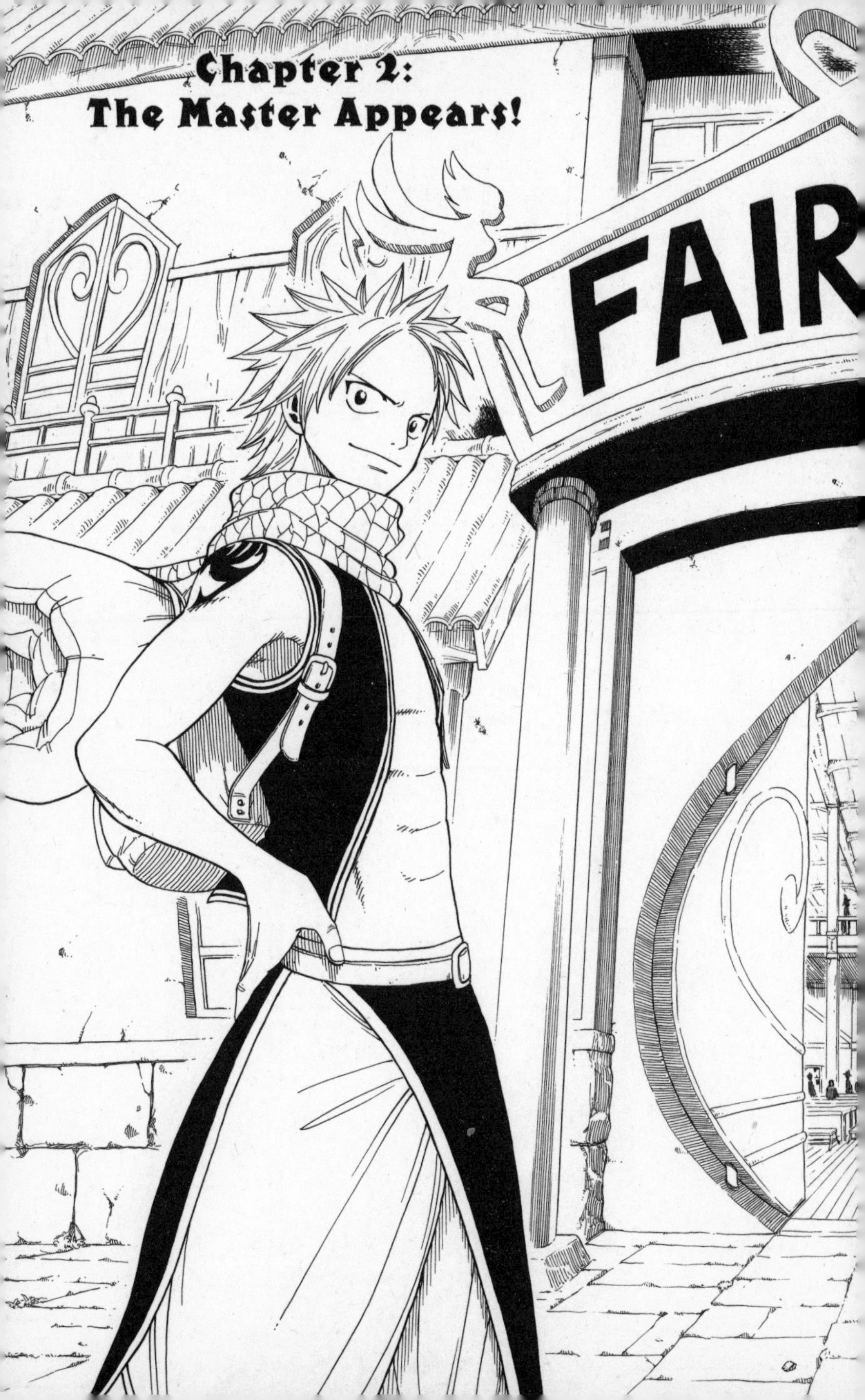
FAIR

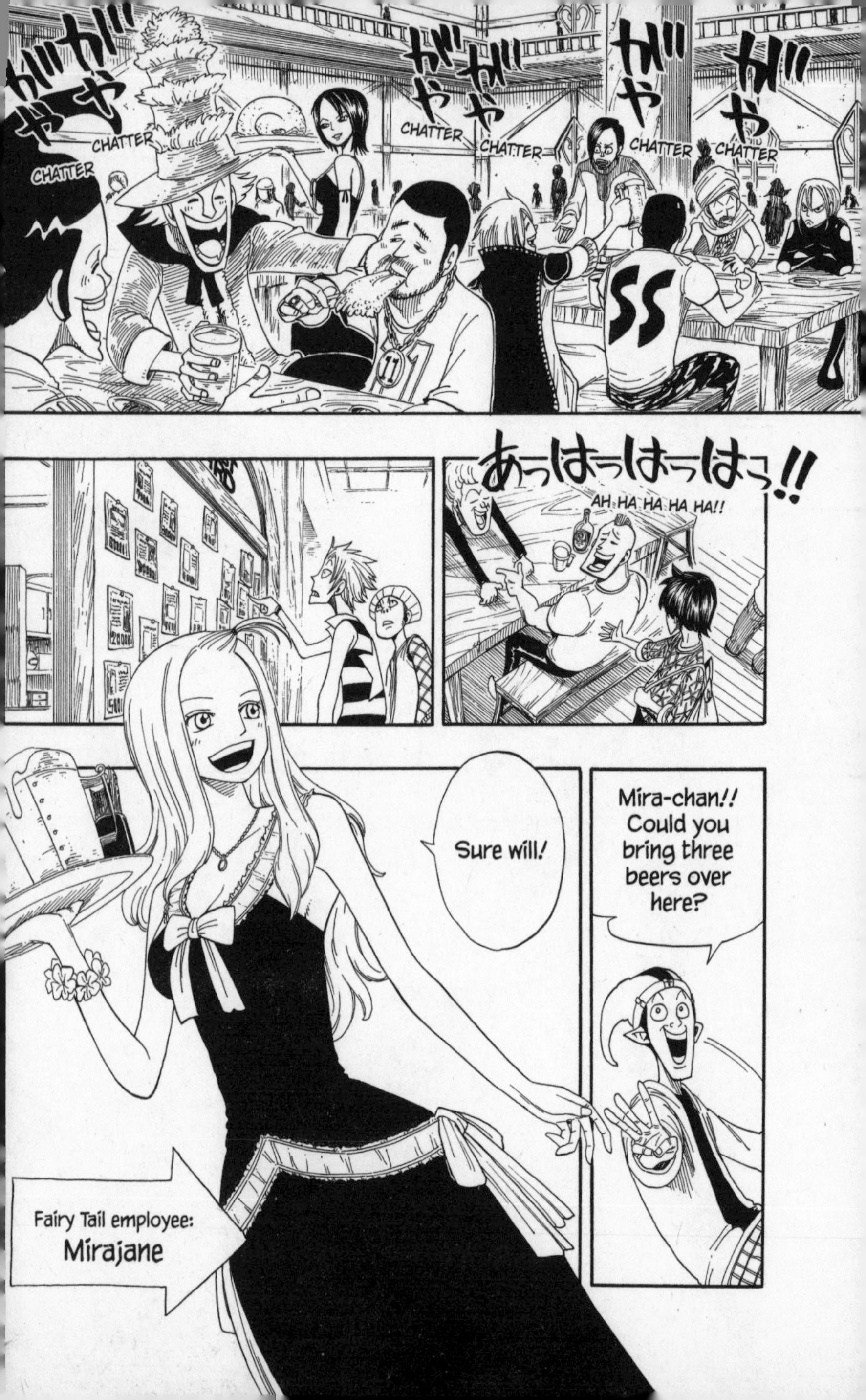

がや
CHATTER
がや
CHATTER
がやがや
CHATTER
CHATTER
がやがや
CHATTER
CHATTER
あっはっはっはっ!!
AH HA HA HA HA!!
Mira-chan!! Could you bring three beers over here?
Sure will!
Fairy Tail employee: Mirajane

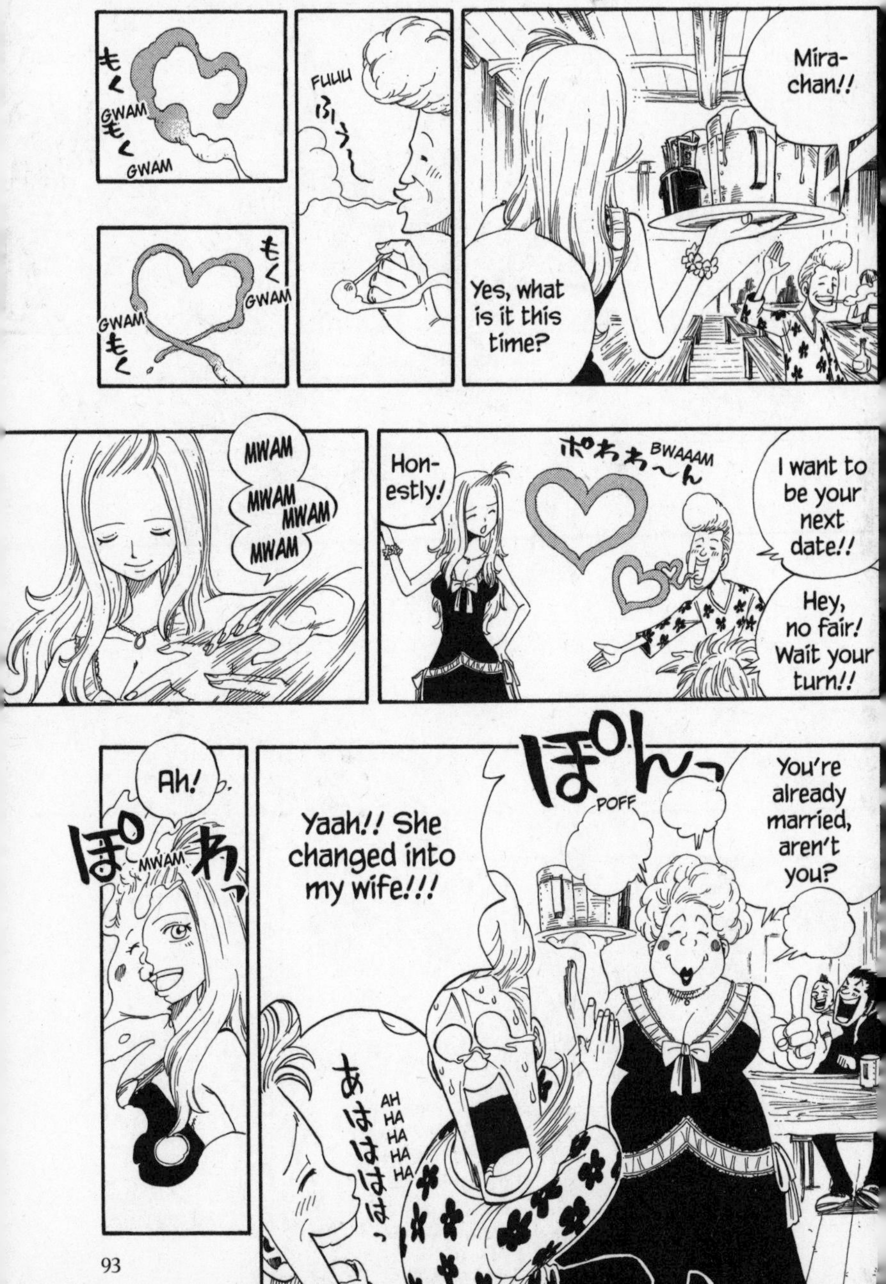
Mira-chan!!
Yes, what is it this time?
ふぅ〜 FUUU
もく GWAM もく GWAM
もく GWAM
GWAM もく
I want to be your next date!!
Hey, no fair! Wait your turn!!
ポわわ〜ん BWAAAM
Hon-estly!
MWAM MWAM MWAM MWAM
ぽんっ POFF
You're already married, aren't you?
Yaah!! She changed into my wife!!!
あはははっ AH HA HA HA HA
Ah!
ぽわっ MWAM

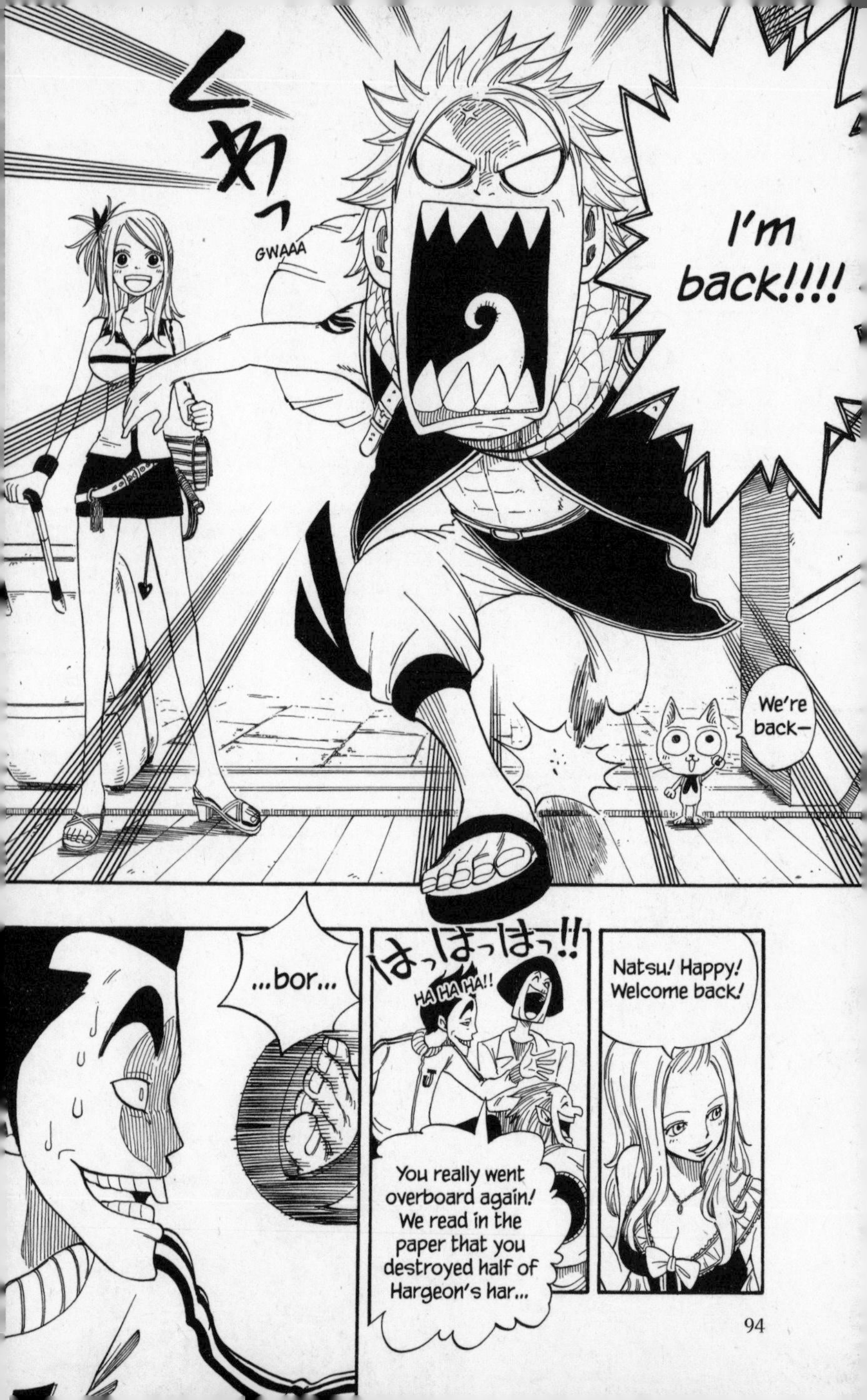
I'm back!!!!
くわっ
GWAAA
We're back—
Natsu! Happy! Welcome back!
はっはっはっ!!
HA HA HA!!
You really went overboard again! We read in the paper that you destroyed half of Hargeon's har...
...bor...

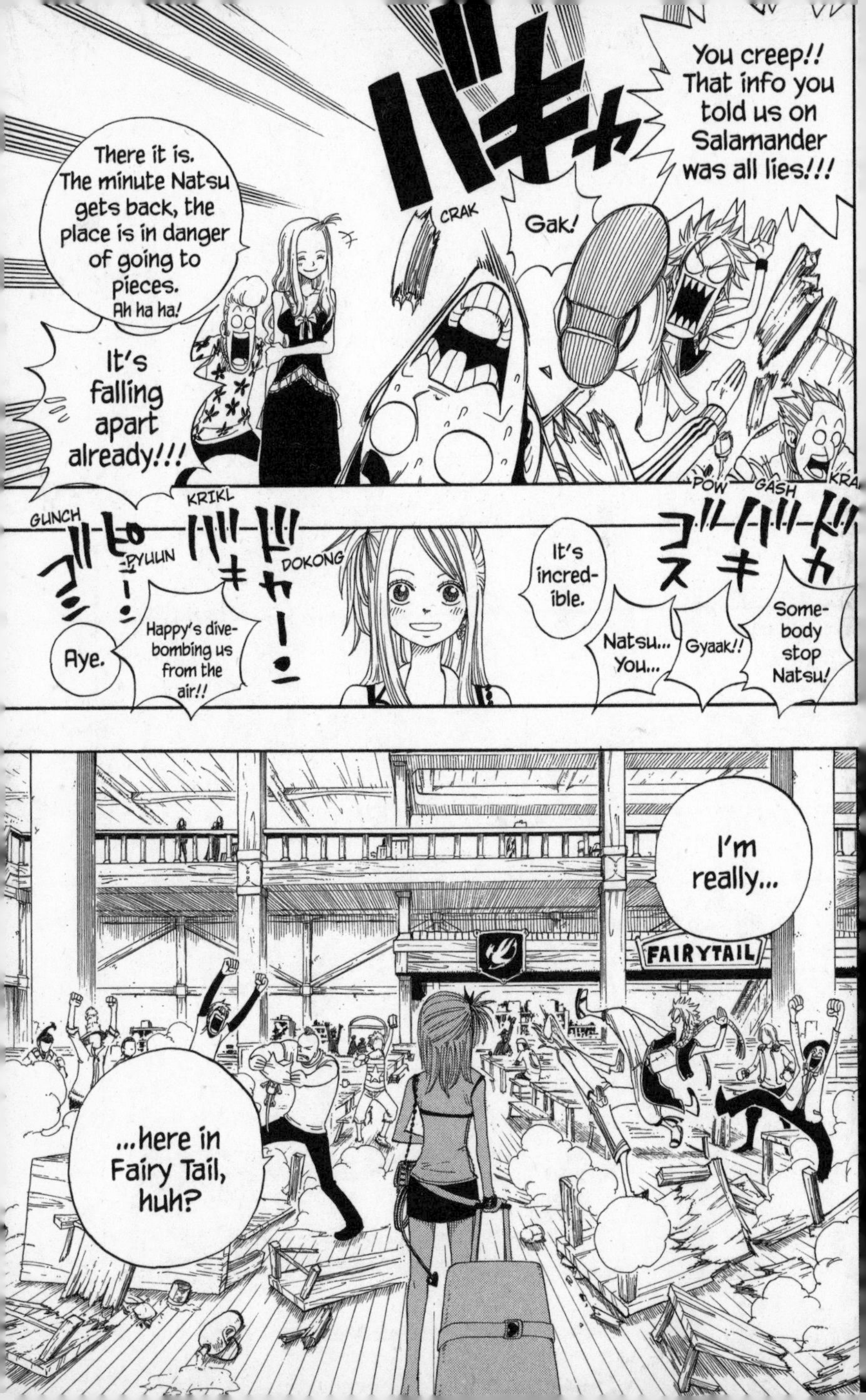

You creep!! That info you told us on Salamander was all lies!!!
CRAK
Gak!
There it is. The minute Natsu gets back, the place is in danger of going to pieces.
Ah ha ha!
It's falling apart already!!!
KRA
Some-body stop Natsu!
GASH
Gyaak!!
POW
Natsu... You...
It's incred-ible.
DOKONG
KRIKL
Happy's dive-bombing us from the air!!
PYUUN
GUNCH
Aye.
I'm really...
FAIRYTAIL
...here in Fairy Tail, huh?

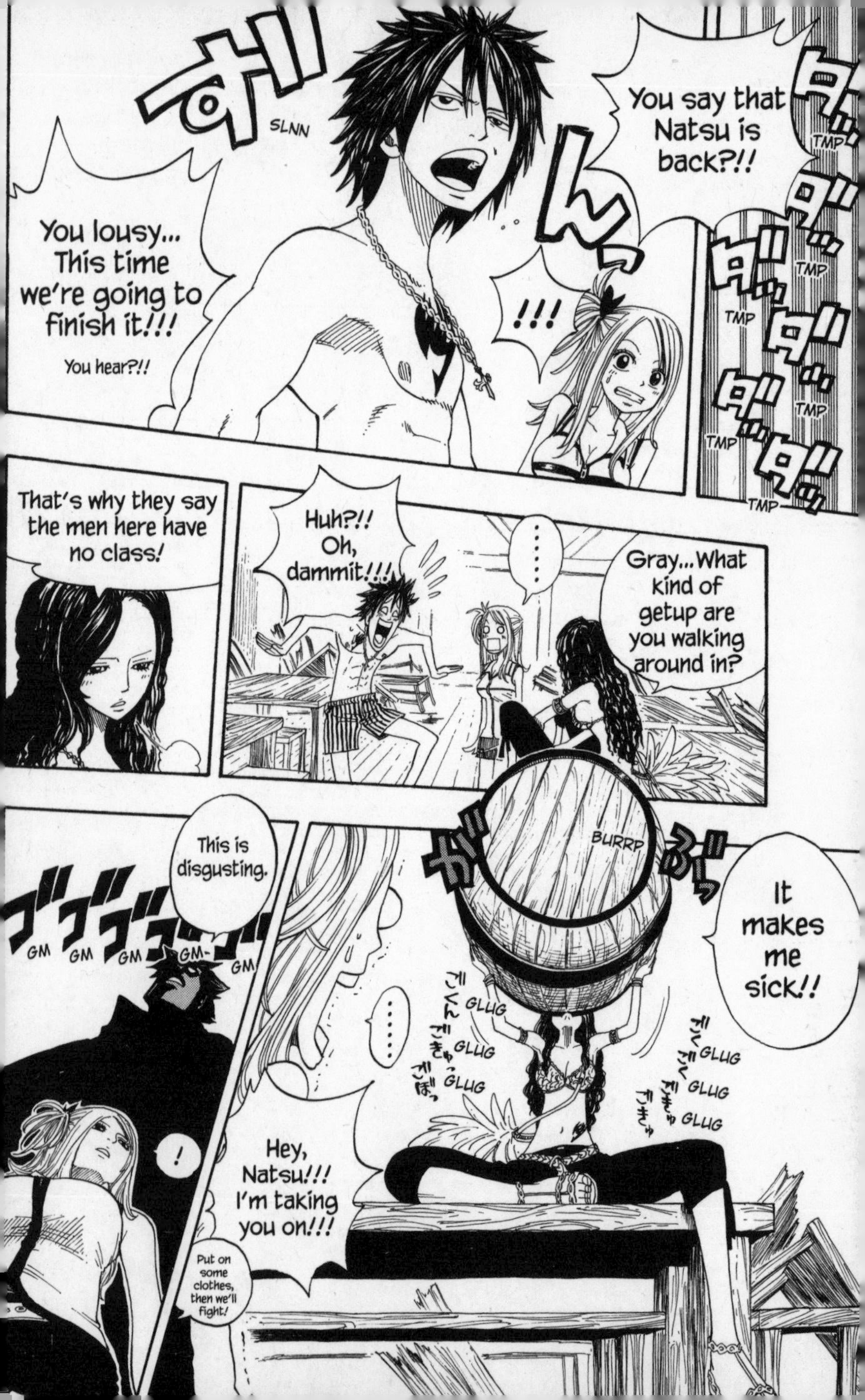
You say that Natsu is back?!!
TMP TMP TMP TMP TMP TMP
!!!
SLNN
You lousy... This time we're going to finish it!!!
You hear?!!
Gray...What kind of getup are you walking around in?
......
Huh?!! Oh, dammit!!!
That's why they say the men here have no class!
BURRP
It makes me sick!!
GLUG GLUG GLUG
GLUG GLUG GLUG
......
Hey, Natsu!!! I'm taking you on!!!
This is disgusting.
GM GM GM GM- GM
!
Put on some clothes, then we'll fight!

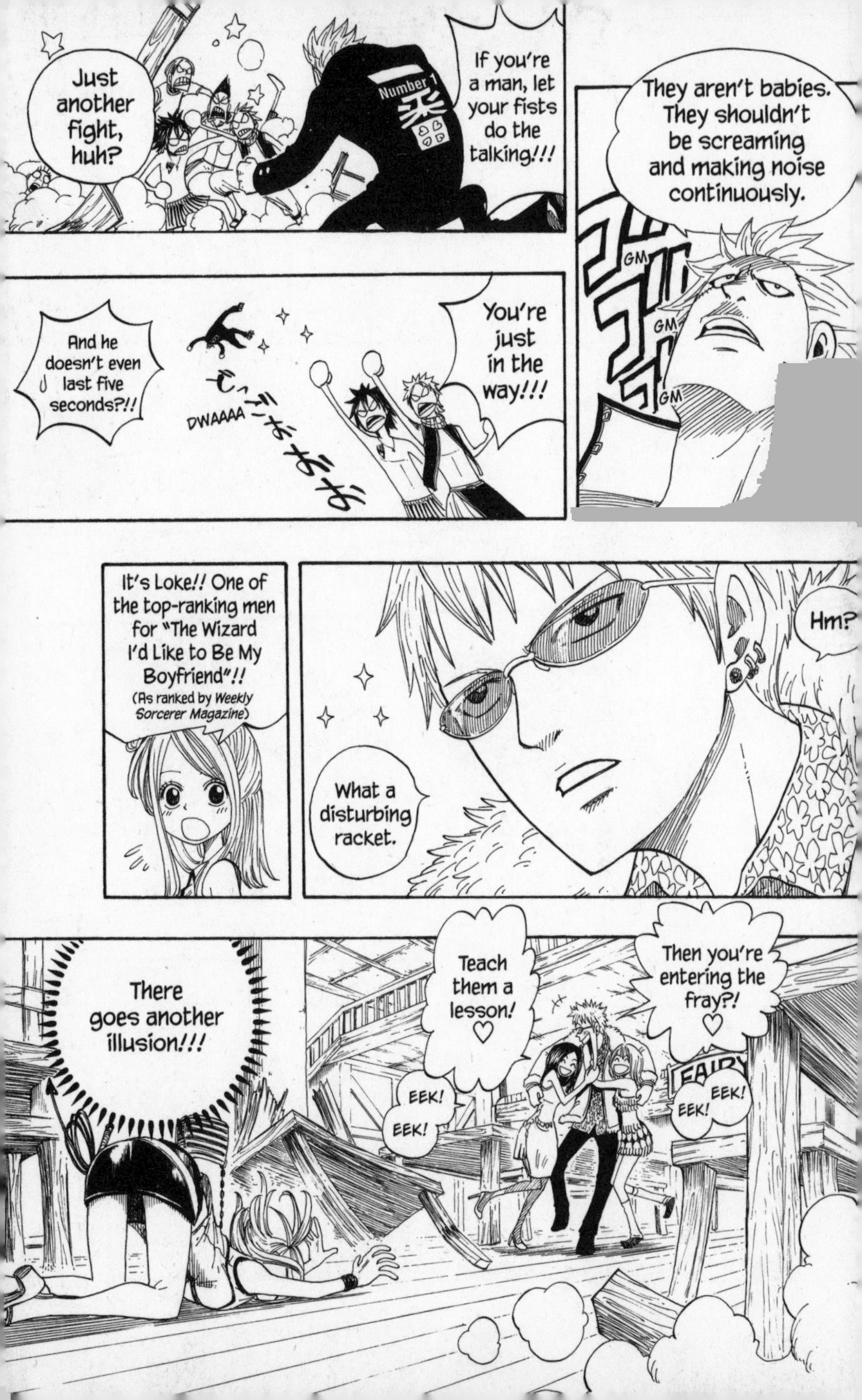
If you're a man, let your fists do the talking!!!
Just another fight, huh?
Number 1
They aren't babies. They shouldn't be screaming and making noise continuously.
GM
GM
GM
You're just in the way!!!
DWAAAA
And he doesn't even last five seconds?!!
Hm?
What a disturbing racket.
It's Loke!! One of the top-ranking men for "The Wizard I'd Like to Be My Boyfriend"!!
(As ranked by Weekly Sorcerer Magazine)
Then you're entering the fray?! ♡
Teach them a lesson! ♡
EEK!
EEK!
EEK!
EEK!
There goes another illusion!!!

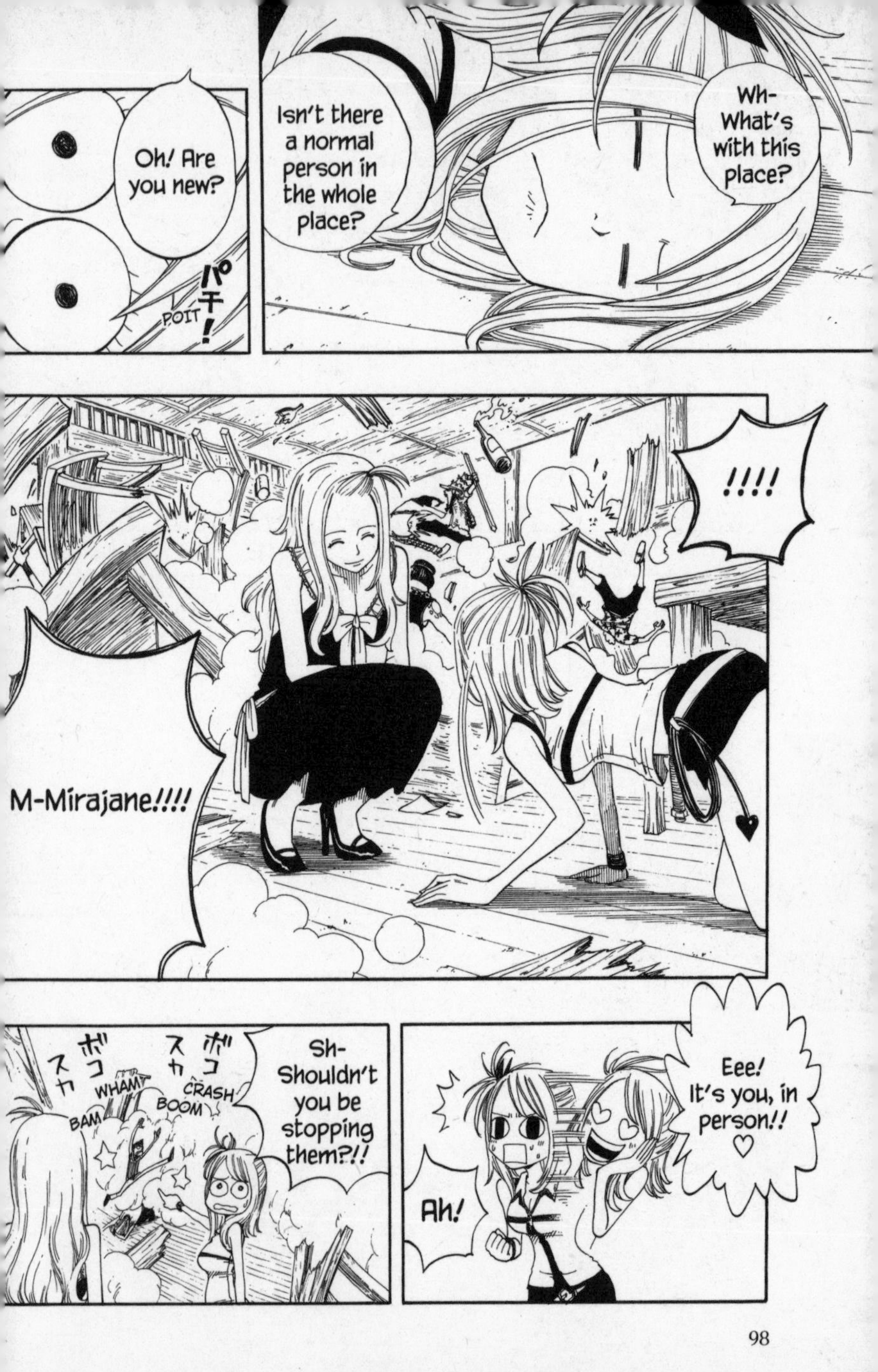
Wh- What's with this place?
Isn't there a normal person in the whole place?
Oh! Are you new?
パチ
POIT
!!!!
M-Mirajane!!!!
Eee! It's you, in person!! ♡
Ah!
Sh- Shouldn't you be stopping them?!!
ボコ
スカ
CRASH
BOOM
ボコ
スカ
WHAM
BAM

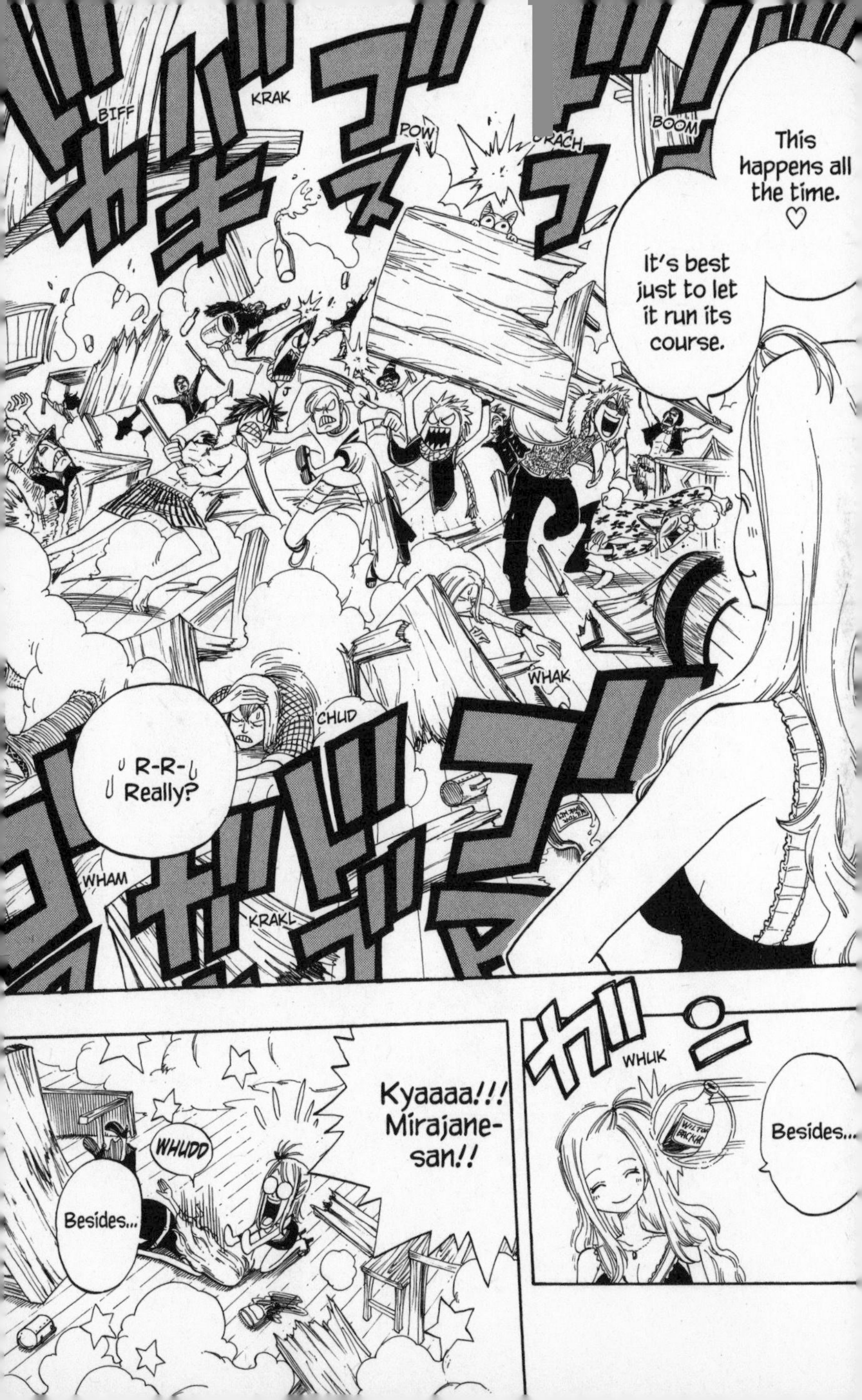
This happens all the time. ♡
It's best just to let it run its course.
BOOM
POW
KRAK
BIFF
WHAK
CHUD
R-R-Really?
KRAKL
WHAM
WHUK
Besides...
Kyaaaa!!! Mirajane-san!!
WHUDD
Besides...

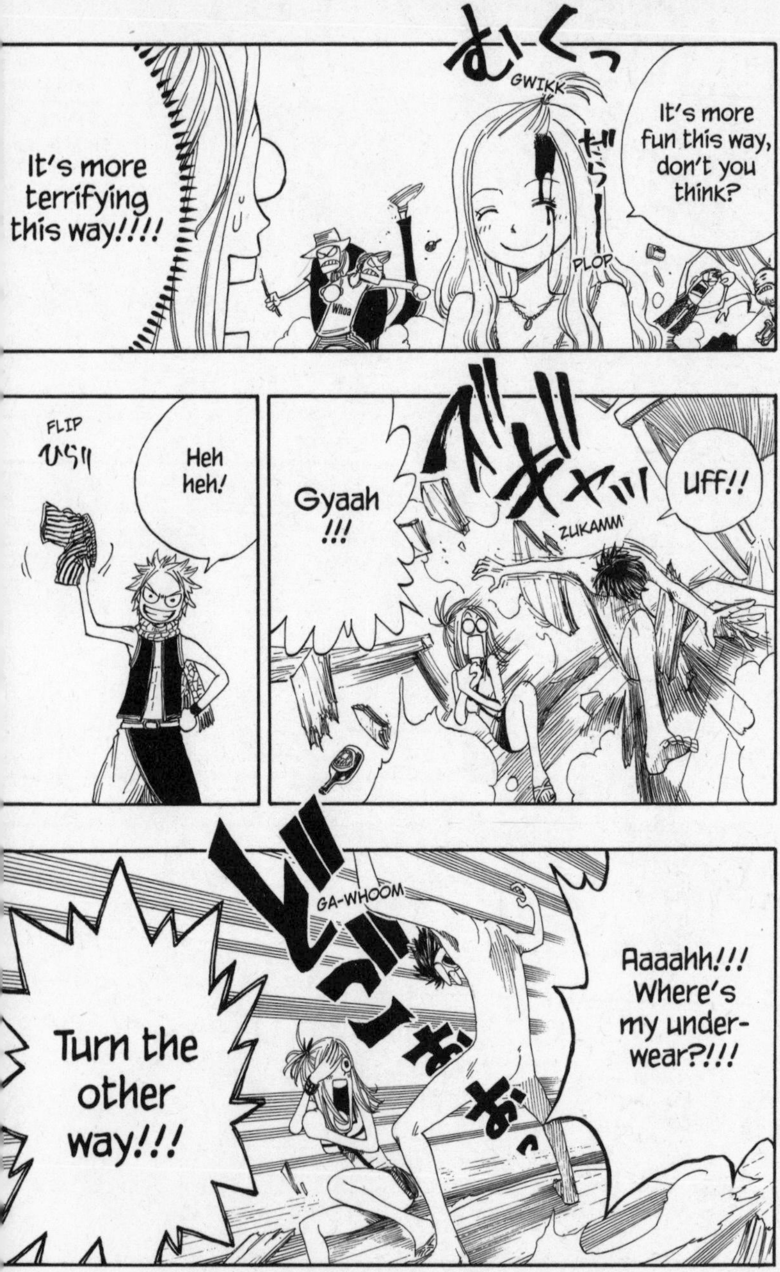
GWIKK
It's more fun this way, don't you think?
PLOP
Whoa
It's more terrifying this way!!!!
Uff!!
ZUKAMM
Gyaah!!!
Heh heh!
FLIP
Aaaahh!!! Where's my under-wear?!!!
GA-WHOOM
Turn the other way!!!

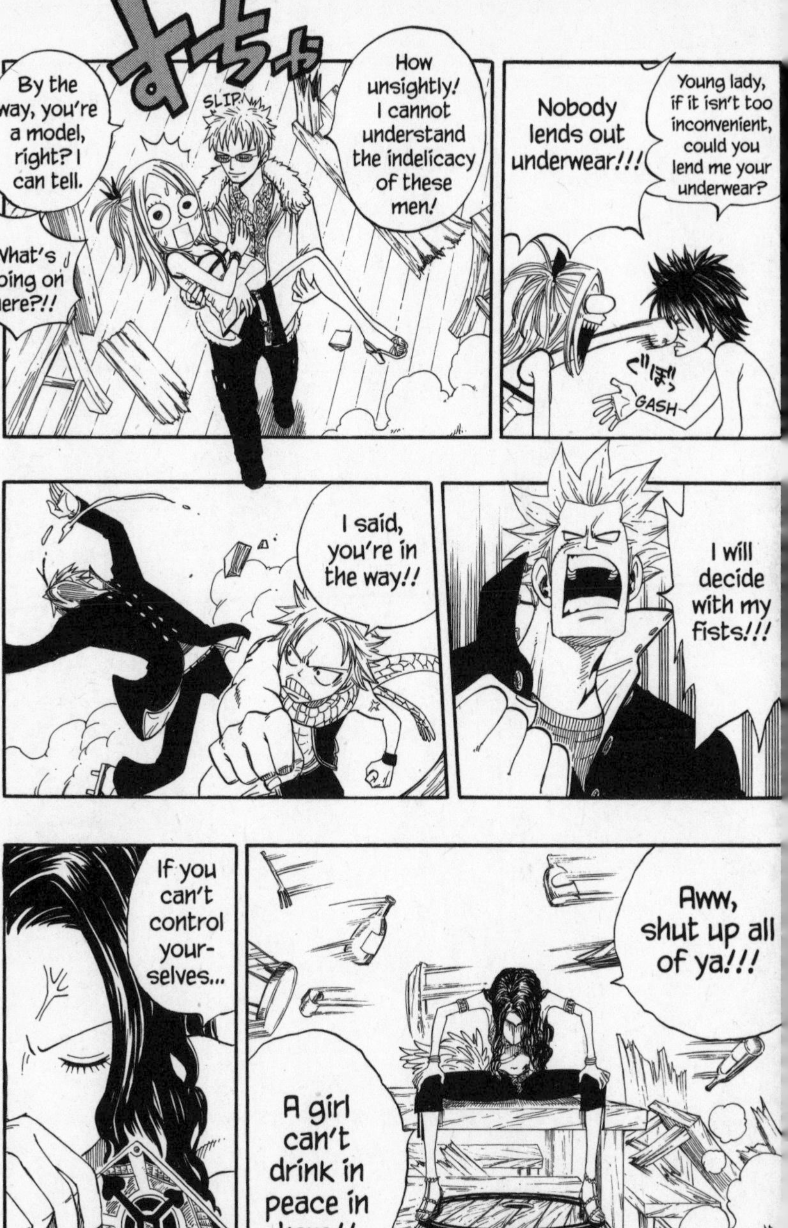
Young lady, if it isn't too inconvenient, could you lend me your underwear?
Nobody lends out underwear!!!
GASH
How unsightly! I cannot understand the indelicacy of these men!
SLIP
By the way, you're a model, right? I can tell.
What's going on here?!!
I will decide with my fists!!!
I said, you're in the way!!
Aww, shut up all of ya!!!
A girl can't drink in peace in here!!
If you can't control yourselves...

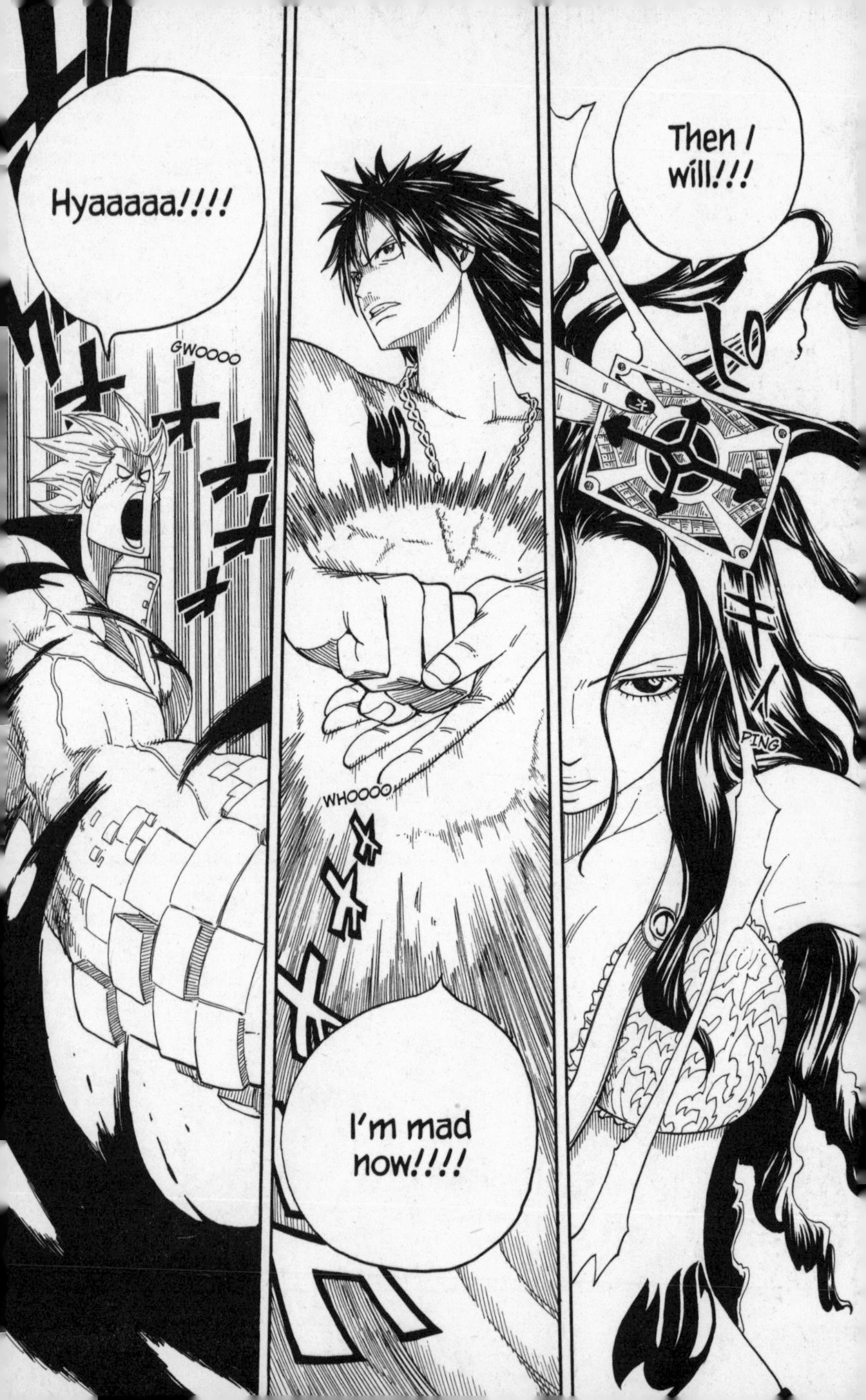
Then I will!!!
PING
WHOOOO
I'm mad now!!!!
Hyaaaaa!!!!
GWOOOO

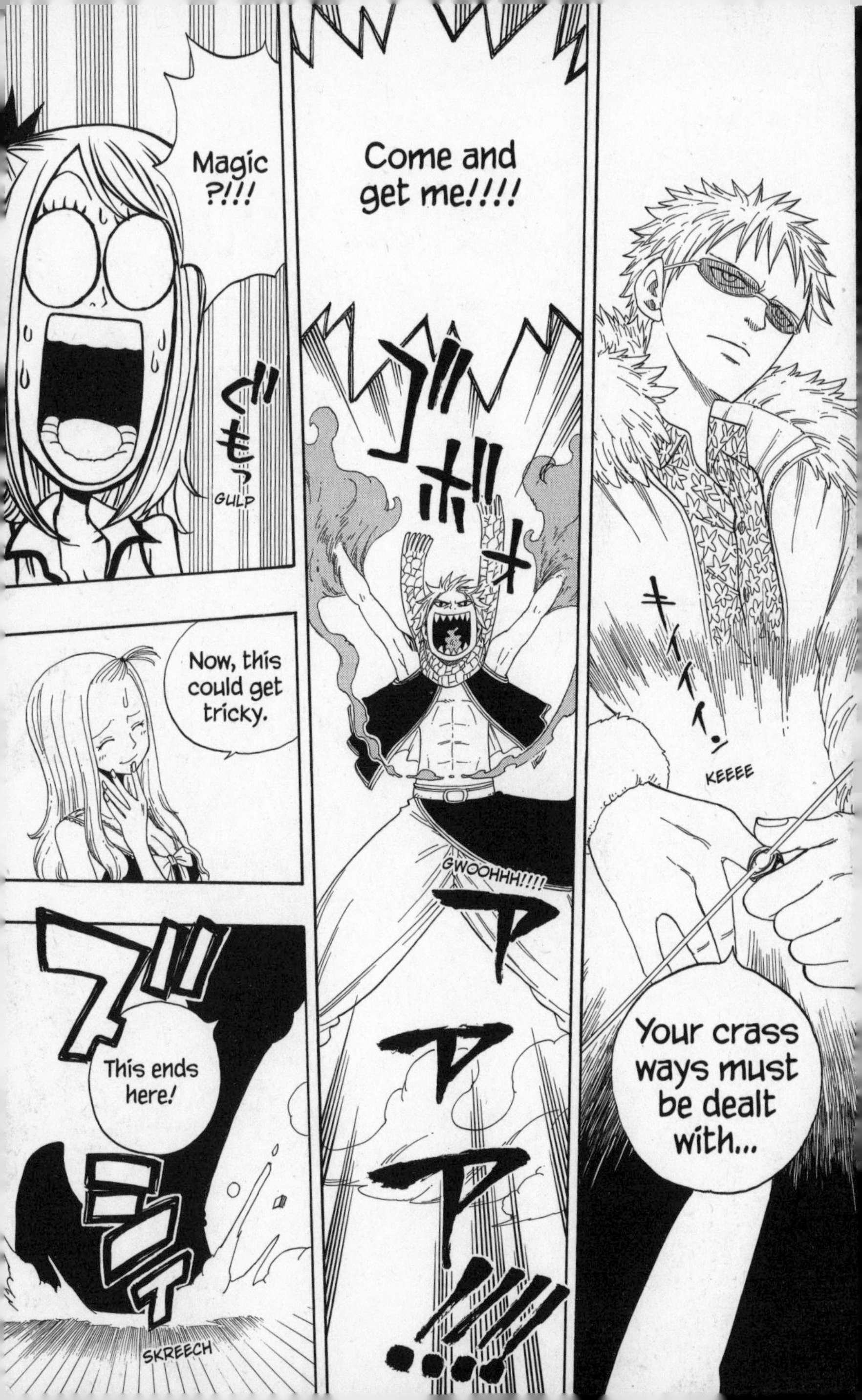
KEEEE
Your crass ways must be dealt with...
Come and get me!!!!
GWOOHHH!!!!
Magic?!!!
GULP
Now, this could get tricky.
This ends here!
SKREECH

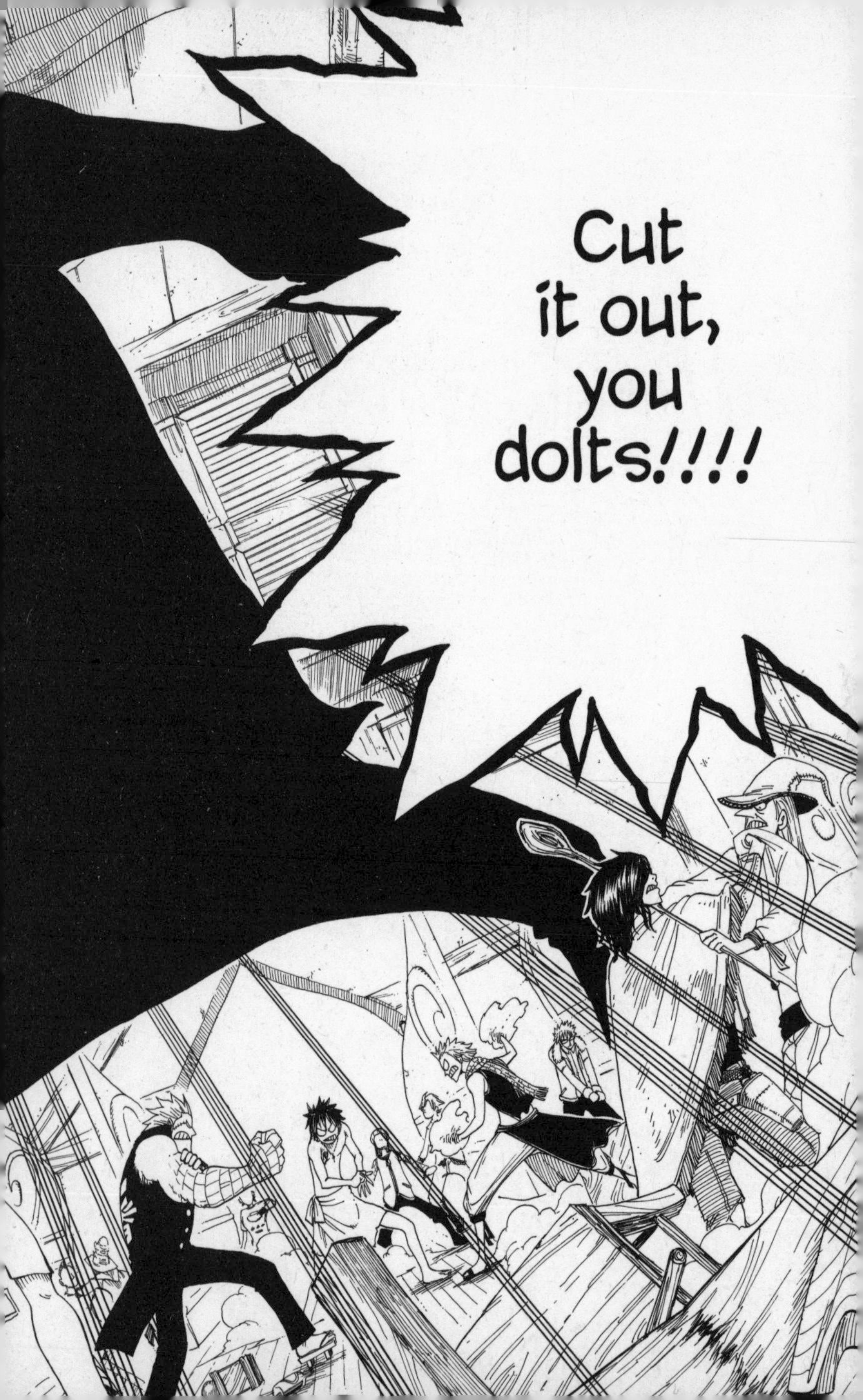
Cut it out, you dolts!!!!

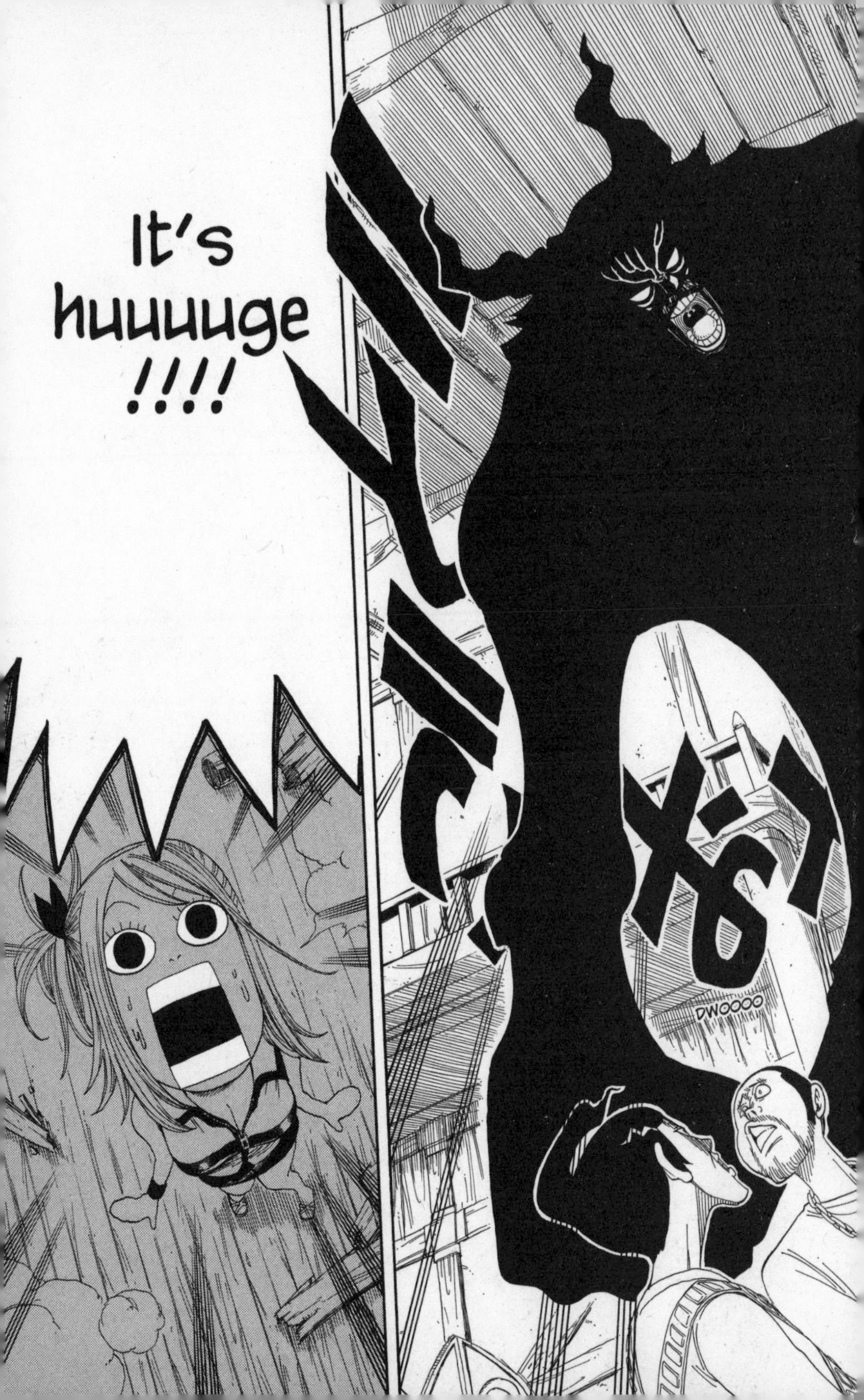
DWOOOO
It's huuuuge!!!!

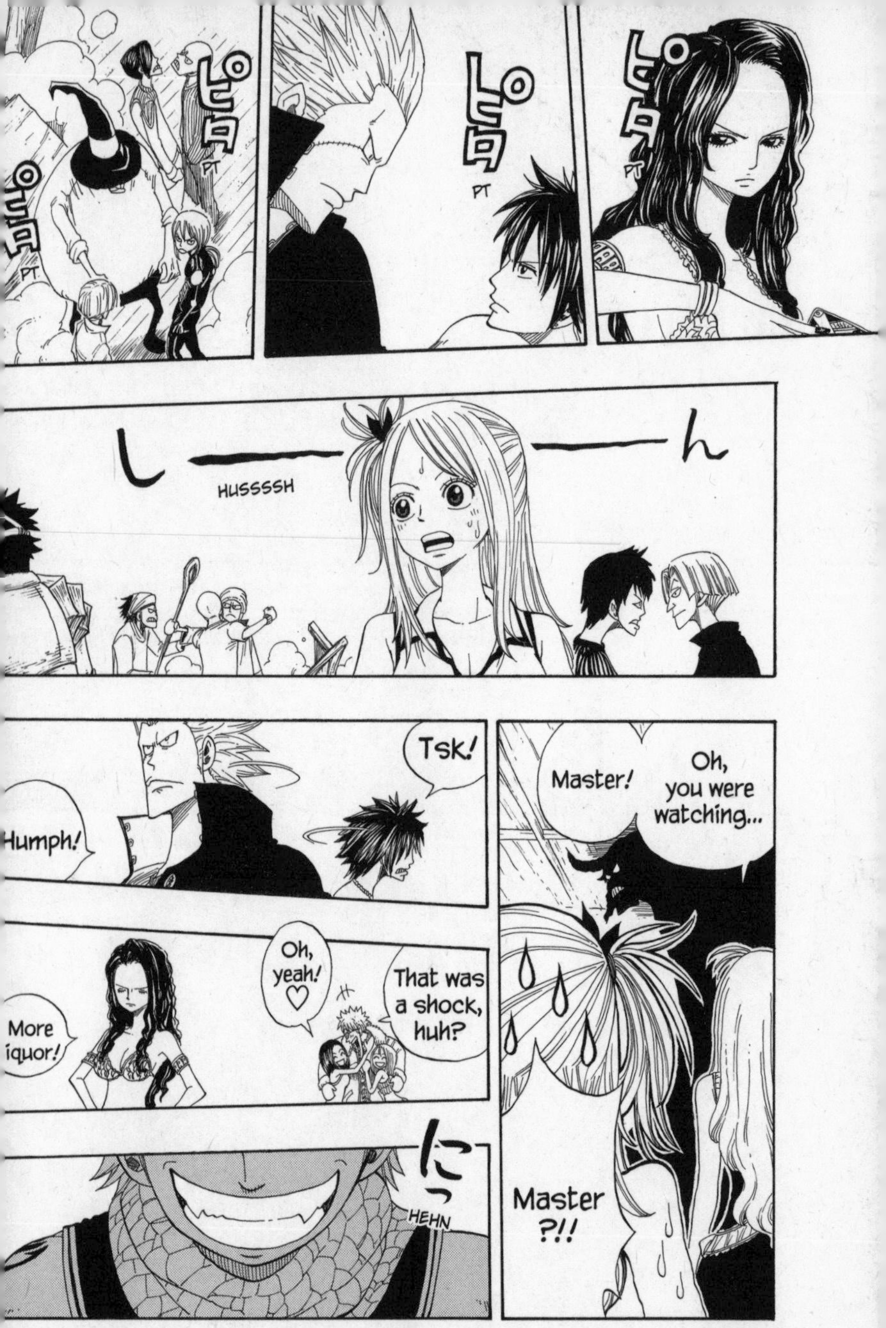
ピタ
PT
ピタ
PT
ピタ
PT
しーーーーん
HUSSSSH
Oh, you were watching...
Master!
Master ?!!
Tsk!
Humph!
That was a shock, huh?
Oh, yeah! ♡
More iquor!
にっ
HEHN

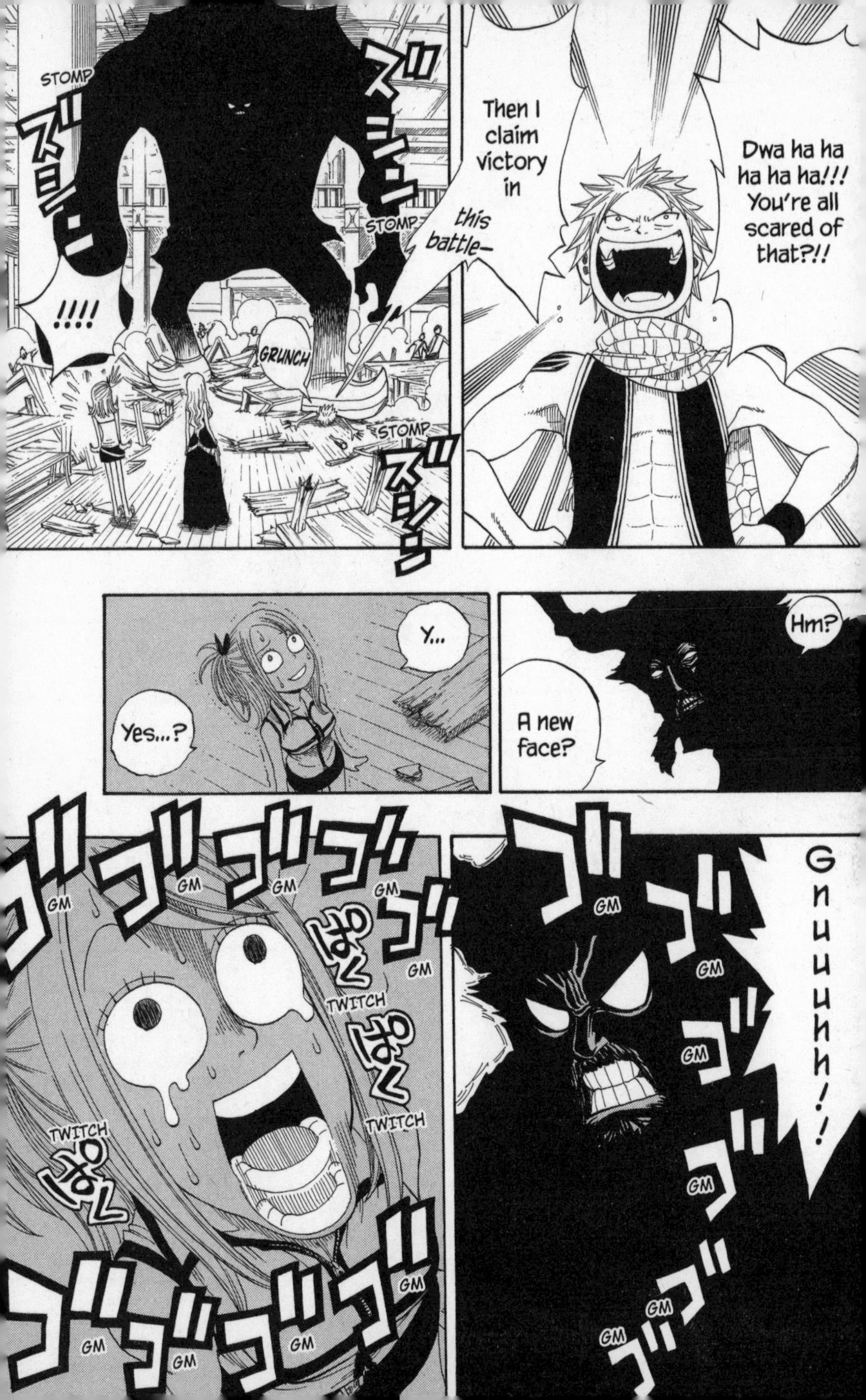
Dwa ha ha ha ha!!! You're all scared of that?!!
Then I claim victory in this battle-
STOMP
STOMP
GRUNCH
STOMP
!!!!
Hm?
A new face?
Y...
Yes...?
GM
GM
GM
GM
GM
Gnuuuuhh!!
GM
GM
GM
GM
GM
GM
TWITCH
TWITCH
TWITCH
GM
GM
GM
GM
GM

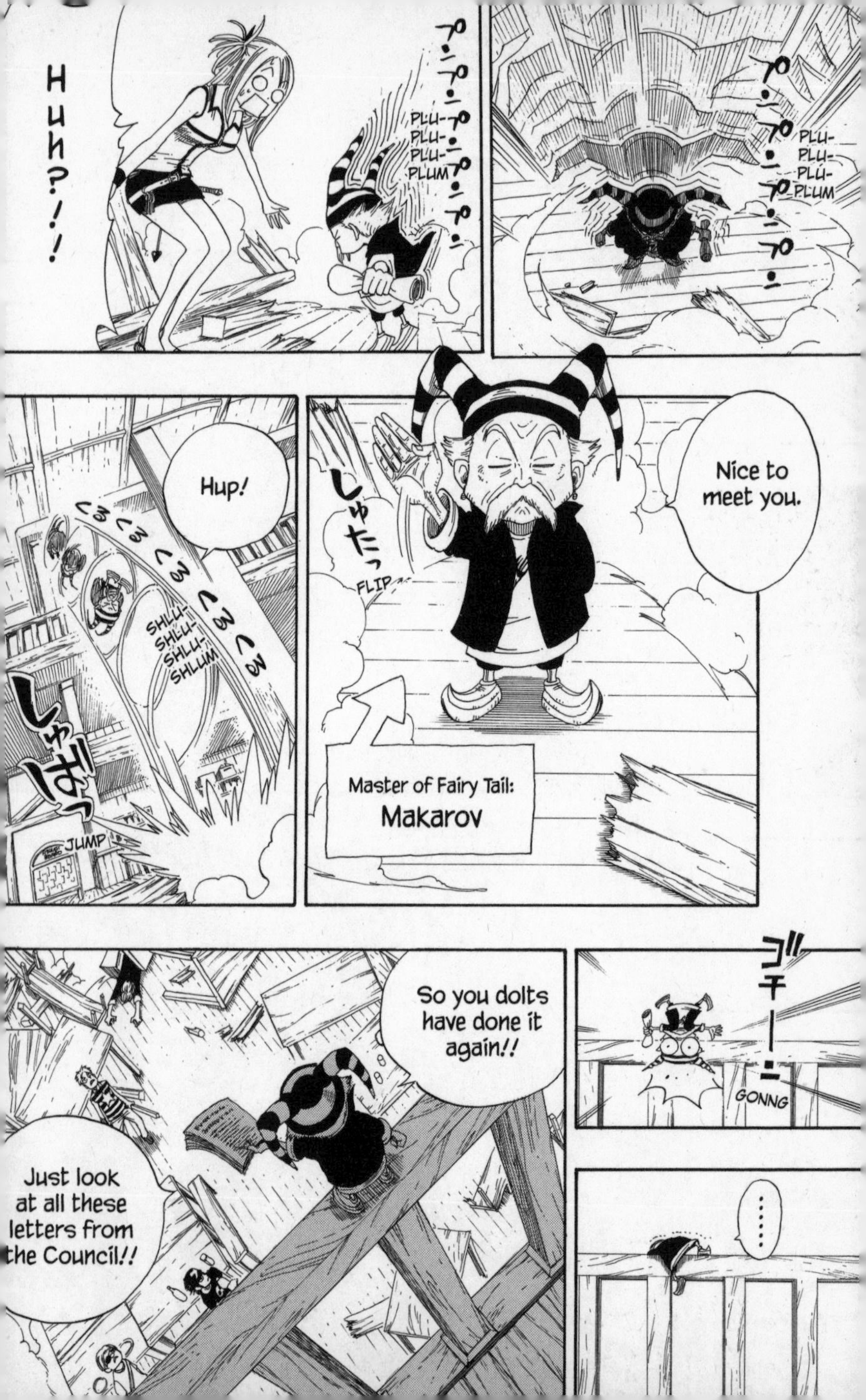
PLU-
PLU-
PLU-
PLUM
PLU-
PLU-
PLU-
PLUM
Huh?!!
Nice to meet you.
FLIP
Master of Fairy Tail:
Makarov
Hup!
SHLU-
SHLU-
SHLU-
SHLUM
JUMP
GONNG
......
So you dolts have done it again!!
Just look at all these letters from the Council!!

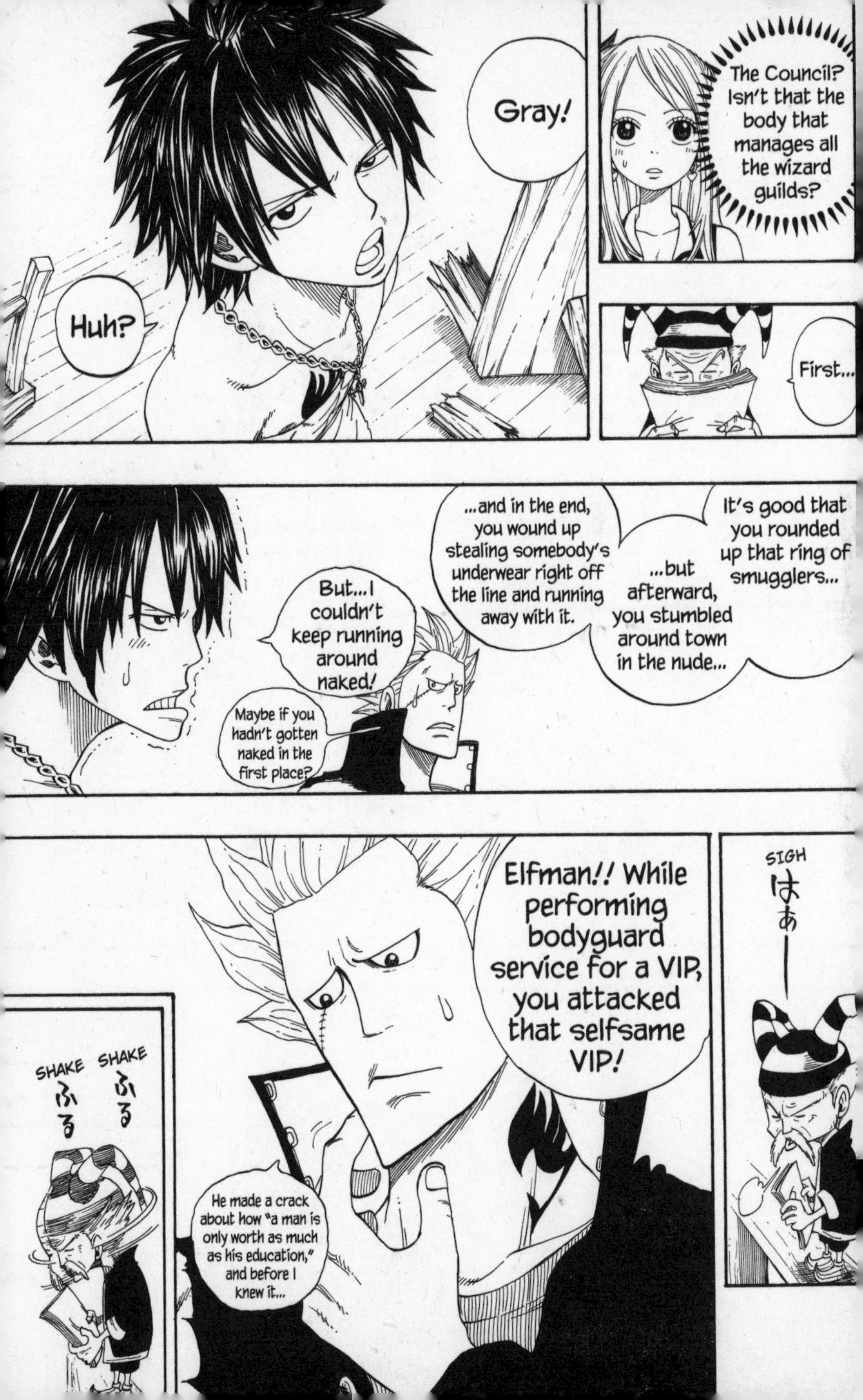
The Council? Isn't that the body that manages all the wizard guilds?
First...
Gray!
Huh?
It's good that you rounded up that ring of smugglers...
...but afterward, you stumbled around town in the nude...
...and in the end, you wound up stealing somebody's underwear right off the line and running away with it.
But...I couldn't keep running around naked!
Maybe if you hadn't gotten naked in the first place?
SIGH
はぁー
Elfman!! While performing bodyguard service for a VIP, you attacked that selfsame VIP!
SHAKE
ふる
SHAKE
ふる
He made a crack about how "a man is only worth as much as his education," and before I knew it...

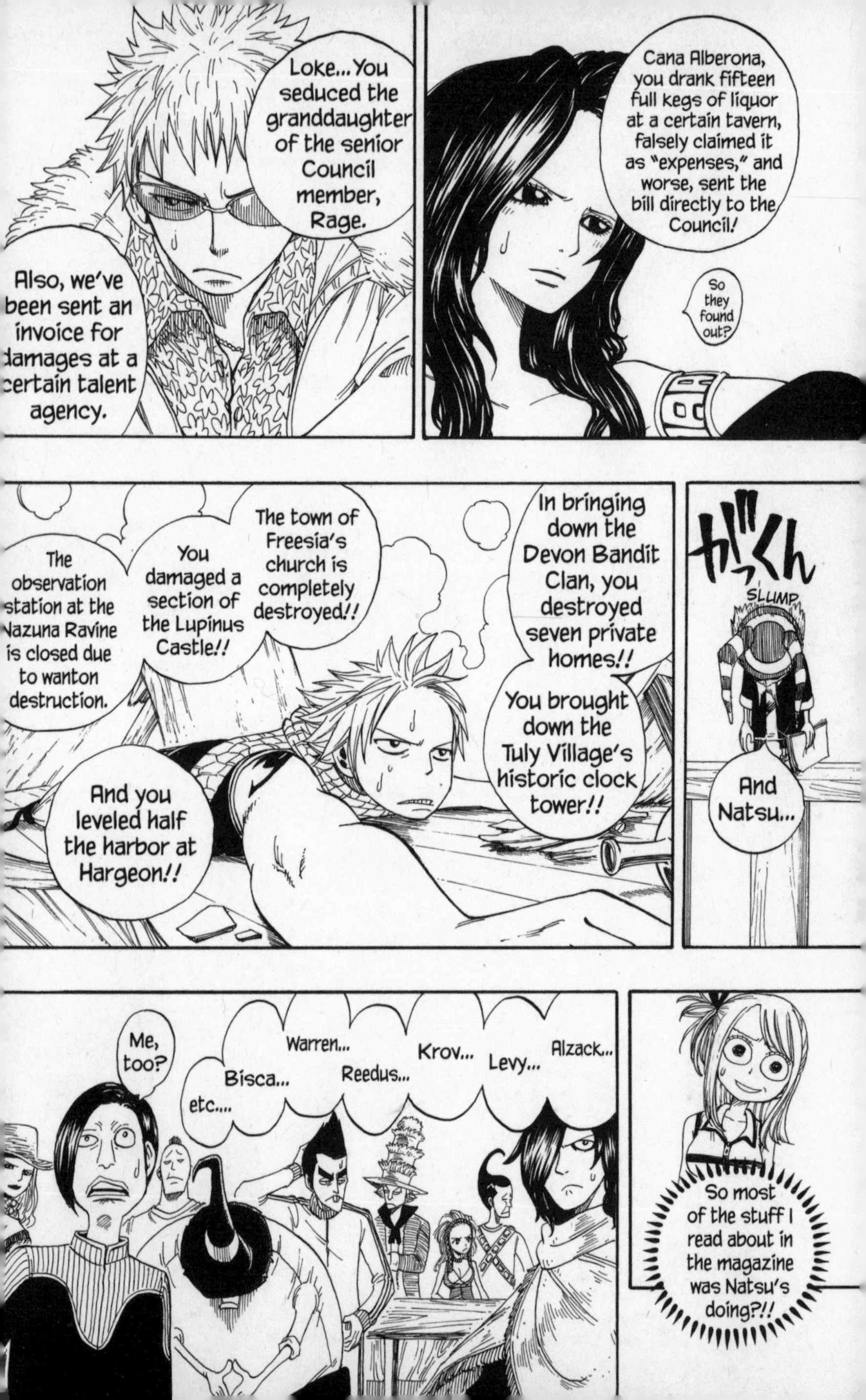

Cana Alberona, you drank fifteen full kegs of liquor at a certain tavern, falsely claimed it as "expenses," and worse, sent the bill directly to the Council!
So they found out?
Loke... You seduced the granddaughter of the senior Council member, Rage.
Also, we've been sent an invoice for damages at a certain talent agency.
がっくん
SLUMP
And Natsu...
In bringing down the Devon Bandit Clan, you destroyed seven private homes!!
The town of Freesia's church is completely destroyed!!
You damaged a section of the Lupinus Castle!!
The observation station at the Nazuna Ravine is closed due to wanton destruction.
You brought down the Tuly Village's historic clock tower!!
And you leveled half the harbor at Hargeon!!
So most of the stuff I read about in the magazine was Natsu's doing?!!
Alzack...
Levy...
Krov...
Reedus...
Warren...
Bisca...
etc....
Me, too?

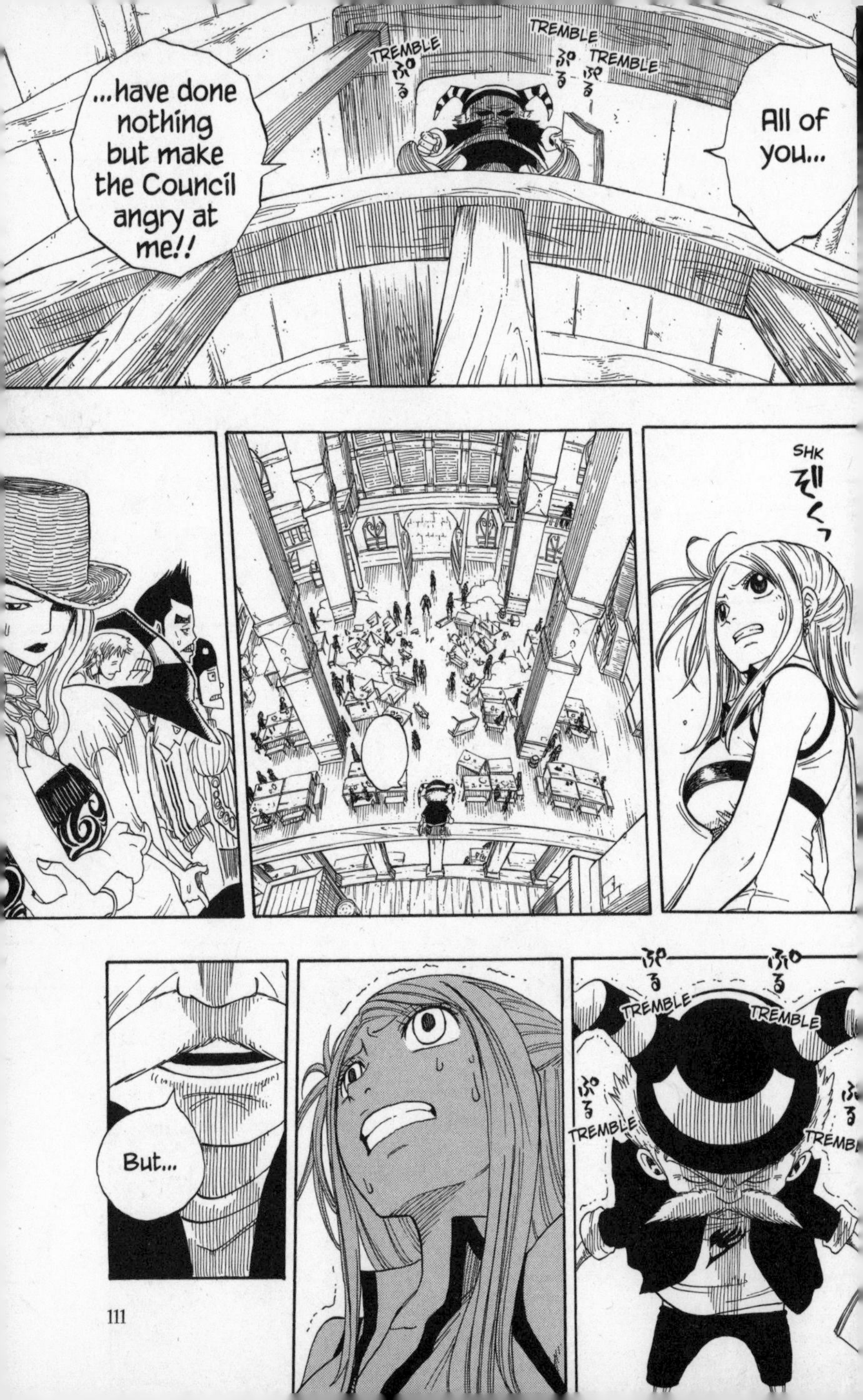
All of you...
TREMBLE ぷる
TREMBLE ぷる
TREMBLE ぷる
...have done nothing but make the Council angry at me!!
SHK ぞくっ
TREMBLE ぷる
TREMBLE ぷる
TREMBLE ぷる
TREMBLE ぷる
But...

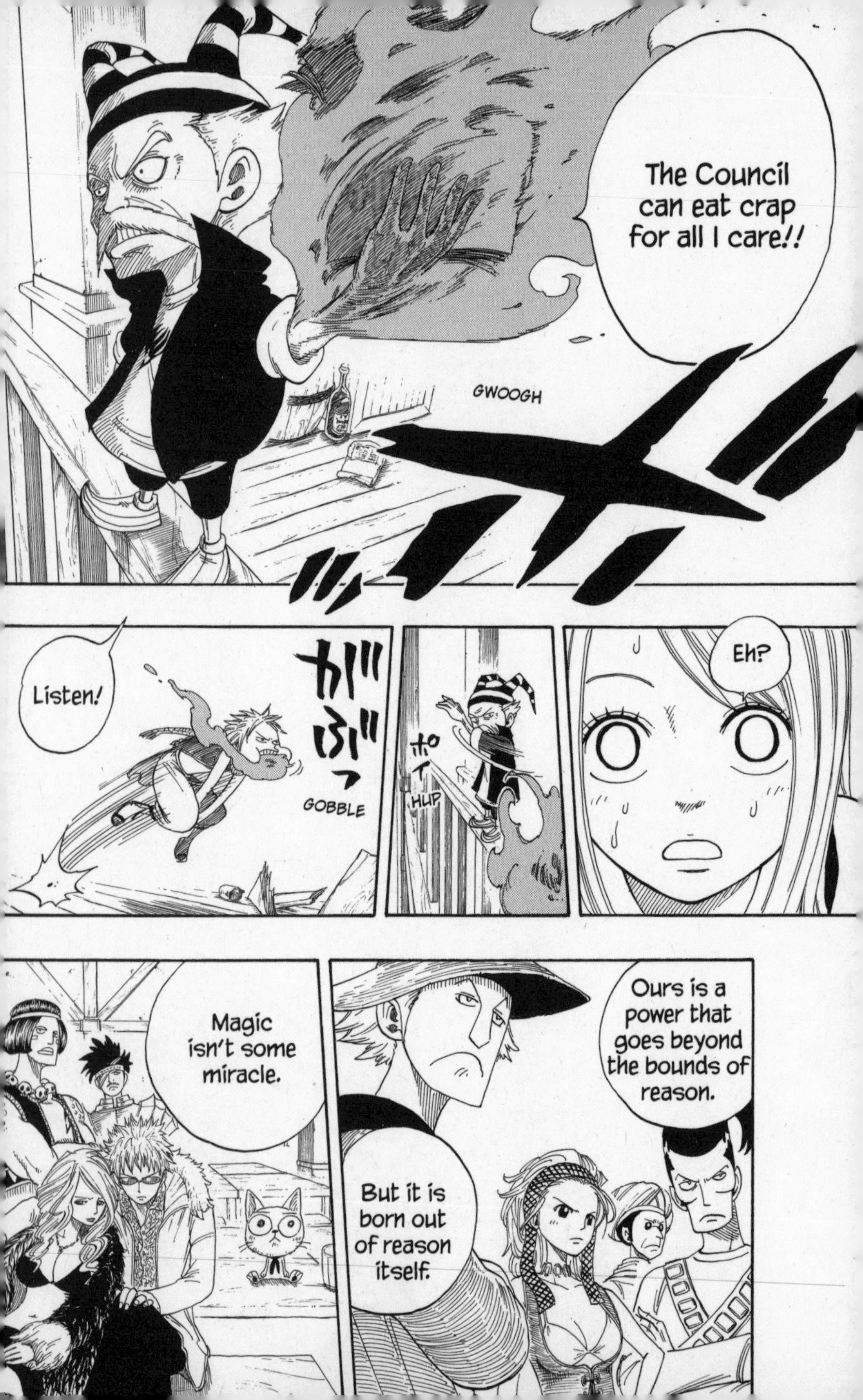
The Council can eat crap for all I care!!
GWOOGH
Eh?
ポイ
HUP
Listen!
がぶっ
GOBBLE
Ours is a power that goes beyond the bounds of reason.
But it is born out of reason itself.
Magic isn't some miracle.

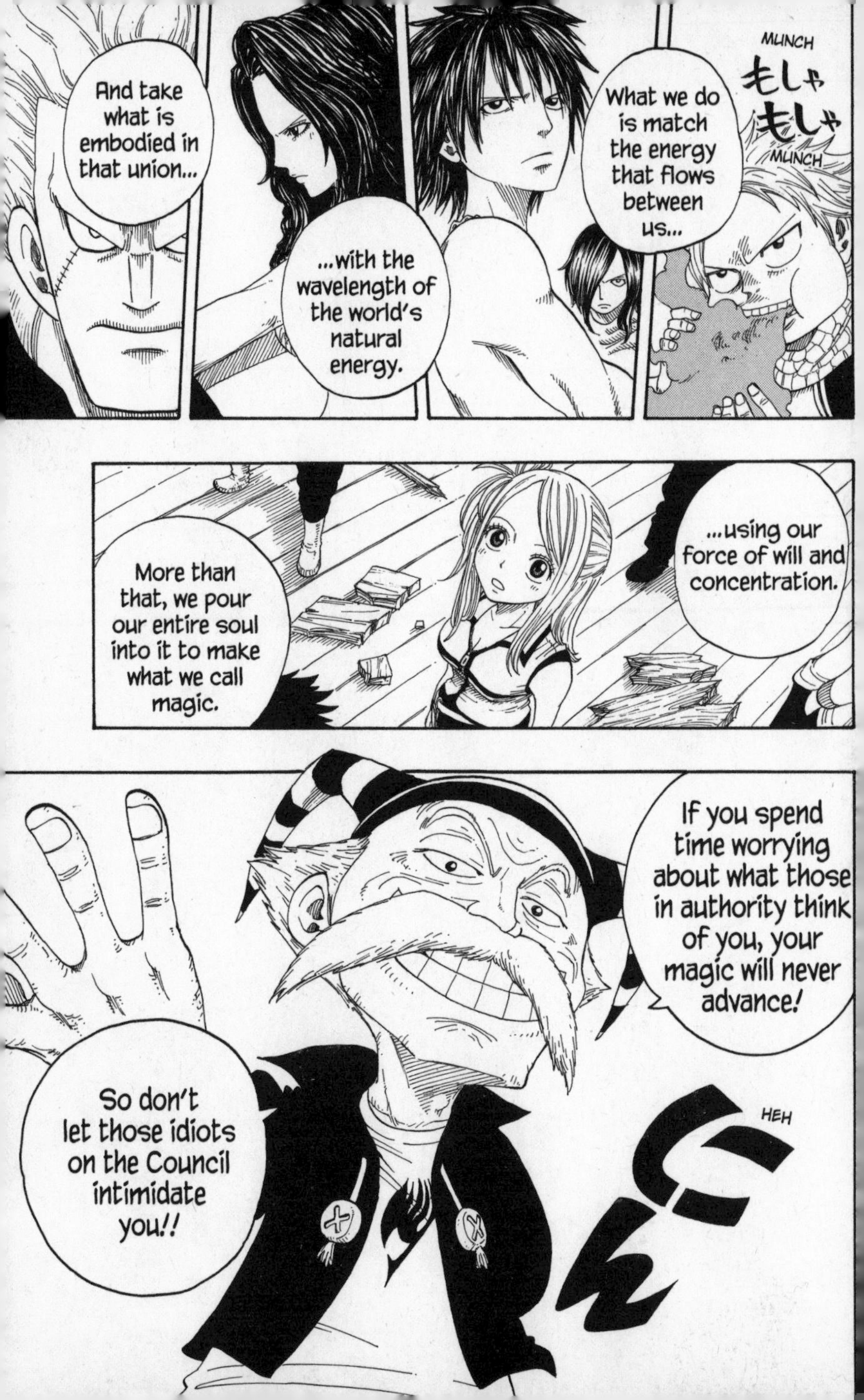
MUNCH
もしゃもしゃ
MUNCH
What we do is match the energy that flows between us...
...with the wavelength of the world's natural energy.
And take what is embodied in that union...
...using our force of will and concentration.
More than that, we pour our entire soul into it to make what we call magic.
If you spend time worrying about what those in authority think of you, your magic will never advance!
HEH
So don't let those idiots on the Council intimidate you!!

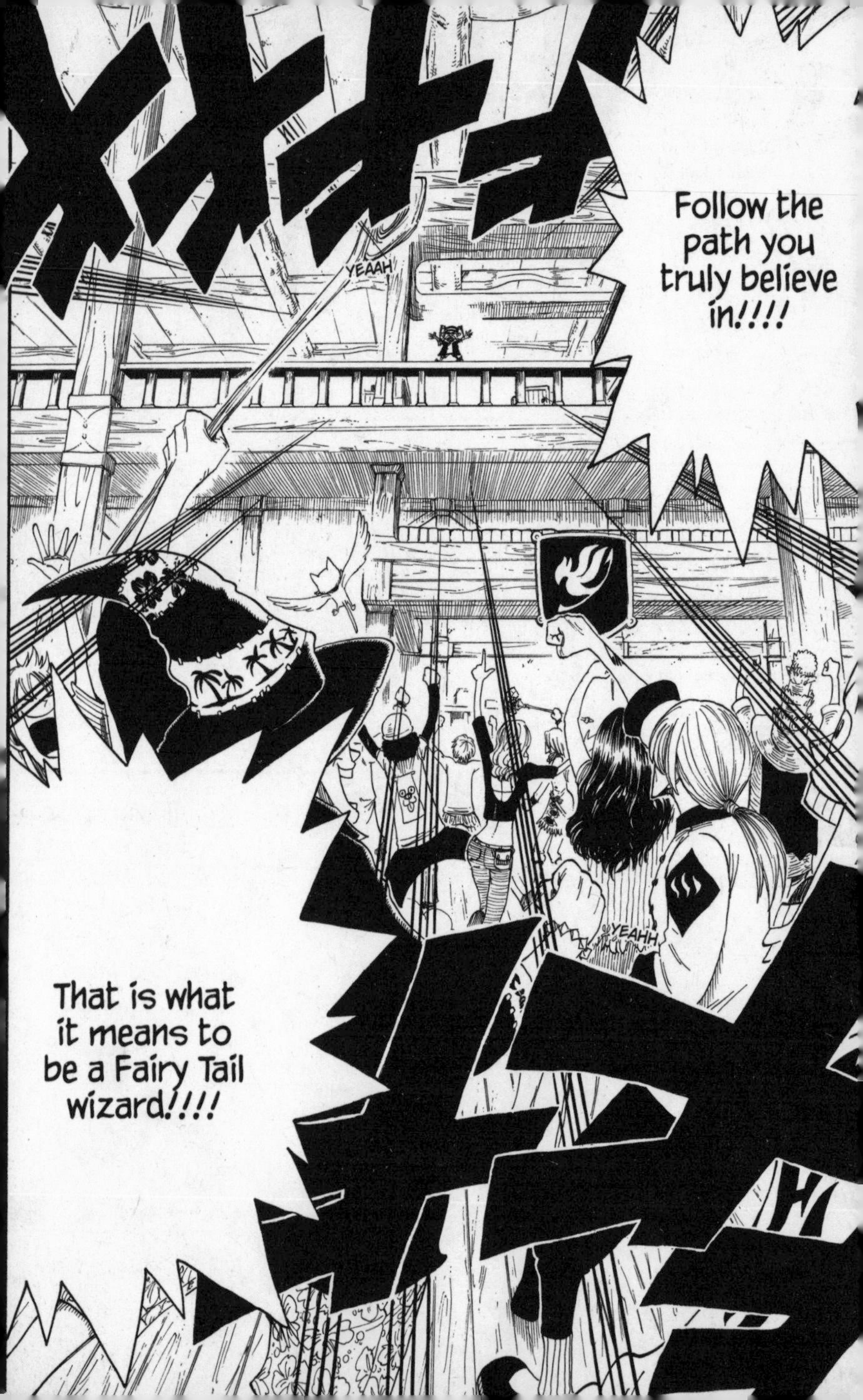
Follow the path you truly believe in!!!!
YEAAH
YEAHH
That is what it means to be a Fairy Tail wizard!!!!

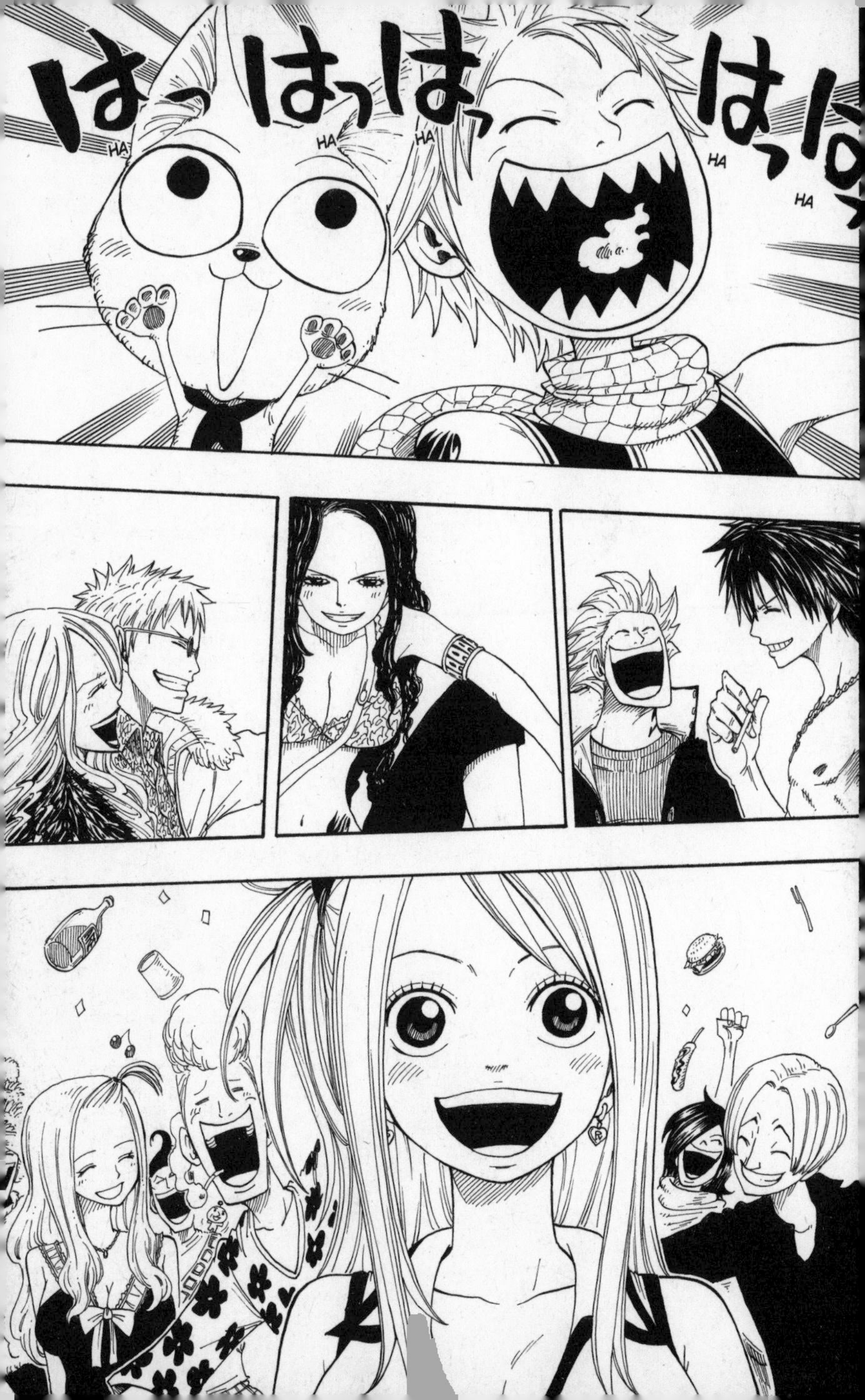
はっはっはっ
HA HA HA
はっは
HA HA

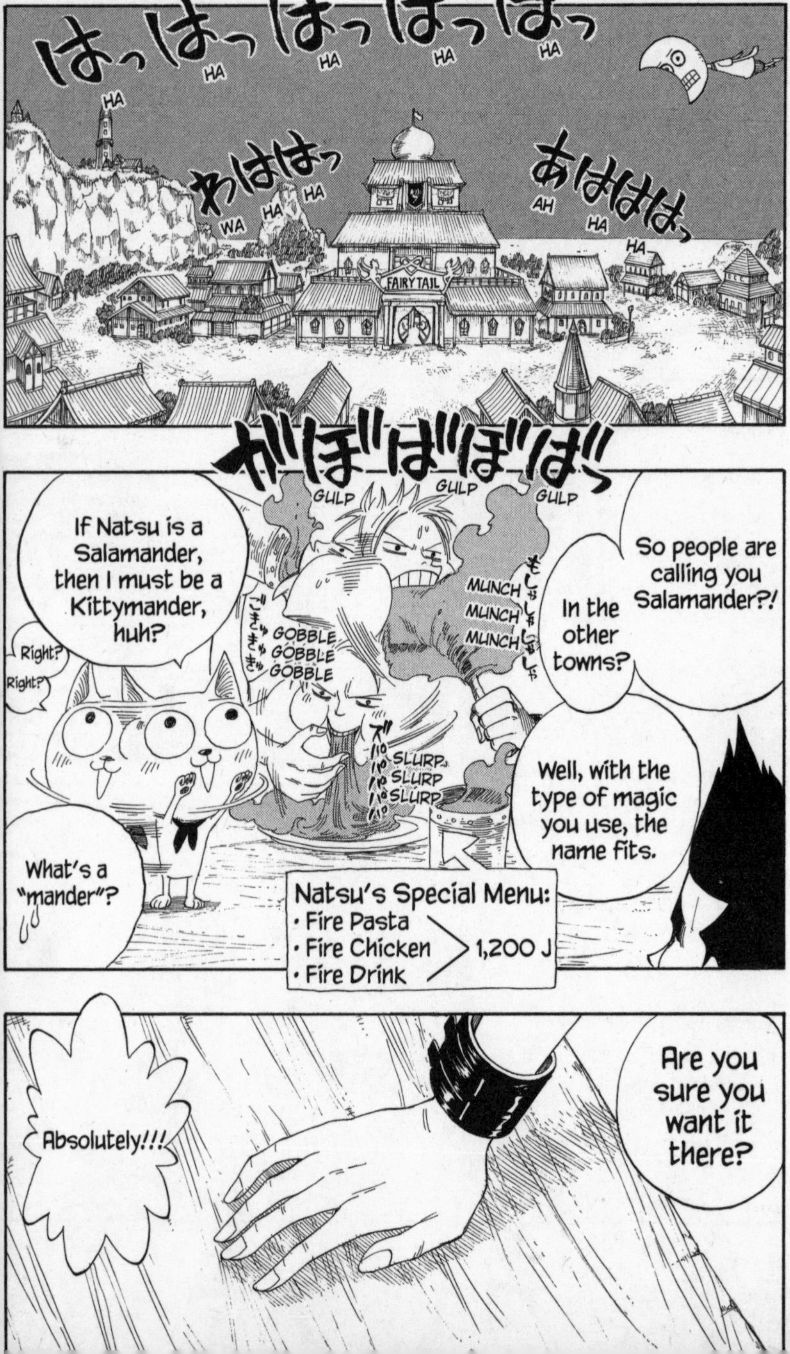
はっはっはっはっはっ
HA HA HA HA HA
あははは
AH HA HA HA
わははっ
WA HA HA
FAIRY TAIL
がぼばぼば
GULP GULP GULP
So people are calling you Salamander?!
In the other towns?
MUNCH MUNCH MUNCH
Well, with the type of magic you use, the name fits.
GOBBLE GOBBLE GOBBLE
SLURP SLURP SLURP
If Natsu is a Salamander, then I must be a Kittymander, huh?
Right? Right?
What's a "mander"?
Natsu's Special Menu:
• Fire Pasta
• Fire Chicken
• Fire Drink
1,200 J
Are you sure you want it there?
Absolutely!!!

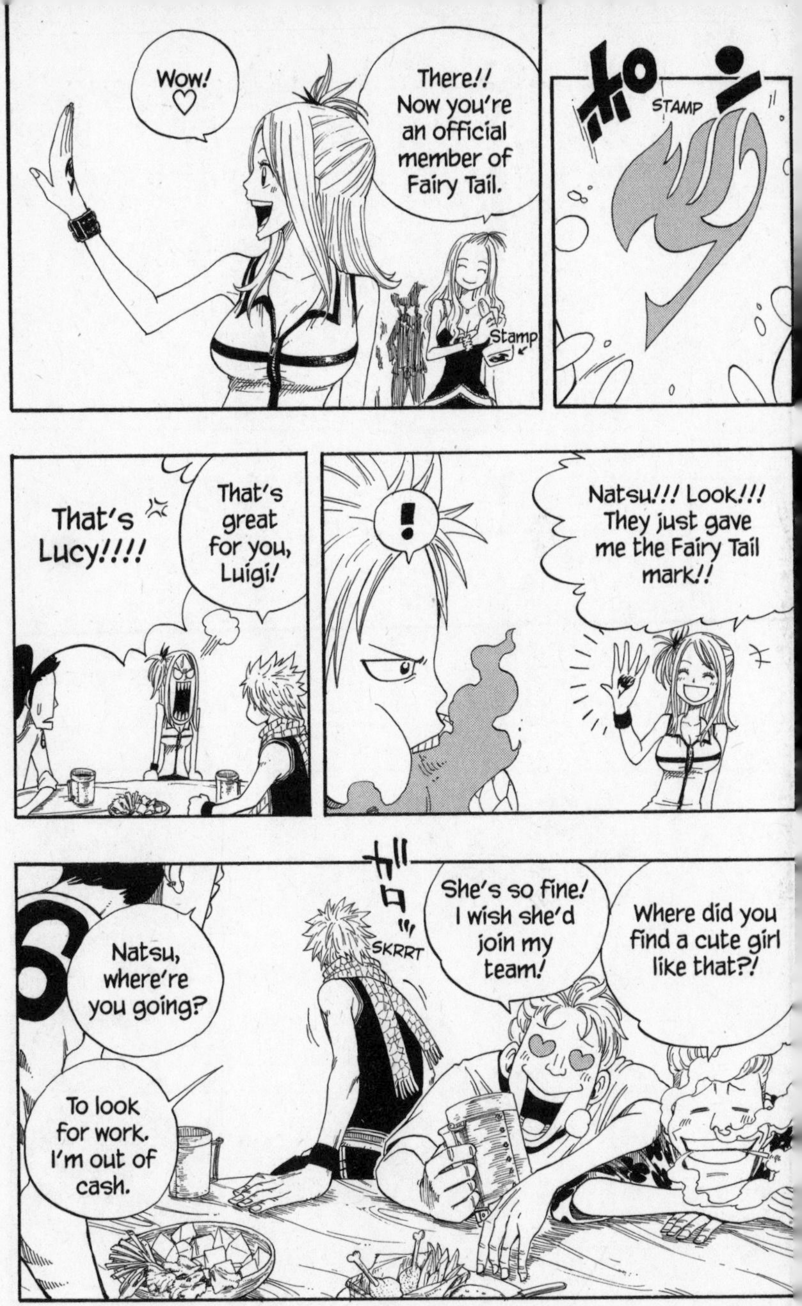
STAMP
There!! Now you're an official member of Fairy Tail.
Wow! ♡
Stamp
Natsu!!! Look!!! They just gave me the Fairy Tail mark!!
That's great for you, Luigi!
That's Lucy!!!!
Where did you find a cute girl like that?!
She's so fine! I wish she'd join my team!
SKRRT
Natsu, where're you going?
To look for work. I'm out of cash.

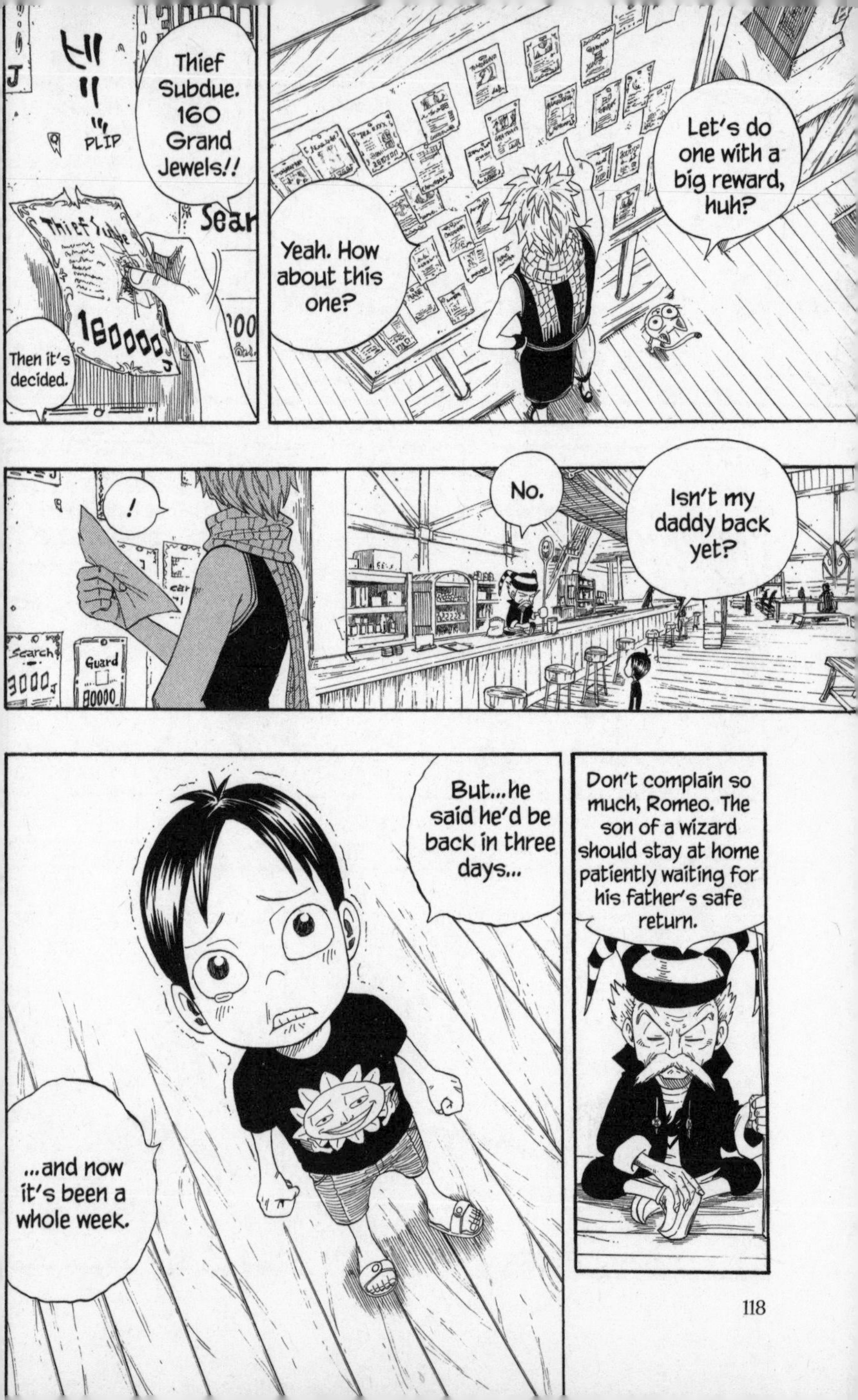
Let's do one with a big reward, huh?
Yeah. How about this one?
Thief Subdue. 160 Grand Jewels!!
PLIP
Then it's decided.
Isn't my daddy back yet?
No.
!
Search
Guard
Don't complain so much, Romeo. The son of a wizard should stay at home patiently waiting for his father's safe return.
But...he said he'd be back in three days...
...and now it's been a whole week.

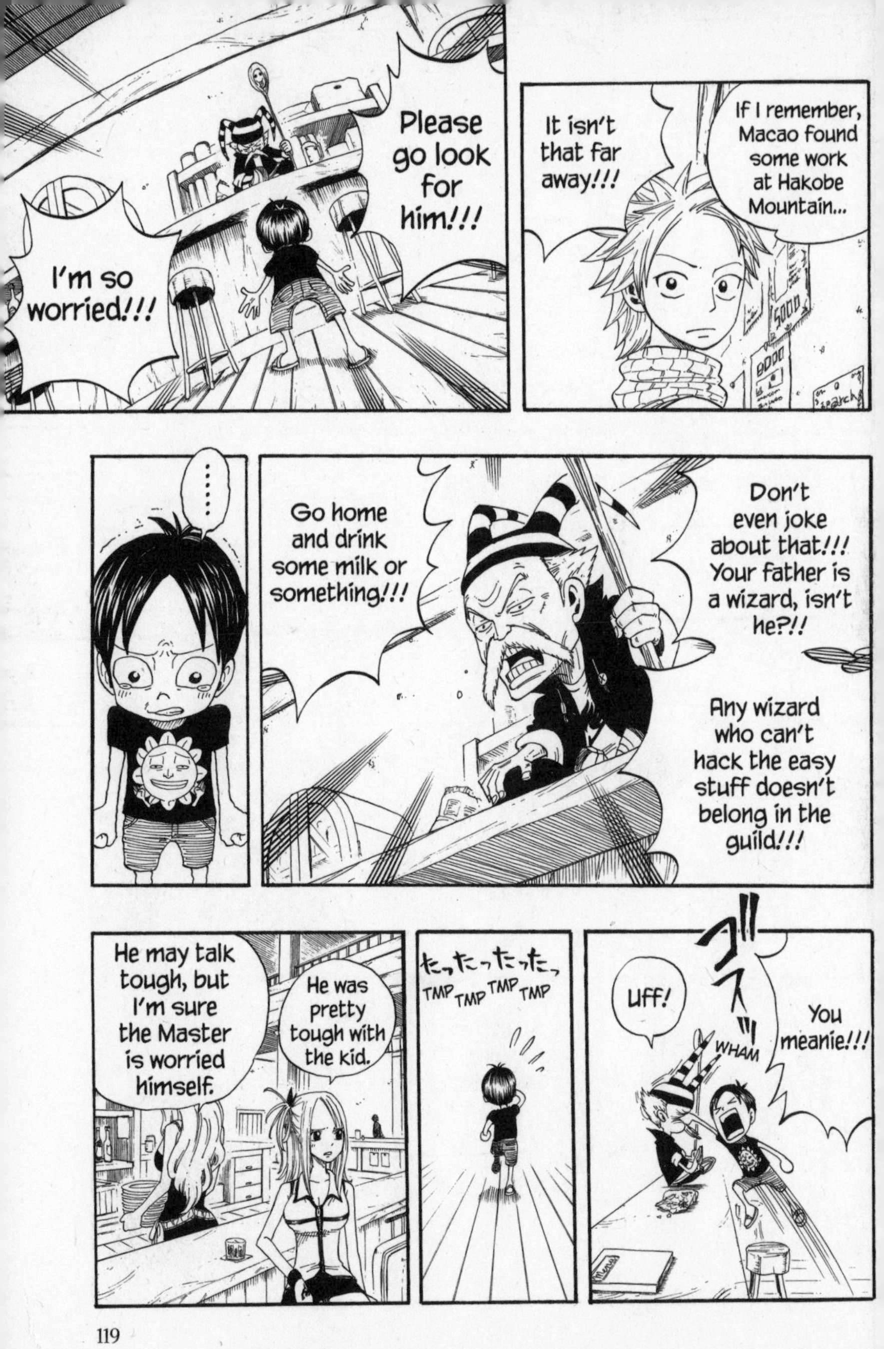
If I remember, Macao found some work at Hakobe Mountain...
It isn't that far away!!!
Please go look for him!!!
I'm so worried!!!
Don't even joke about that!!! Your father is a wizard, isn't he?!!
Any wizard who can't hack the easy stuff doesn't belong in the guild!!!
Go home and drink some milk or something!!!
......
You meanie!!!
ゴスッ
WHAM
Uff!
たったったったっ
TMP TMP TMP TMP
He was pretty tough with the kid.
He may talk tough, but I'm sure the Master is worried himself.

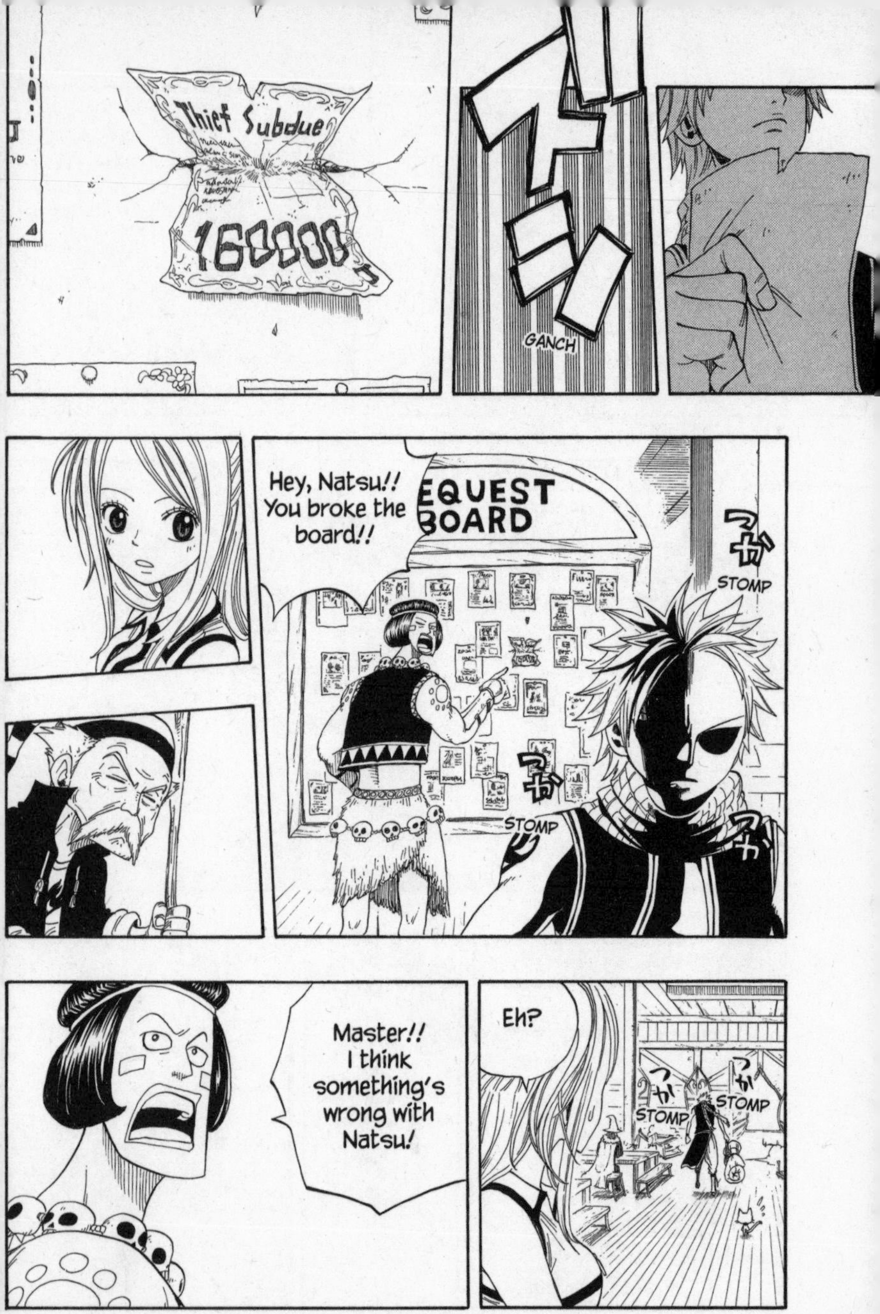
GANCH
Thief Subdue
160000
Hey, Natsu!! You broke the board!!
EQUEST BOARD
STOMP
STOMP
Eh?
STOMP
STOMP
Master!! I think something's wrong with Natsu!

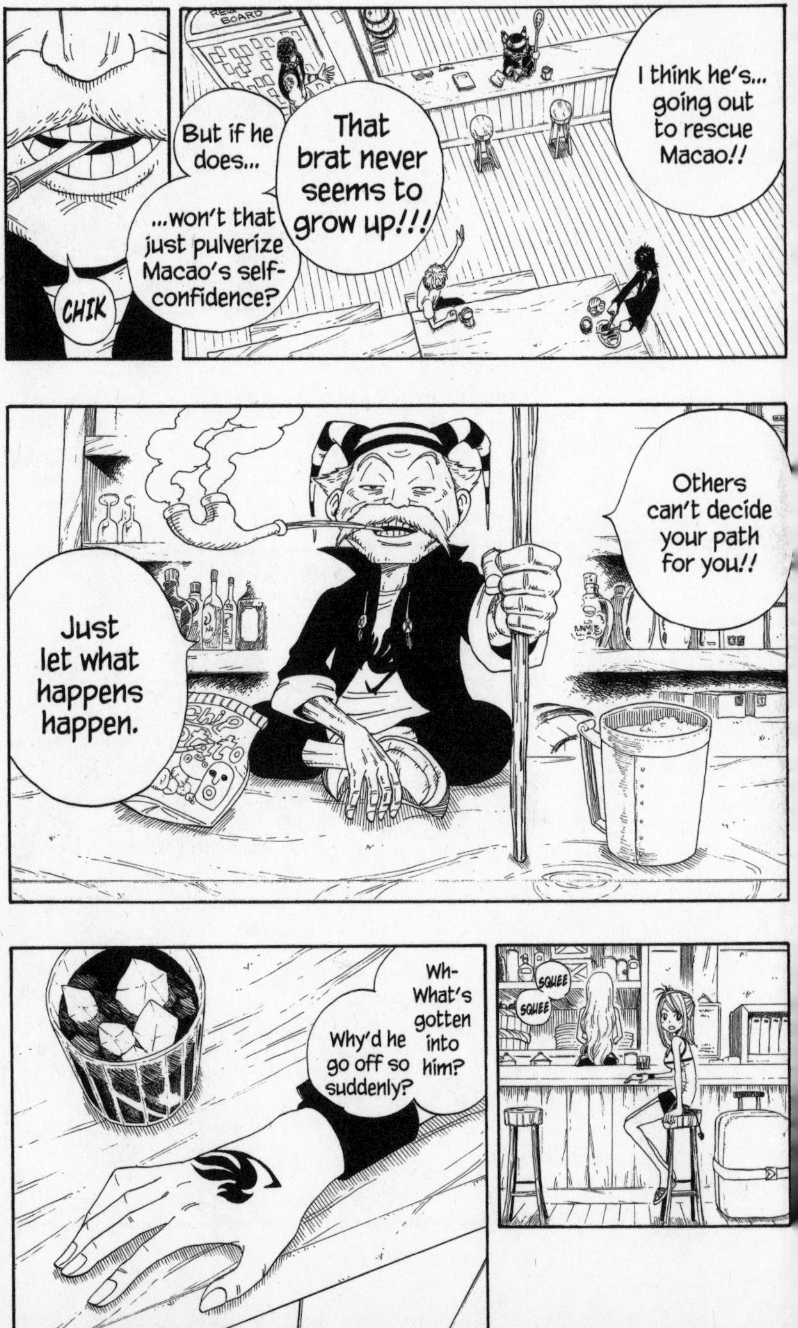
I think he's... going out to rescue Macao!!
That brat never seems to grow up!!!
But if he does...
...won't that just pulverize Macao's self-confidence?
CHIK
Others can't decide your path for you!!
Just let what happens happen.
SQUEE
SQUEE
Wh- What's gotten into him?
Why'd he go off so suddenly?

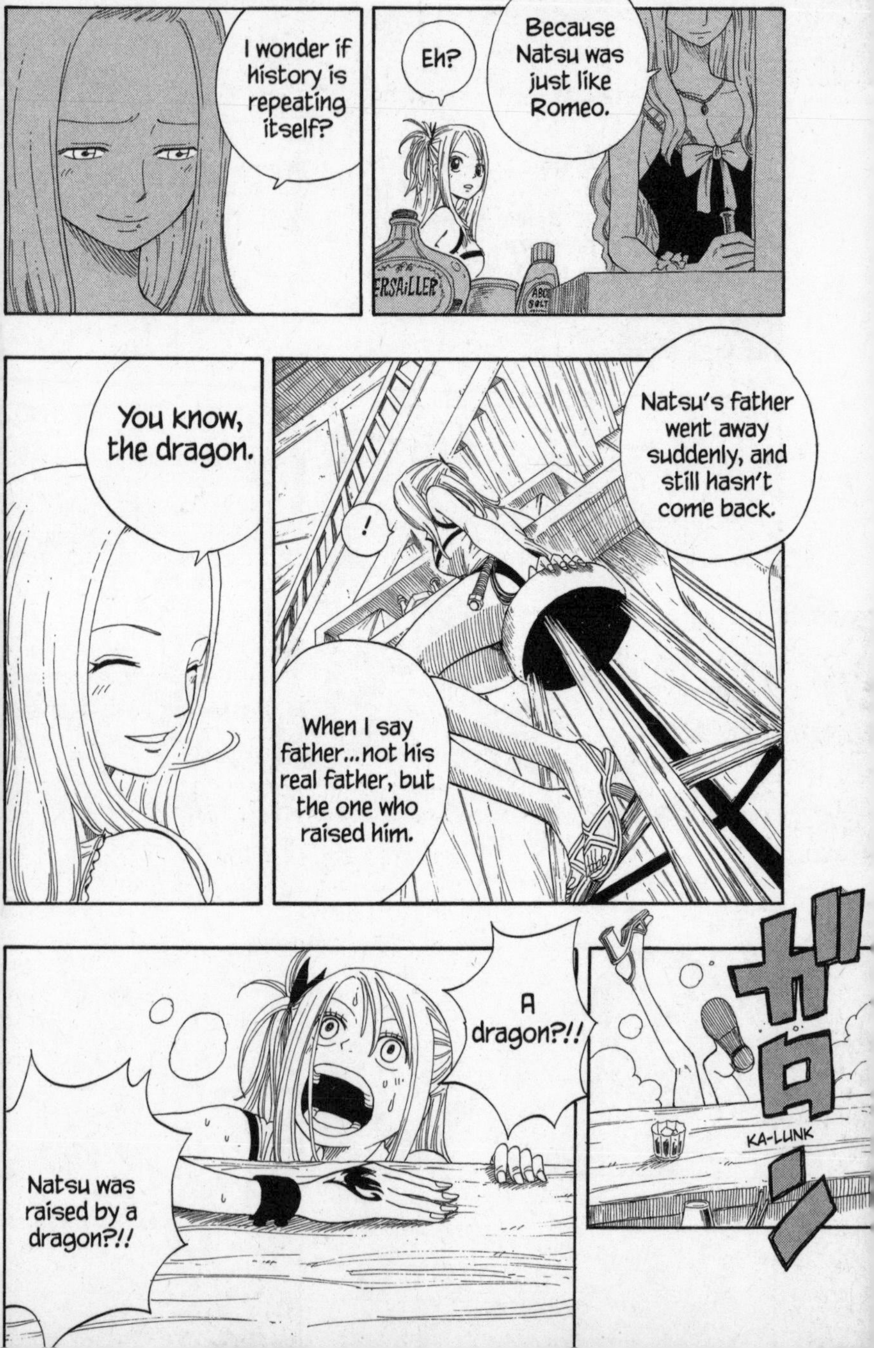
Because Natsu was just like Romeo.
Eh?
I wonder if history is repeating itself?
Natsu's father went away suddenly, and still hasn't come back.
!
When I say father...not his real father, but the one who raised him.
You know, the dragon.
KA-LUNK
A dragon?!!
Natsu was raised by a dragon?!!

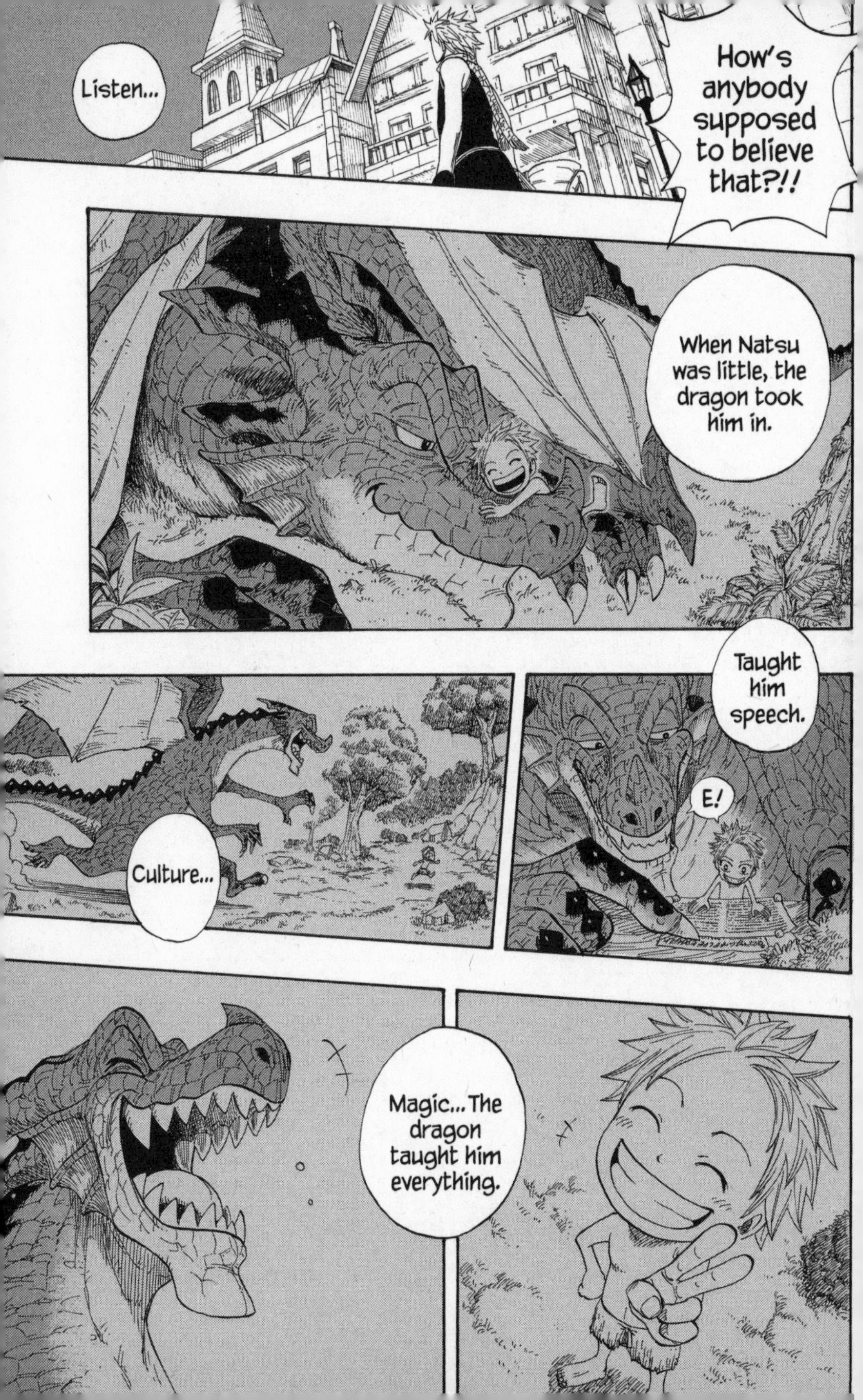
How's anybody supposed to believe that?!!
Listen...
When Natsu was little, the dragon took him in.
Taught him speech.
E!
Culture...
Magic... The dragon taught him everything.

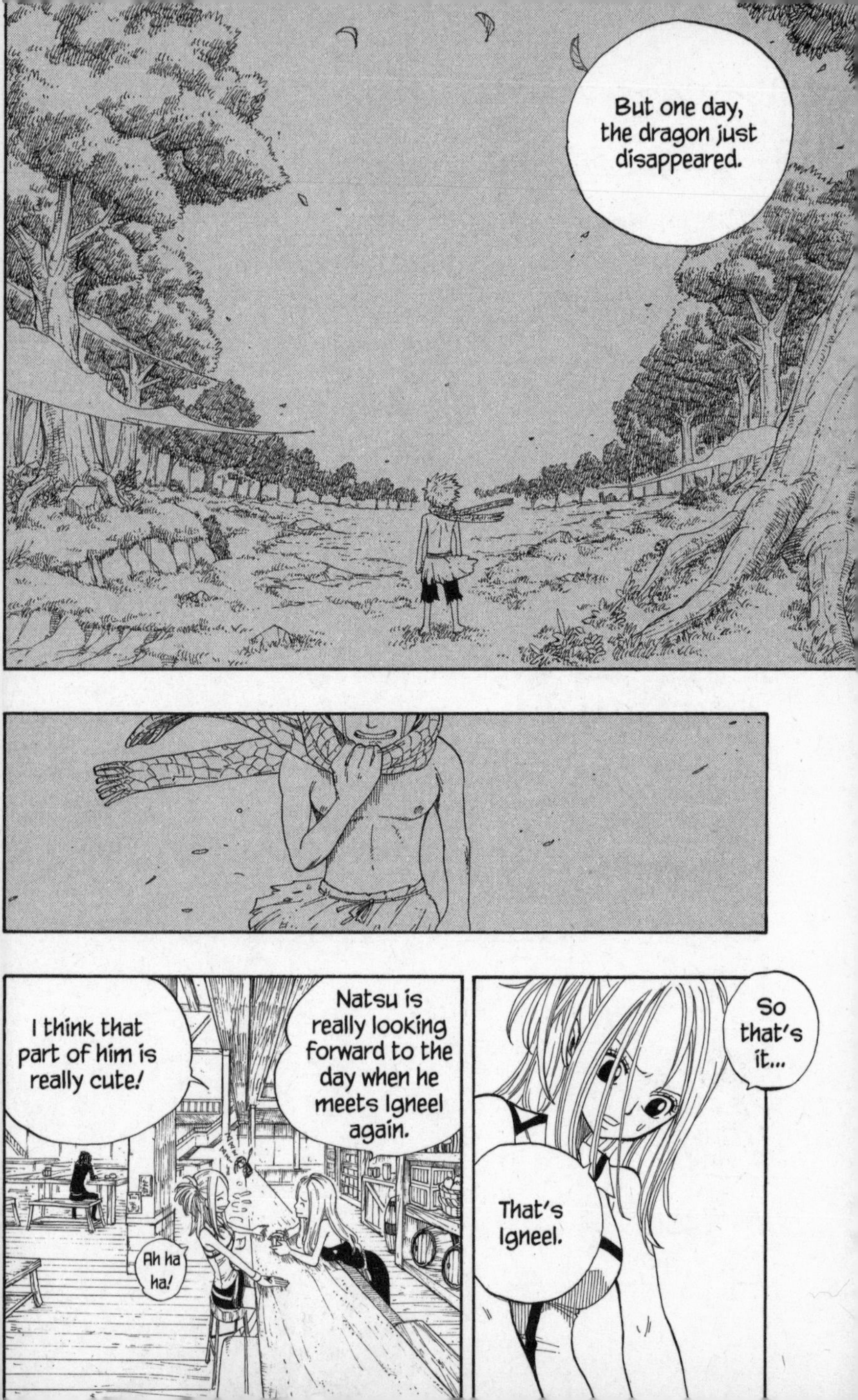
But one day, the dragon just disappeared.
So that's it...
That's Igneel.
Natsu is really looking forward to the day when he meets Igneel again.
I think that part of him is really cute!
Ah ha ha!

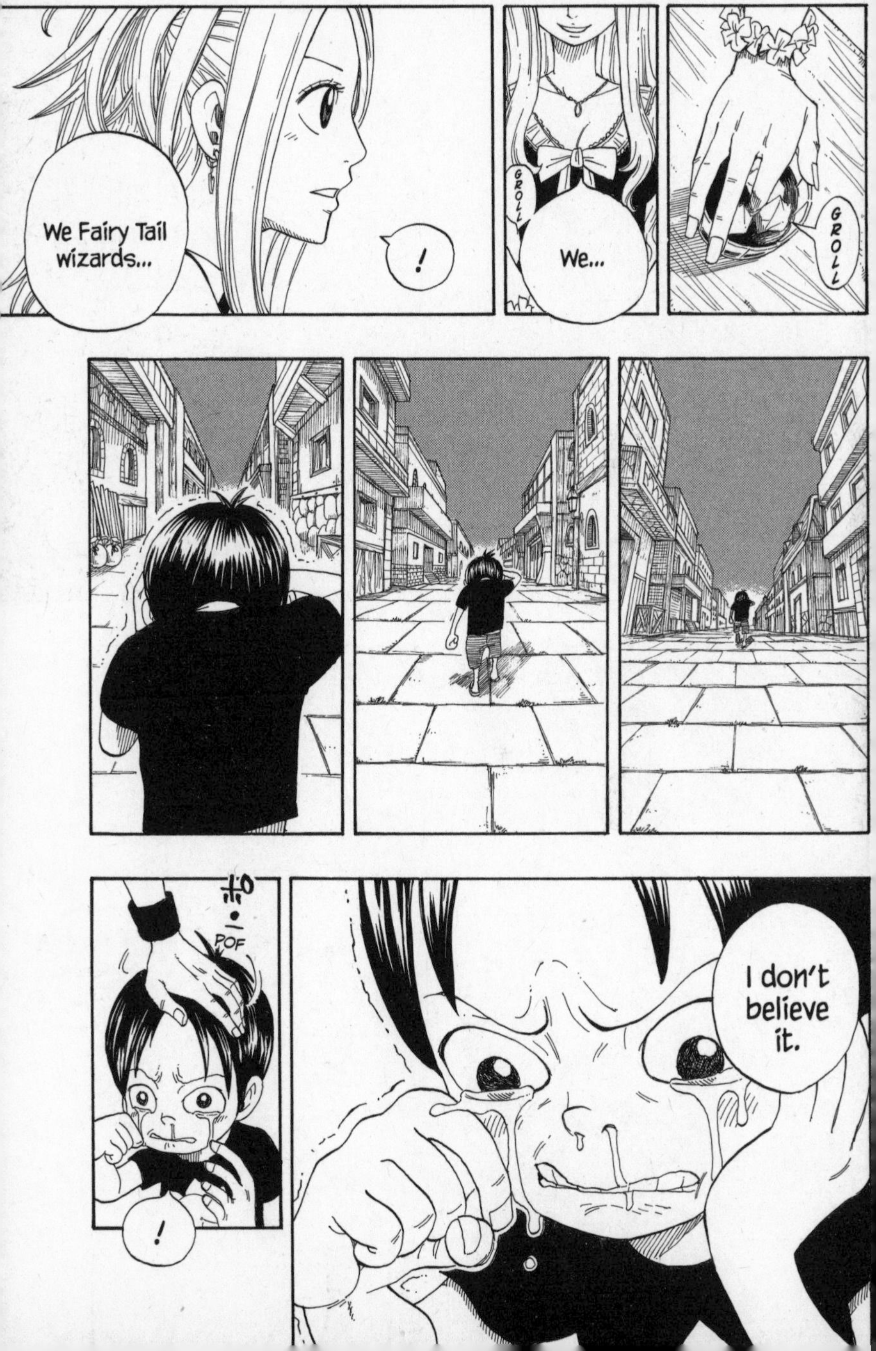
GROLL
GROLL
We...
We Fairy Tail wizards...
!
I don't believe it.
POF
!

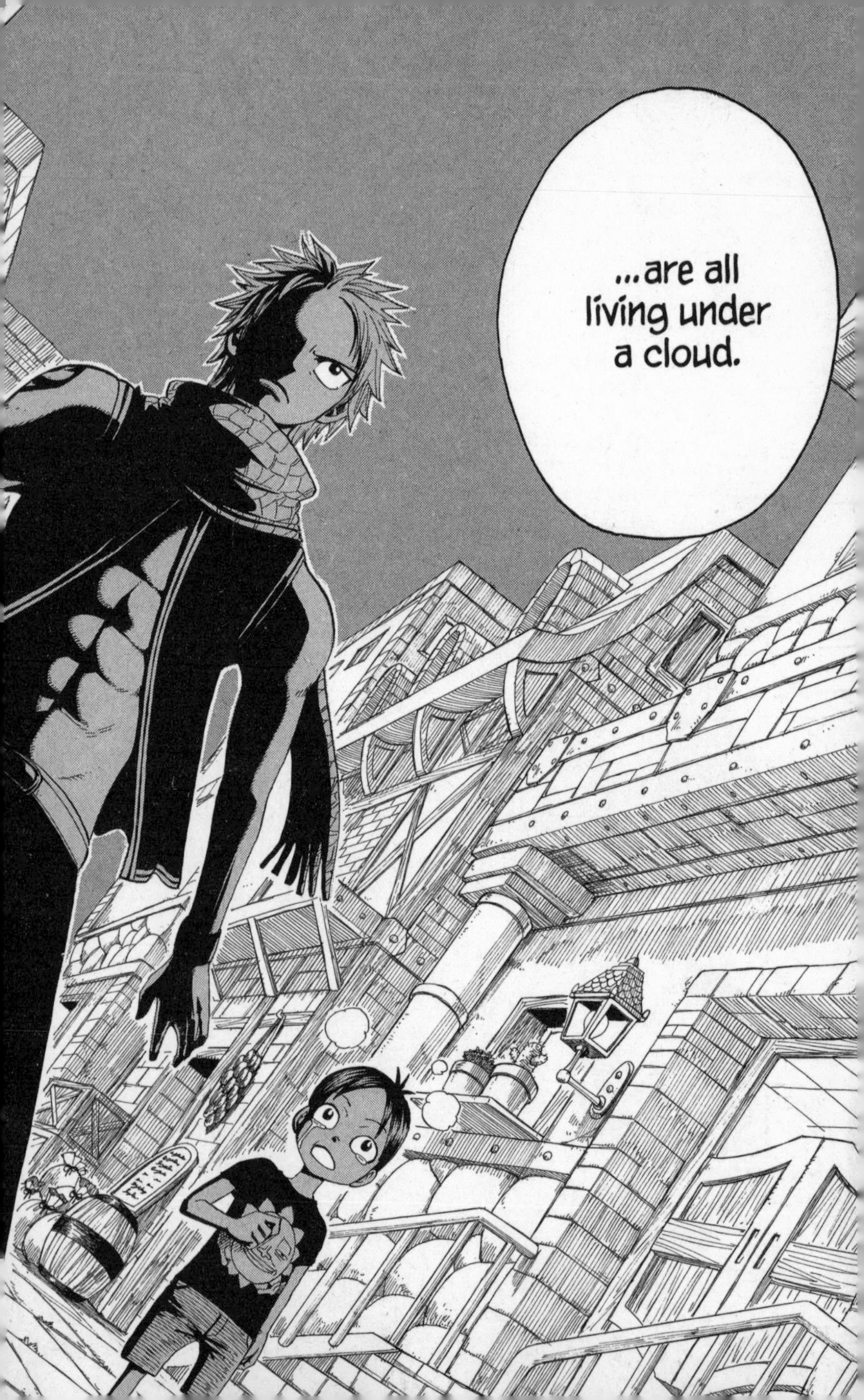
...are all living under a cloud.

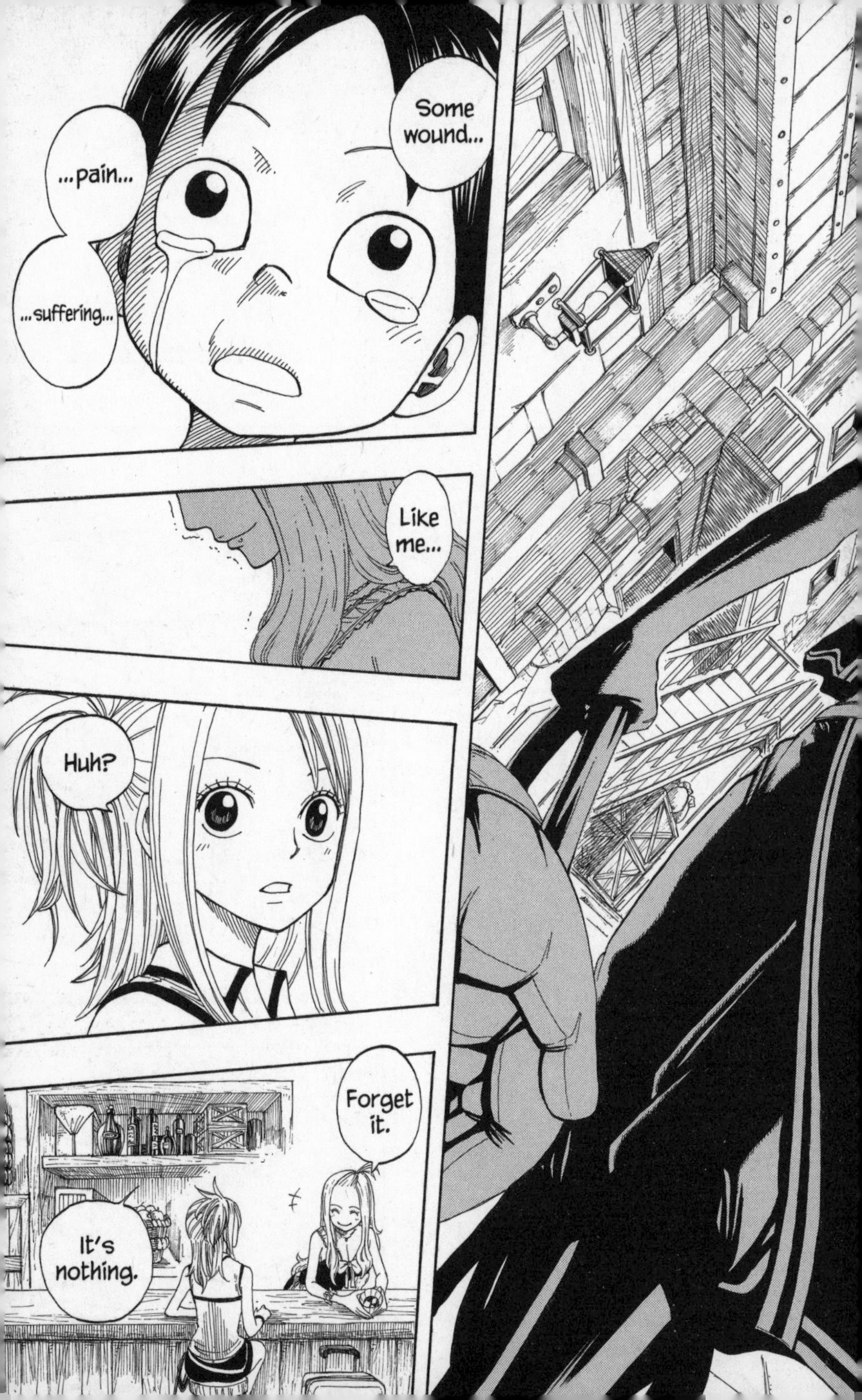
Some wound...
...pain...
...suffering...
Like me...
Huh?
Forget it.
It's nothing.

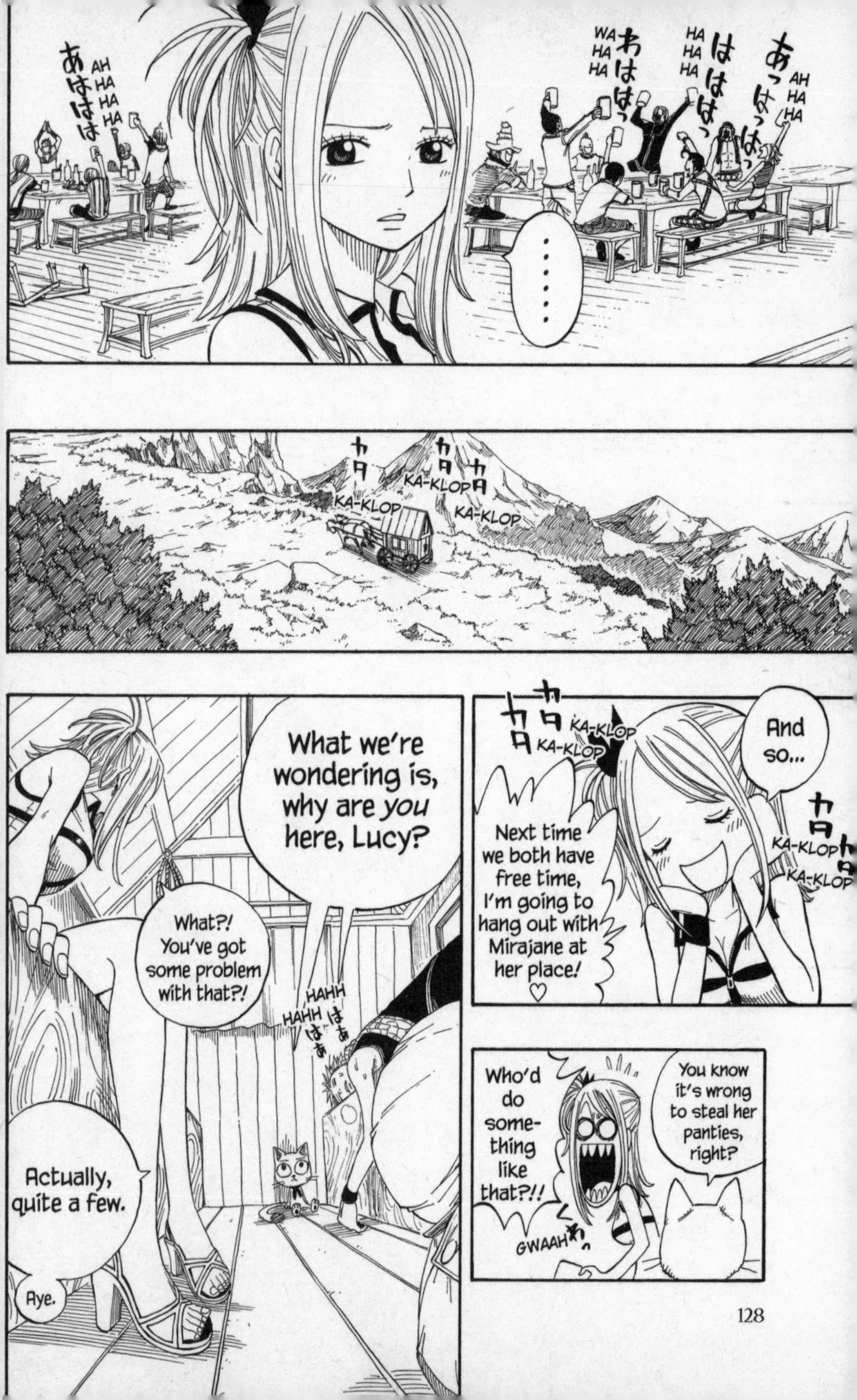

AH HA HA
HA HA HA
WA HA HA
AH HA HA HA
......
KA-KLOP
KA-KLOP
KA-KLOP
KA-KLOP
And so...
KA-KLOP
KA-KLOP
Next time we both have free time, I'm going to hang out with Mirajane at her place! ♡
KA-KLOP
KA-KLOP
You know it's wrong to steal her panties, right?
Who'd do something like that?!!
GWAAH
What we're wondering is, why are *you* here, Lucy?
What?! You've got some problem with that?!
HAHH HAHH
Actually, quite a few.
Aye.

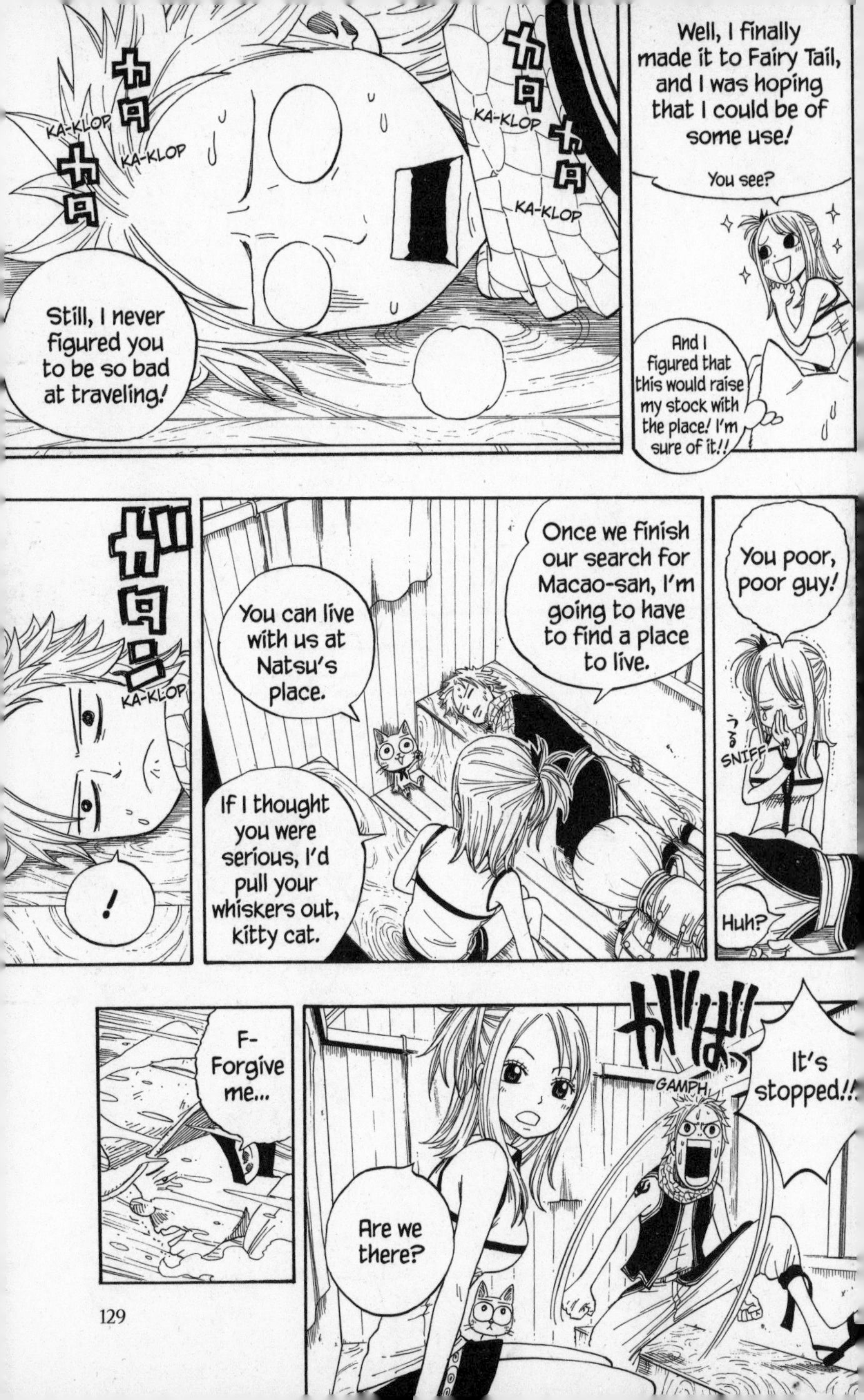
Well, I finally made it to Fairy Tail, and I was hoping that I could be of some use!
You see?
And I figured that this would raise my stock with the place! I'm sure of it!!
KA-KLOP
KA-KLOP
KA-KLOP
KA-KLOP
Still, I never figured you to be so bad at traveling!
You poor, poor guy!
SNIFF
Huh?
Once we finish our search for Macao-san, I'm going to have to find a place to live.
You can live with us at Natsu's place.
If I thought you were serious, I'd pull your whiskers out, kitty cat.
KA-KLOP
!
It's stopped!!
GAMPH
Are we there?
F-Forgive me...

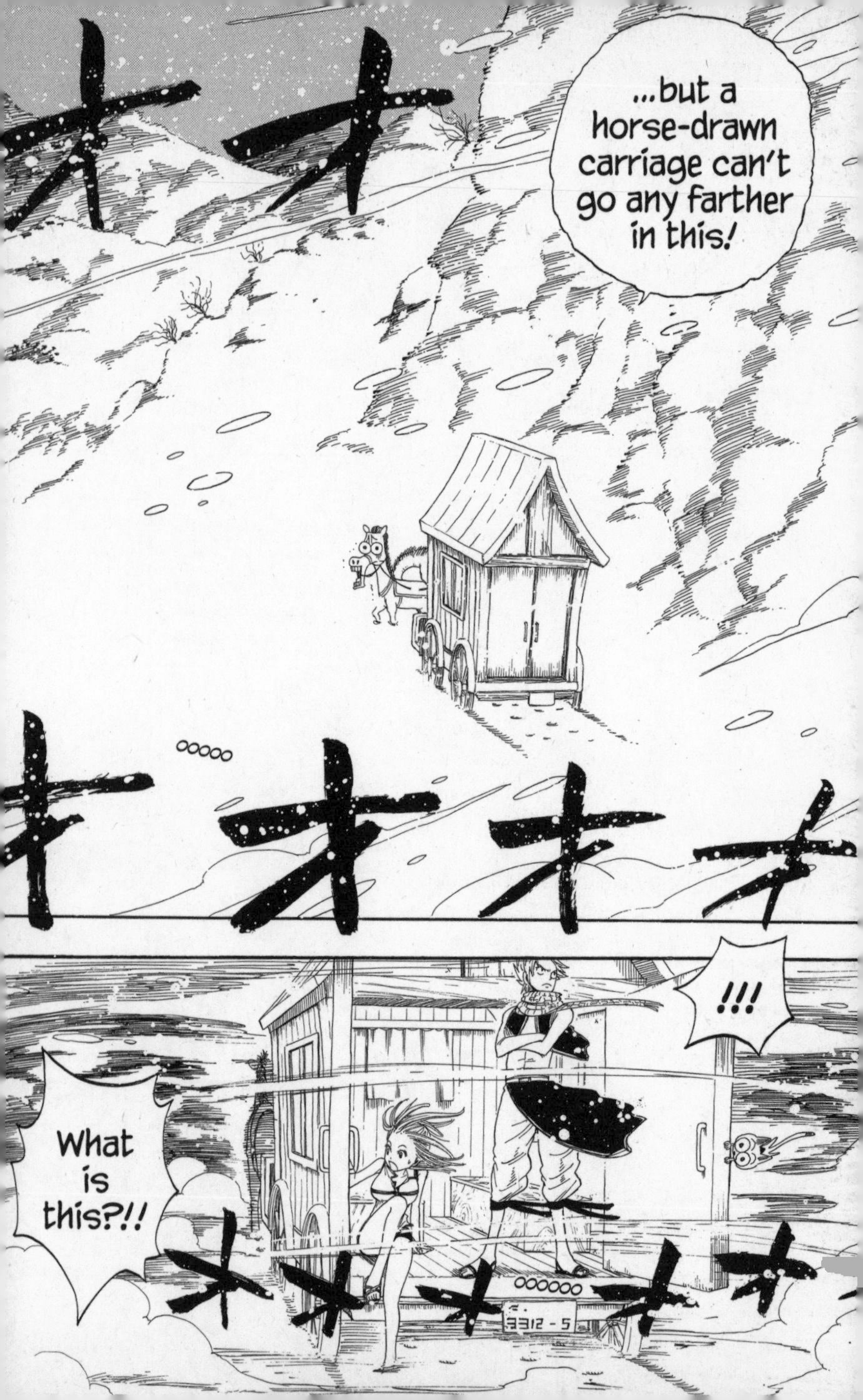
...but a horse-drawn carriage can't go any farther in this!
ooooo
!!!
What is this?!!
oooooo

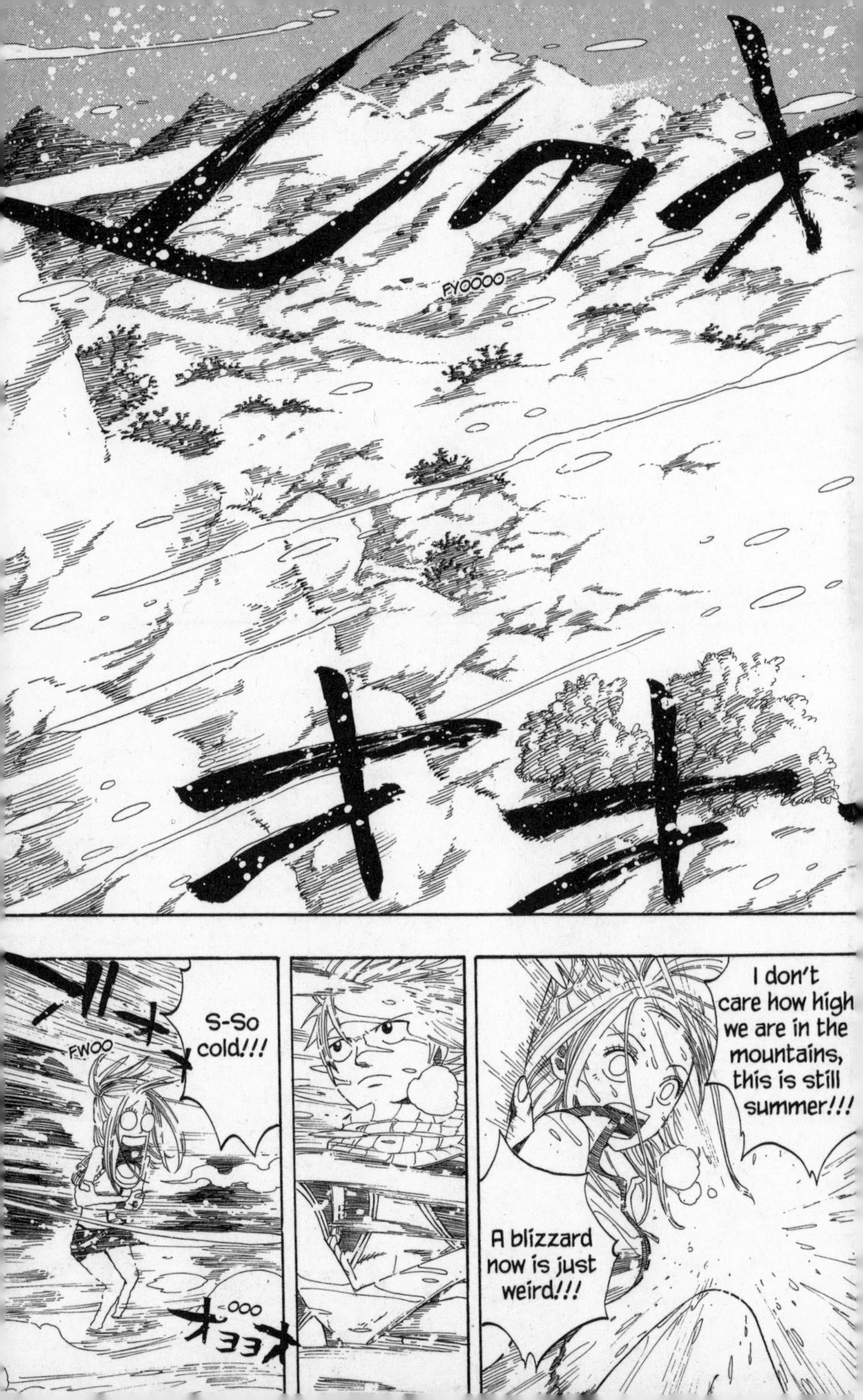
FYOOOO
I don't care how high we are in the mountains, this is still summer!!!
A blizzard now is just weird!!!
S-So cold!!!
FWOO
-OOO

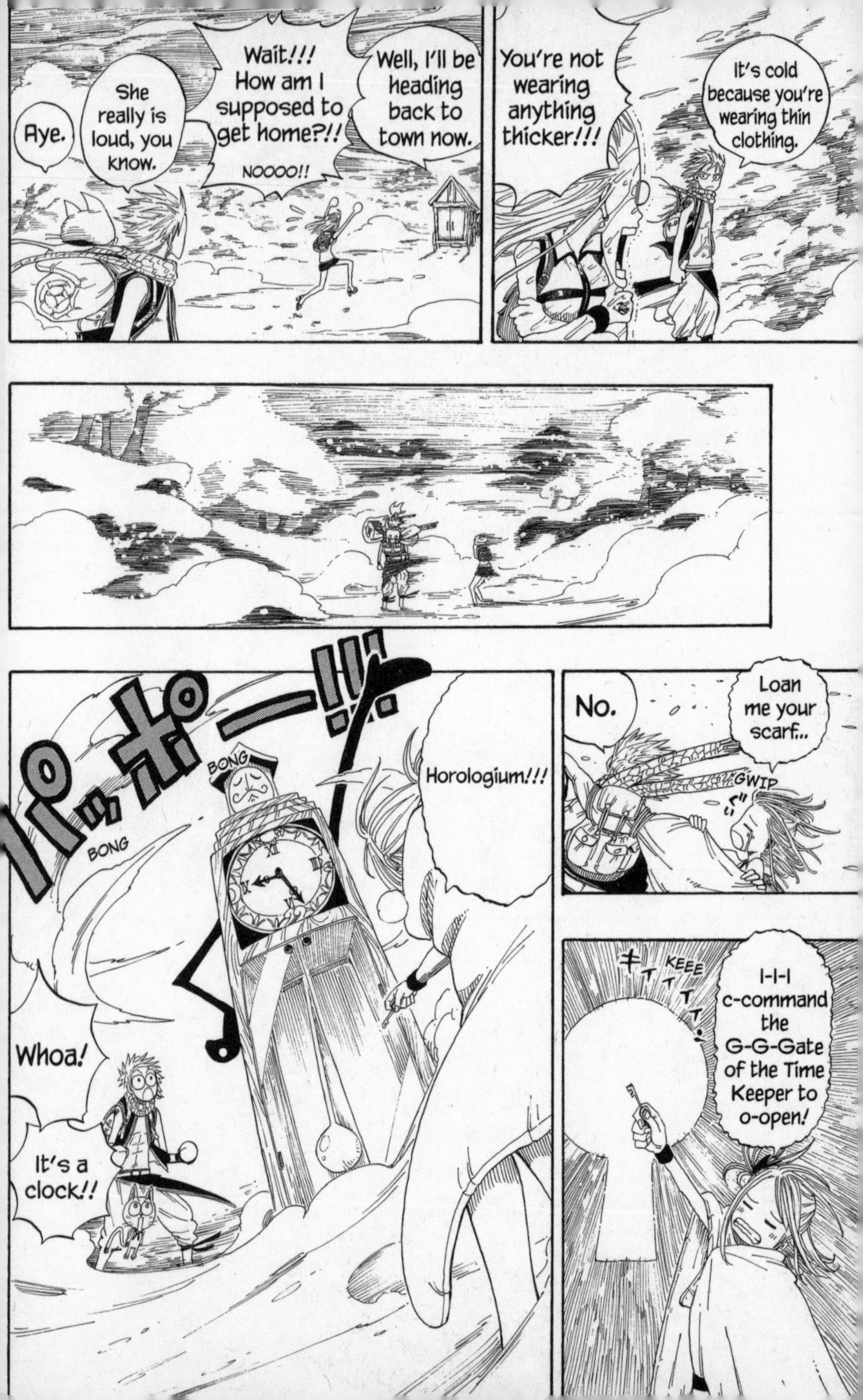
It's cold because you're wearing thin clothing.
You're not wearing anything thicker!!!
Well, I'll be heading back to town now.
Wait!!! How am I supposed to get home?!!
NOOOO!!
She really is loud, you know.
Aye.
Loan me your scarf...
GWIP
No.
KEEE
I-I-I c-command the G-G-Gate of the Time Keeper to o-open!
Horologium!!!
パッポー!!!
BONG
BONG
Whoa!
It's a clock!!

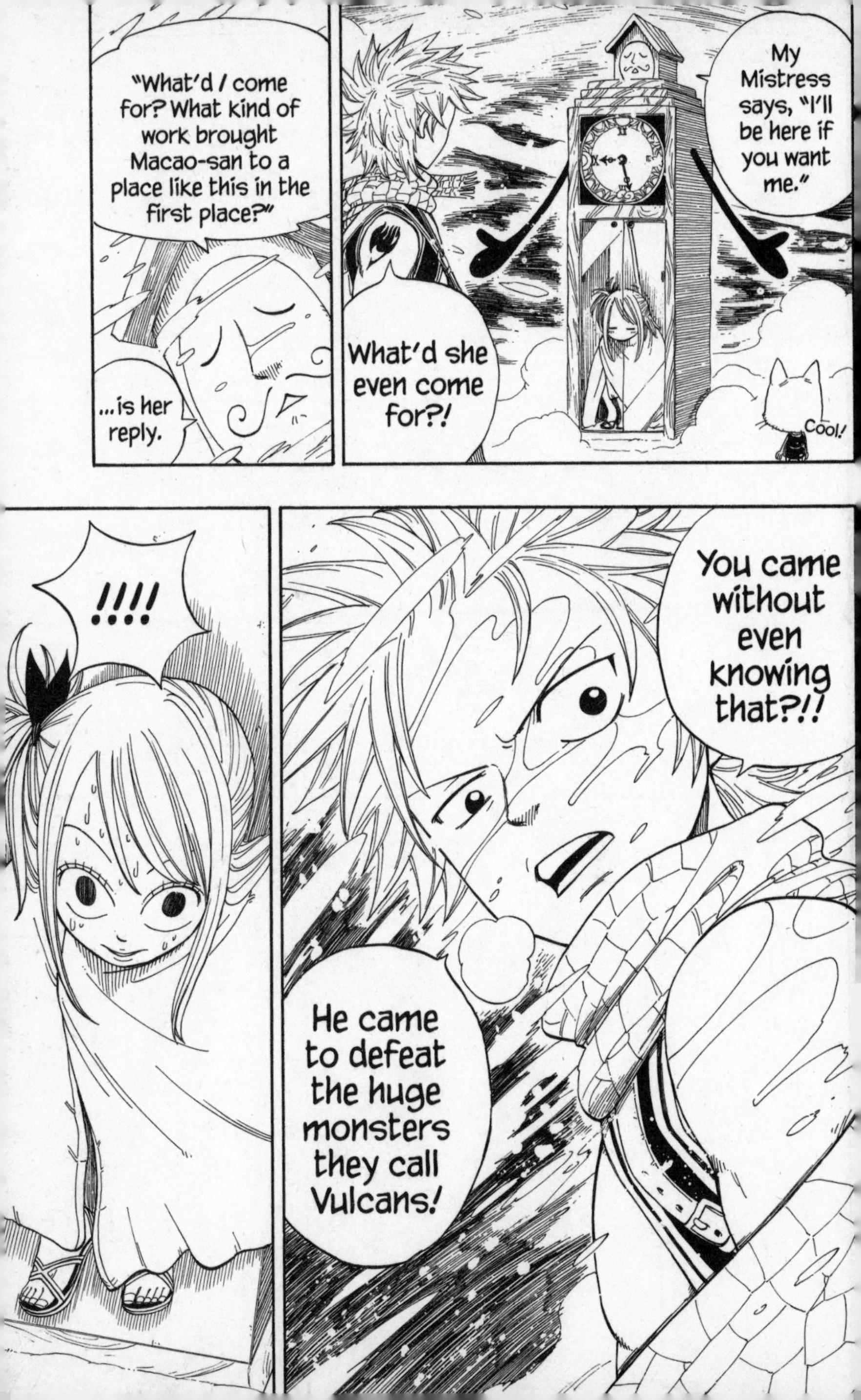
My Mistress says, "I'll be here if you want me."
What'd she even come for?!
Cool!
"What'd I come for? What kind of work brought Macao-san to a place like this in the first place?"
...is her reply.
You came without even knowing that?!!
He came to defeat the huge monsters they call Vulcans!
!!!!

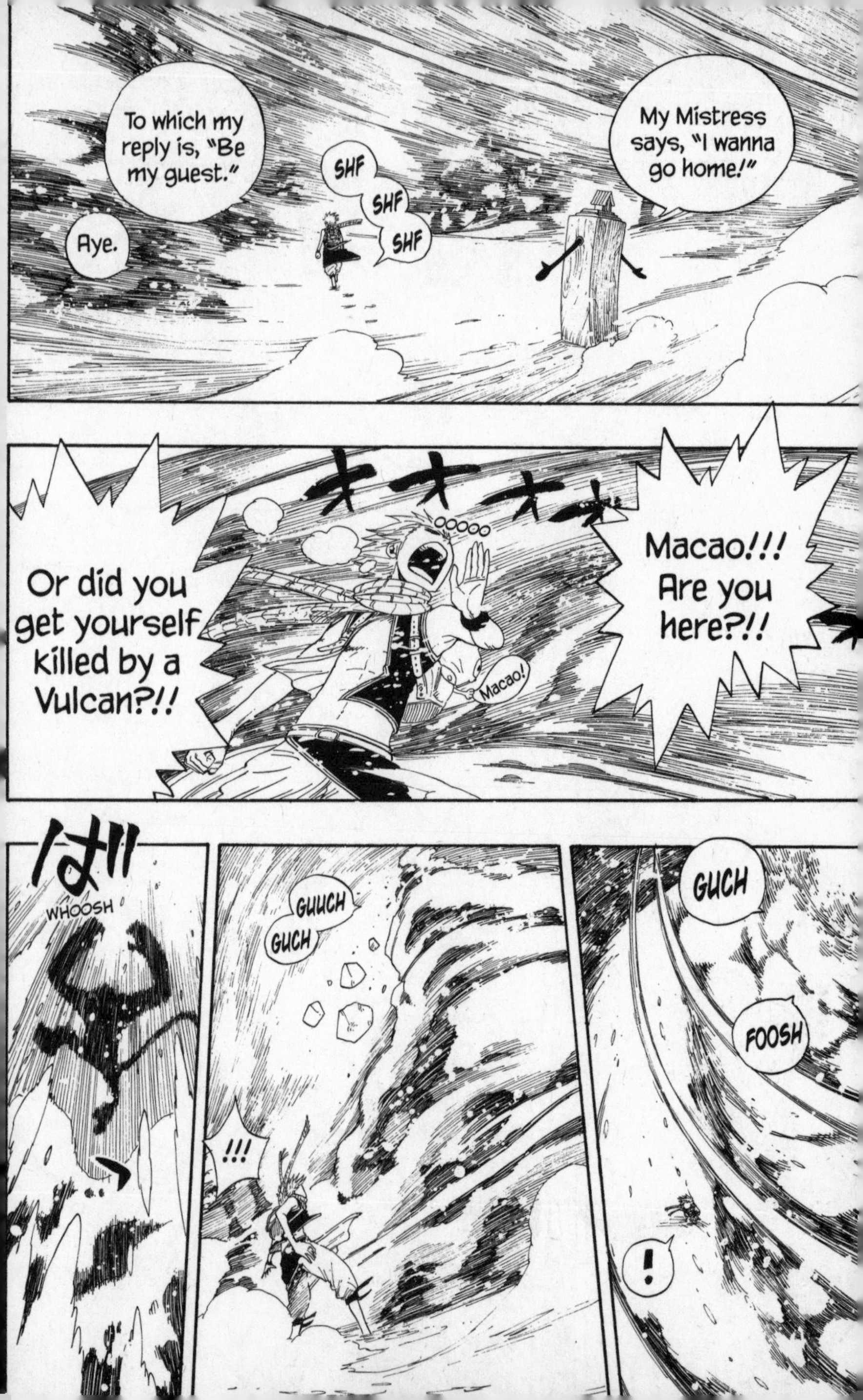
My Mistress says, "I wanna go home!"
SHF
SHF
SHF
To which my reply is, "Be my guest."
Aye.
Macao!!! Are you here?!!
Ooooo
Macao!
Or did you get yourself killed by a Vulcan?!!
GUCH
FOOSH
!
GUUCH
GUCH
!!!
WHOOSH

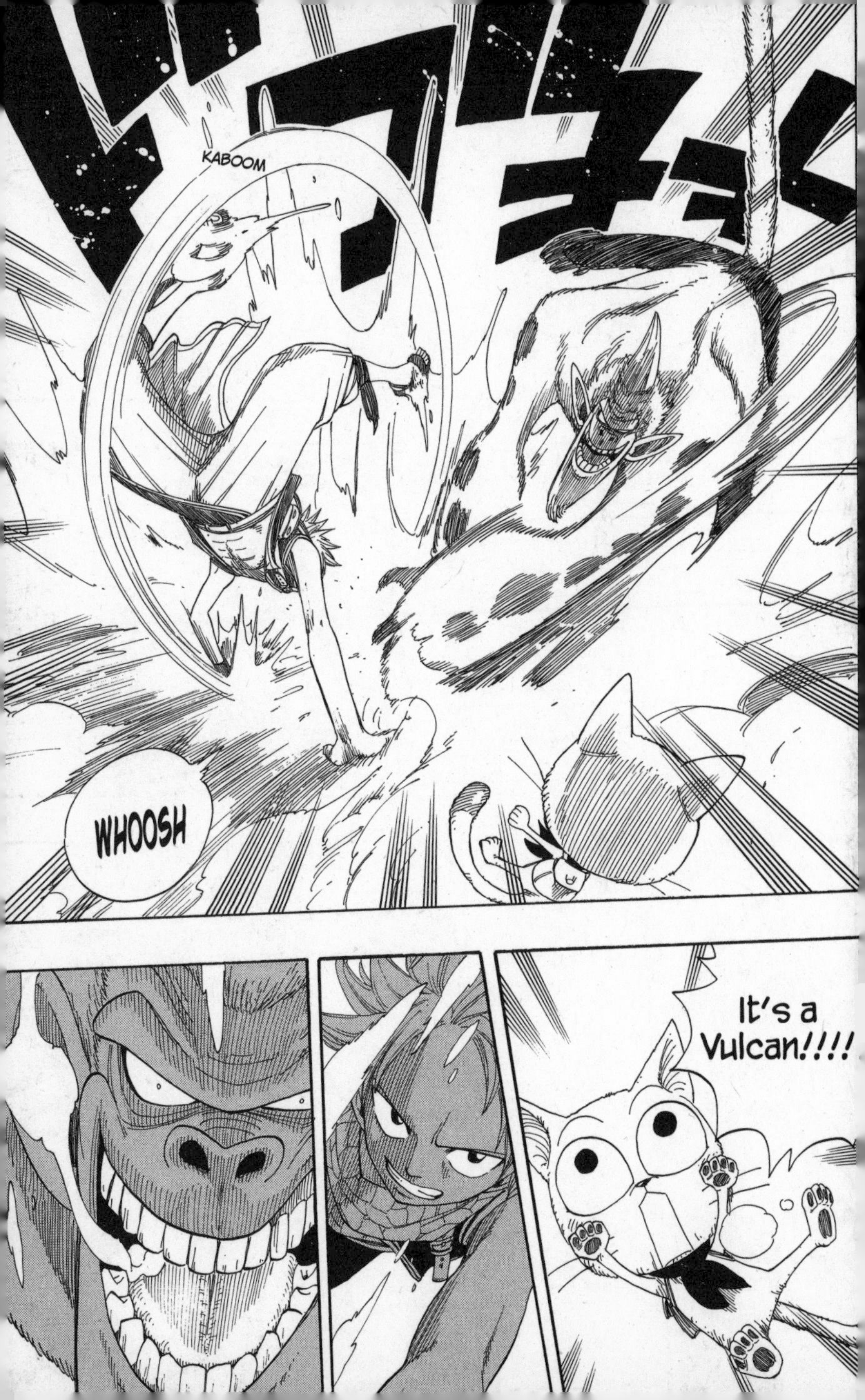
KABOOM
WHOOSH
It's a Vulcan!!!!

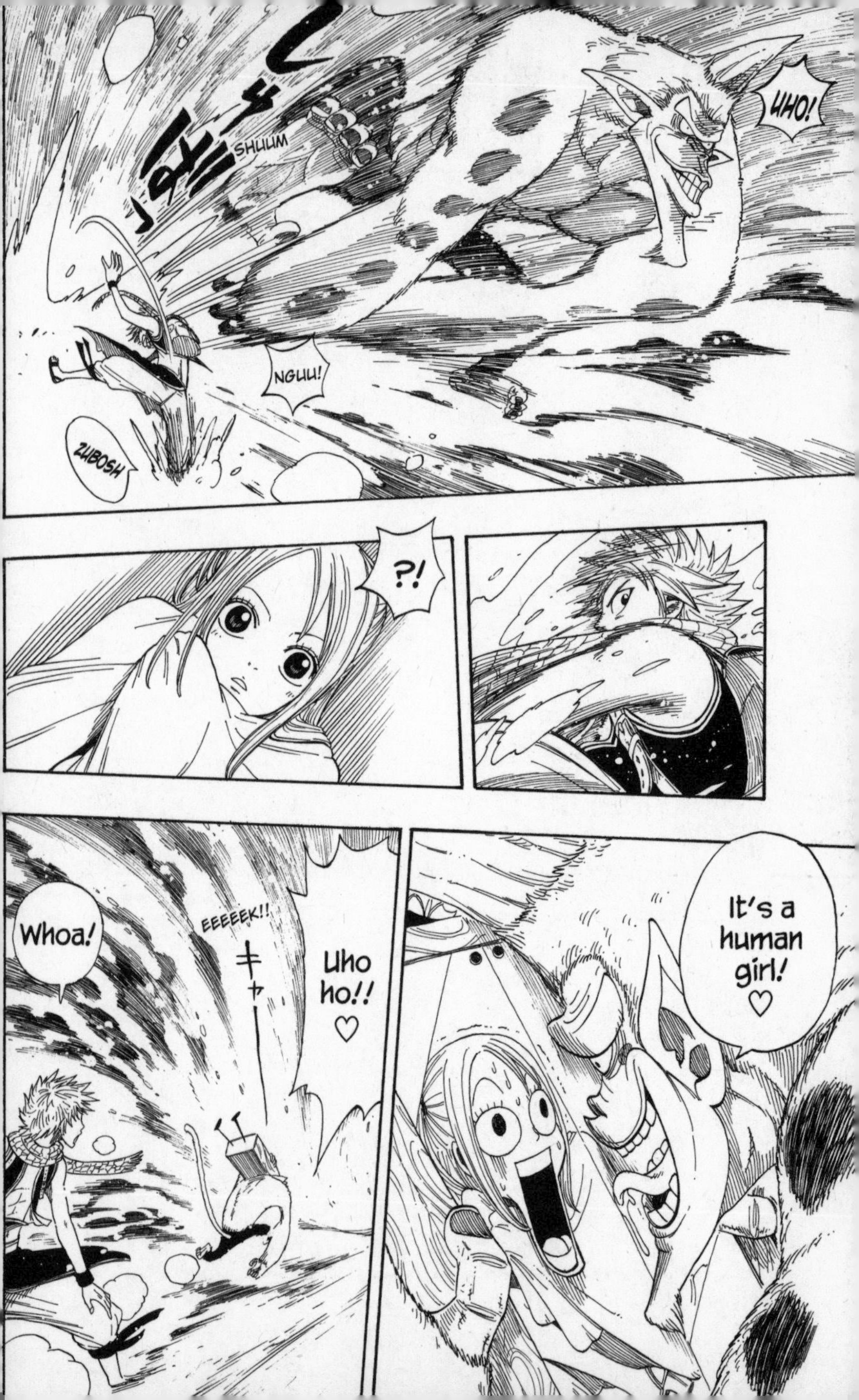
UHO!
SHUUM
NGUU!
ZUBOSH
?!
It's a human girl! ♡
Uho ho!! ♡
EEEEEK!!
キャー
Whoa!

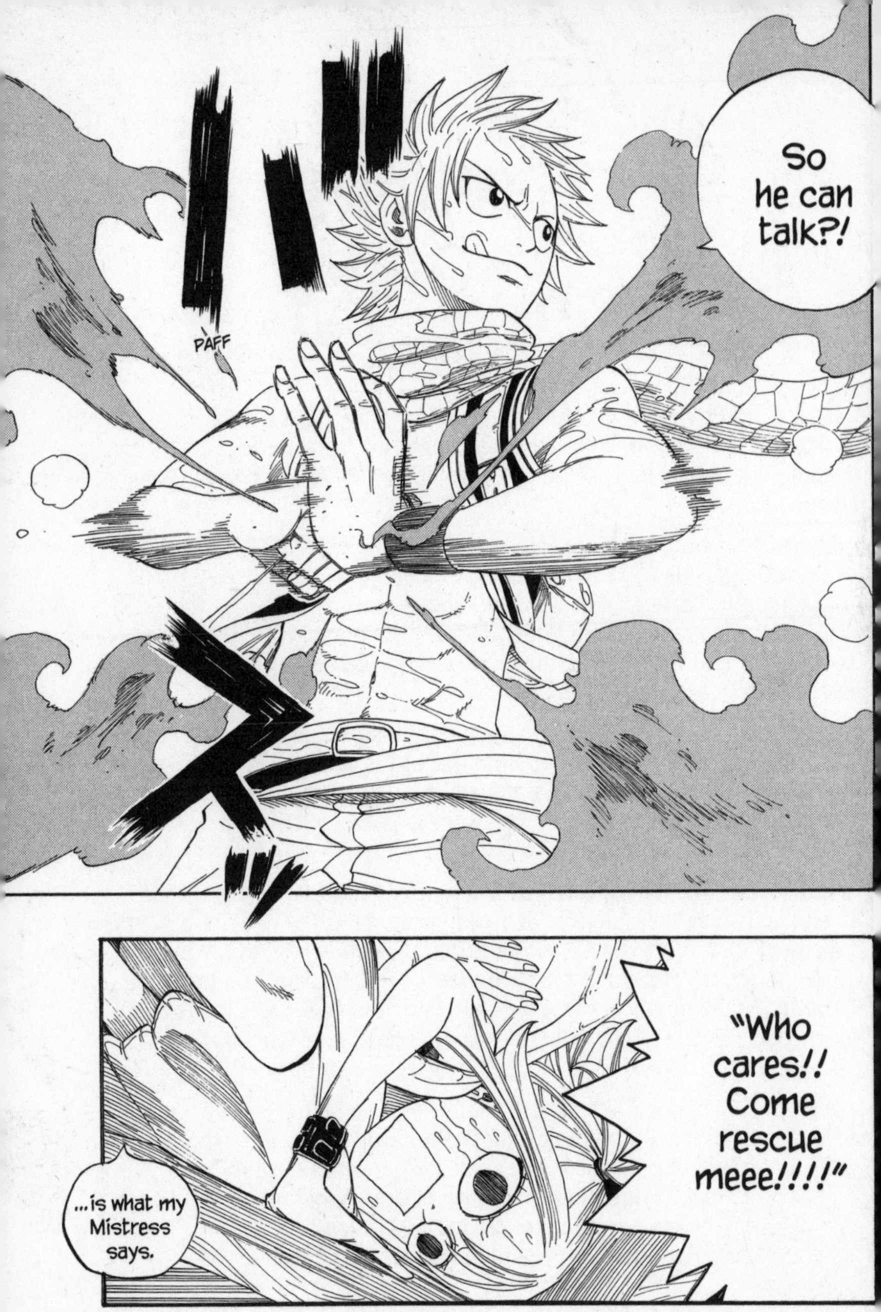
So he can talk?!
PAFF
"Who cares!! Come rescue meee!!!!"
...is what my Mistress says.

What Is a Guild?

It's a word you don't hear much nowadays, huh? They gave an explanation in the book already, but there may be somebody out there who still doesn't get it, so for that person, I'd like to go into a little more detail.

Originally, guilds began in Europe in the Middle Ages. You can think of them as groups of people working in a single type of industry who join forces and act on their decisions together. At the time, guilds were only for tradesmen and craftsmen, but for the purposes of this story, we thought, "What the heck? Let's make a story about craftsmen whose craft is wizardry!" And thus, this book.

So why did guilds arise in the first place? It's because the world is full of dangers. Tradesmen cross mountains and oceans to sell their wares. But there are pirates on the oceans and bandits in the mountains who are after the tradesmen's goods. Hiring soldiers costs a lot of money. So what to do? Well, why shouldn't everyone go together?!

And that's how many people with the same objective first gathered together. The danger never really went away, but they had more strength together than alone, right? One additional benefit was that the guild would take care of a tradesman's house when he was off on business. Eventually, the guilds became too powerful, and they were the causes of wars. But if you're really interested in that part, go do some studying. (Ha ha!)

In other words, a guild is where people with similar objectives congregate. In this story, the people are a group of wizards who earn their living by using magic to help solve other people's problems. "Earn your living" may sound a little too "grown-up" for some of you, but it means that wizards have a lot of adventures to look forward to. That's what the wizard guild is all about!

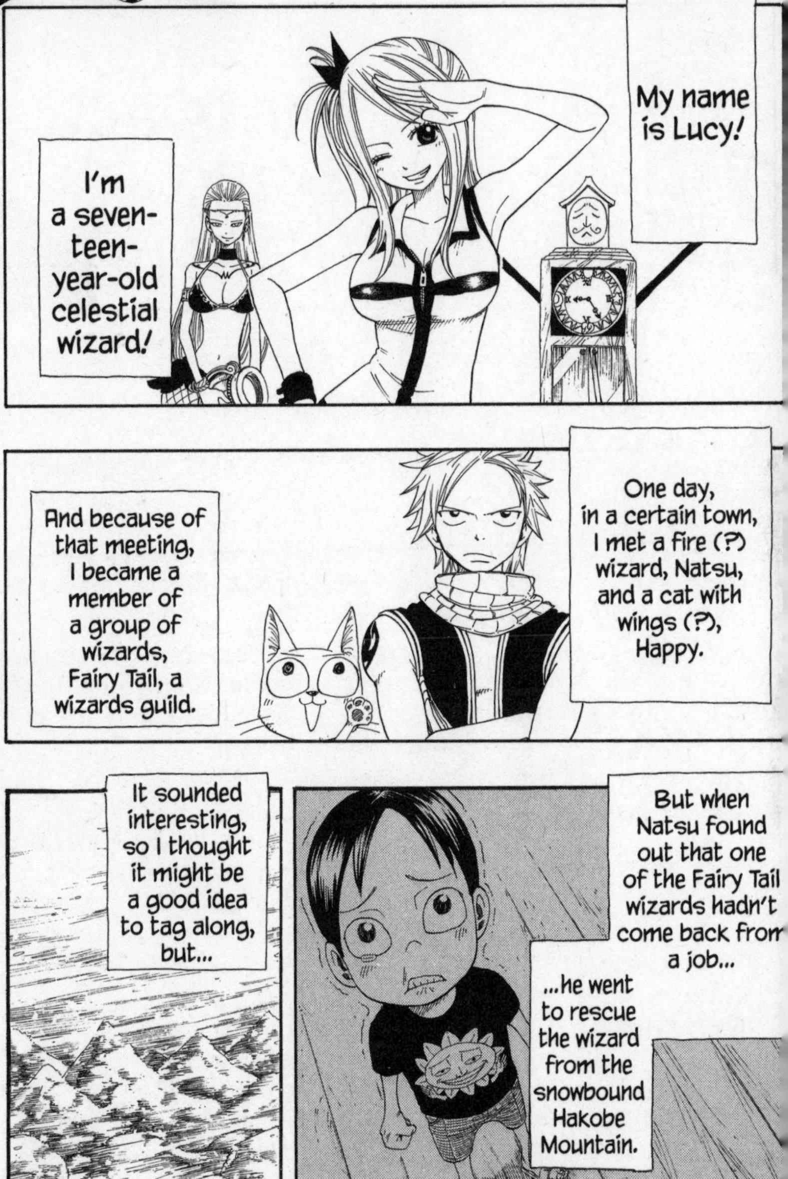
My name is Lucy!
I'm a seventeen-year-old celestial wizard!
One day, in a certain town, I met a fire (?) wizard, Natsu, and a cat with wings (?), Happy.
And because of that meeting, I became a member of a group of wizards, Fairy Tail, a wizards guild.
But when Natsu found out that one of the Fairy Tail wizards hadn't come back from a job...
...he went to rescue the wizard from the snowbound Hakobe Mountain.
It sounded interesting, so I thought it might be a good idea to tag along, but...

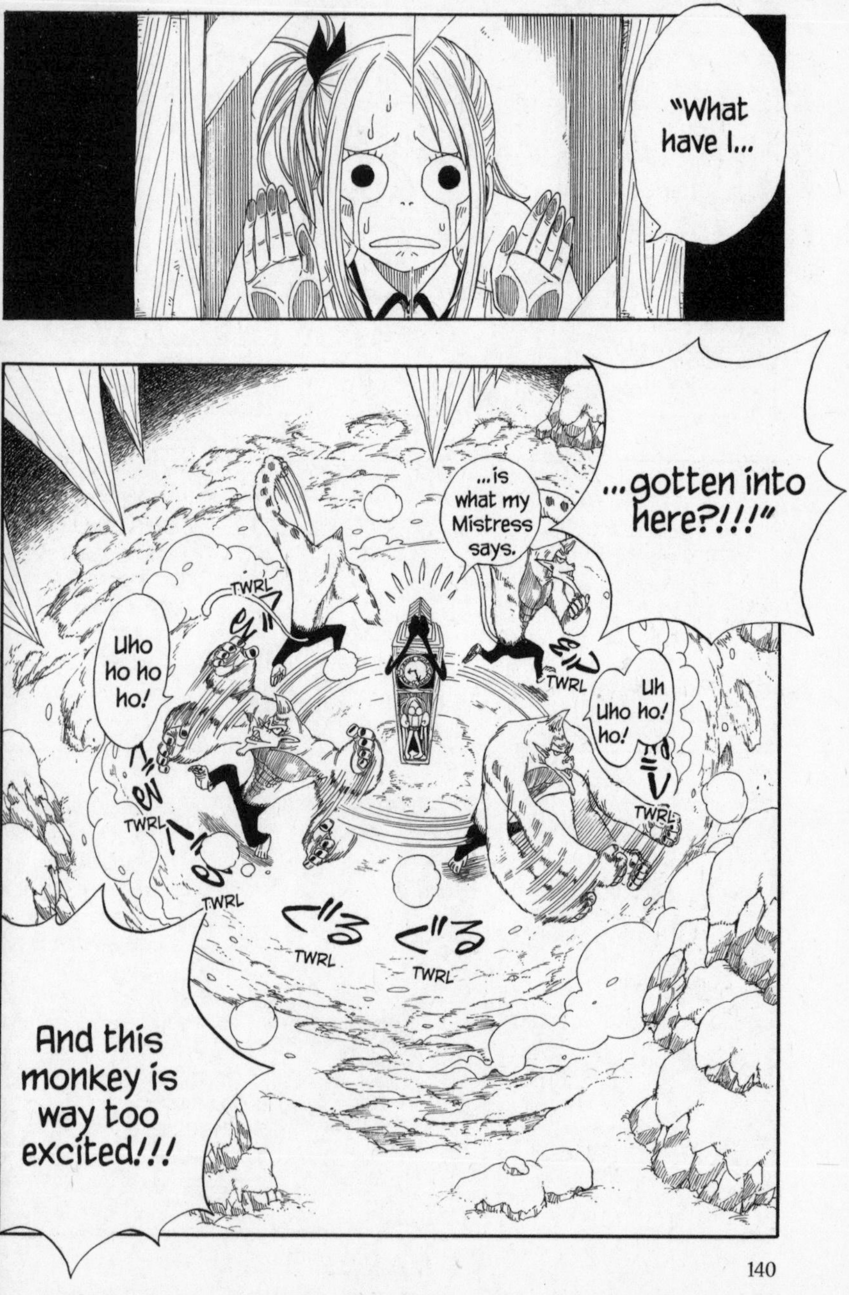
"What have I...
...gotten into here?!!!"
...is what my Mistress says.
Uh Uho ho! ho!
TWRL
TWRL
Uho ho ho ho!
TWRL
TWRL
TWRL
TWRL
TWRL
And this monkey is way too excited!!!

FAIRY TAIL

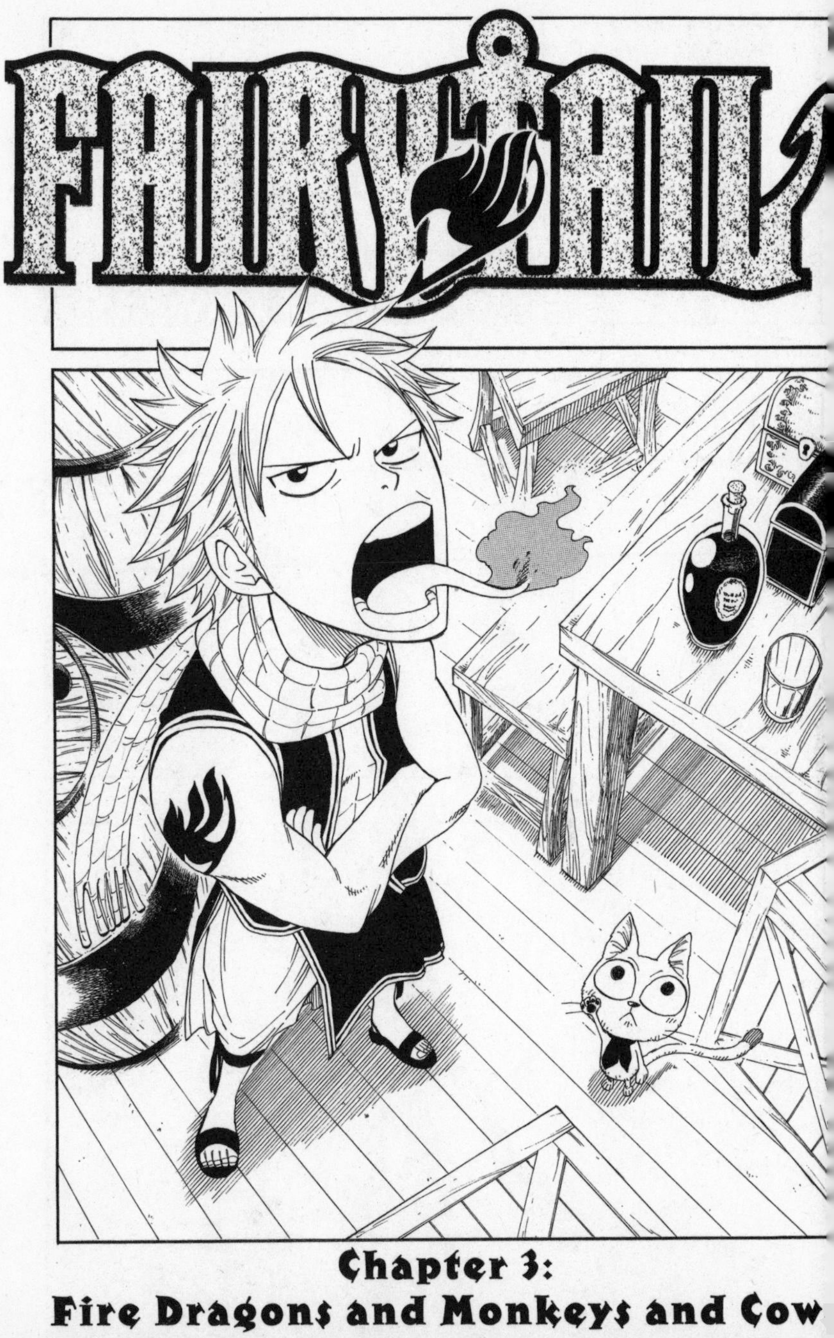

Chapter 3:
Fire Dragons and Monkeys and Cow

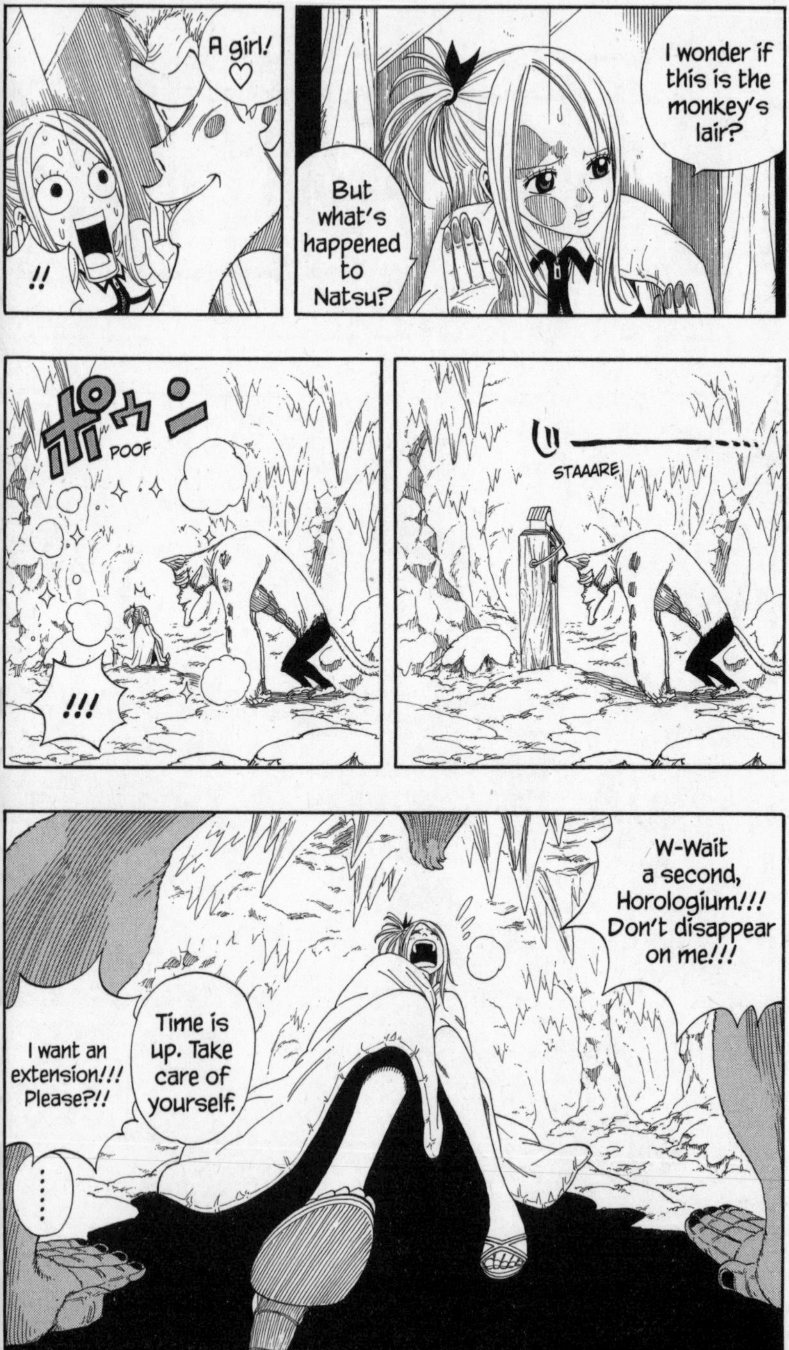
I wonder if this is the monkey's lair?
But what's happened to Natsu?
A girl! ♡
!!
STAARE
POOF
!!!
W-Wait a second, Horologium!!! Don't disappear on me!!!
Time is up. Take care of yourself.
I want an extension!!! Please?!!
......

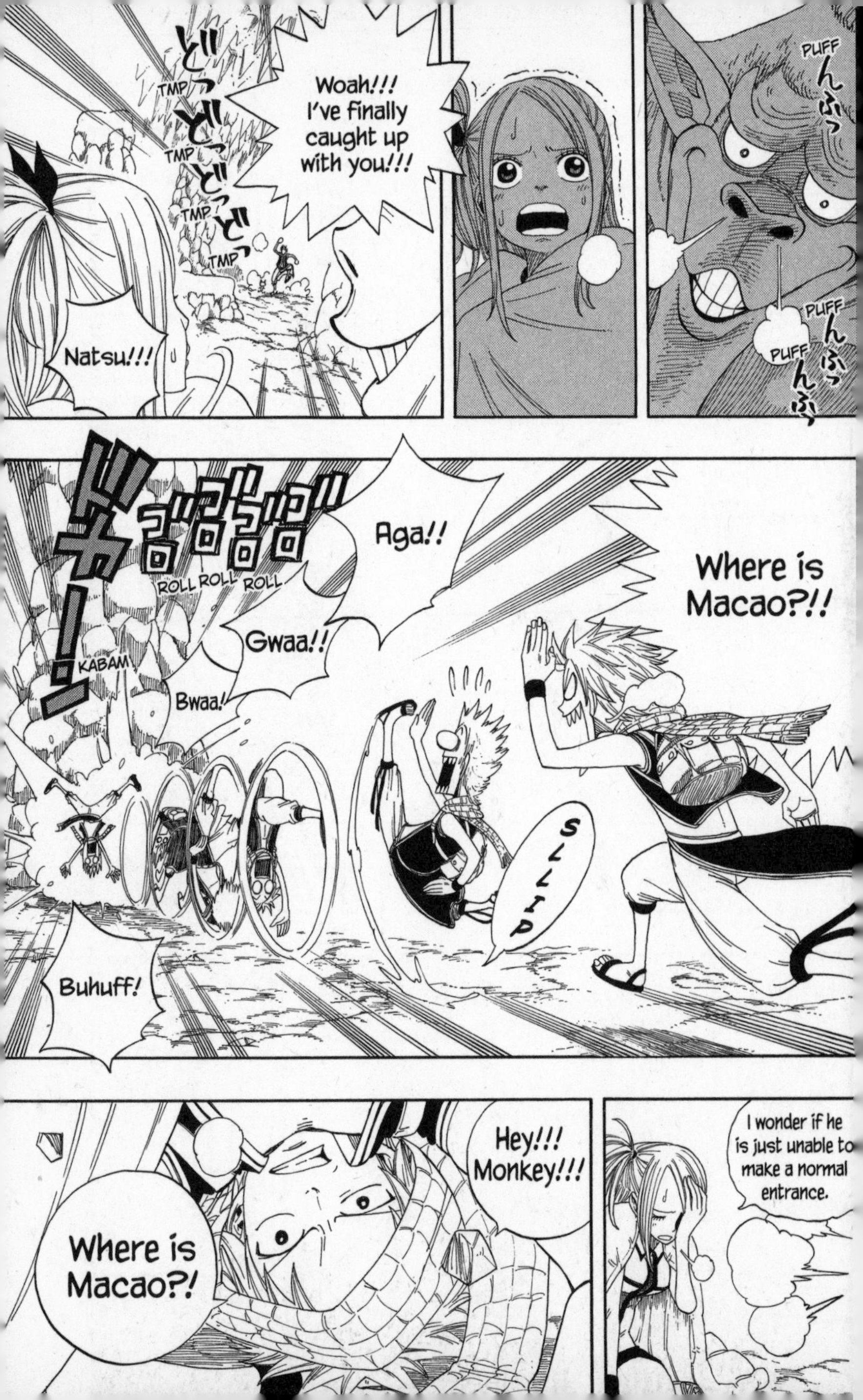
PUFF
んふっ
PUFF
んふっ
PUFF
んふっ
Woah!!! I've finally caught up with you!!!
TMP
TMP
TMP
TMP
Natsu!!!
Where is Macao?!!
Aga!!
ROLL ROLL ROLL
Gwaa!!
KABAM
SLLIP
Bwaa!
Buhuff!
I wonder if he is just unable to make a normal entrance.
Hey!!! Monkey!!!
Where is Macao?!

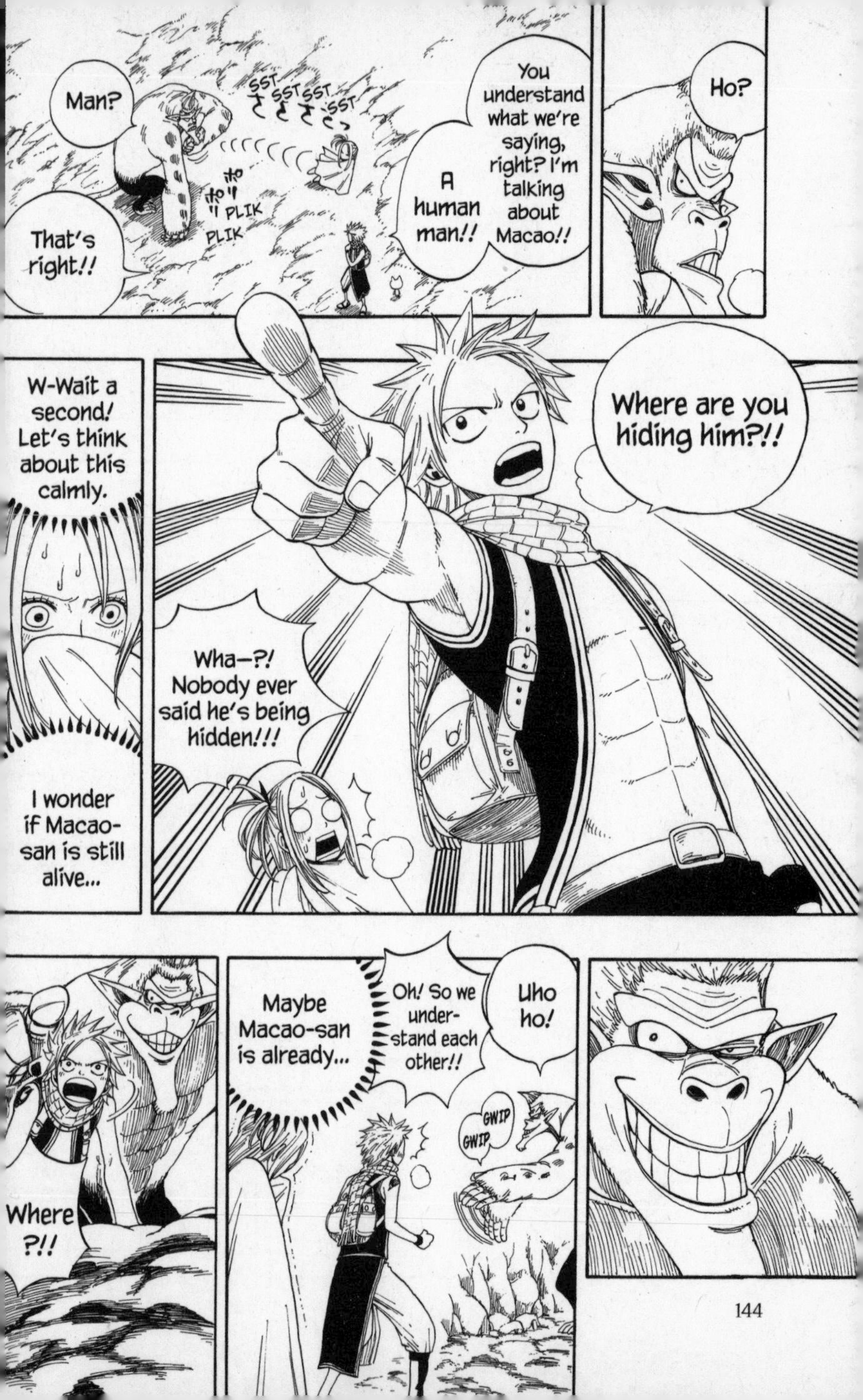
Ho?
You understand what we're saying, right? I'm talking about Macao!!
A human man!!
SST SST SST SST
Man?
PLIK PLIK
That's right!!
Where are you hiding him?!!
Wha–?! Nobody ever said he's being hidden!!!
W-Wait a second! Let's think about this calmly.
I wonder if Macao-san is still alive...
Uho ho!
Oh! So we under-stand each other!!
Maybe Macao-san is already...
GWIP GWIP
Where?!!

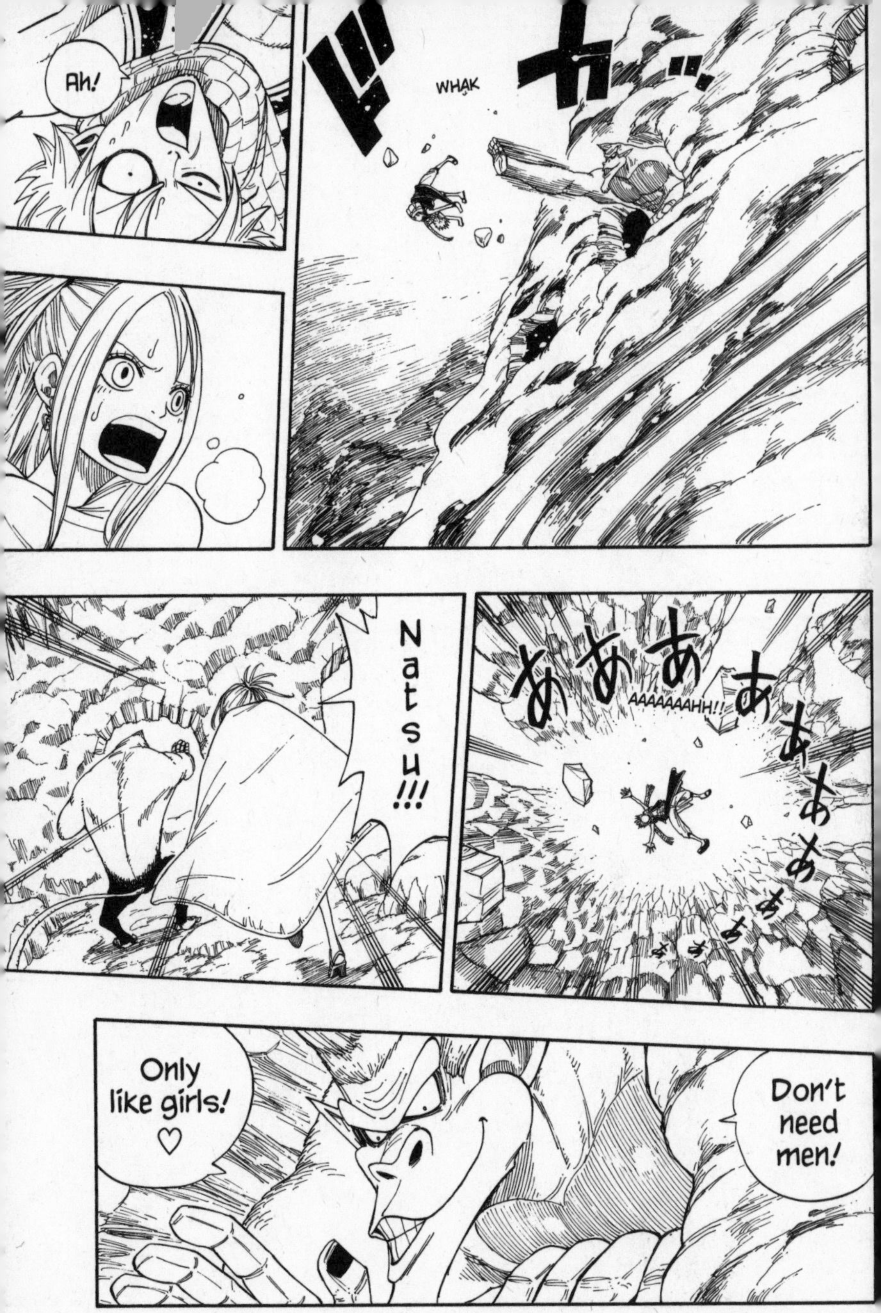
WHAK
Ah!
AAAAAAAAHH!!!
Natsu!!!
Don't need men!
Only like girls! ♡

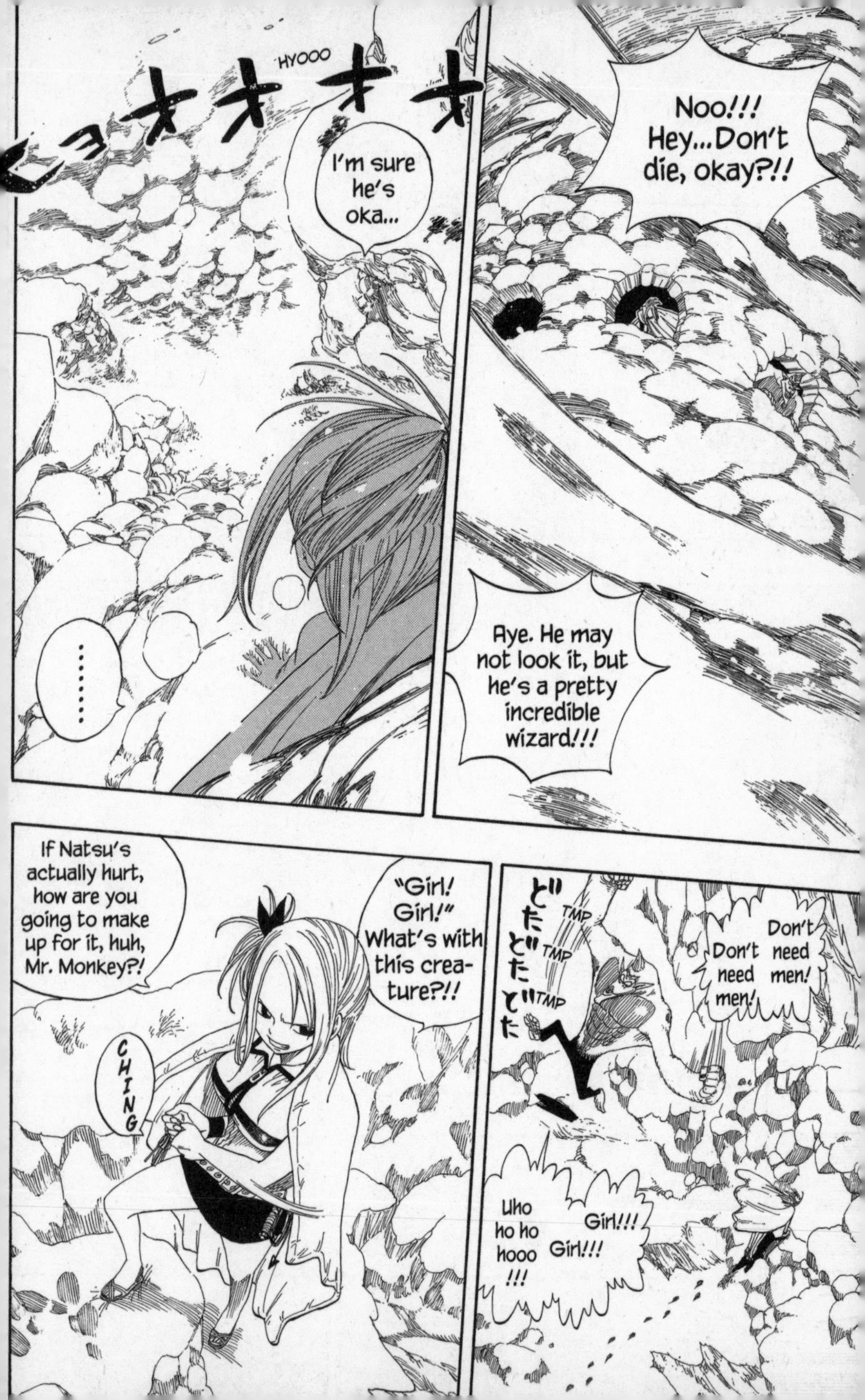
Noo!!! Hey...Don't die, okay?!!
Aye. He may not look it, but he's a pretty incredible wizard!!!
HYOOO
I'm sure he's oka...
......
Don't need men!
Don't need men!
TMP TMP TMP
Girl!!!
Girl!!!
Uho ho ho hooo !!!
"Girl! Girl!" What's with this crea-ture?!!
If Natsu's actually hurt, how are you going to make up for it, huh, Mr. Monkey?!
CHING

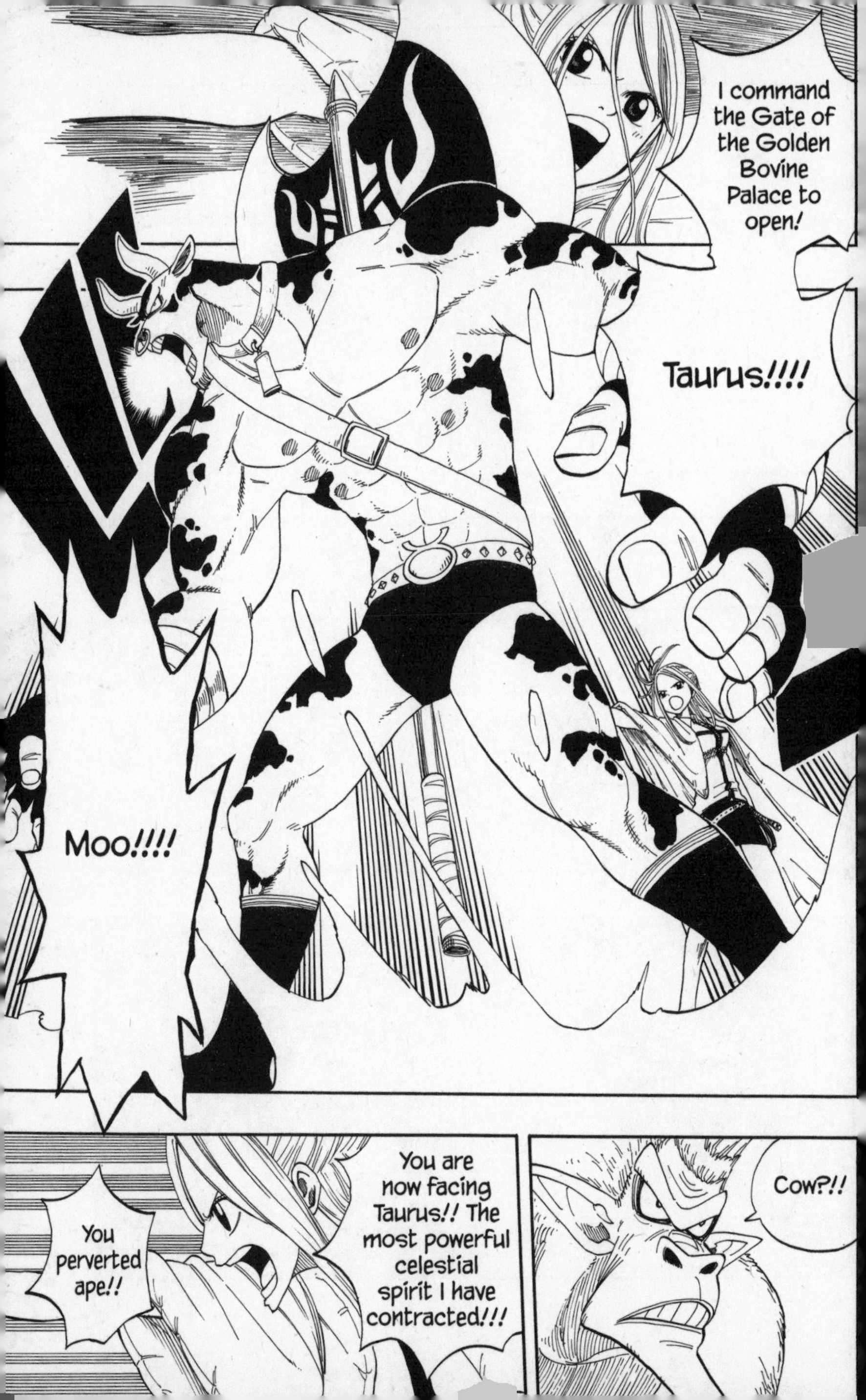
I command the Gate of the Golden Bovine Palace to open!
Taurus!!!!
Moo!!!!
Cow?!!
You are now facing Taurus!! The most powerful celestial spirit I have contracted!!!
You perverted ape!!

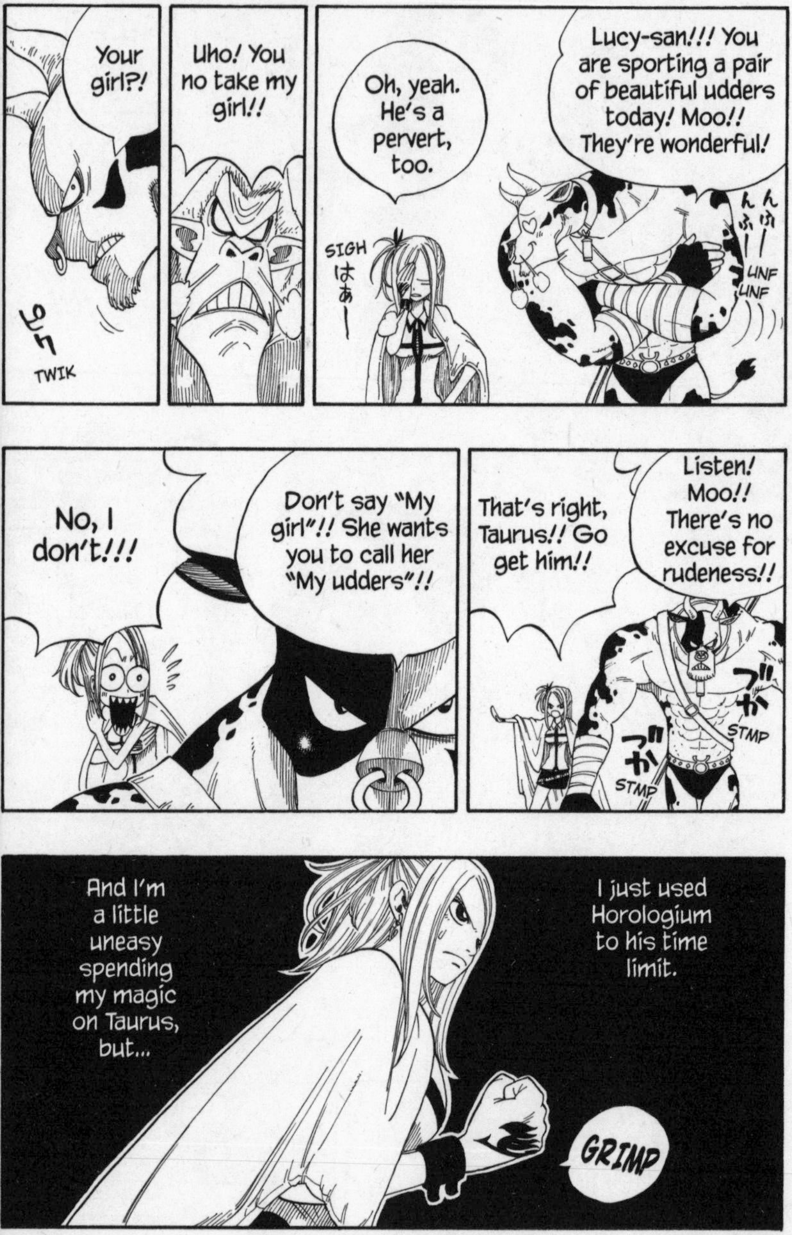
Lucy-san!!! You are sporting a pair of beautiful udders today! Moo!! They're wonderful!
んふー んふー
UNF UNF
Oh, yeah. He's a pervert, too.
SIGH
はあー
Uho! You no take my girl!!
Your girl?!
ピク
TWIK
Listen! Moo!! There's no excuse for rudeness!!
That's right, Taurus!! Go get him!!
づが
STMP
づが
STMP
Don't say "My girl"!! She wants you to call her "My udders"!!
No, I don't!!!
I just used Horologium to his time limit.
And I'm a little uneasy spending my magic on Taurus, but...
GRIMP

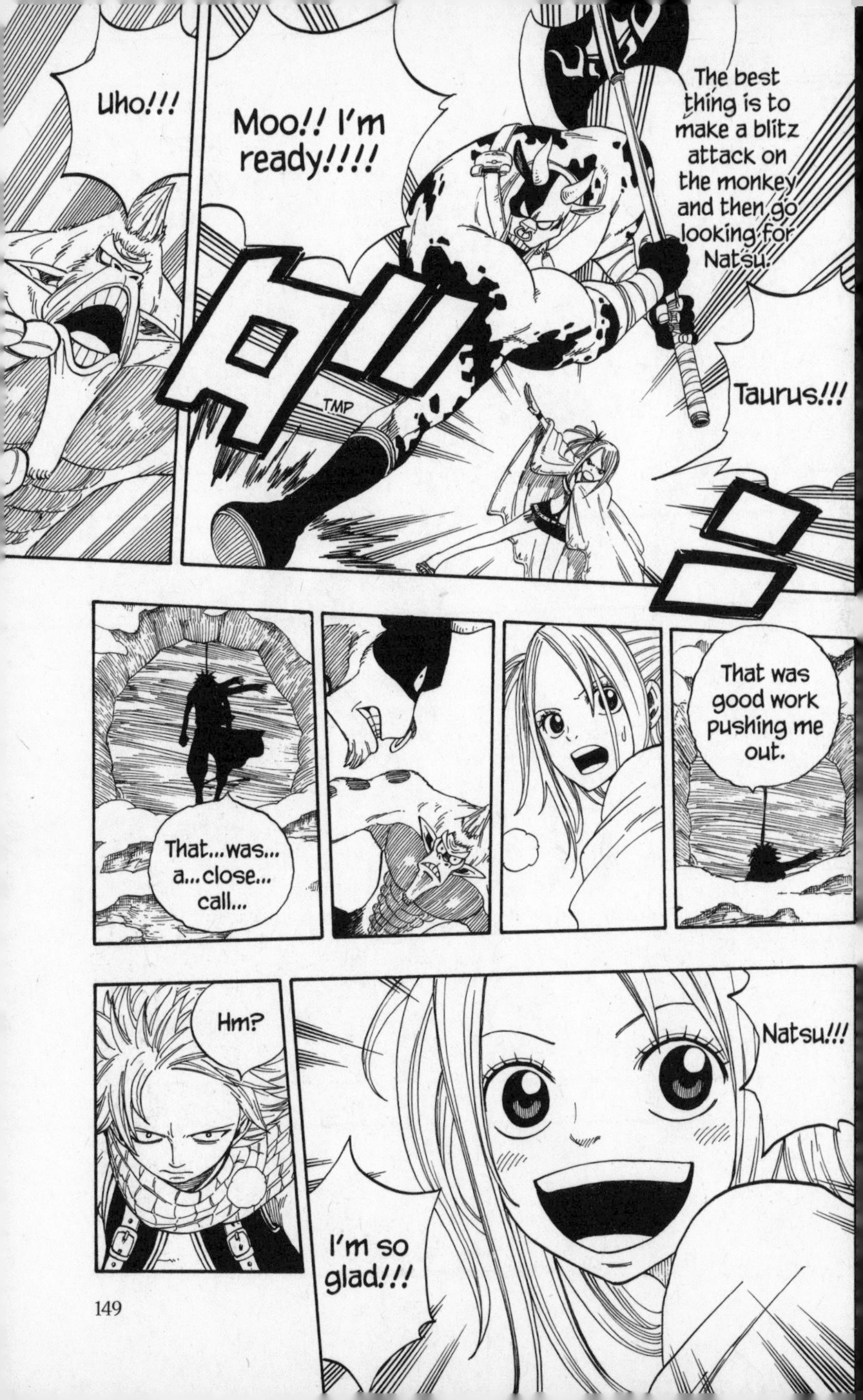
The best thing is to make a blitz attack on the monkey and then go looking for Natsu.
Taurus!!!
Moo!! I'm ready!!!!
TMP
Uho!!!
That was good work pushing me out.
That...was... a...close... call...
Natsu!!!
I'm so glad!!!
Hm?

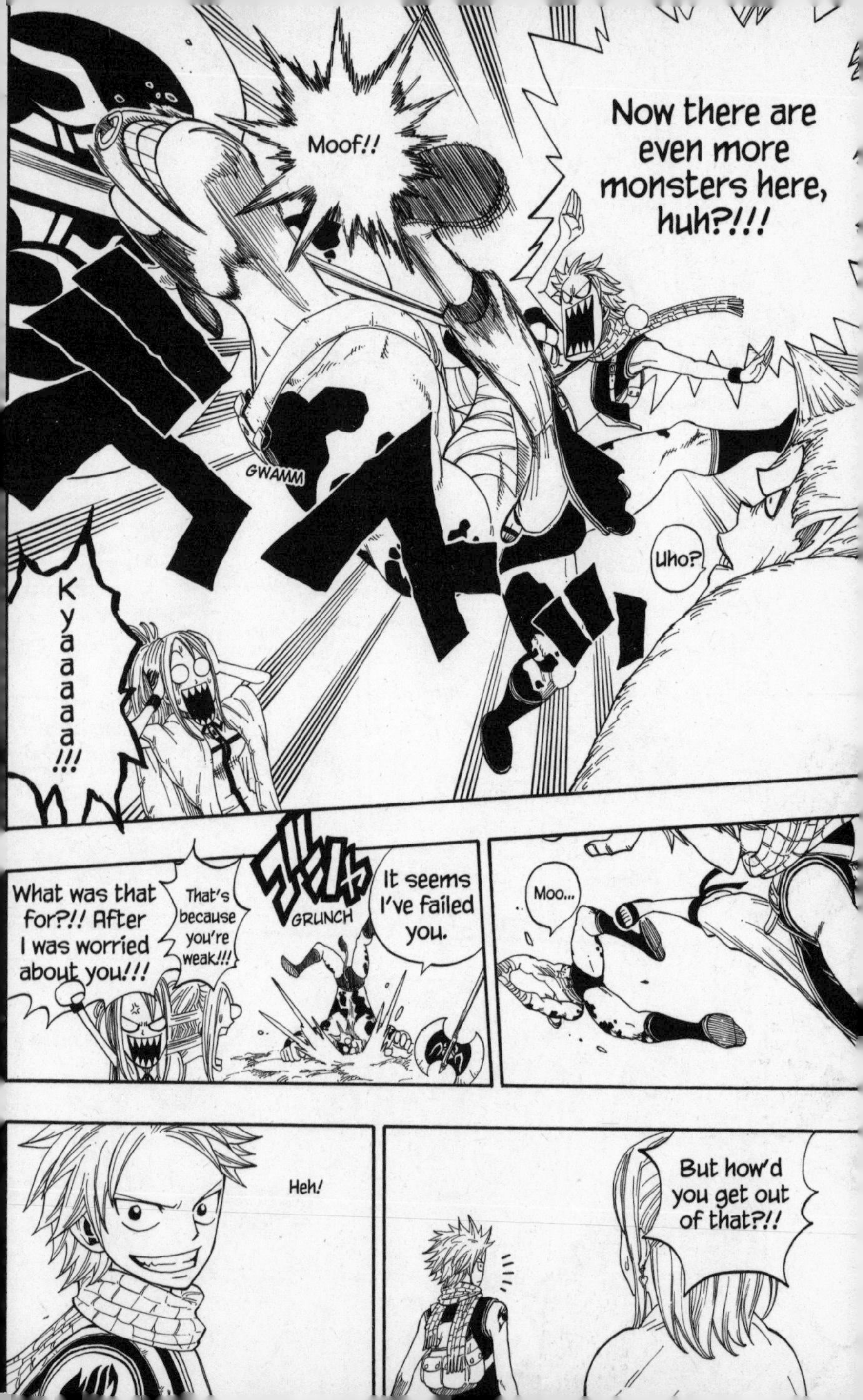
Now there are even more monsters here, huh?!!!
Moof!!
Uho?
GWAMM
Kyaaaaaa!!!
Moo...
It seems I've failed you.
GRUNCH
That's because you're weak!!!
What was that for?!! After I was worried about you!!!
But how'd you get out of that?!!
Heh!

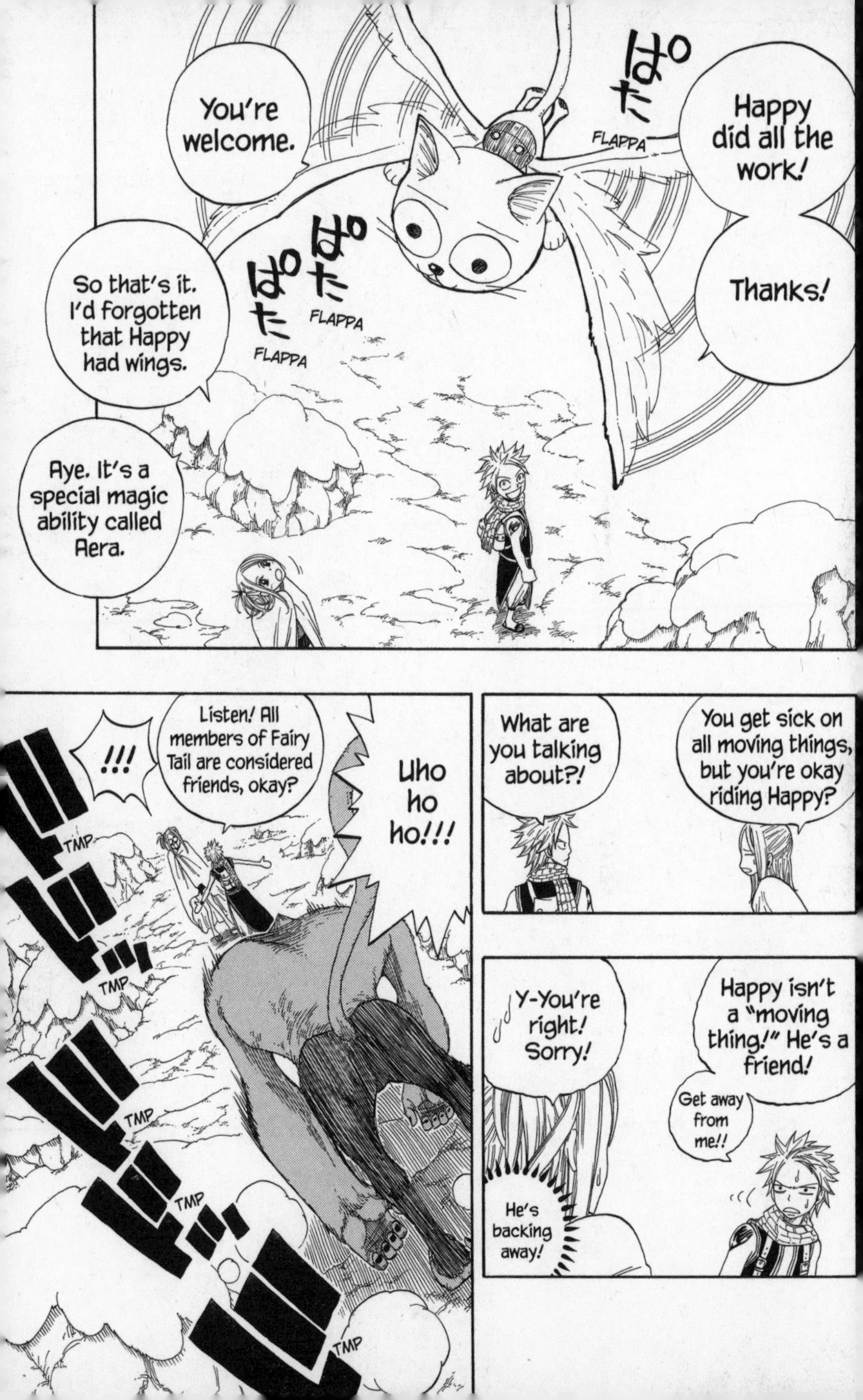
Happy did all the work!
Thanks!
ぱた
FLAPPA
You're welcome.
ぱた
FLAPPA
ぱた
FLAPPA
So that's it. I'd forgotten that Happy had wings.
Aye. It's a special magic ability called Aera.
You get sick on all moving things, but you're okay riding Happy?
What are you talking about?!
Happy isn't a "moving thing!" He's a friend!
Get away from me!!
Y-You're right! Sorry!
He's backing away!
Uho ho ho!!!
Listen! All members of Fairy Tail are considered friends, okay?
!!!
TMP
TMP
TMP
TMP
TMP

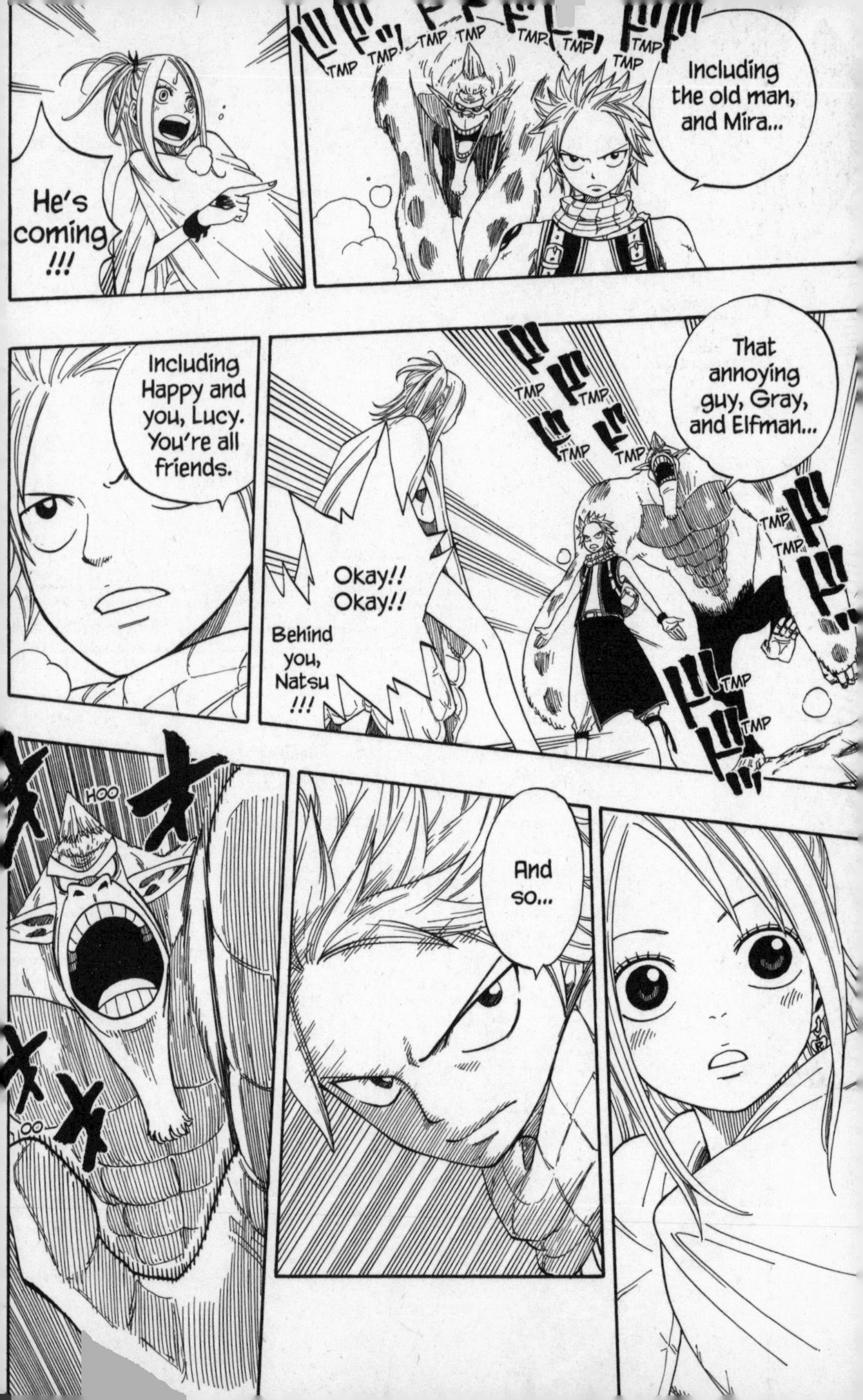

TMP TMP TMP TMP TMP TMP TMP TMP
Including the old man, and Mira...
He's coming!!!
That annoying guy, Gray, and Elfman...
TMP TMP TMP TMP TMP TMP TMP TMP
Okay!! Okay!!
Behind you, Natsu!!!
Including Happy and you, Lucy. You're all friends.
And so...
HOO
OO

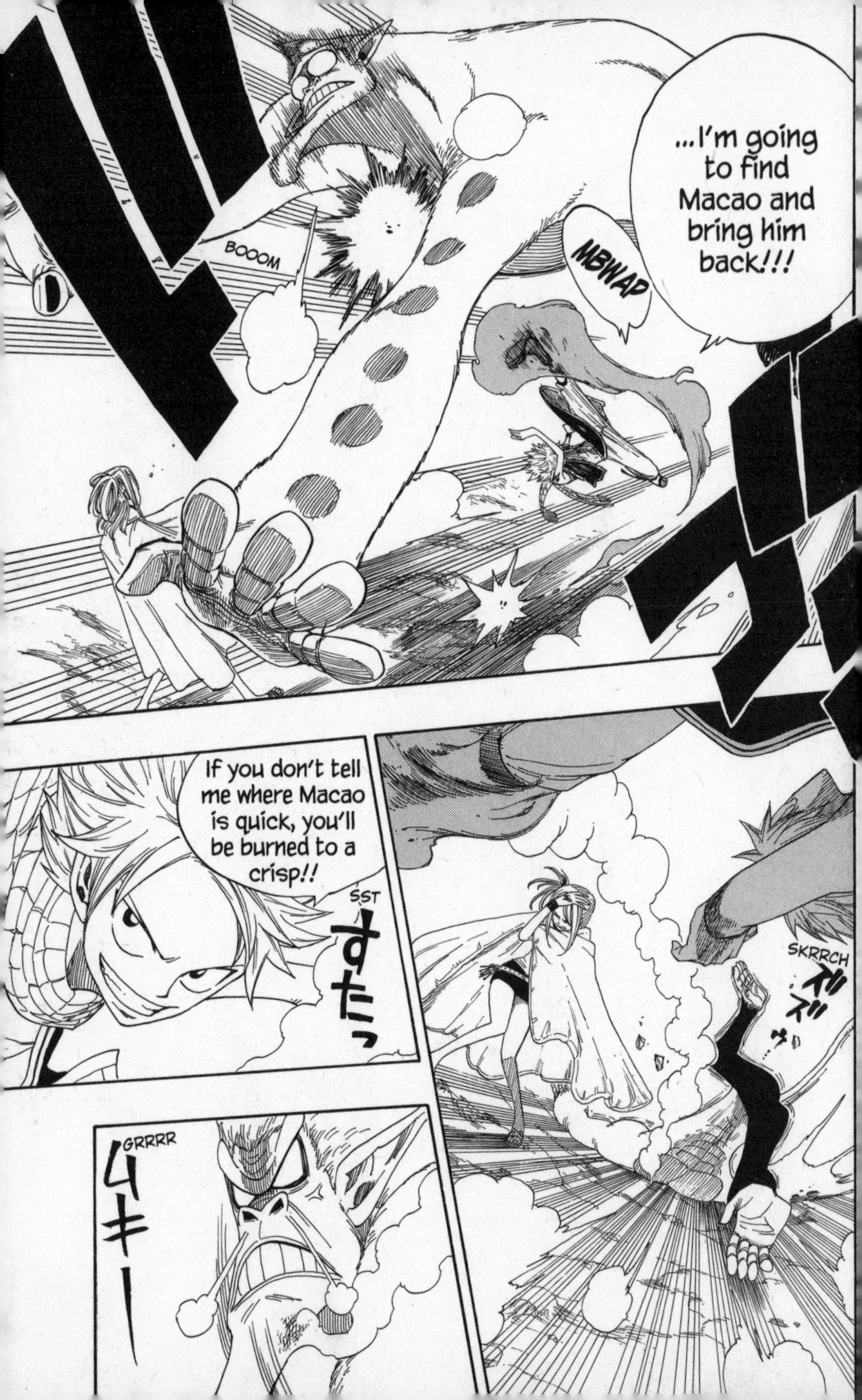
...I'm going to find Macao and bring him back!!!
MBWAP
BOOOM
SKRRCH
ズズッ
If you don't tell me where Macao is quick, you'll be burned to a crisp!!
SST
すたっ
GRRRR
ムキー

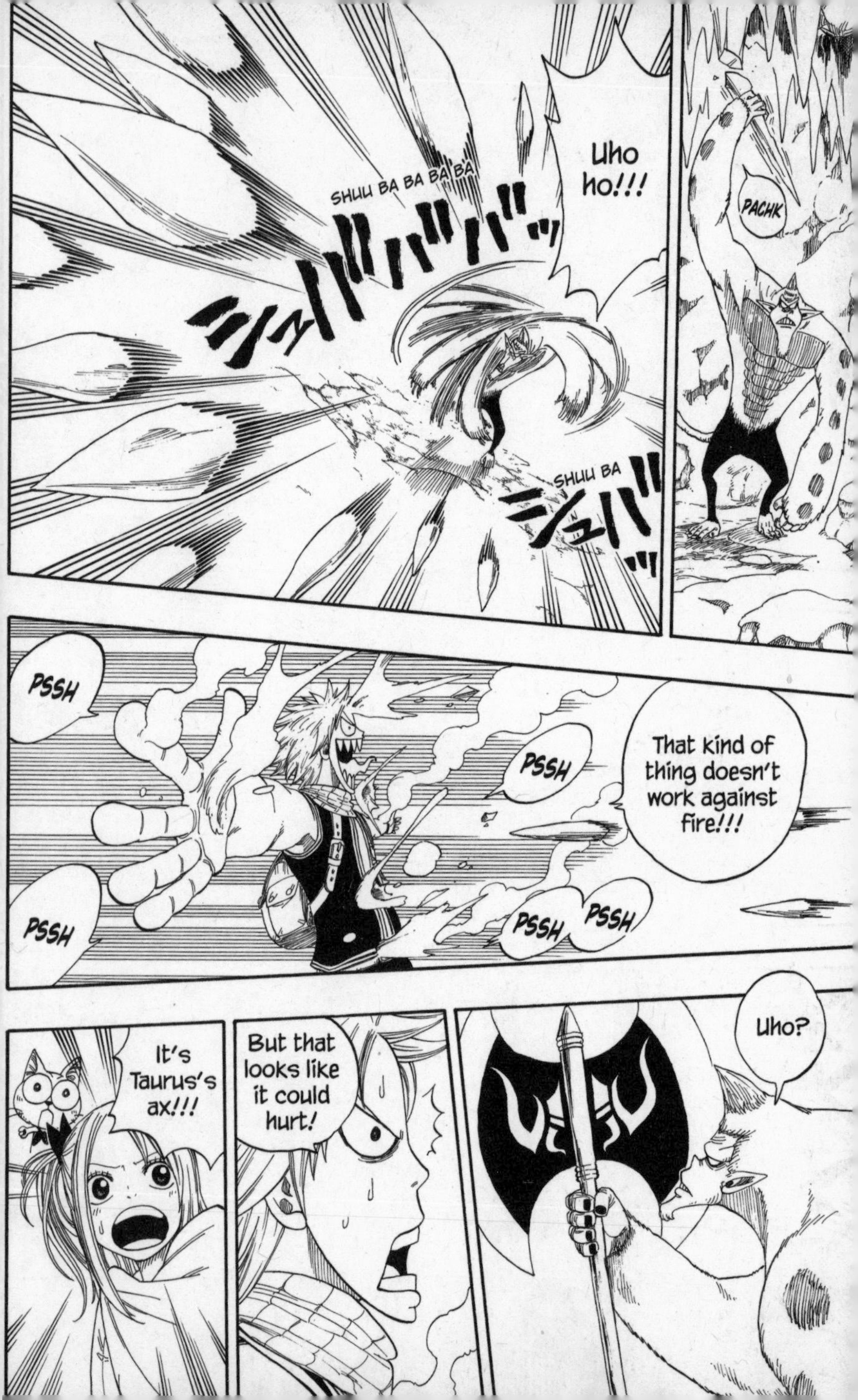
PACHK
Uho ho!!!
SHUU BA BA BA BA
SHUU BA
That kind of thing doesn't work against fire!!!
PSSH
PSSH
PSSH
PSSH
PSSH
Uho?
But that looks like it could hurt!
It's Taurus's ax!!!

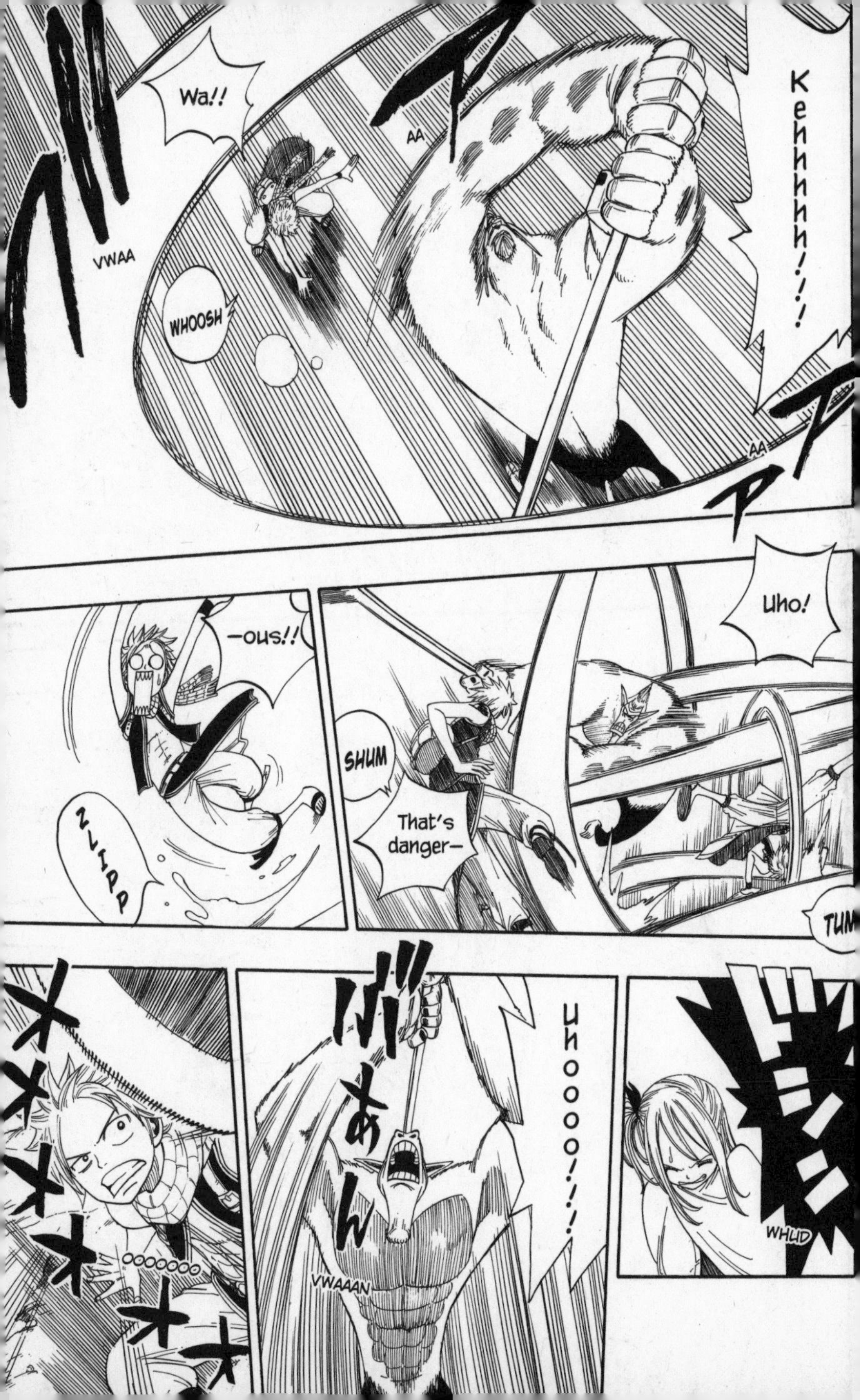
Kehhhhh!!!
AA
AA
Wa!!
WHOOSH
VWAA
Uho!
TUM
That's danger-
SHUM
-ous!!
ZLIPP
WHUD
Uhoooooo!!!
VWAAAN
OOOOOOO

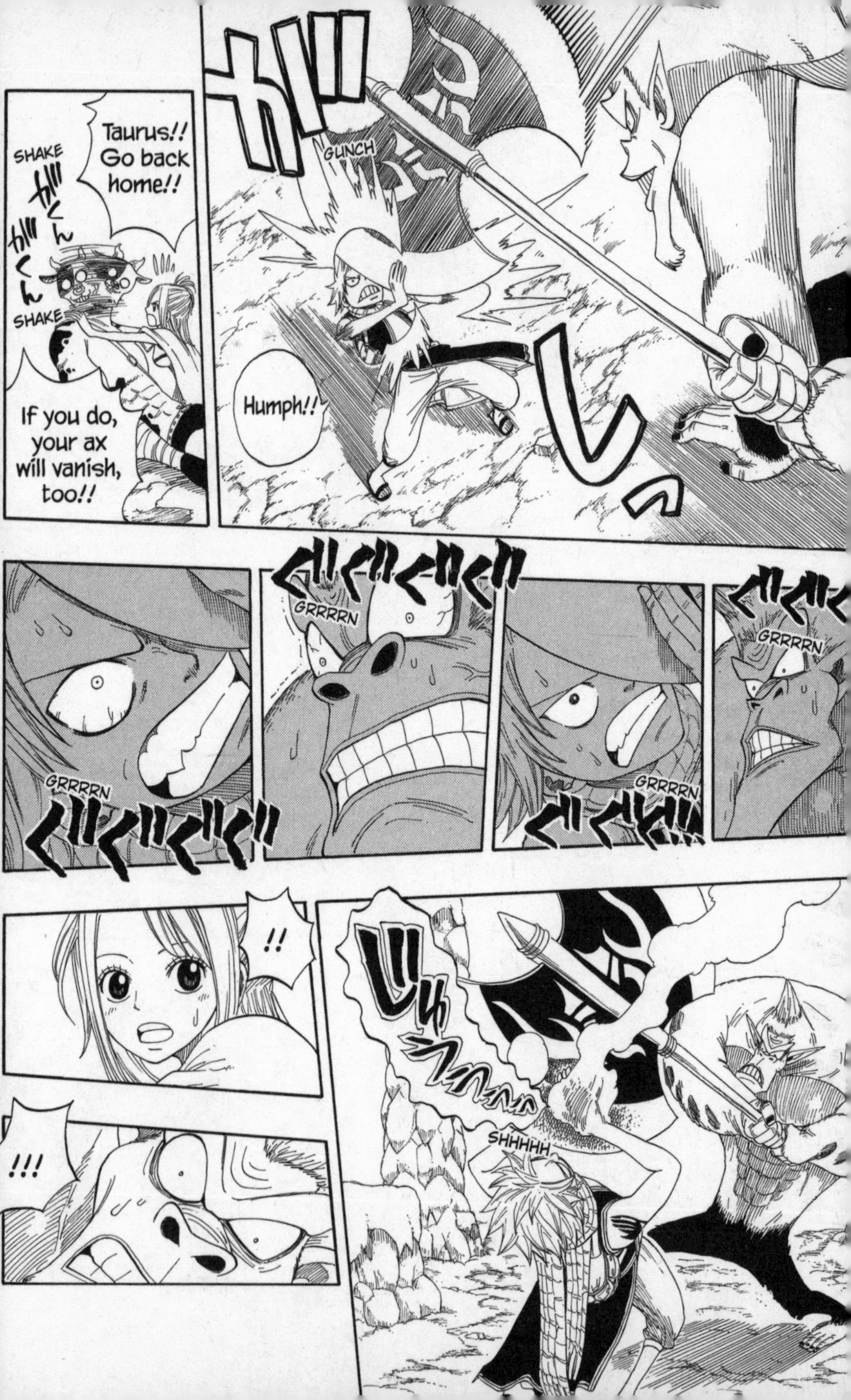
GUNCH
Humph!!
Taurus!! Go back home!!
SHAKE
SHAKE
If you do, your ax will vanish, too!!
GRRRRN
GRRRRN
GRRRRN
GRRRRN
SHHHHH
!!
!!!

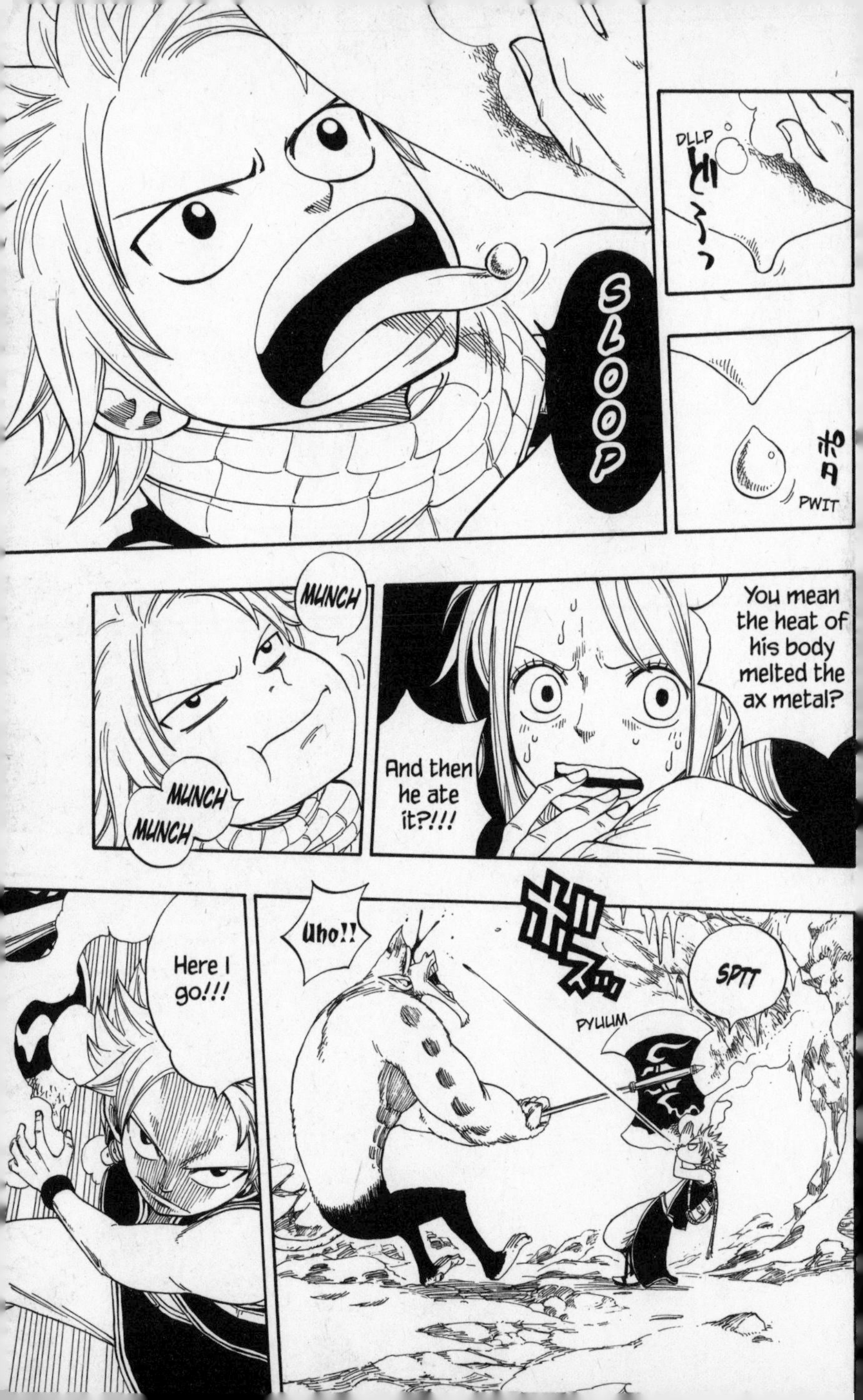
DLLP
どろっ
ポタ
PWIT
SLOOP
You mean the heat of his body melted the ax metal?
And then he ate it?!!!
MUNCH
MUNCH
MUNCH
SPTT
Uho!!
PYUUM
Here I go!!!

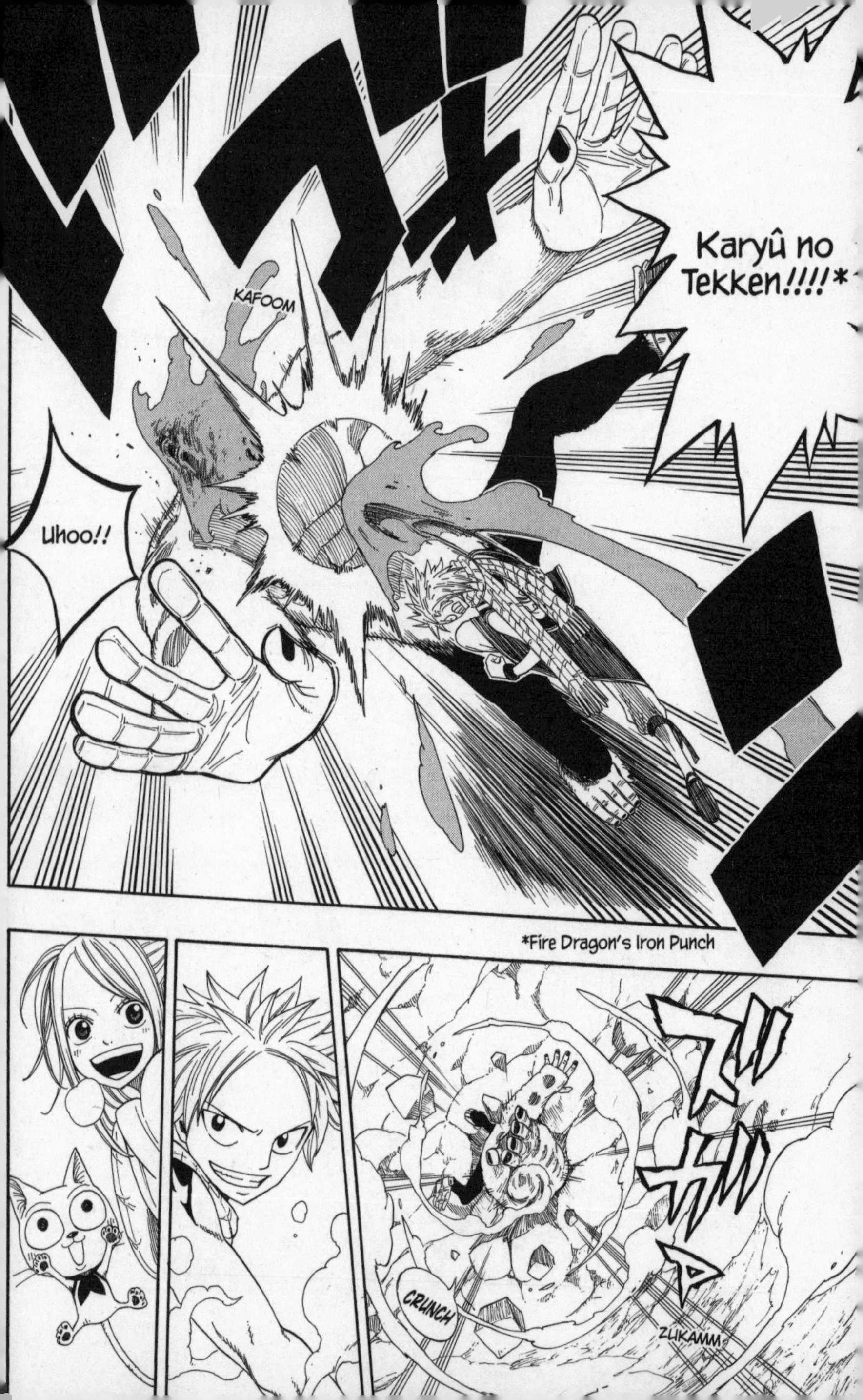
Karyû no Tekken!!!!*
KAFOOM
Uhoo!!
CRUNCH
ZUKAMM
*Fire Dragon's Iron Punch

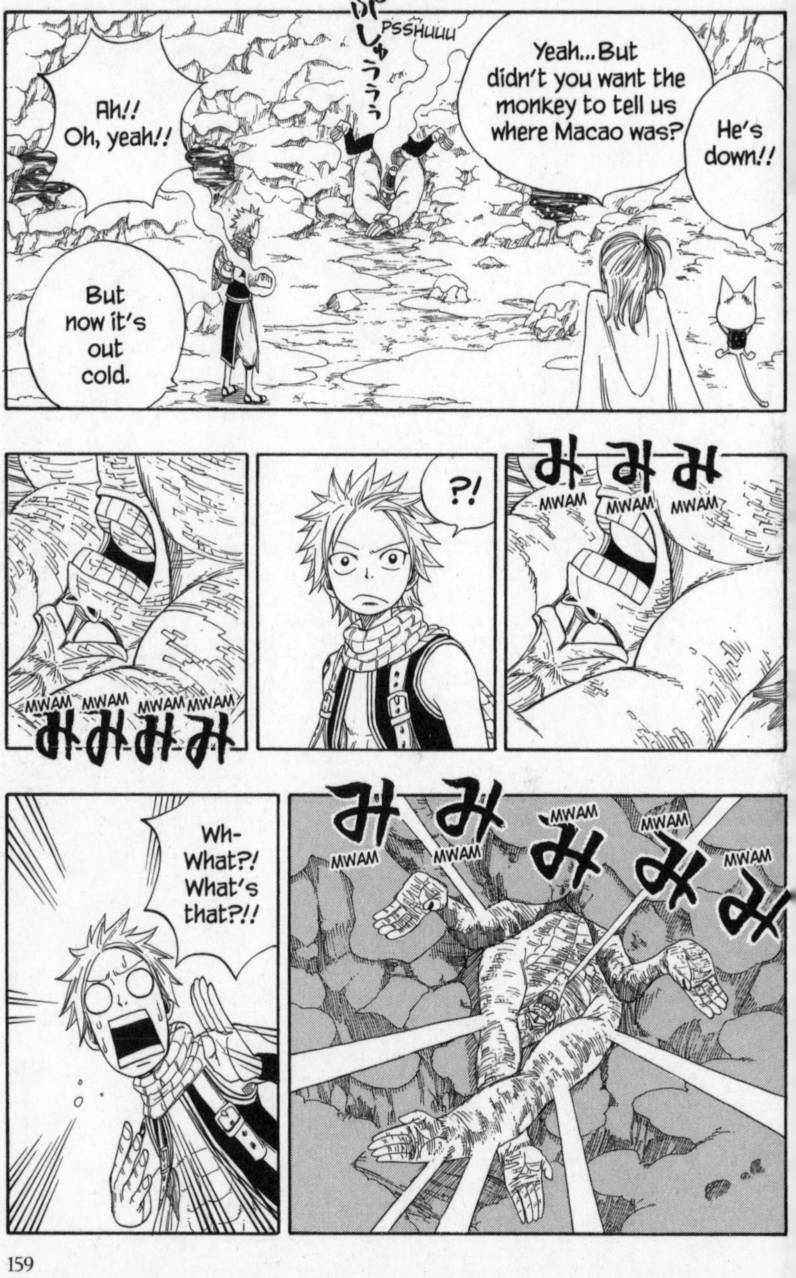
He's down!!
Yeah...But didn't you want the monkey to tell us where Macao was?
PSSHUUU
Ah!! Oh, yeah!!
But now it's out cold.
みみみ
MWAM MWAM MWAM
?!
MWAM MWAM MWAM MWAM
みみみみ
みみみみみ
MWAM MWAM MWAM MWAM MWAM
Wh- What?! What's that?!!

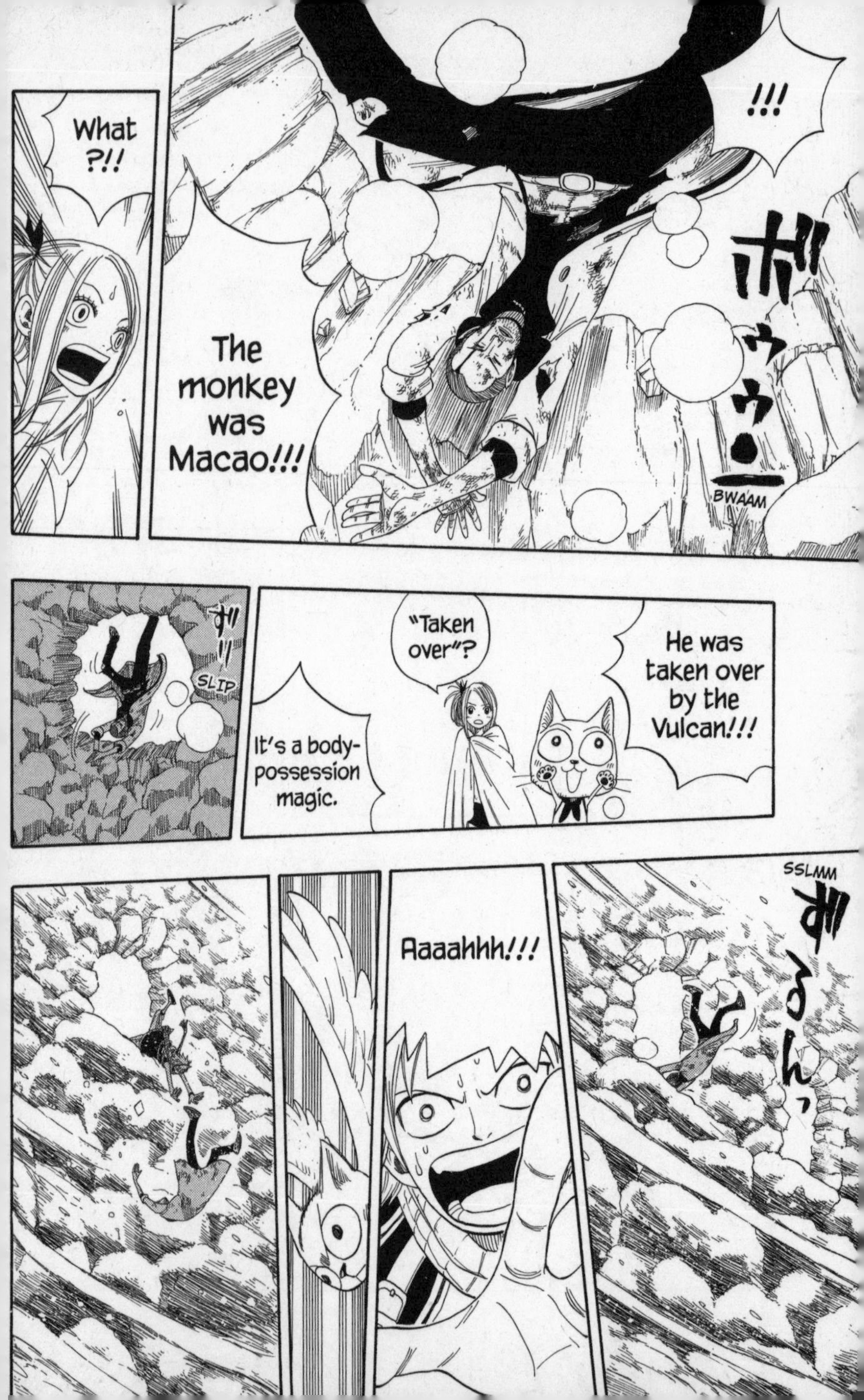
!!!
ボウウ
BWAAM
The monkey was Macao!!!
What ?!!
He was taken over by the Vulcan!!!
"Taken over"?
It's a body-possession magic.
SLIP
SSLMM
するん
Aaaahhh!!!

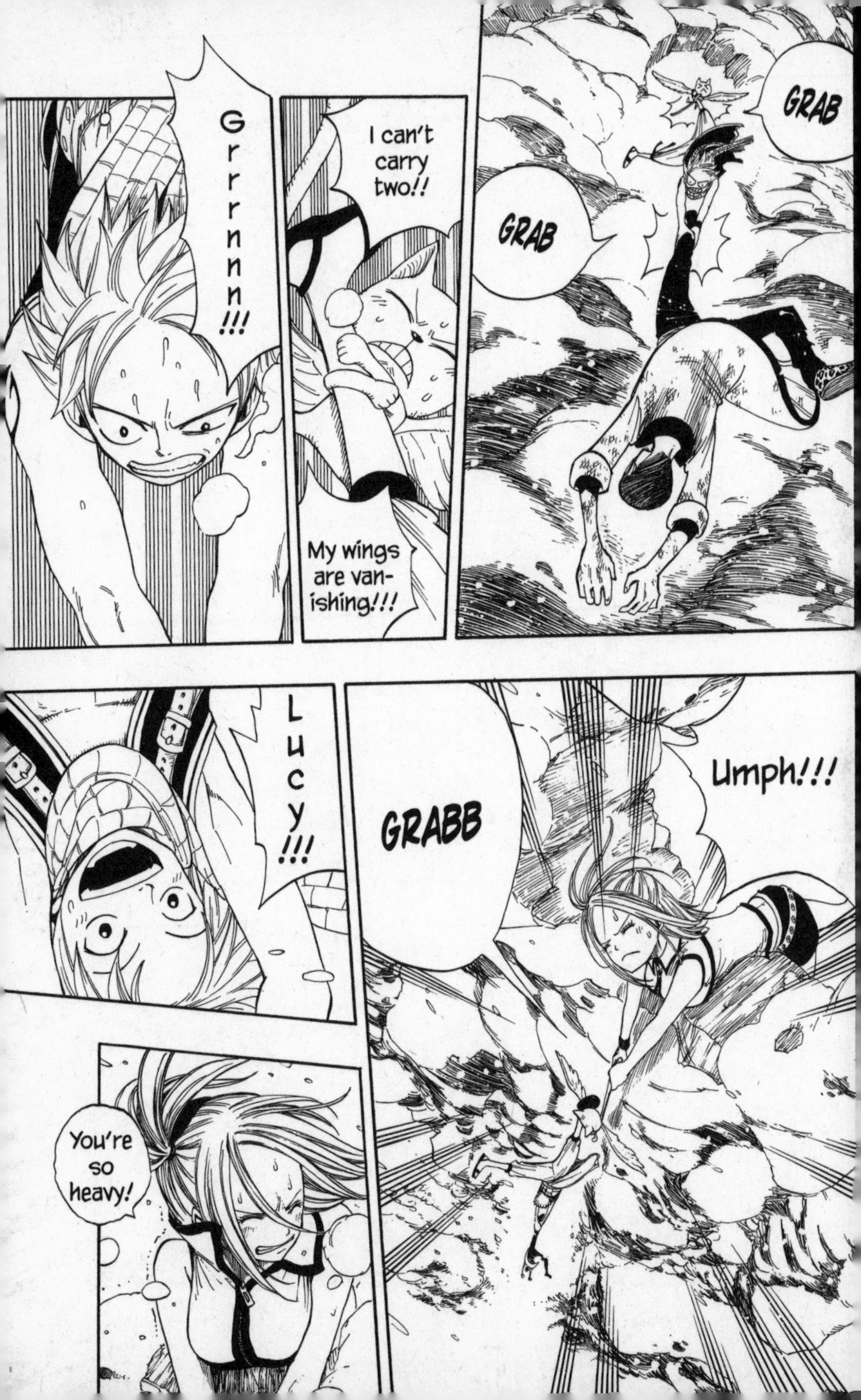
GRAB
GRAB
I can't carry two!!
My wings are van-ishing!!!
Grrrnnn!!!
Umph!!!
GRABB
Lucy!!!
You're so heavy!

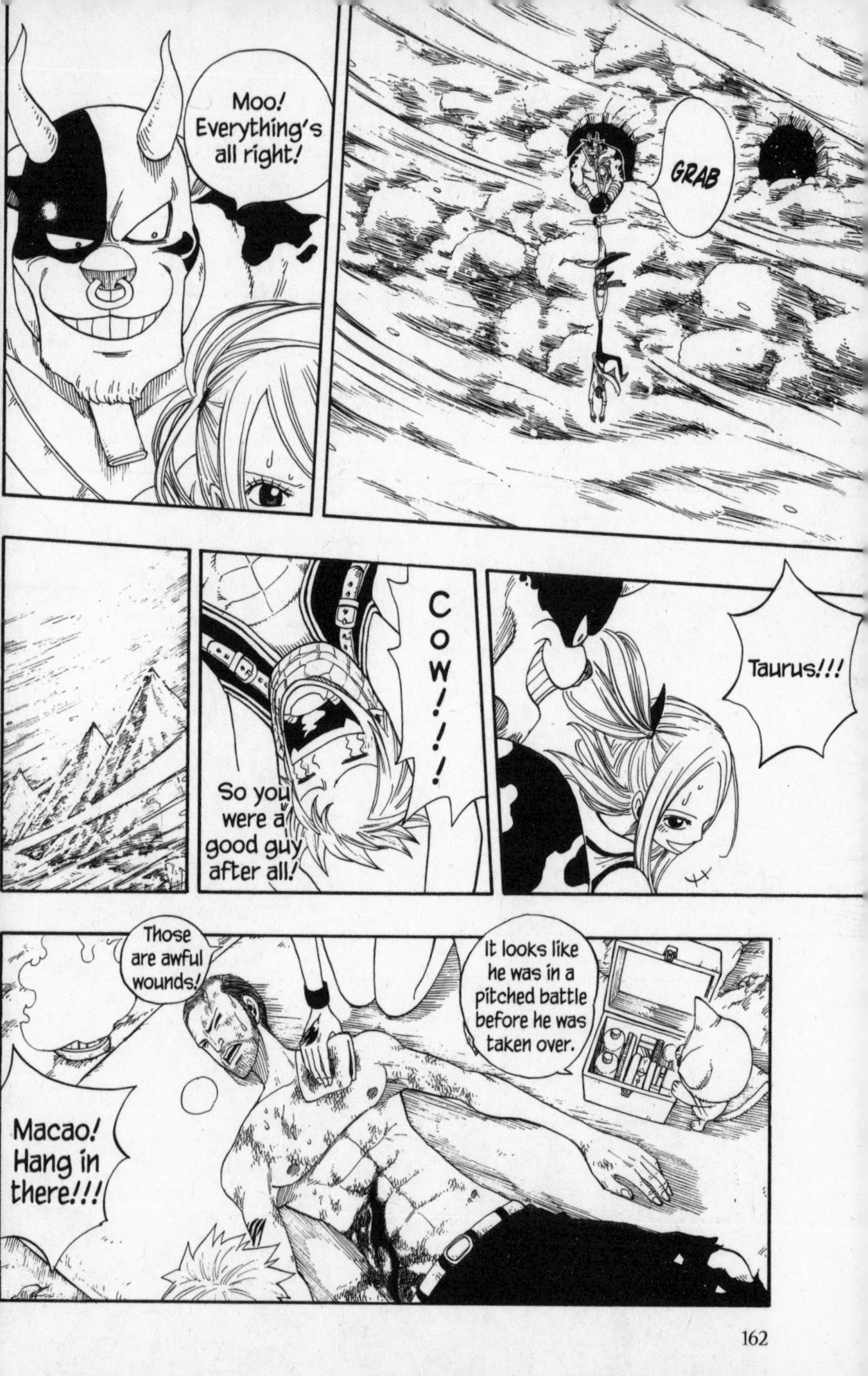
GRAB
Moo! Everything's all right!
Taurus!!!
COW!!!
So you were a good guy after all!
It looks like he was in a pitched battle before he was taken over.
Those are awful wounds!
Macao! Hang in there!!!

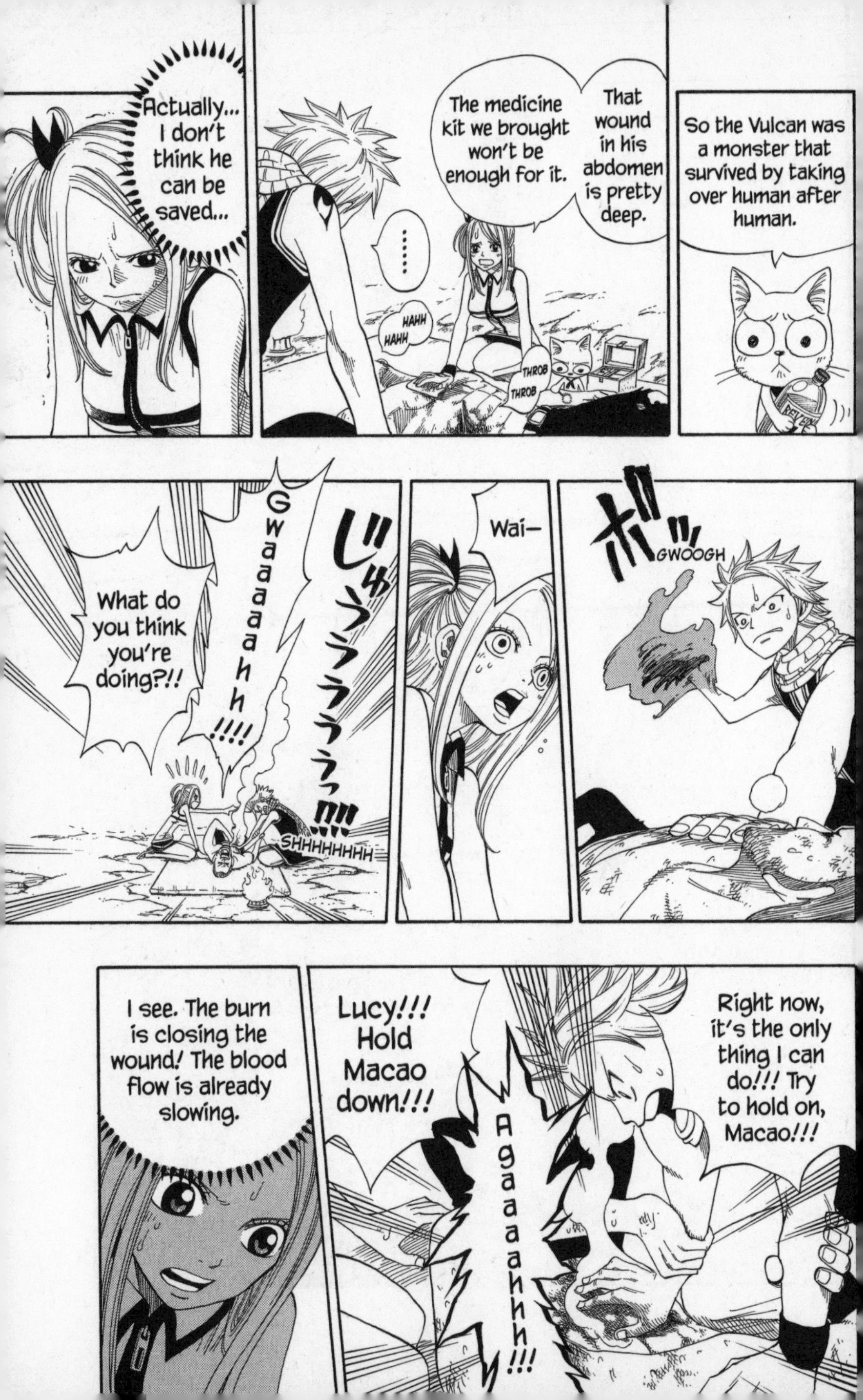
So the Vulcan was a monster that survived by taking over human after human.
That wound in his abdomen is pretty deep.
The medicine kit we brought won't be enough for it.
......
HAHH HAHH
THROB THROB
Actually... I don't think he can be saved...
GWOOGH
Wai–
Gwaaaaaahh!!!!
What do you think you're doing?!!
SHHHHHHHH
Right now, it's the only thing I can do!!! Try to hold on, Macao!!!
Lucy!!! Hold Macao down!!!
Agaaaaahhh!!!
I see. The burn is closing the wound! The blood flow is already slowing.

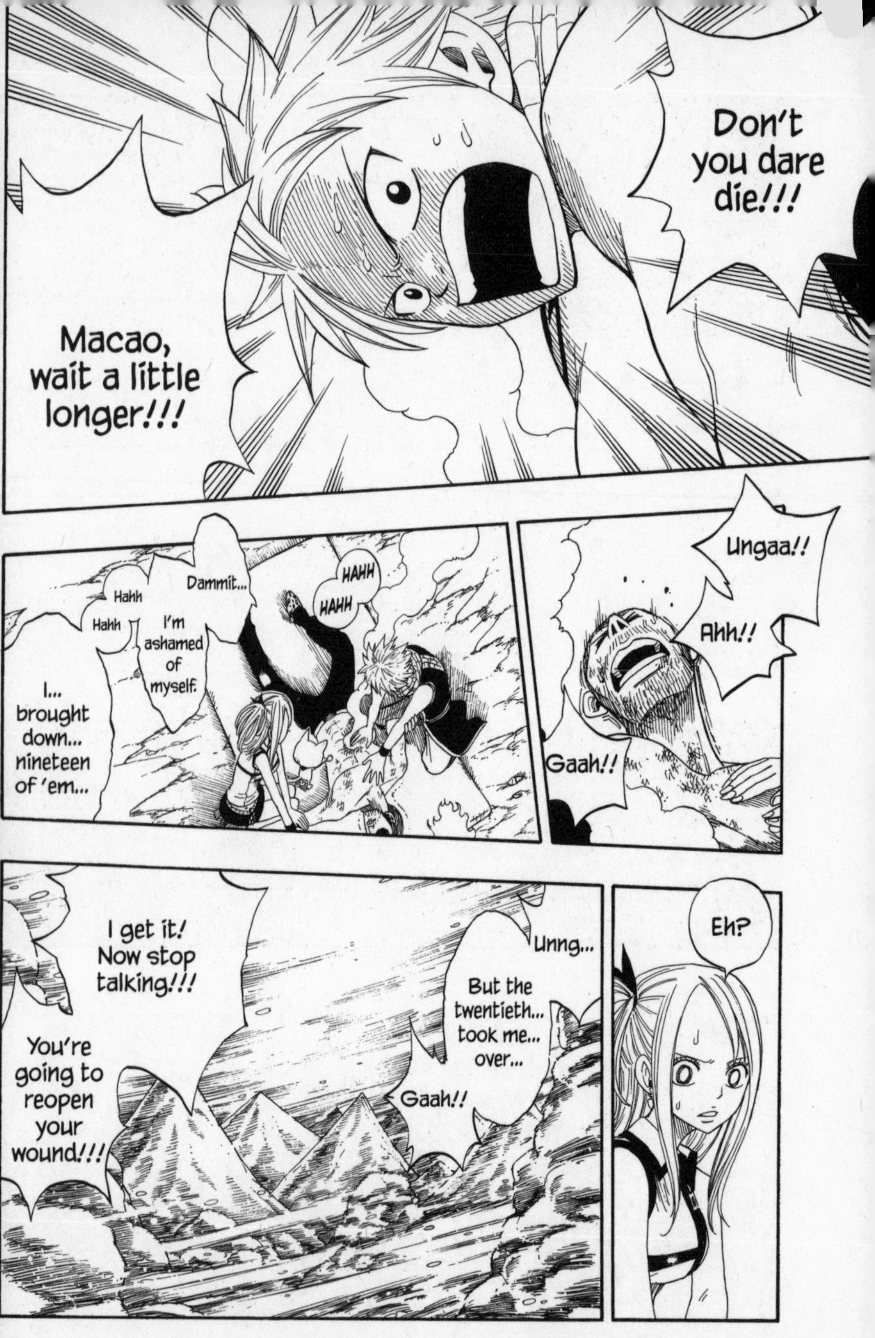
Don't you dare die!!!
Macao, wait a little longer!!!
Ungaa!!
Ahh!!
Gaah!!
HAHH HAHH
Dammit... I'm ashamed of myself.
Hahh Hahh
I... brought down... nineteen of 'em...
Eh?
Unng...
But the twentieth... took me... over...
Gaah!!
I get it! Now stop talking!!!
You're going to reopen your wound!!!

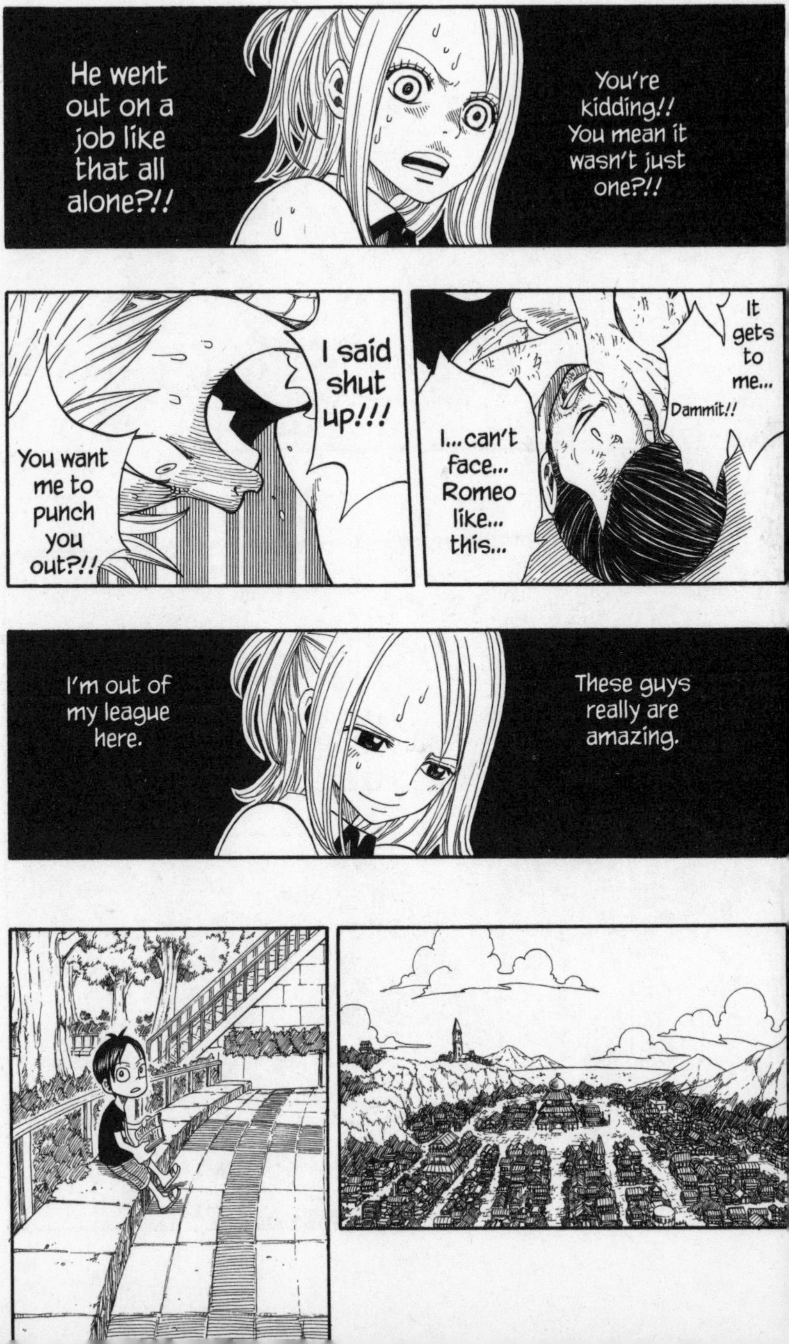
You're kidding!! You mean it wasn't just one?!!
He went out on a job like that all alone?!!
It gets to me...
Dammit!!
I...can't face... Romeo like... this...
I said shut up!!!
You want me to punch you out?!!
These guys really are amazing.
I'm out of my league here.

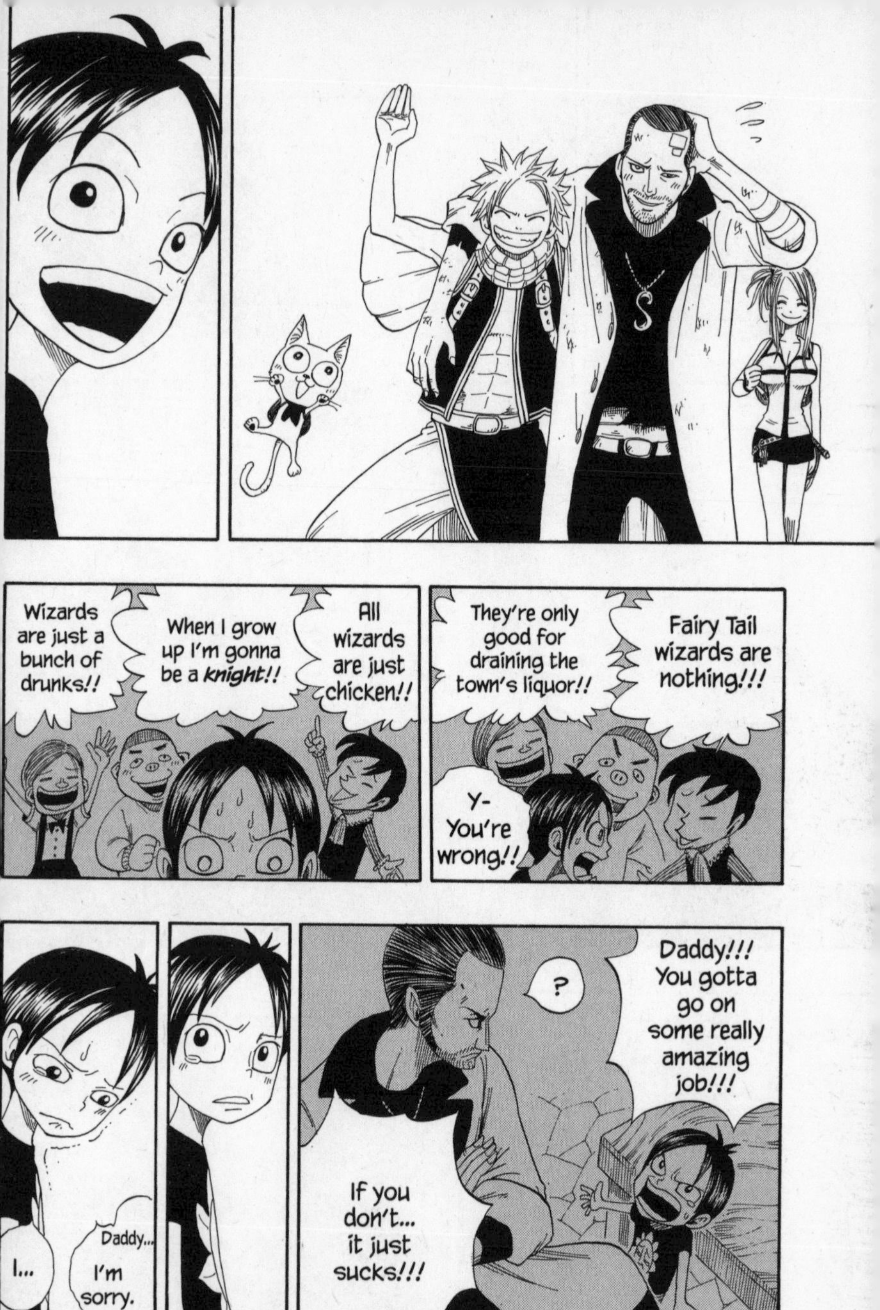
Fairy Tail wizards are nothing!!!
They're only good for draining the town's liquor!!
Y- You're wrong!!
All wizards are just chicken!!
When I grow up I'm gonna be a *knight*!!
Wizards are just a bunch of drunks!!
Daddy!!! You gotta go on some really amazing job!!!
?
If you don't... it just sucks!!!
Daddy... I'm sorry.
I...

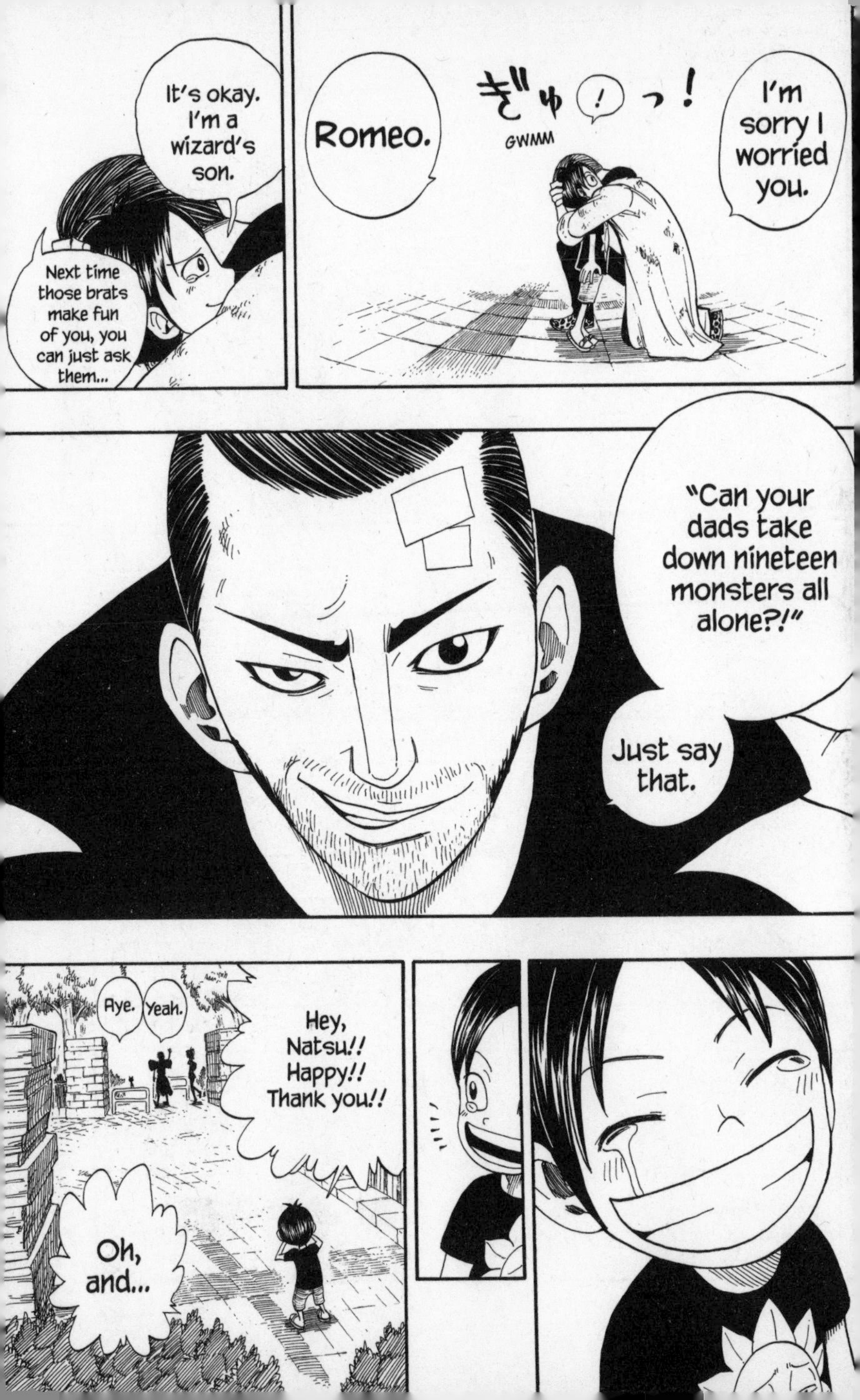
I'm sorry I worried you.
ぎゅっ!
GWMM
!
Romeo.
It's okay. I'm a wizard's son.
Next time those brats make fun of you, you can just ask them...
"Can your dads take down nineteen monsters all alone?!"
Just say that.
Hey, Natsu!! Happy!! Thank you!!
Aye.
Yeah.
Oh, and...

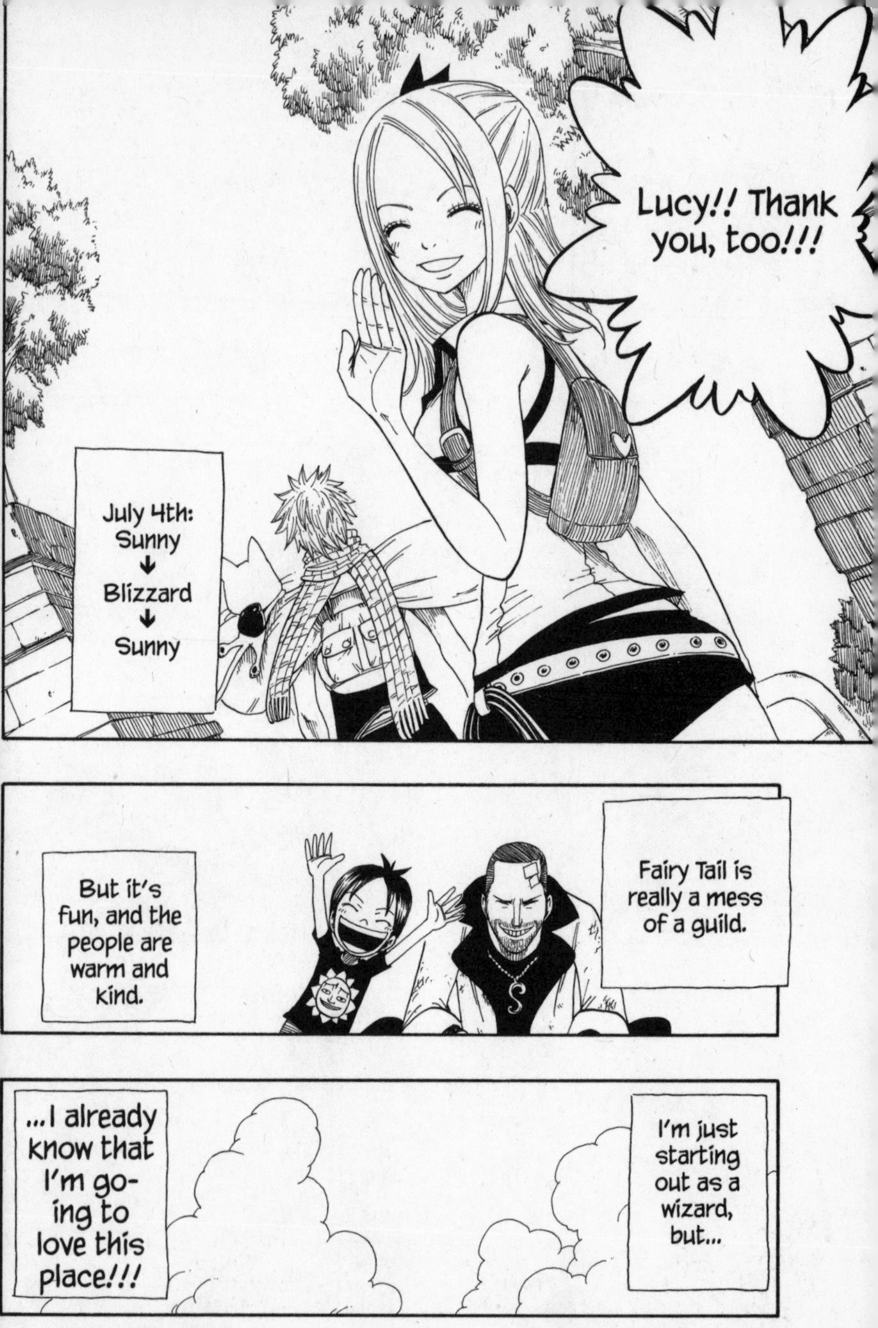
Lucy!! Thank you, too!!!
July 4th: Sunny ↓ Blizzard ↓ Sunny
Fairy Tail is really a mess of a guild.
But it's fun, and the people are warm and kind.
I'm just starting out as a wizard, but...
...I already know that I'm going to love this place!!!

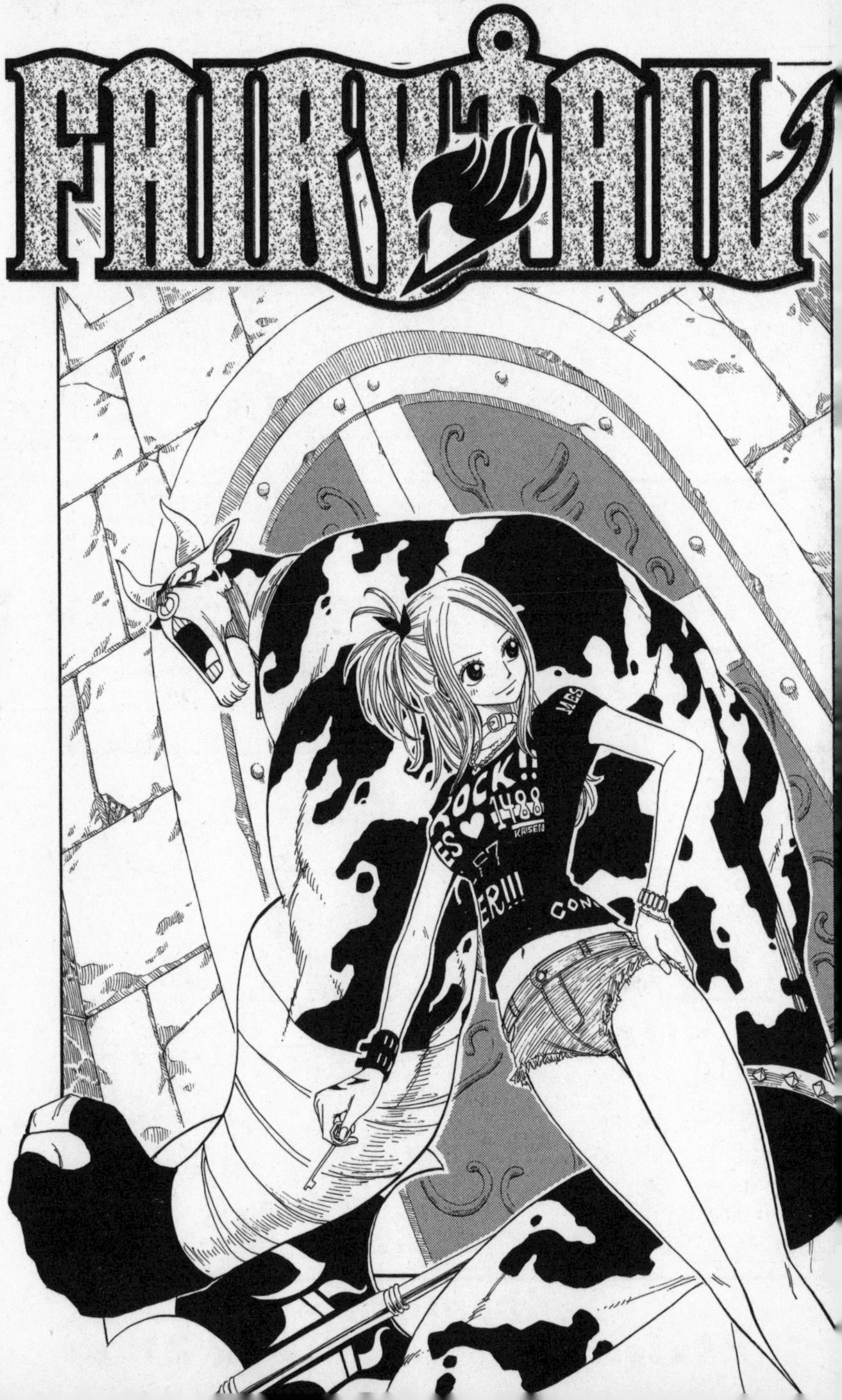
FAIRY TAIL
ROCK!!
1488
KAISEN

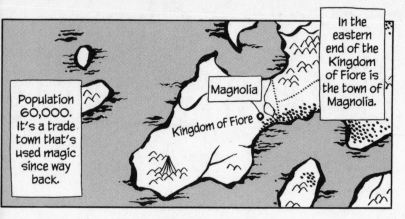

In the eastern end of the Kingdom of Fiore is the town of Magnolia.

Population 60,000. It's a trade town that's used magic since way back.

Magnolia

Kingdom of Fiore

Go past Kardia Cathedral, which towers above the center of town...

...and you'll find the only wizard guild in the area, Fairy Tail.

Fairy Tail

Kardia Cathedral

And!!

This is where I've taken up residence. (Rent: 70,000 J)

It's a little expensive, but the shopping district is close, so it's very convenient.

Chapter 4: The Celestial Spirit of Canis Minor

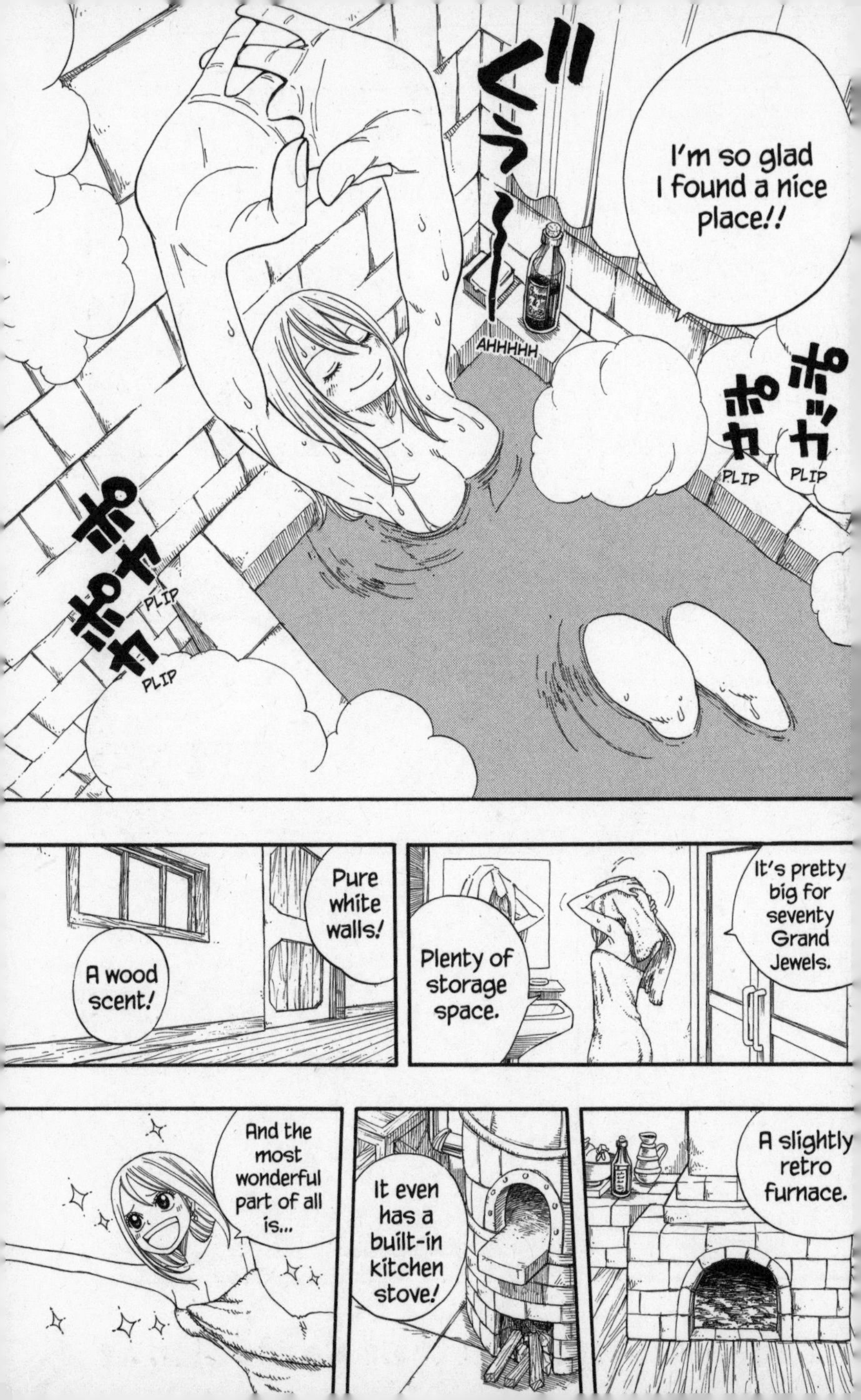
AHHHHH
I'm so glad I found a nice place!!
PLIP
PLIP
PLIP
PLIP
It's pretty big for seventy Grand Jewels.
Plenty of storage space.
Pure white walls!
A wood scent!
A slightly retro furnace.
It even has a built-in kitchen stove!
And the most wonderful part of all is...

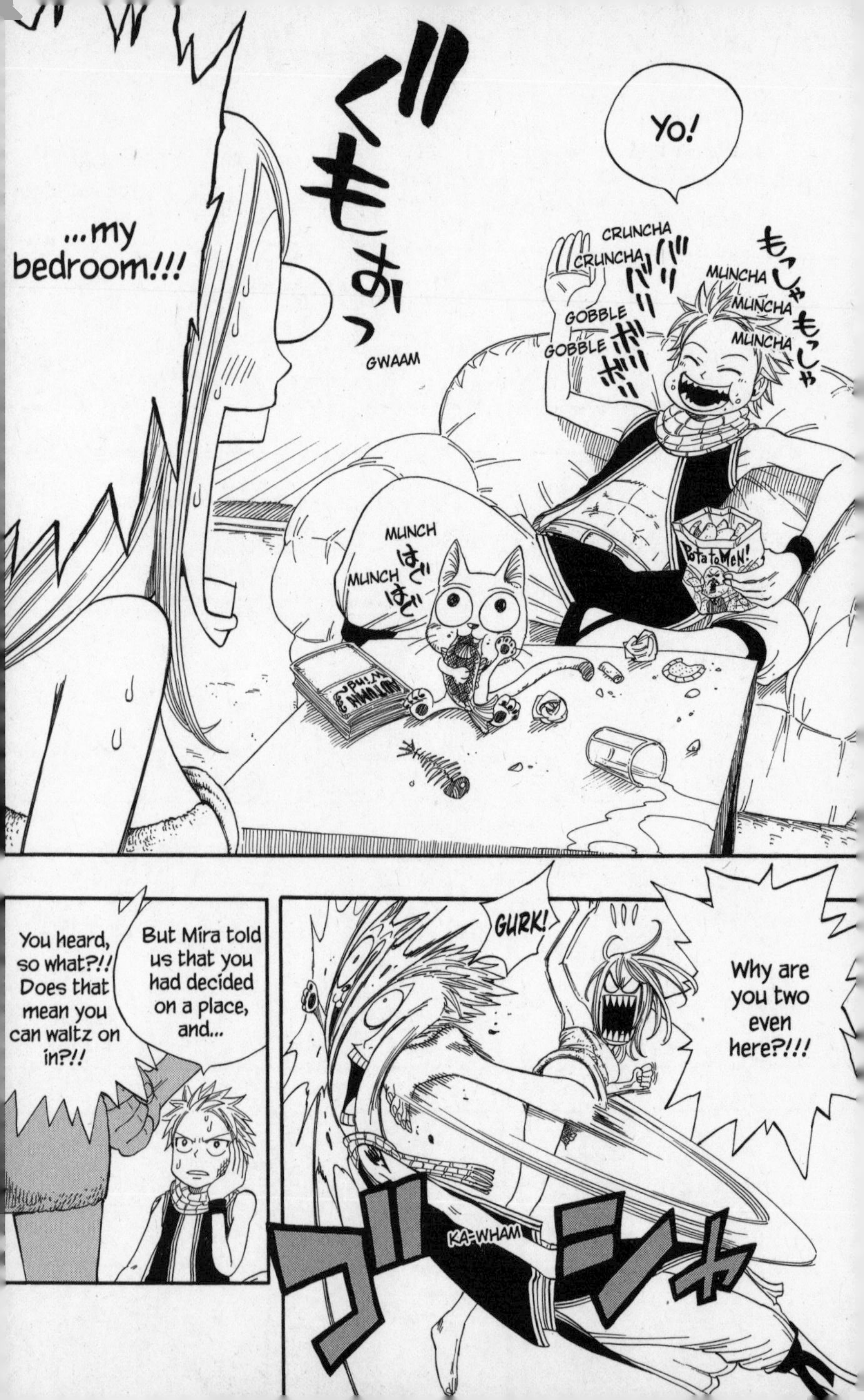
Yo!
CRUNCHA
CRUNCHA
バリバリ
MUNCHA
MUNCHA
MUNCHA
もっしゃもっしゃ
GOBBLE
GOBBLE
ボリボリ
ぐもぉっ
GWAAM
...my bedroom!!!
MUNCH
MUNCH
はぐはぐ
Why are you two even here?!!!
GURK!
KA-WHAM
But Mira told us that you had decided on a place, and...
You heard, so what?!! Does that mean you can waltz on in?!!

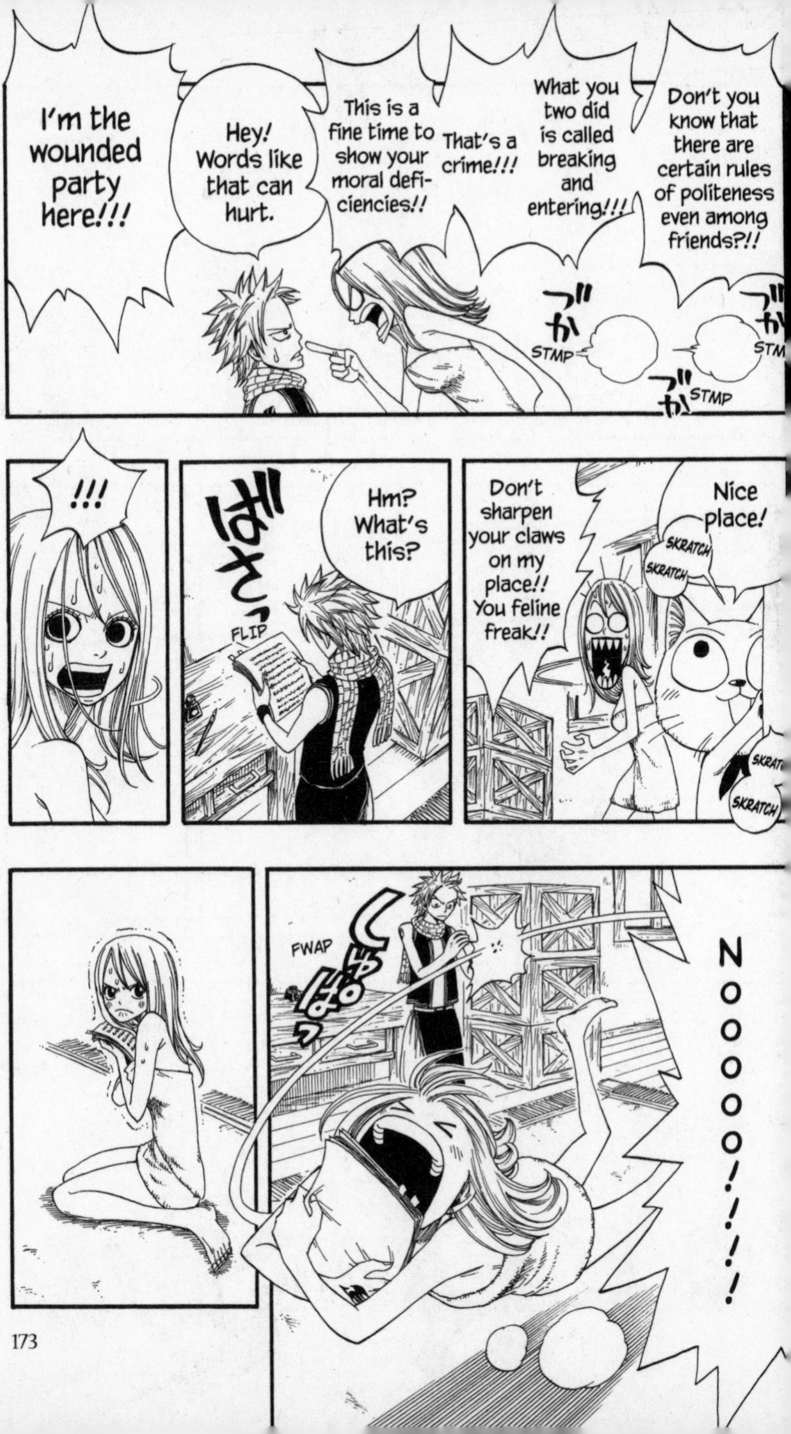
Don't you know that there are certain rules of politeness even among friends?!!
What you two did is called breaking and entering!!!
That's a crime!!!
This is a fine time to show your moral deficiencies!!
Hey! Words like that can hurt.
I'm the wounded party here!!!
STMP
STMP
STMP
Nice place!
SKRATCH
SKRATCH
SKRATCH
SKRATCH
Don't sharpen your claws on my place!! You feline freak!!
FLIP
Hm? What's this?
!!!
NOOOOOO!!!!!
FWAP

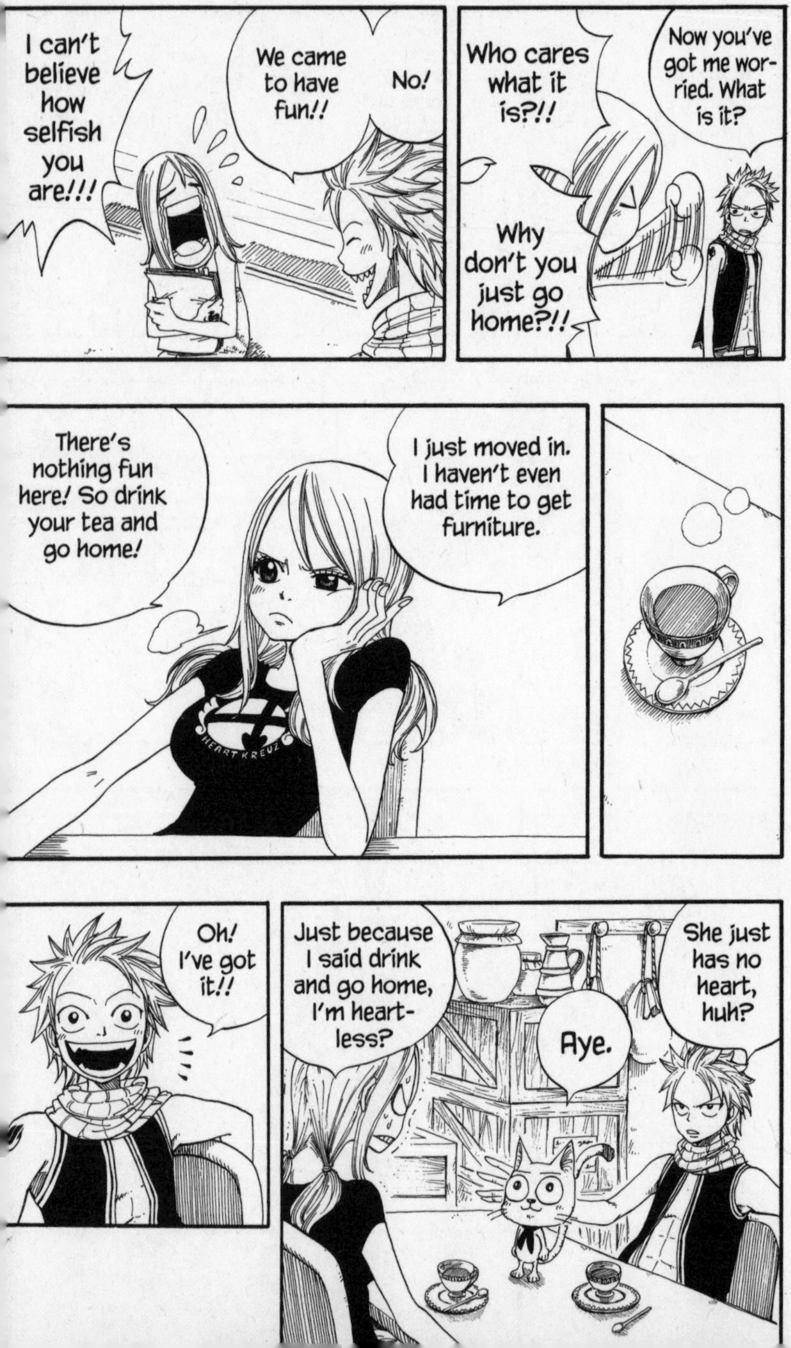

Now you've got me worried. What is it?
Who cares what it is?!!
Why don't you just go home?!!
No!
We came to have fun!!
I can't believe how selfish you are!!!
I just moved in. I haven't even had time to get furniture.
There's nothing fun here! So drink your tea and go home!
HEART KREUZ
She just has no heart, huh?
Aye.
Just because I said drink and go home, I'm heartless?
Oh! I've got it!!

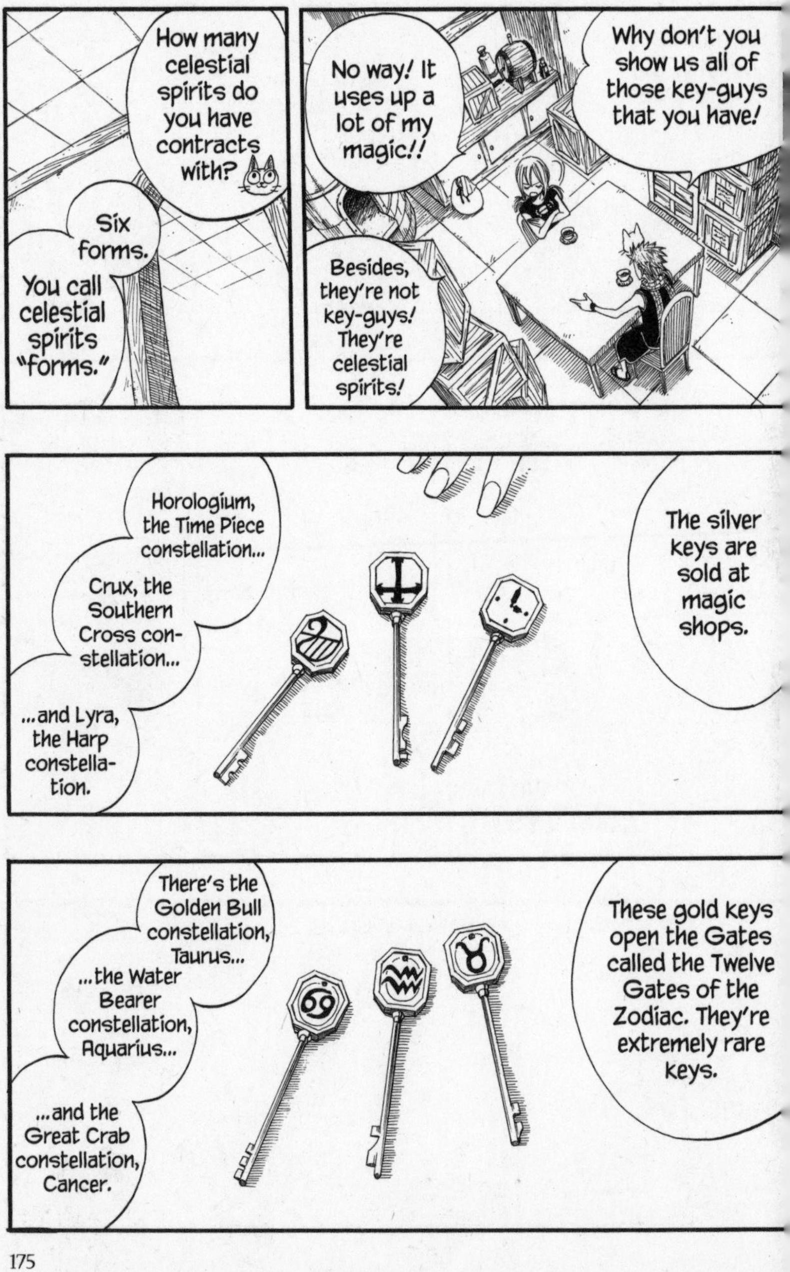
Why don't you show us all of those key-guys that you have!
No way! It uses up a lot of my magic!!
Besides, they're not key-guys! They're celestial spirits!
How many celestial spirits do you have contracts with?
Six forms.
You call celestial spirits "forms."
The silver keys are sold at magic shops.
Horologium, the Time Piece constellation...
Crux, the Southern Cross con-stellation...
...and Lyra, the Harp constella-tion.
These gold keys open the Gates called the Twelve Gates of the Zodiac. They're extremely rare keys.
There's the Golden Bull constellation, Taurus...
...the Water Bearer constellation, Aquarius...
...and the Great Crab constellation, Cancer.

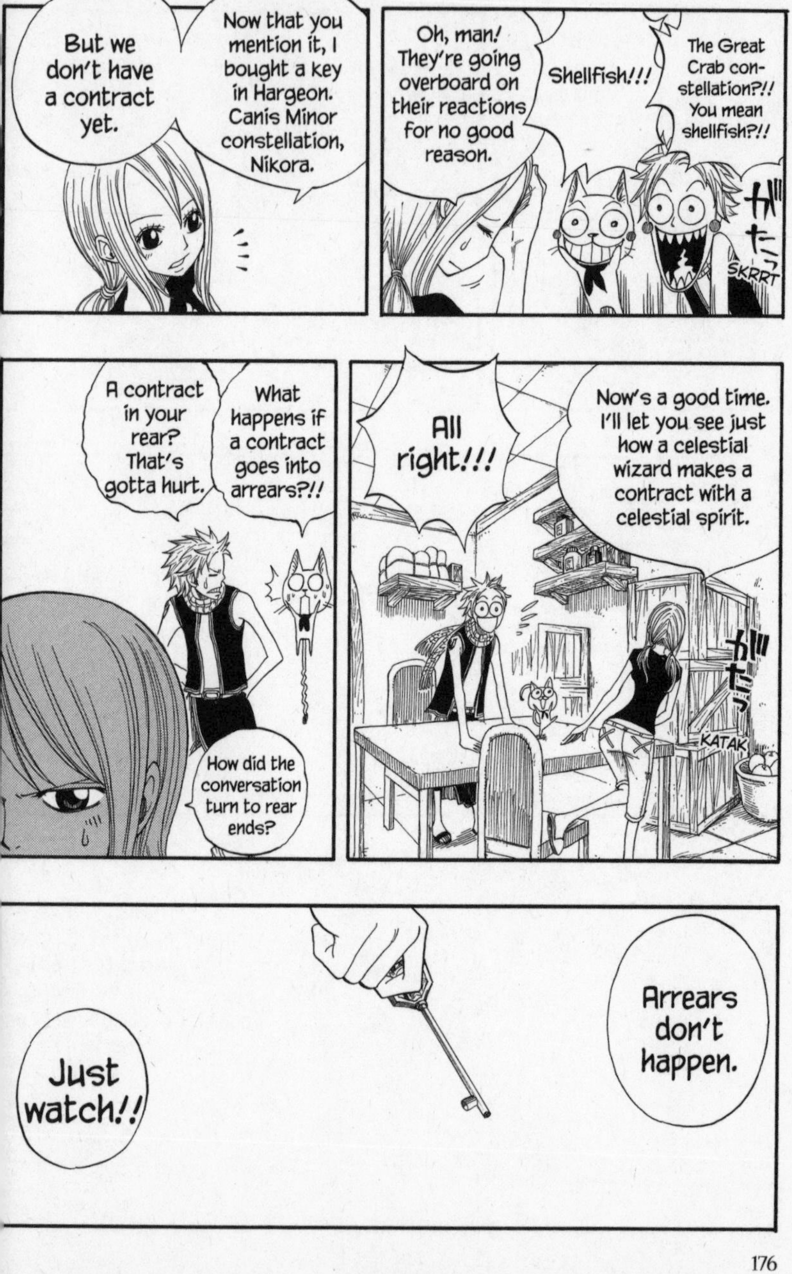
The Great Crab constellation?!! You mean shellfish?!!
Shellfish!!!
Oh, man! They're going overboard on their reactions for no good reason.
SKRRT
Now that you mention it, I bought a key in Hargeon. Canis Minor constellation, Nikora.
But we don't have a contract yet.
Now's a good time. I'll let you see just how a celestial wizard makes a contract with a celestial spirit.
All right!!!
KATAK
What happens if a contract goes into arrears?!!
A contract in your rear? That's gotta hurt.
How did the conversation turn to rear ends?
Arrears don't happen.
Just watch!!

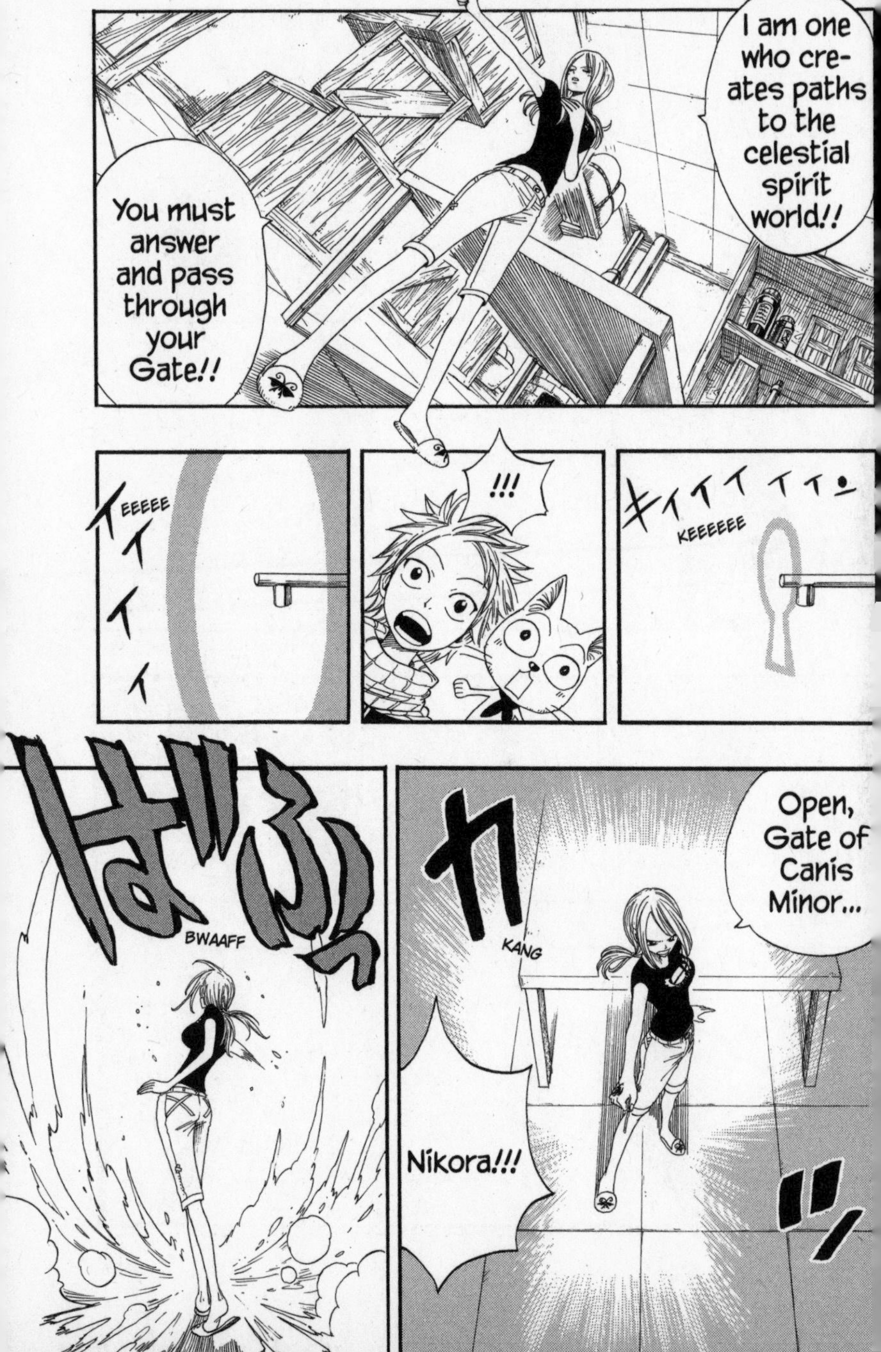
I am one who cre-ates paths to the celestial spirit world!!
You must answer and pass through your Gate!!
KEEEEEE
!!!
EEEEE
Open, Gate of Canis Minor...
KANG
Nikora!!!
BWAAFF

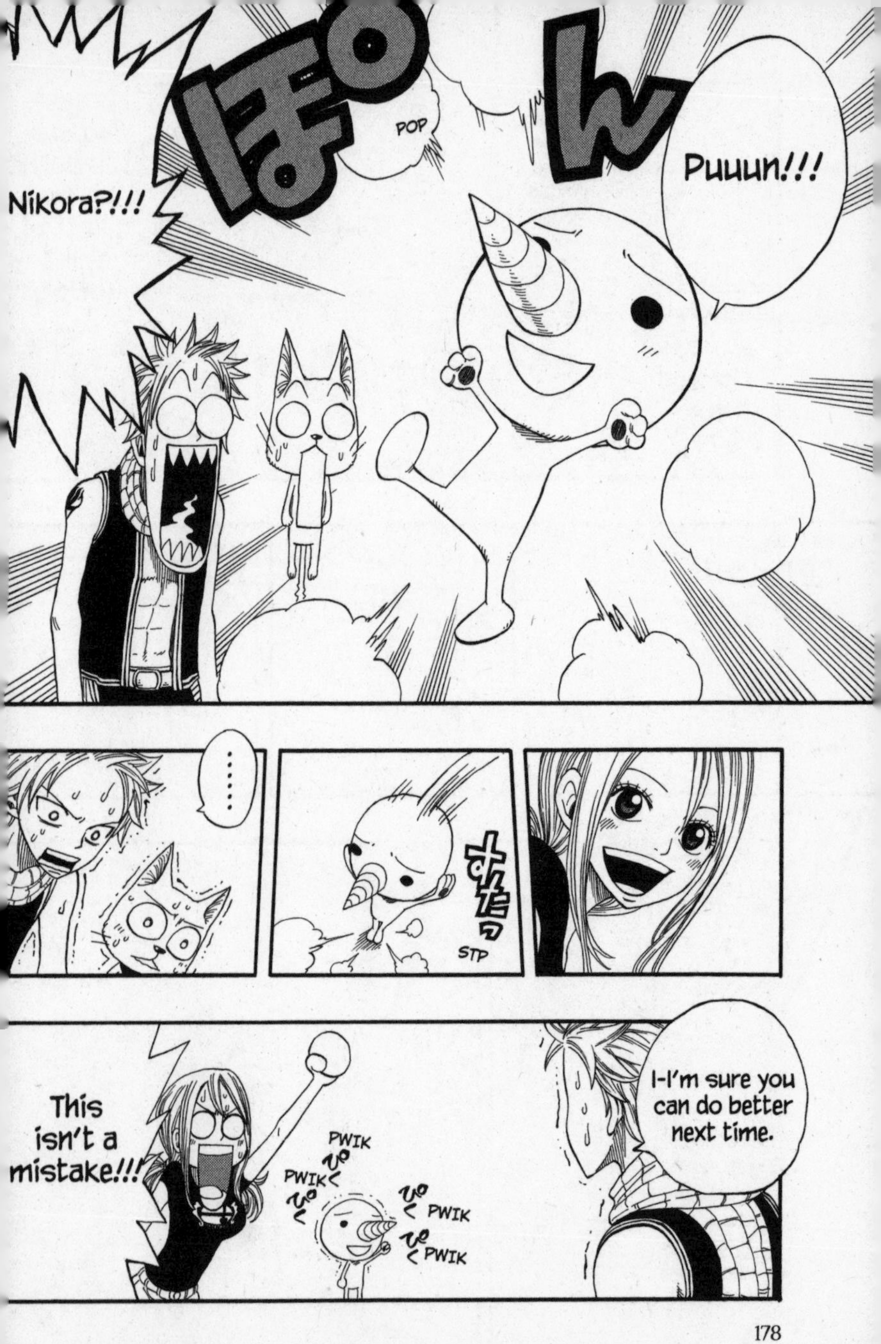
Puuun!!!
ぽん
POP
Nikora?!!!
すたっ
STP
......
I-I'm sure you can do better next time.
This isn't a mistake!!!
ぴく
PWIK
ぴく
PWIK
ぴく
PWIK
ぴく
PWIK

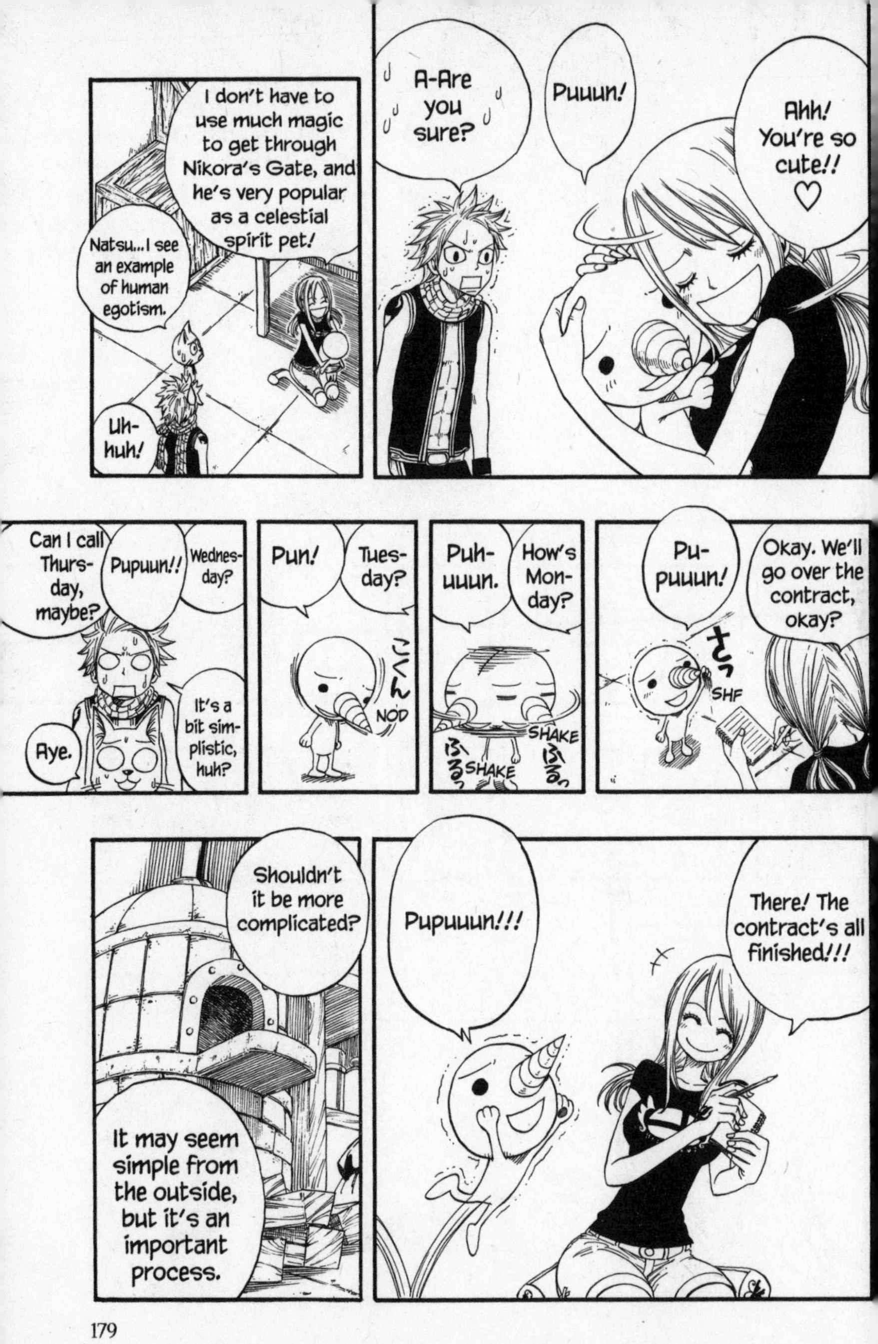
Ahh! You're so cute!! ♡
Puuun!
A-Are you sure?
I don't have to use much magic to get through Nikora's Gate, and he's very popular as a celestial spirit pet!
Natsu...I see an example of human egotism.
Uh-huh!
Okay. We'll go over the contract, okay?
Pu-puuun!
SHF
How's Mon-day?
Puh-uuun.
SHAKE
SHAKE
Tues-day?
Pun!
NOD
Wednes-day?
Pupuun!!
Can I call Thurs-day, maybe?
It's a bit sim-plistic, huh?
Aye.
There! The contract's all finished!!!
Pupuuun!!!
Shouldn't it be more complicated?
It may seem simple from the outside, but it's an important process.

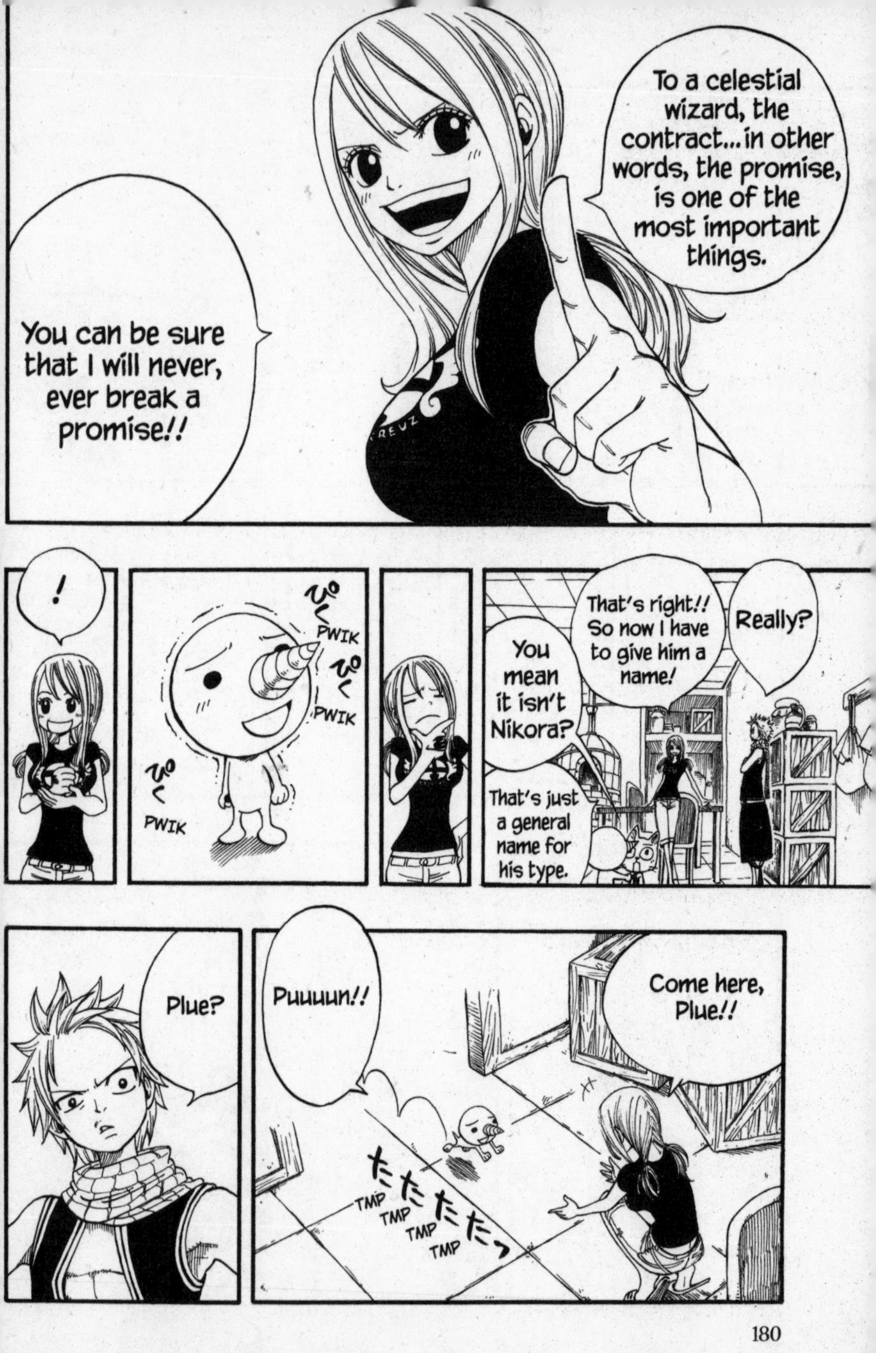
To a celestial wizard, the contract...in other words, the promise, is one of the most important things.
You can be sure that I will never, ever break a promise!!
Really?
That's right!! So now I have to give him a name!
You mean it isn't Nikora?
That's just a general name for his type.
ぴく PWIK
ぴく PWIK
ぴく PWIK
!
Come here, Plue!!
Puuuun!!
たたたたっ TMP TMP TMP TMP
Plue?

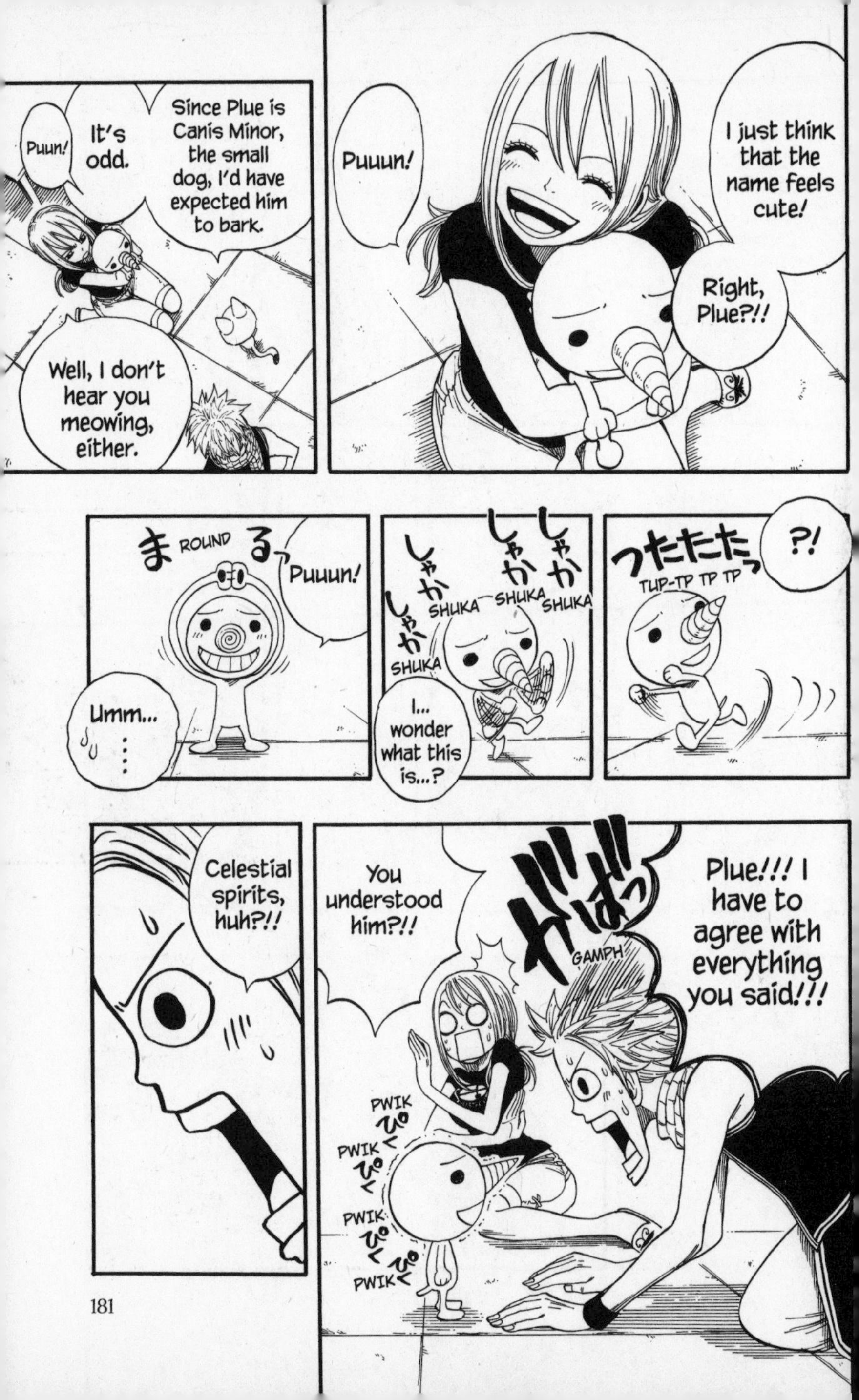
I just think that the name feels cute!
Right, Plue?!!
Puuun!
Since Plue is Canis Minor, the small dog, I'd have expected him to bark.
It's odd.
Puun!
Well, I don't hear you meowing, either.
?!
つたたたっ
TUP-TP TP TP
しゃか しゃか しゃか しゃか
SHUKA SHUKA SHUKA SHUKA
I... wonder what this is...?
まるっ
ROUND
Puuun!
Umm... ...
Plue!!! I have to agree with everything you said!!!
がばっ
GAMPH
You understood him?!!
ぴく ぴく ぴく ぴく
PWIK PWIK PWIK PWIK
Celestial spirits, huh?!!

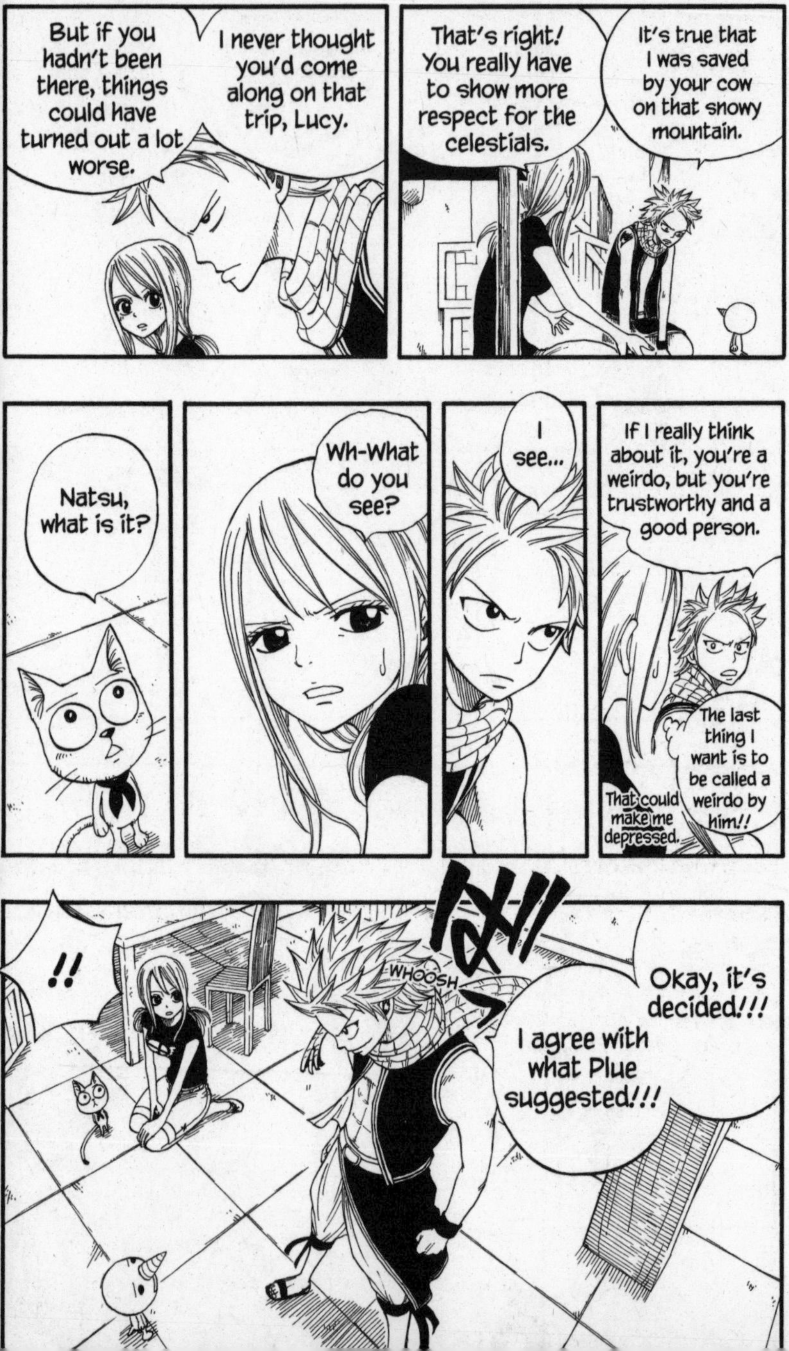
It's true that I was saved by your cow on that snowy mountain.
That's right! You really have to show more respect for the celestials.
I never thought you'd come along on that trip, Lucy.
But if you hadn't been there, things could have turned out a lot worse.
If I really think about it, you're a weirdo, but you're trustworthy and a good person.
The last thing I want is to be called a weirdo by him!!
That could make me depressed.
I see...
Wh-What do you see?
Natsu, what is it?
Okay, it's decided!!!
I agree with what Plue suggested!!!
WHOOSH
!!

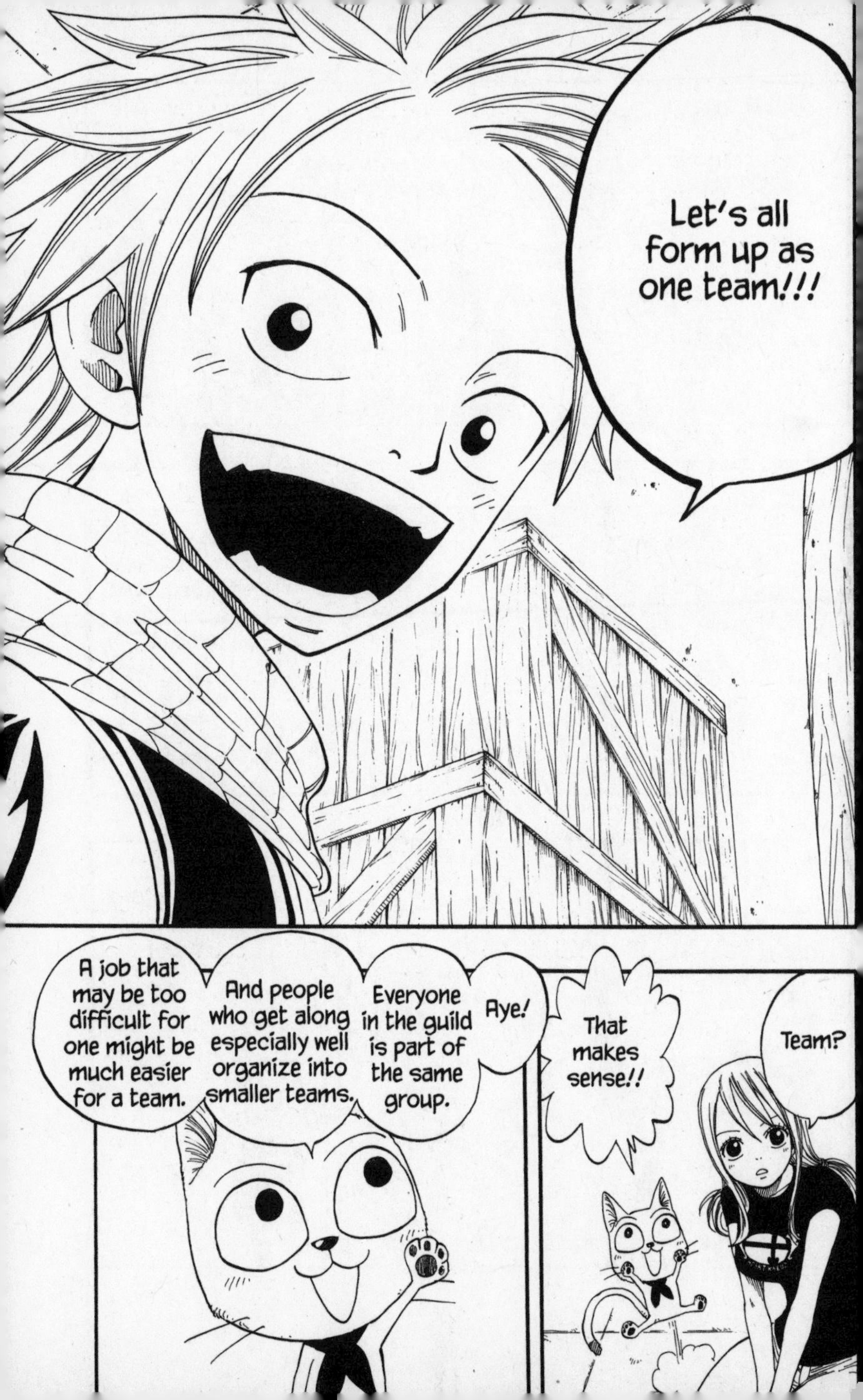
Let's all form up as one team!!!
Team?
That makes sense!!
Aye!
Everyone in the guild is part of the same group.
And people who get along especially well organize into smaller teams.
A job that may be too difficult for one might be much easier for a team.

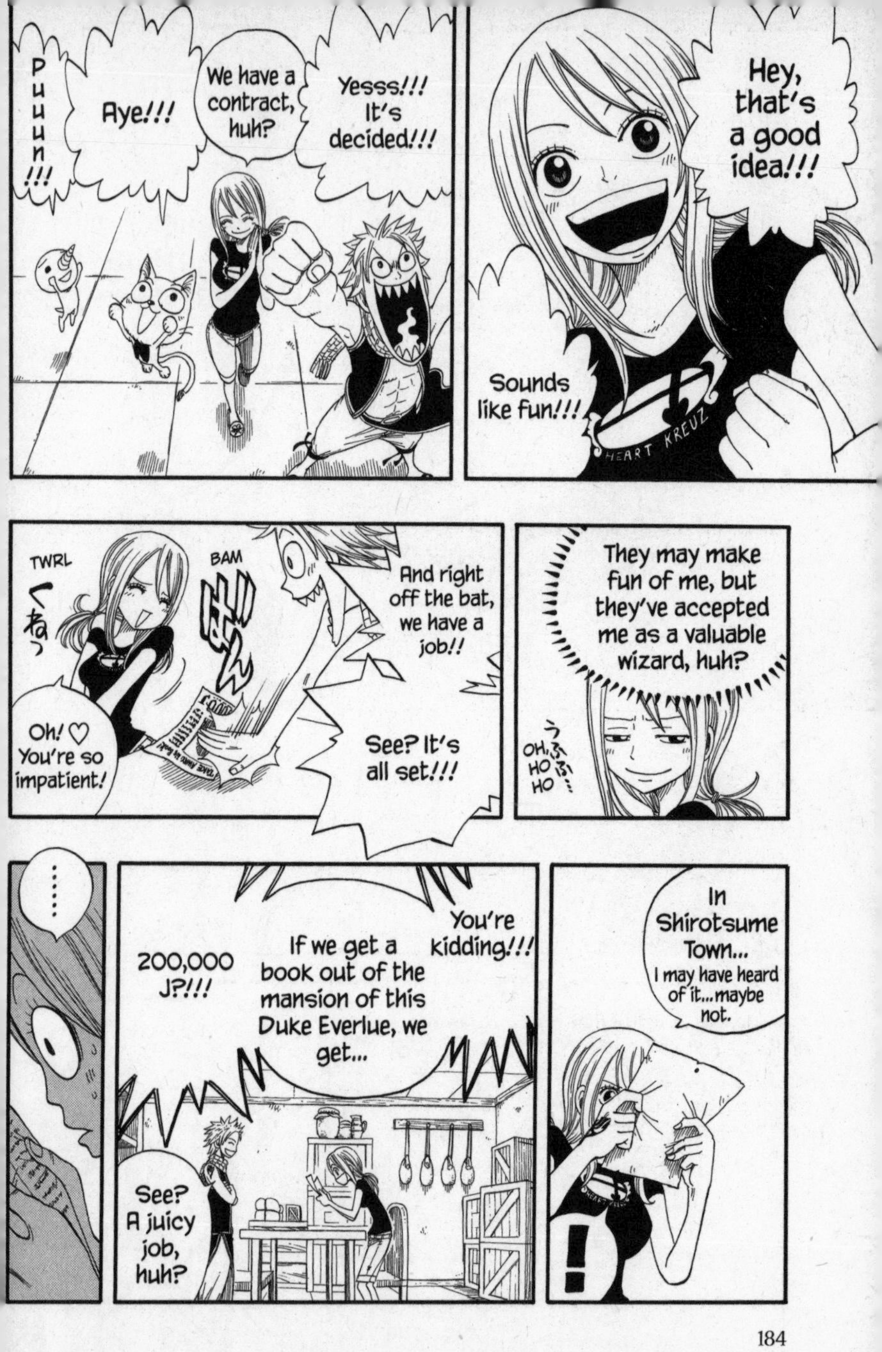
Hey, that's a good idea!!!
Sounds like fun!!!
Yesss!!! It's decided!!!
We have a contract, huh?
Aye!!!
Puuun!!!
They may make fun of me, but they've accepted me as a valuable wizard, huh?
OH, HO HO
And right off the bat, we have a job!!
BAM
See? It's all set!!!
TWRL
Oh! ♡ You're so impatient!
In Shirotsume Town... I may have heard of it...maybe not.
!
You're kidding!!!
If we get a book out of the mansion of this Duke Everlue, we get...
200,000 J?!!!
See? A juicy job, huh?
......

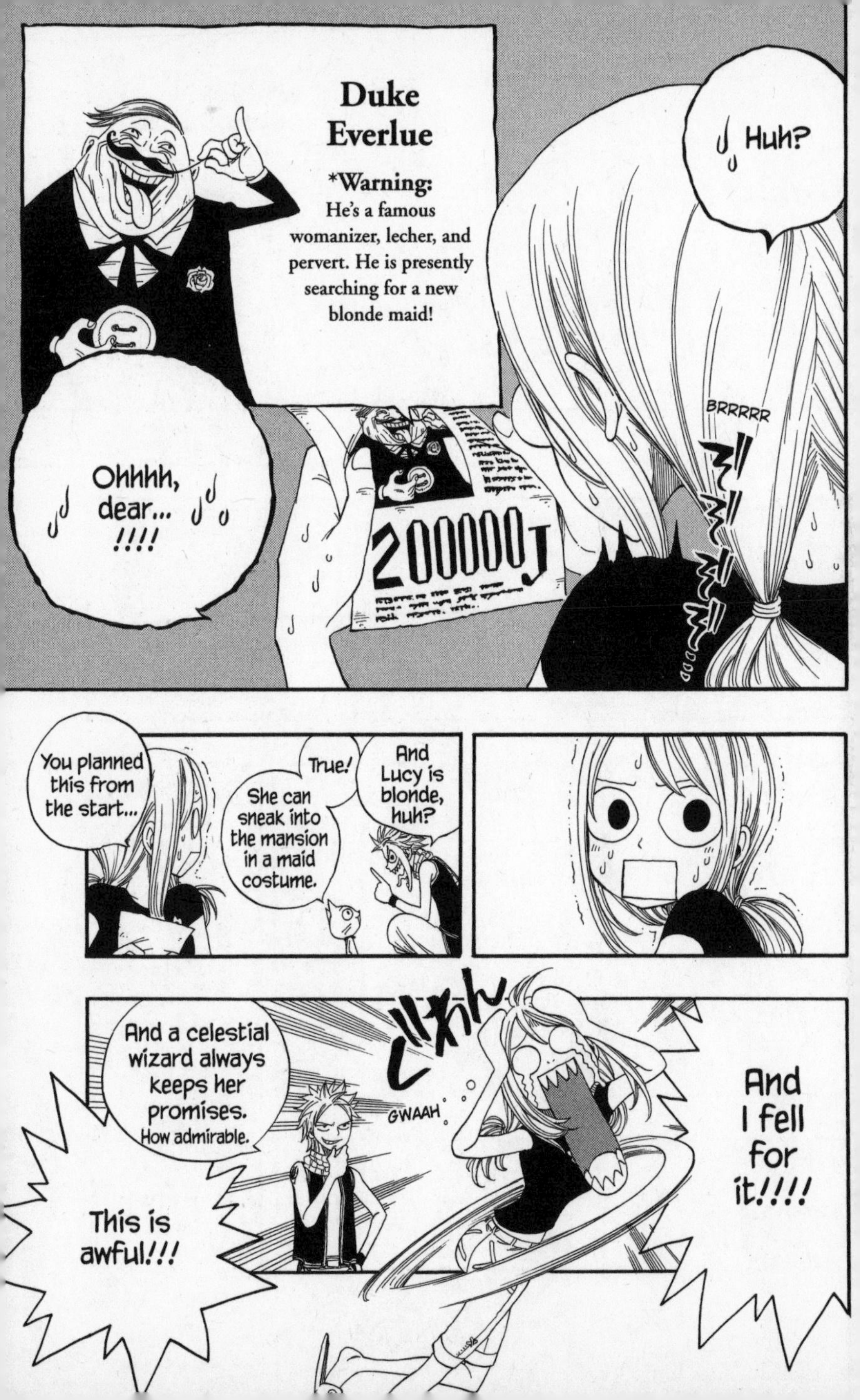
Huh?
Duke Everlue
*Warning:
He's a famous womanizer, lecher, and pervert. He is presently searching for a new blonde maid!
BRRRRR
200000J
Ohhhh, dear... !!!!
And Lucy is blonde, huh?
True!
She can sneak into the mansion in a maid costume.
You planned this from the start...
And I fell for it!!!!
GWAAH
And a celestial wizard always keeps her promises. How admirable.
This is awful!!!

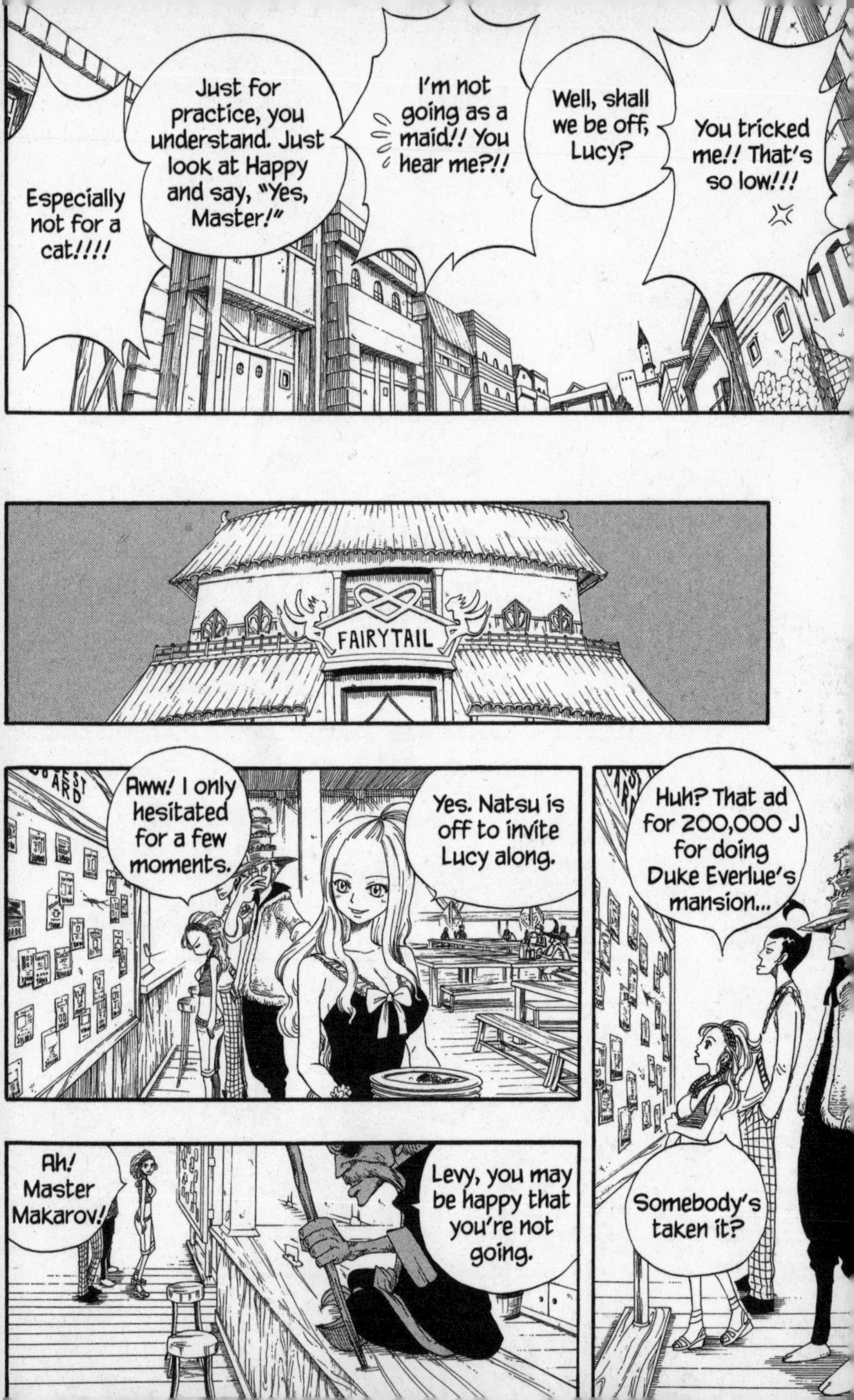
You tricked me!! That's so low!!!
Well, shall we be off, Lucy?
I'm not going as a maid!! You hear me?!!
Just for practice, you understand. Just look at Happy and say, "Yes, Master!"
Especially not for a cat!!!!
FAIRYTAIL
Huh? That ad for 200,000 J for doing Duke Everlue's mansion...
Somebody's taken it?
Yes. Natsu is off to invite Lucy along.
Aww! I only hesitated for a few moments.
Levy, you may be happy that you're not going.
Ah! Master Makarov!

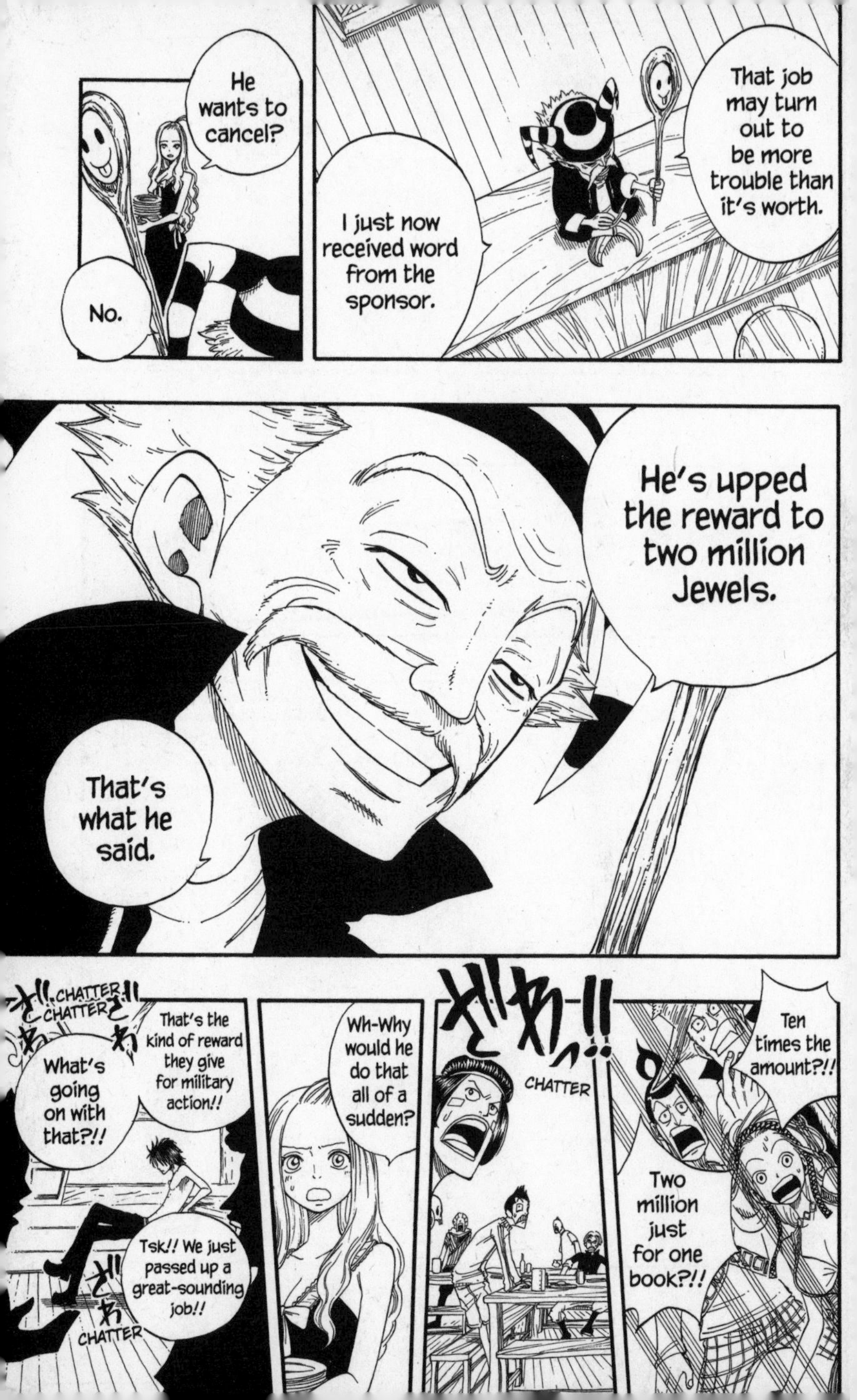

That job may turn out to be more trouble than it's worth.
I just now received word from the sponsor.
He wants to cancel?
No.
He's upped the reward to two million Jewels.
That's what he said.
Ten times the amount?!!
Two million just for one book?!!
CHATTER
Wh-Why would he do that all of a sudden?
CHATTER CHATTER
That's the kind of reward they give for military action!!
What's going on with that?!!
Tsk!! We just passed up a great-sounding job!!
CHATTER

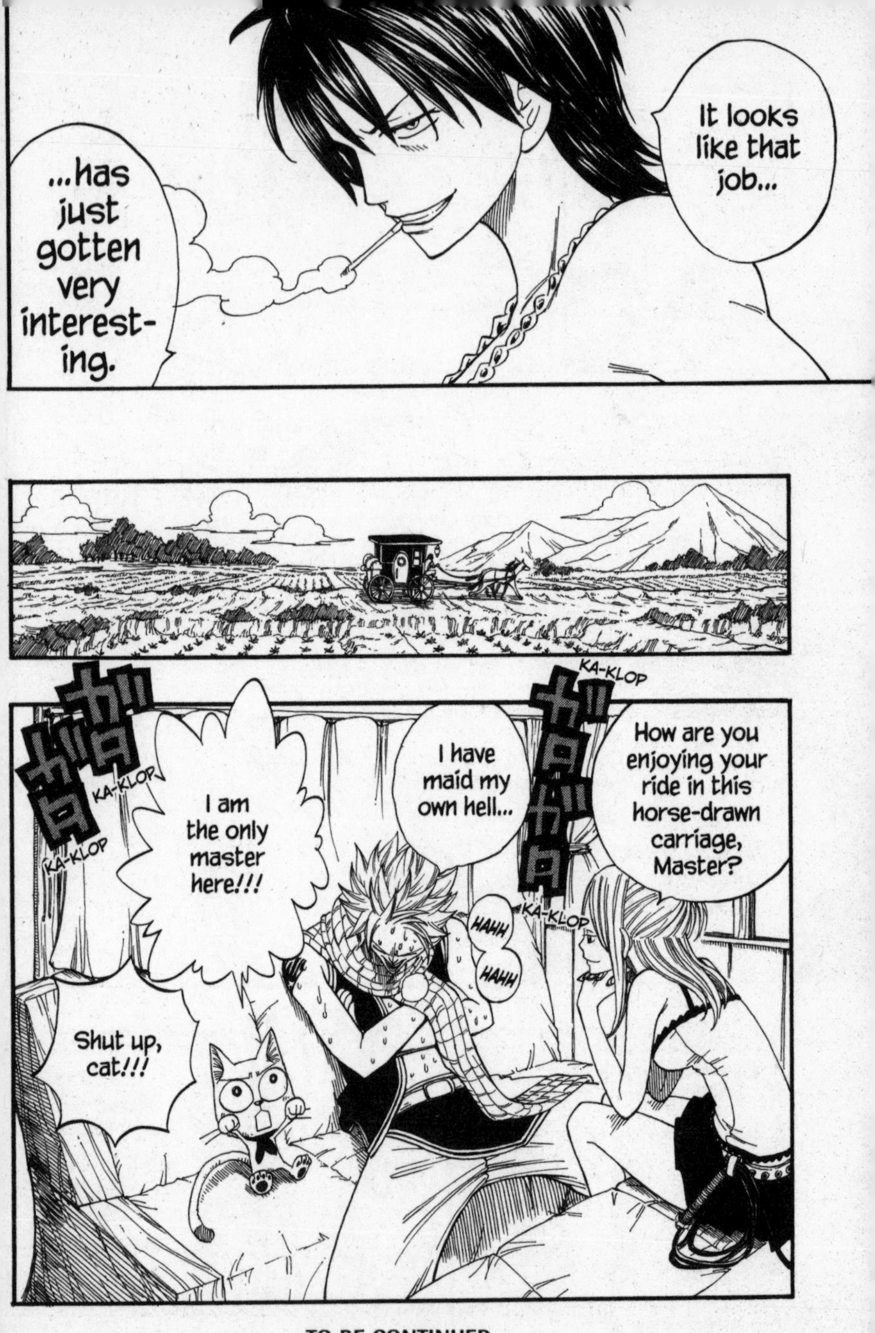
It looks like that job...
...has just gotten very interest-ing.
KA-KLOP
How are you enjoying your ride in this horse-drawn carriage, Master?
KA-KLOP
I have maid my own hell...
HAHH
HAHH
I am the only master here!!!
KA-KLOP
KA-KLOP
Shut up, cat!!!

TO BE CONTINUED

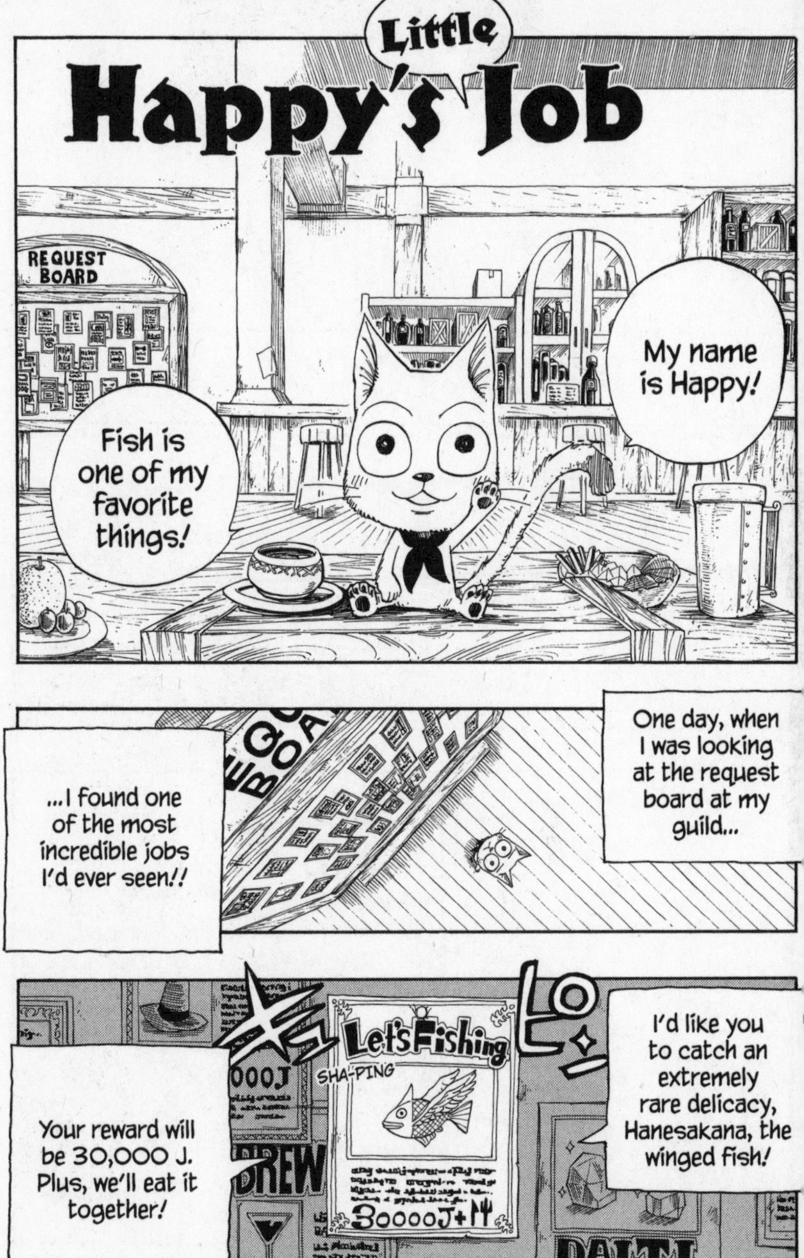
Little Happy's Job
REQUEST BOARD
My name is Happy!
Fish is one of my favorite things!
One day, when I was looking at the request board at my guild...
...I found one of the most incredible jobs I'd ever seen!!
I'd like you to catch an extremely rare delicacy, Hanesakana, the winged fish!
Let'sFishing
SHA-PING
30000J+
Your reward will be 30,000 J. Plus, we'll eat it together!

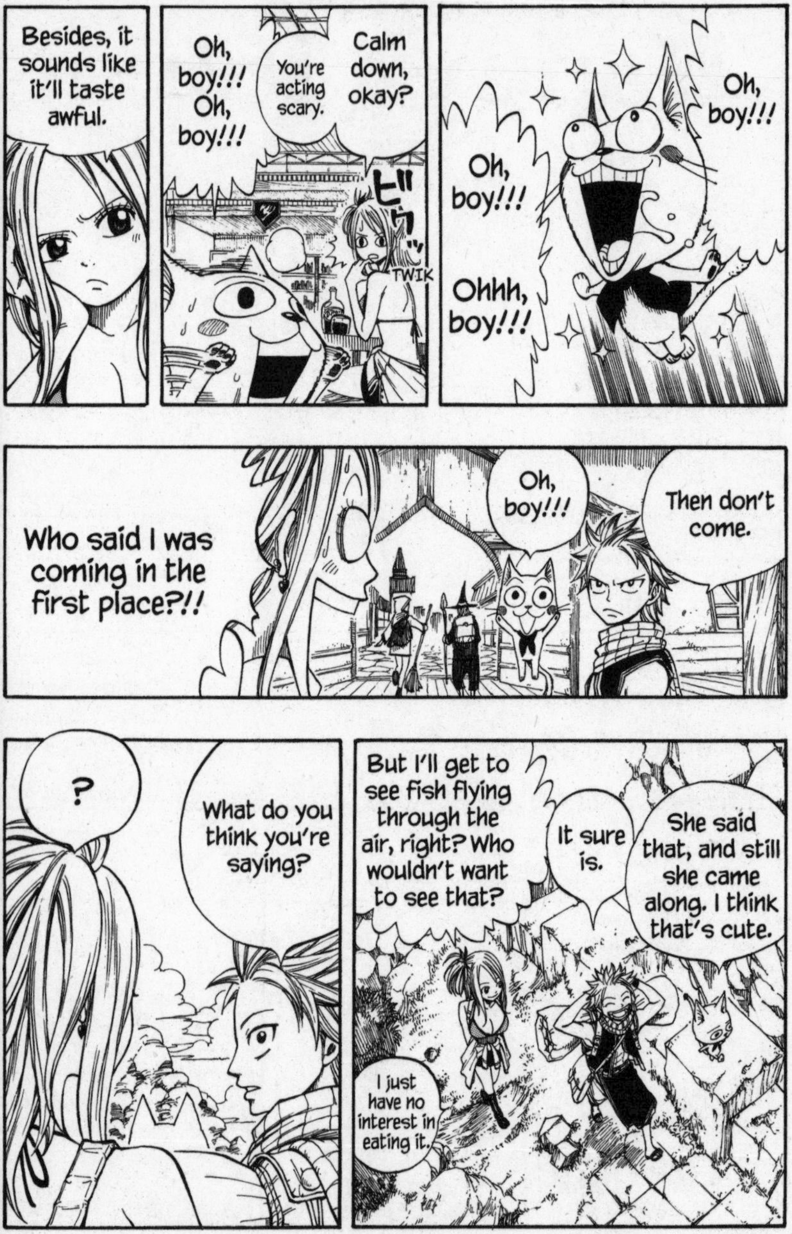
Oh, boy!!!
Oh, boy!!!
Ohhh, boy!!!
Calm down, okay?
You're acting scary.
Oh, boy!!! Oh, boy!!!
ビクッ
TWIK
Besides, it sounds like it'll taste awful.
Then don't come.
Oh, boy!!!
Who said I was coming in the first place?!!
She said that, and still she came along. I think that's cute.
It sure is.
But I'll get to see fish flying through the air, right? Who wouldn't want to see that?
I just have no interest in eating it.
What do you think you're saying?
?

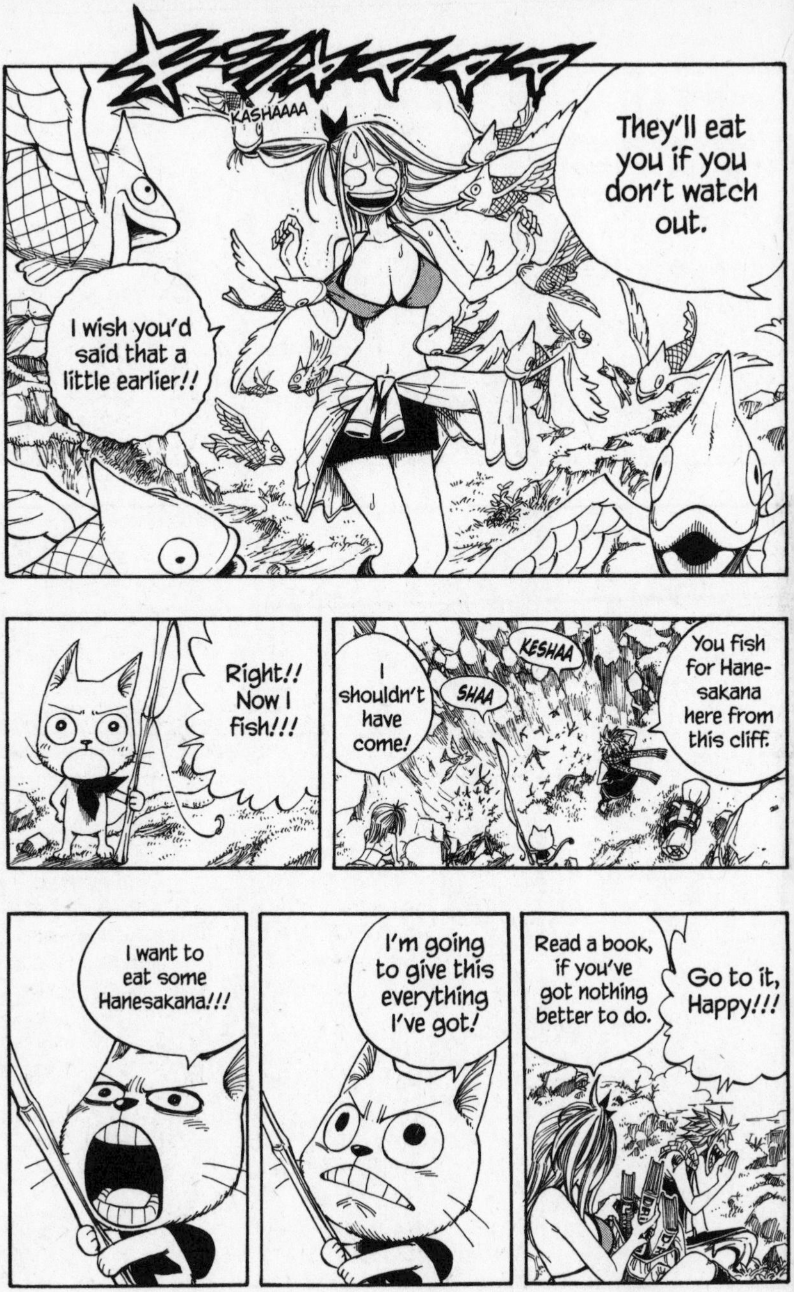
KASHAAAA
They'll eat you if you don't watch out.
I wish you'd said that a little earlier!!
You fish for Hane-sakana here from this cliff.
KESHAA
SHAA
I shouldn't have come!
Right!! Now I fish!!!
Go to it, Happy!!!
Read a book, if you've got nothing better to do.
I'm going to give this everything I've got!
I want to eat some Hanesakana!!!

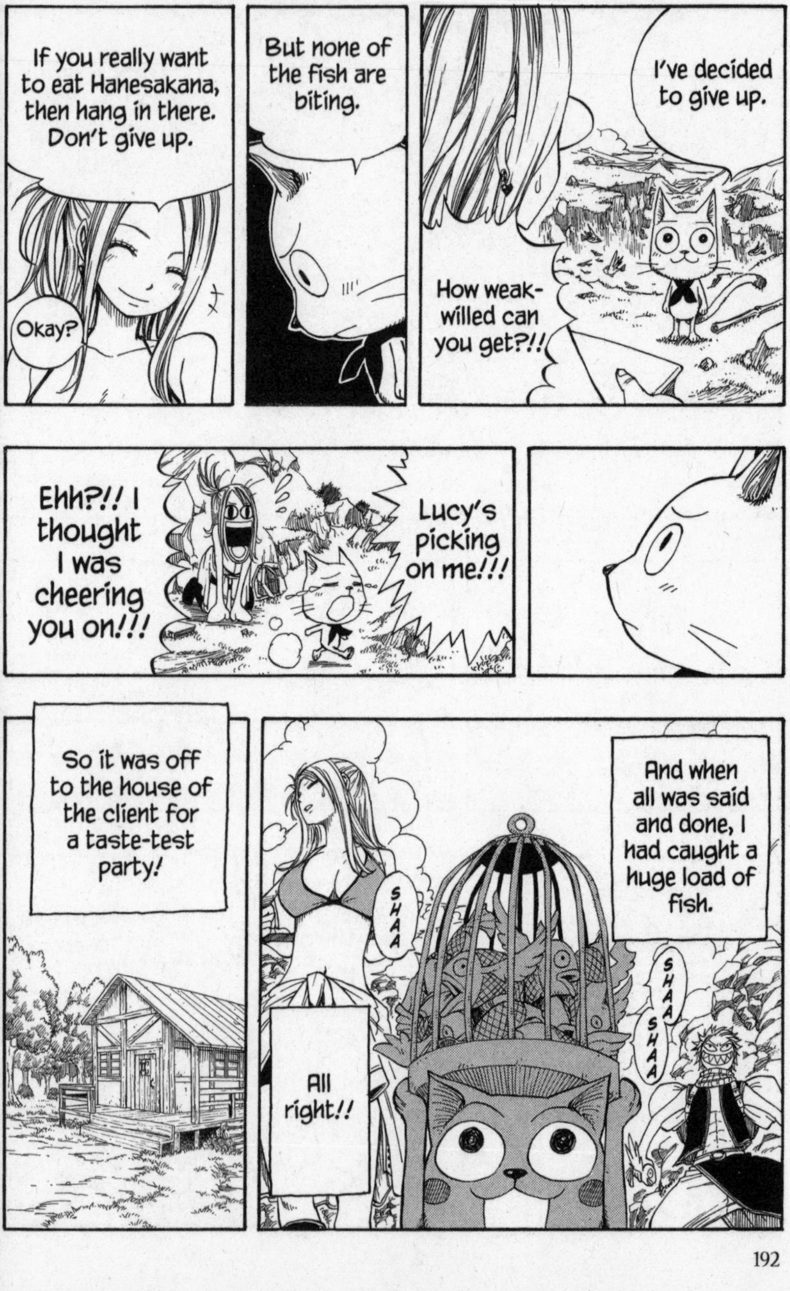
I've decided to give up.
How weak-willed can you get?!!
But none of the fish are biting.
If you really want to eat Hanesakana, then hang in there. Don't give up.
Okay?
Lucy's picking on me!!!
Ehh?!! I thought I was cheering you on!!!
And when all was said and done, I had caught a huge load of fish.
SHAA SHAA
SHAA
SHAA
All right!!
So it was off to the house of the client for a taste-test party!

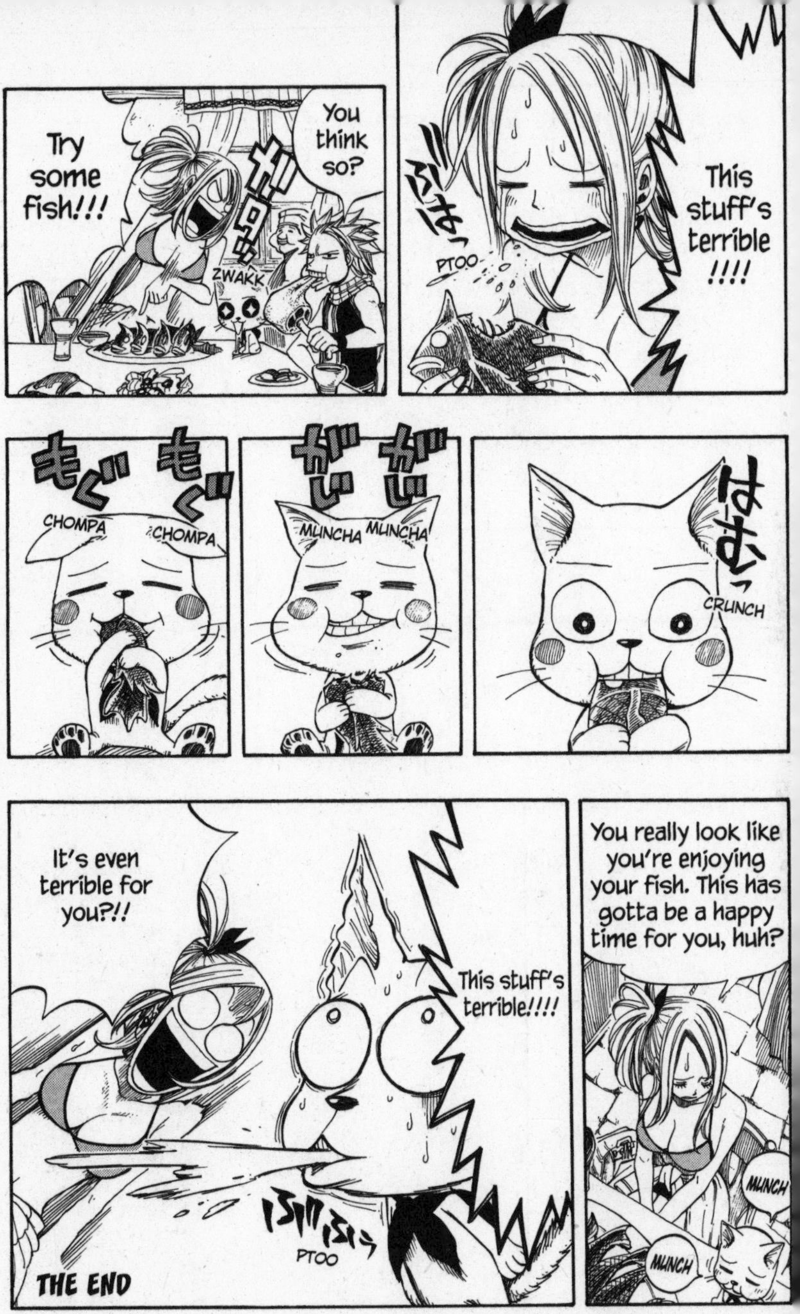

ぶはっ
PTOO
This stuff's terrible!!!!
You think so?
Try some fish!!!
ZWAKK
はむっ
CRUNCH
がじがじ
MUNCHA MUNCHA
もぐもぐ
CHOMPA CHOMPA
You really look like you're enjoying your fish. This has gotta be a happy time for you, huh?
MUNCH
MUNCH
This stuff's terrible!!!!
It's even terrible for you?!!
PTOO
THE END

Natsu's Design... Huh? He had horns?

This is what the main character for the short-story version of *Fairy Tail* (actually, it's *Fairy Tale*) looks like. In the short-story version, he was a spirit, but this time he's human, and he's lost the horns.

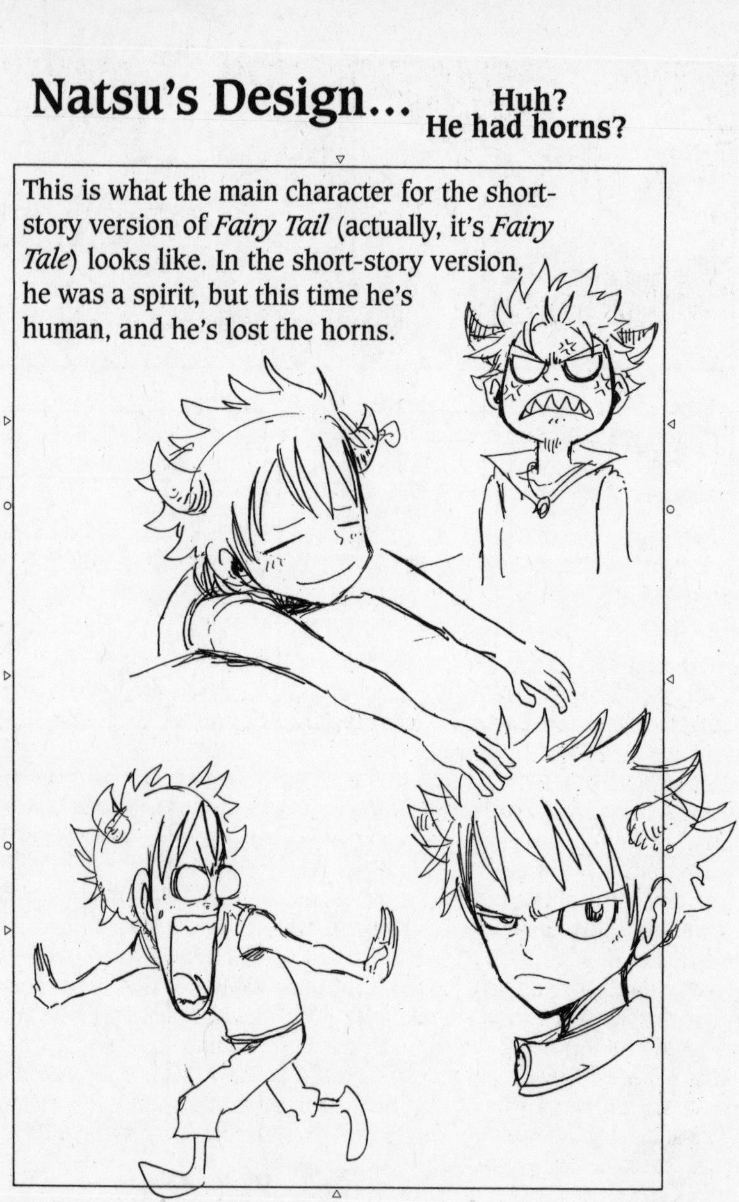

( )

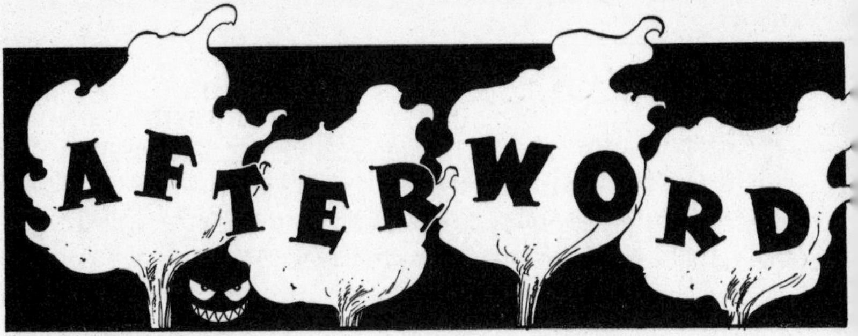
AFTERWORD

Nice to meet you! Or, long time no see! I'm the author, Mashima. First, let me say thank you for reading the first volume of *Fairy Tail*. Did you enjoy it? I'm planning on making things more and more interesting as we go along, so please join me for the ride.

In this portion of the book, I'm thinking that I'll use the space to talk a little about the behind-the-scenes parts of the manga, recent events in my life, weird things about my editor, or just silly stuff that means nothing. So read it when you have some free time.

For the first volume, I'll tell you the behind-the-scenes story of how *Fairy Tail* was born. Well, it really isn't all that "behind-the-scenes," but...At the very start, it was a story about a guild of couriers and how the fire-using main character, Natsu, carried various things on all kinds of assignments. Even though he's a courier, he gets motion sickness very easily. Natsu of *Fairy Tail* had his motion sickness as a part of his design from the start. The story of how he went from courier to wizard is like this: I pondered how to make the story about a man with a dream. I had the first story about the courier guild pretty much finished, but I became more and more intrigued. And when I came up with the wizard guild idea, and how all sorts of wizards could be gathered in one place, I had pretty much decided to change it to a story about wizards. I can't explain just how excited I was with the thought. One idea after another kept popping into my head. I practically forced my editor to allow me to do it, and I started over from scratch. That's how *Fairy Tail* was born. By the way, the title isn't supposed to be a once-upon-a-time story. It means the tail of a fairy. That may prove to be a pivotal point, but it may not. Well, who cares, really? [*laughs*]

So, from here on, I'm going to do my best to write an interesting story. We'll fly from one thing to the next. (What the hell is that supposed to mean?!!) So expect magic! Let's meet again in volume 2!

About the Creator

HIRO MASHIMA was born May 3, 1977, in Nagano prefecture. His series *Rave Master* has made him one of the most popular manga artists in America. *Fairy Tail,* currently being serialized in *Weekly Shonen Magazine,* is his latest creation.

Translation Notes

Japanese is a tricky language for most Westerners, and translation is often more art than science. For your edification and reading pleasure, here are notes on some of the places where we could have gone in a different direction in our translation of the work, or where a Japanese cultural reference is used.

General Note: Wizard

In the original Japanese version of *Fairy Tail*, you'll find panels in which the English word "wizard" is part of the original illustration. So this translation has taken that as its inspiration and translates the word *madôshi* as "wizard." But *madôshi*'s meaning is similar to certain Japanese words that have been borrowed by the English language, such as *judo* ("the soft way") and *kendo* ("the way of the sword"). *Madô* is "the way of magic," and *madôshi* are those who follow the way of magic. So although the word "wizard" is used in the original dialogue, a Japanese reader would be likely to think not of traditional Western wizards such as Merlin or Gandalf, but of martial artists.

Jewels and calculating money, page 12

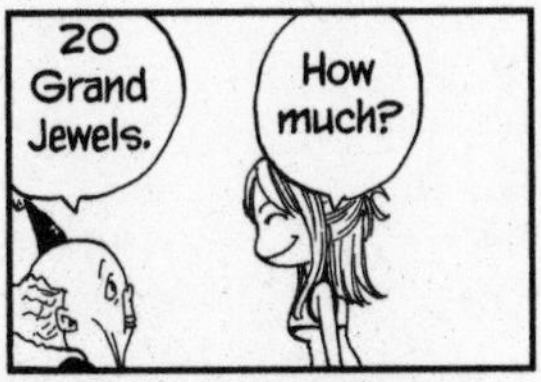
How much?
20 Grand Jewels.

In fantasy tales, no small part of the story's unique magical world is that world's imaginary currency. In America, fantasy writers tend to depend on their readers' familiarity with American money, attaching a phrase like "silver pieces" to an amount that would be wholly plausible in U.S. dollars. In Japan, the same convention is used, except that the imaginary currency is a substitute for yen. So, in *Fairy Tail*, merchants quote sums like 20,000 Jewels that sound ridiculously huge to American readers but are fairly reasonable to the Japanese. A rough-but-quick currency conversion is 100 yen to the dollar, so when Lucy is told that the White Doggy key is 20,000 J, that would be roughly equivalent to ¥20,000 in Japanese money, or about $200 U.S. Keeping the amounts so close to the yen/dollar amounts that readers already know makes it easy for them to understand how expensive things are in the fantasy world.

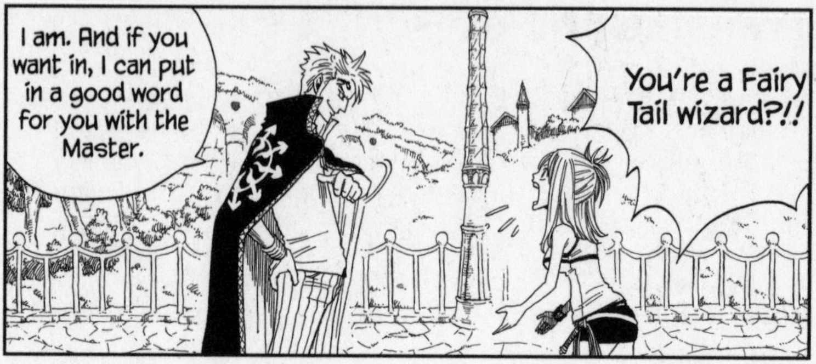
You're a Fairy Tail wizard?!!
I am. And if you want in, I can put in a good word for you with the Master.

Master, page 32

"Master" is an English loan word that the Japanese have added to their language, but like many loan words, "master" has acquired an entirely different meaning than its English one. In Japan, the owner or manager of a bar or other similar establishment is called the master of the business. The nuances of the word "master" as we know it—that it implies advanced knowledge or skill—have disappeared in its Japanese usage, nor does it imply the "slave owner" definition. It is simply what one calls the person who runs a business.

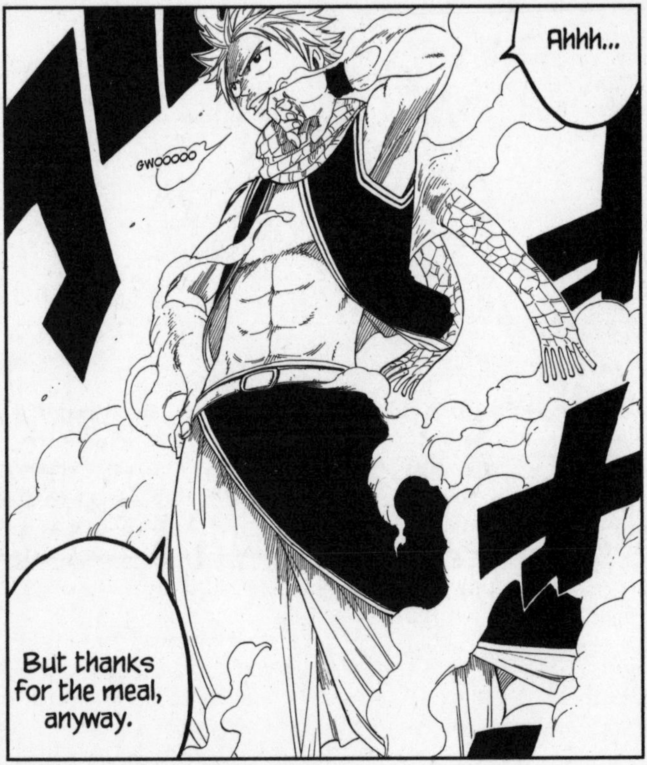
Ahhh...
GWOOOOO
But thanks for the meal, anyway.

Thanks for the meal, page 64

This is a rough translation of a ritualistic Japanese phrase. This phrase, *Gochisô-sama*, is said at the end of every meal. It literally means "It was a feast," and it is usually said to the person who cooked the meal or the one who provided it (for example, the person who pays the bill at a restaurant). So ingrained is this habit that one often says it to oneself even after finishing eating a self-prepared meal alone.

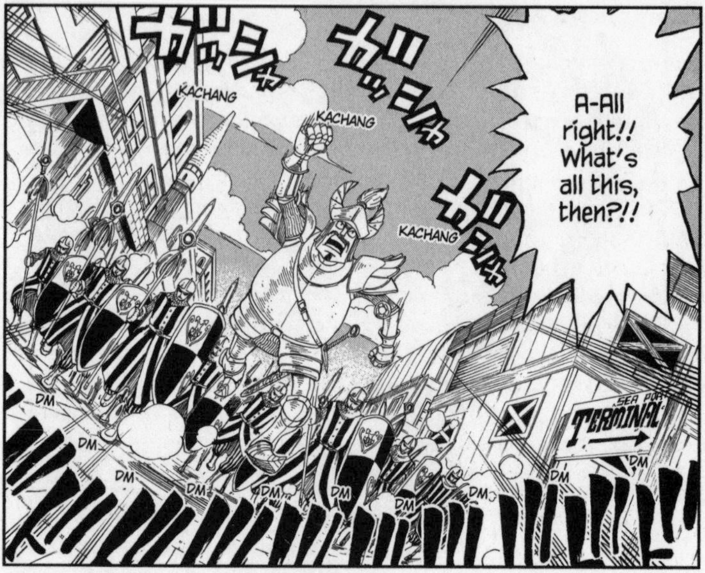
A-All right!! What's all this, then?!!
KACHANG
KACHANG
KACHANG
SEA PORT
TERMINAL
DM

What's all this, then? page 77

Yes, this is an old, worn-out cliché that British police are famous for saying when arriving at a crime scene (although I doubt that all that many of them actually use it these days). But it is, in fact, a pretty accurate translation of what was said in Japanese.

Nekomander, page 112

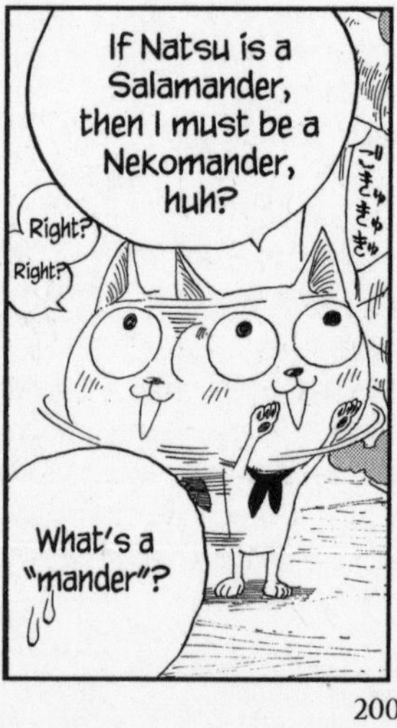
If Natsu is a Salamander, then I must be a Nekomander, huh?
Right?
Right?
What's a "mander"?

This is a joking play on the name of the villain. The Japanese version used the English word "salamander" as the name of the villain. The Japanese word for cat is *neko*. As translator, I suppose I could have used the translation "catmander" or "kittymander" for Happy's dialogue, but the Japanese word that Happy used, *nekomander*, just had a nice ring to it.

"Forms," page 171

In the original, Lucy is actually explaining how to count celestial spirits. English sometimes uses special counter words for some items. For example, when saying how much paper one has, one counts by pieces or sheets. When saying how many cows one has, one counts by heads of cattle. This is a matter of custom and established usage. The same is true for Japanese, but on a much wider scale. Nearly everything has a special counter word. In the previous panel, Happy asks how many spirits Lucy has, but he asks using the same counter that is used for counting people. So Lucy corrects Happy by telling him they're counted with the counter *tai* (which uses the kanji that means "body"). Although, because they are spirits, "body" is not the most appropriate translation; the somewhat synonymous word "form" can indicate both corporeal bodies and noncorporeal manifestations. It isn't a perfect translation, since English doesn't allow for Happy to make his counter mistake without his dialogue sounding very awkward. But fortunately for the translator, it's in Lucy's character to explain a lot of things for no particular reason.

Nikor, page 172

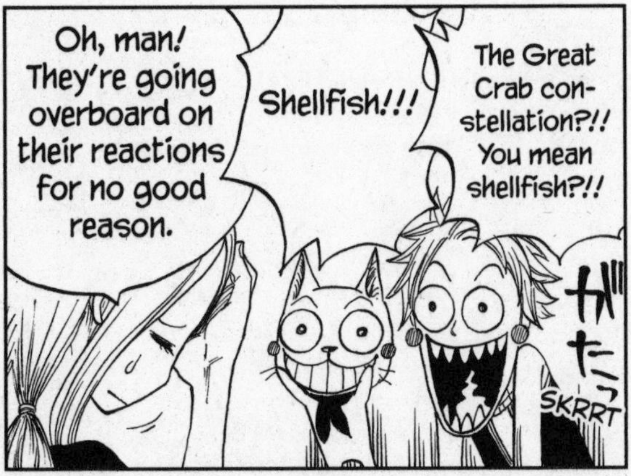
The Great Crab constellation?!! You mean shellfish?!!
Shellfish!!!
Oh, man! They're going overboard on their reactions for no good reason.
SKRRT

The constellation Taurus is called Taurus, and the constellation Aquarius is called Aquarius, so why is Canis Minor called Nikora? I have to admit that I don't know. The famous astronomer Nicolas Louis de Lacaille discovered and coined the names to many constellations, and the Japanese transliterate his first name as Nikora. But he did not name Canis Minor, and he seems to have no other relation to the constellation. If you readers know the answer, please write in to Kodansha and let us know.

Arrears, page 172

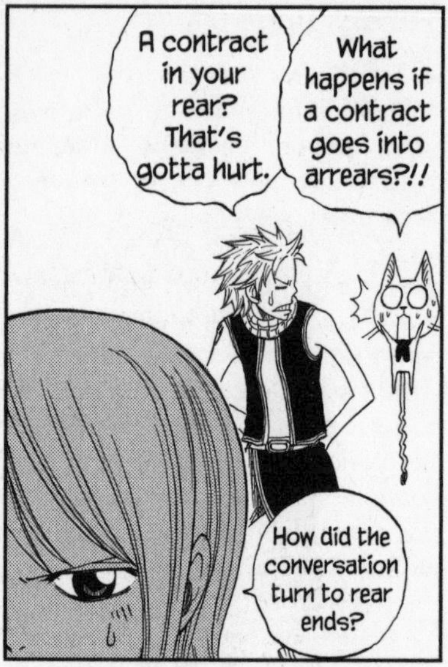
What happens if a contract goes into arrears?!!
A contract in your rear? That's gotta hurt.
How did the conversation turn to rear ends?

This was a pun. When translating a pun, one usually has to choose one of the two meanings to put into the translation (since it is rare that one word can contain the same two meanings in both languages). In this case, Happy asked if one must sign in blood (*ketsuban*), and Natsu misinterpreted the statement, saying that such a thing can hurt one's rear end (*ketsu*). As translator, I decided to take the low road by keeping the "rear end" meaning rather than the "blood contract" meaning. As it turns out, one does not have to sign in blood (nor does one ever come into arrears).

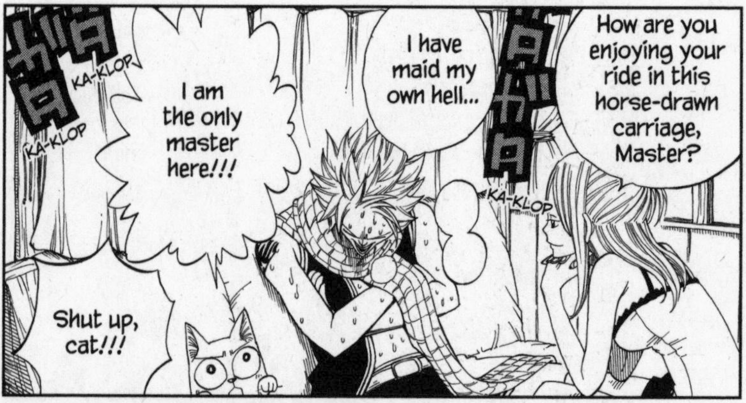
How are you enjoying your ride in this horse-drawn carriage, Master?
KA-KLOP
I have maid my own hell...
I am the only master here!!!
KA-KLOP
KA-KLOP
Shut up, cat!!!

Maid my own hell, page 184

Another pun. In Japanese, one of the words for the underworld is *meido*, which also happens to be the way the Japanese say the English word "maid." I simply took advantage of the fact that "made" and "maid" are homophones in English to make a pun that is still a pretty close equivalent to the Japanese.

Preview of Volume 2

We're pleased to present you with a preview from volume 2, now available from Kodansha Comics. Check out our Web site (www.kodanshacomics.com) for more details!

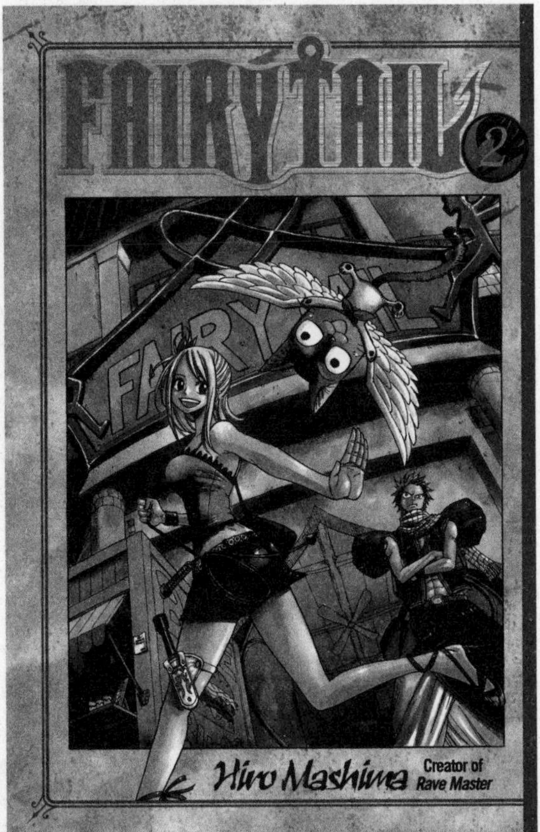

FAIRY TAIL
2
FAIRY TAIL
Hiro Mashima
Creator of Rave Master

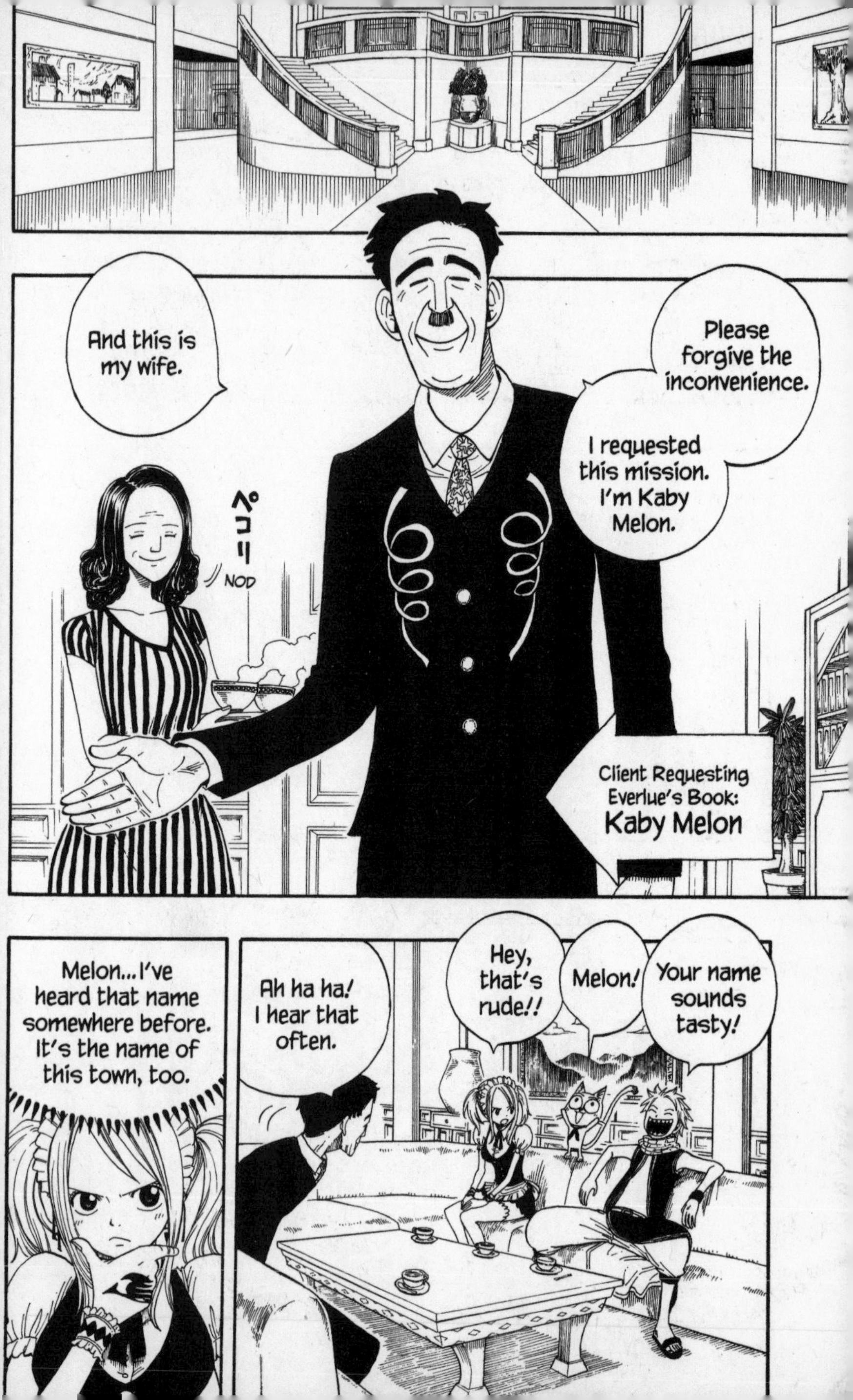

Please forgive the inconvenience.
I requested this mission. I'm Kaby Melon.
Client Requesting Everlue's Book: Kaby Melon
And this is my wife.
ペコリ NOD
Your name sounds tasty!
Melon!
Hey, that's rude!!
Ah ha ha! I hear that often.
Melon...I've heard that name somewhere before. It's the name of this town, too.

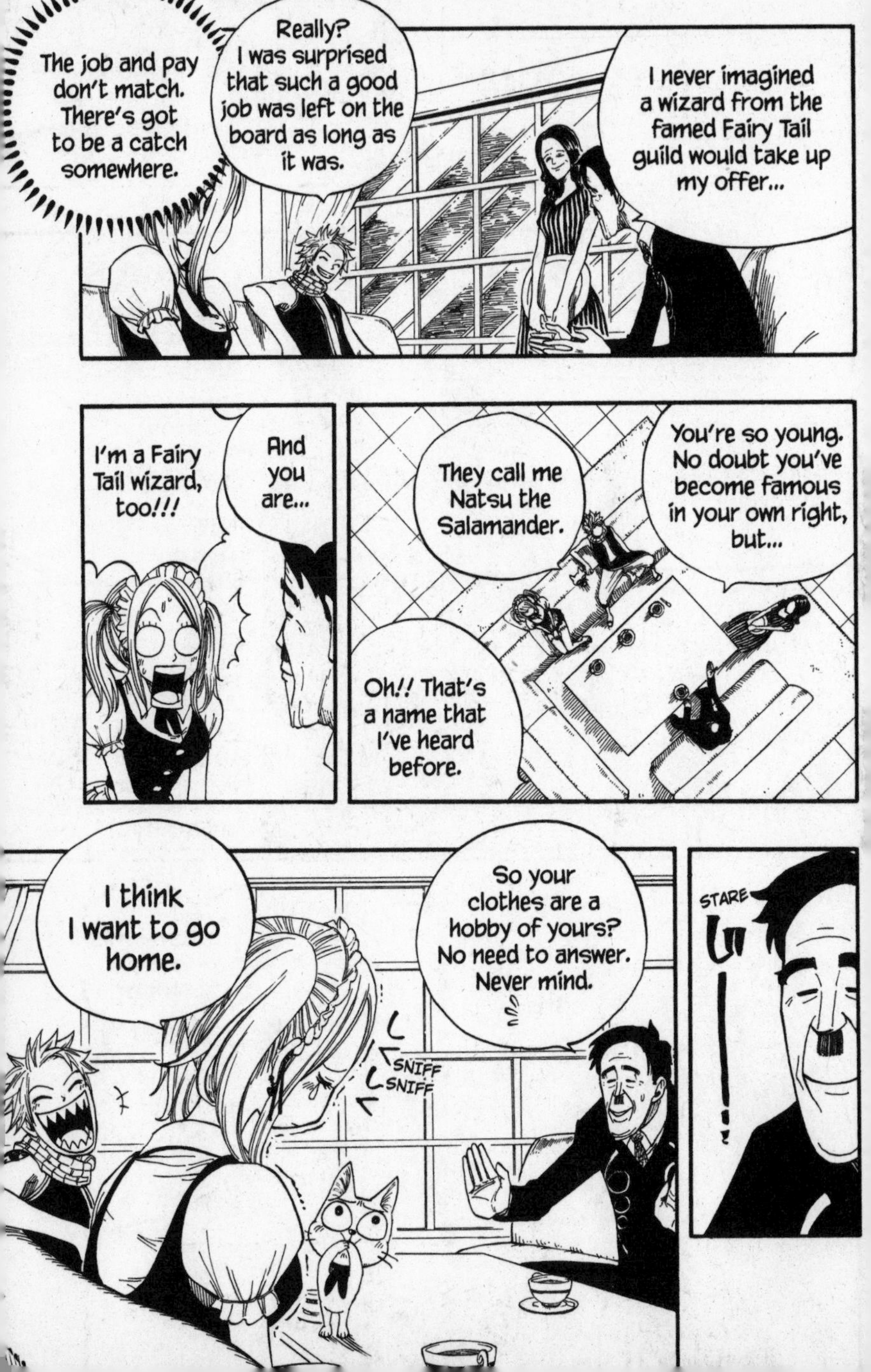
I never imagined a wizard from the famed Fairy Tail guild would take up my offer...
Really? I was surprised that such a good job was left on the board as long as it was.
The job and pay don't match. There's got to be a catch somewhere.
You're so young. No doubt you've become famous in your own right, but...
They call me Natsu the Salamander.
Oh!! That's a name that I've heard before.
And you are...
I'm a Fairy Tail wizard, too!!!
STARE
So your clothes are a hobby of yours? No need to answer. Never mind.
SNIFF
SNIFF
I think I want to go home.

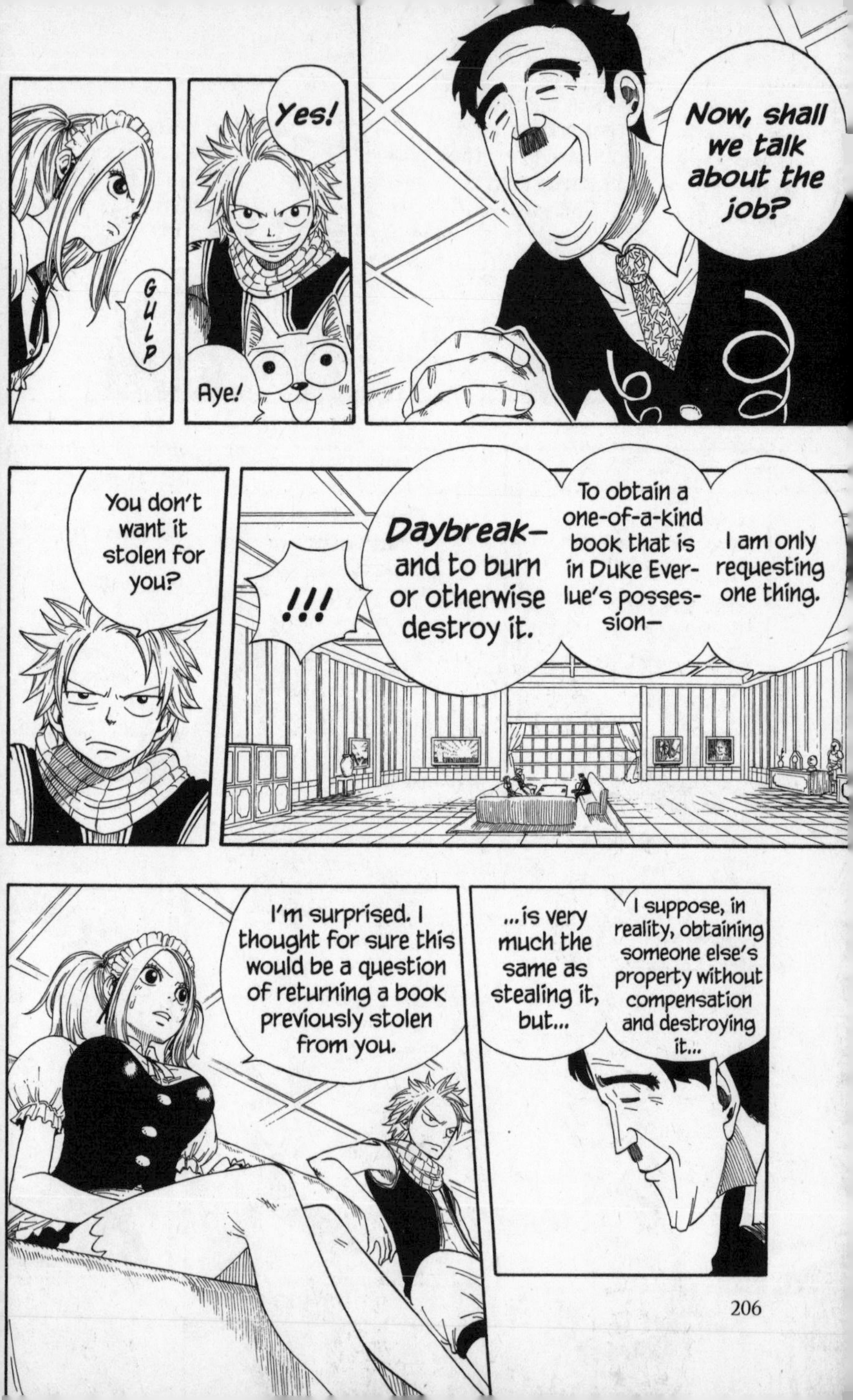
Now, shall we talk about the job?
Yes!
Aye!
GULP
I am only requesting one thing.
To obtain a one-of-a-kind book that is in Duke Everlue's possession—
Daybreak—and to burn or otherwise destroy it.
!!!
You don't want it stolen for you?
I suppose, in reality, obtaining someone else's property without compensation and destroying it...
...is very much the same as stealing it, but...
I'm surprised. I thought for sure this would be a question of returning a book previously stolen from you.

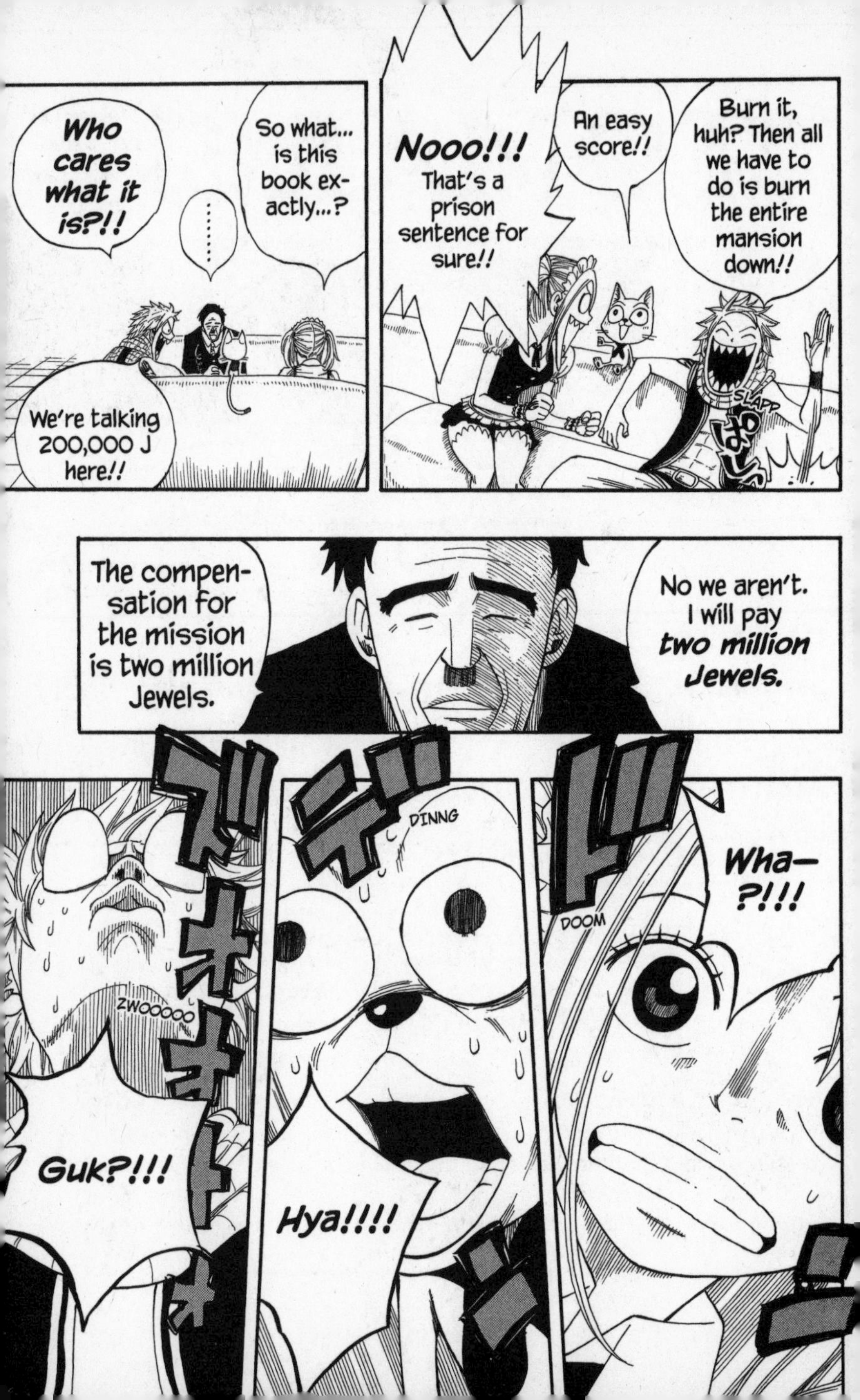
Burn it, huh? Then all we have to do is burn the entire mansion down!!
SLAPP
An easy score!!
Nooo!!! That's a prison sentence for sure!!
So what... is this book exactly...?
......
Who cares what it is?!!
We're talking 200,000 J here!!
No we aren't. I will pay two million Jewels.
The compensation for the mission is two million Jewels.
DOOM
Wha—?!!!
DINNG
Hya!!!!
ZWOOOOO
Guk?!!!

TOMARE!

止まれ

[STOP!]

You're going the wrong way!

Manga is a completely different type of reading experience.

To start at the *beginning*,
go to the *end*!

That's right! Authentic manga is read the traditional Japanese way—from right to left, exactly the opposite of how American books are read. It's easy to follow: Just go to the other end of the book, and read each page—and each panel—from right side to left side, starting at the top right. Now you're experiencing manga as it was meant to be!